SB

Shojo Beat

# VAMPIRE KNIGHT

**Story & Art by**
**Matsuri**
**Hino**

**Vol. 4**

# VAMPIRE KNIGHT

## Contents

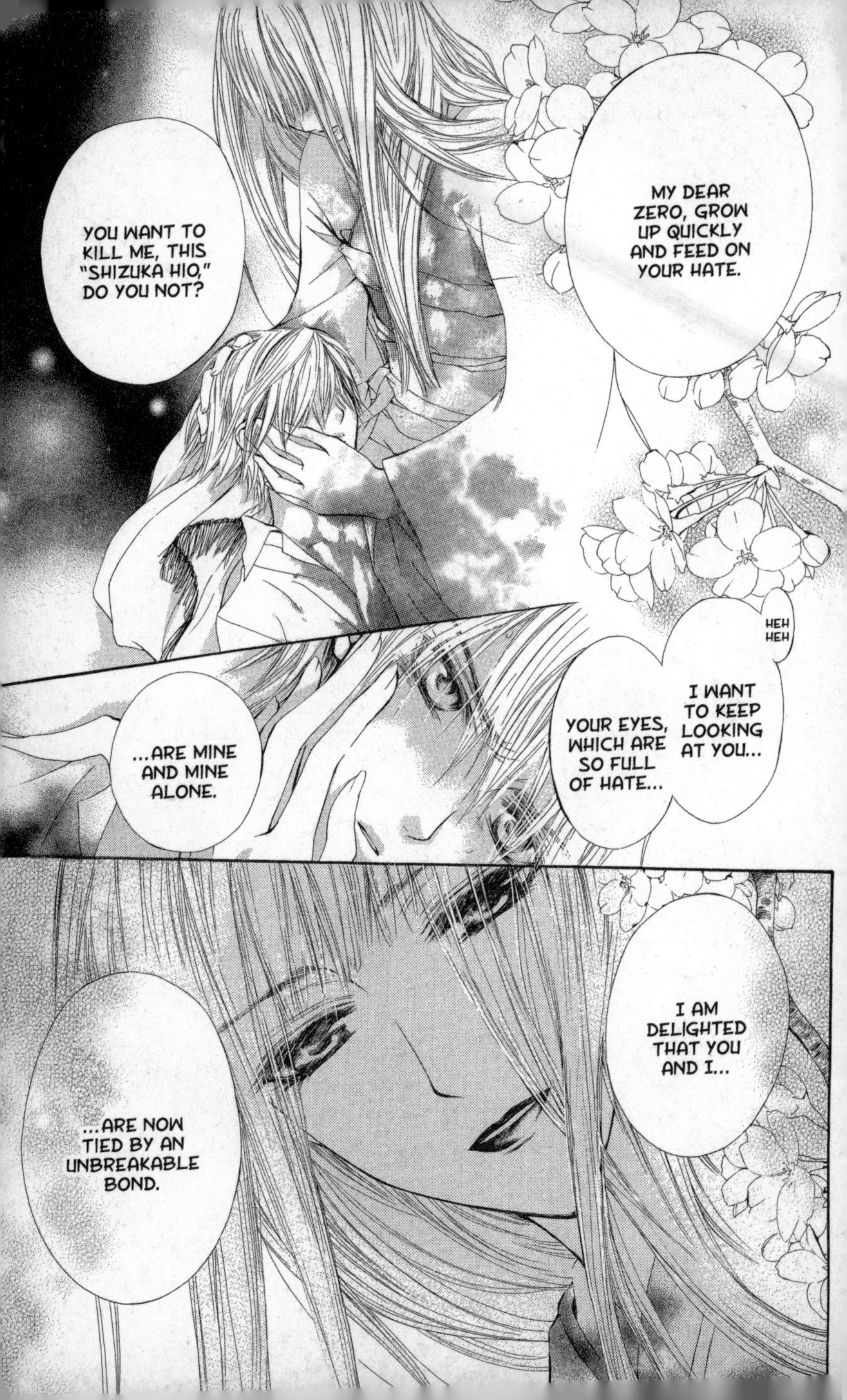
MY DEAR ZERO, GROW UP QUICKLY AND FEED ON YOUR HATE.
YOU WANT TO KILL ME, THIS "SHIZUKA HIO," DO YOU NOT?
HEH HEH
I WANT TO KEEP LOOKING AT YOU...
YOUR EYES, WHICH ARE SO FULL OF HATE...
...ARE MINE AND MINE ALONE.
I AM DELIGHTED THAT YOU AND I...
...ARE NOW TIED BY AN UNBREAKABLE BOND.

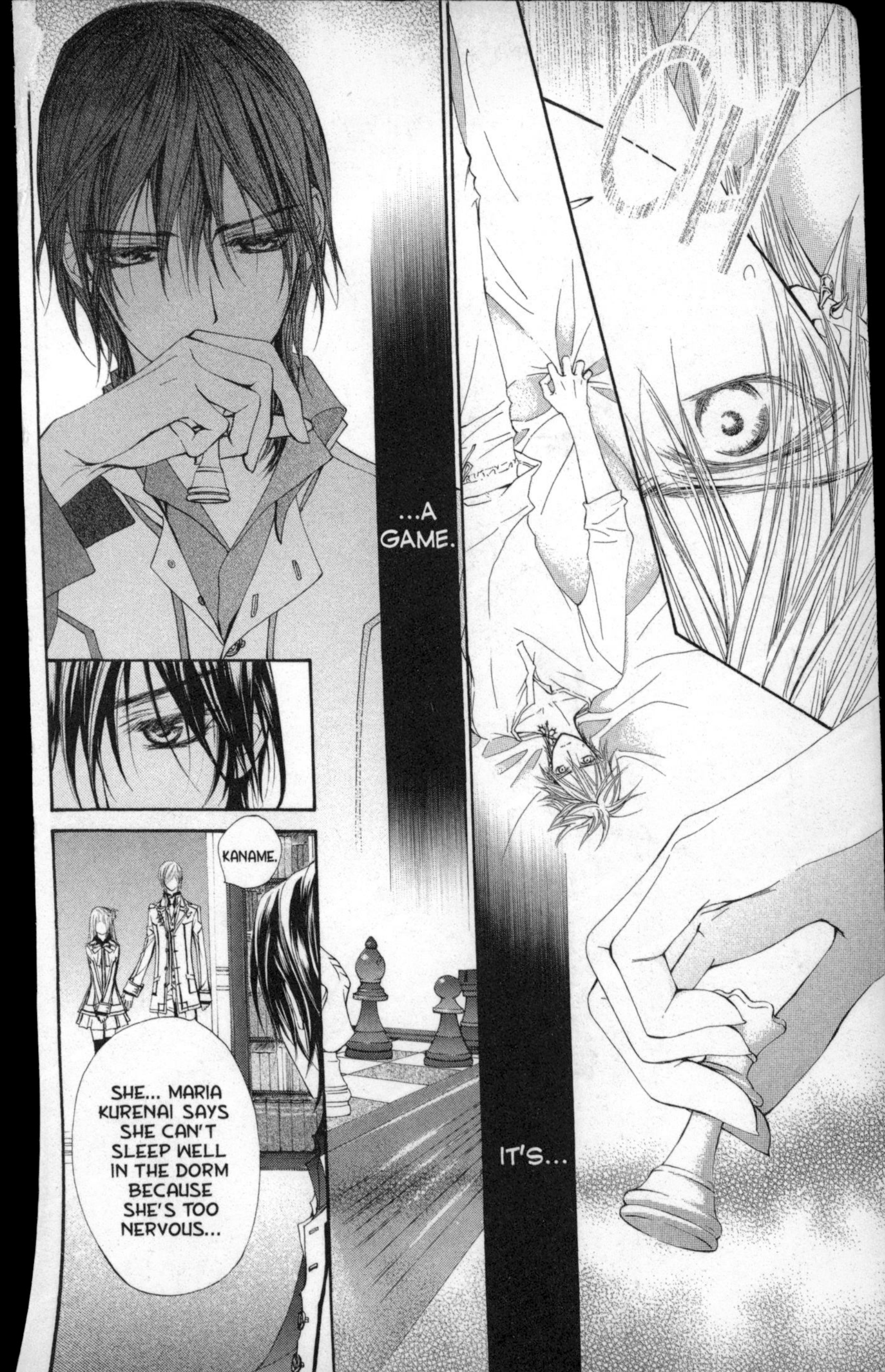
IT'S...
...A GAME.
KANAME.
SHE... MARIA KURENAI SAYS SHE CAN'T SLEEP WELL IN THE DORM BECAUSE SHE'S TOO NERVOUS...

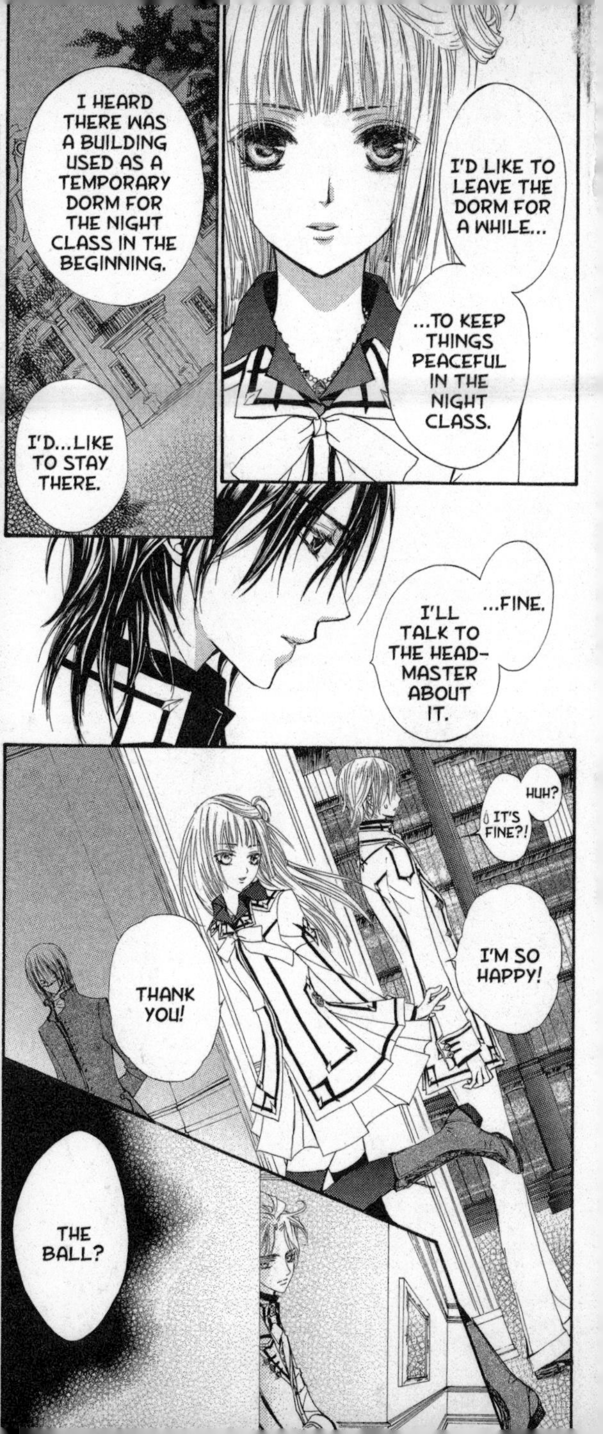
I'D LIKE TO LEAVE THE DORM FOR A WHILE...
...TO KEEP THINGS PEACEFUL IN THE NIGHT CLASS.
I HEARD THERE WAS A BUILDING USED AS A TEMPORARY DORM FOR THE NIGHT CLASS IN THE BEGINNING.
I'D...LIKE TO STAY THERE.
...FINE.
I'LL TALK TO THE HEAD-MASTER ABOUT IT.
HUH? IT'S FINE?!
I'M SO HAPPY!
THANK YOU!
THE BALL?

# I

Thank you for waiting. It's been six months since the last Vampire Knight volume!

This is volume 4, and it's coming out right before the 2nd anniversary. This has been the fastest pace ever for me...

I was able to make it this far because of you, the readers who cheer me on, and because of all the people who support me. Thank you! Thank you!

Due to the number of pages, I couldn't draw much bonus stuff this time either (I did... a lot of corrections.) I apologize to everyone who was looking forward to them. The bonus manga I drew for vols. 1 and 2 were more popular than I thought they would be. I was happy. So I will look for opportunities to draw more. Definitely!

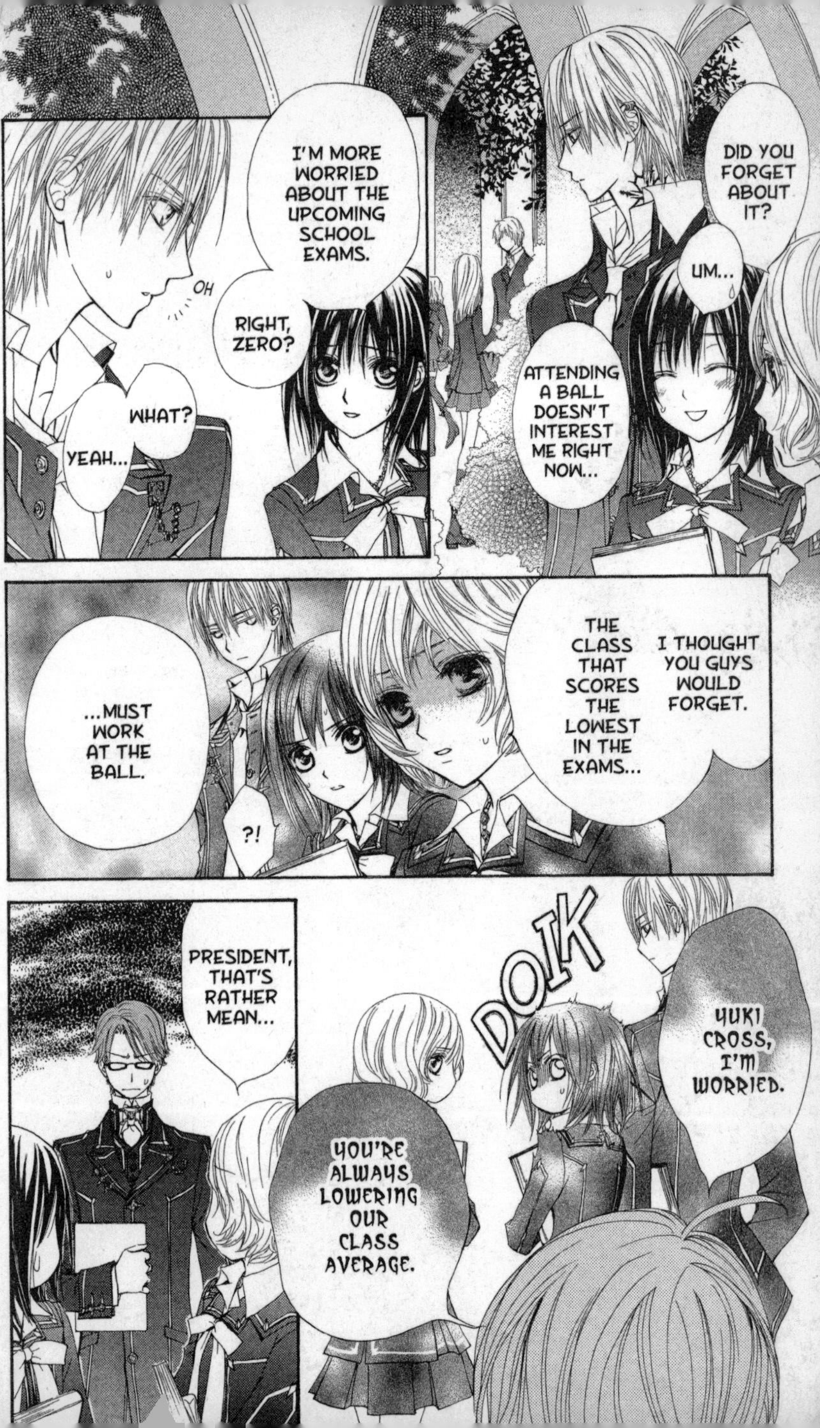
DID YOU FORGET ABOUT IT?
UM...
ATTENDING A BALL DOESN'T INTEREST ME RIGHT NOW...
I'M MORE WORRIED ABOUT THE UPCOMING SCHOOL EXAMS.
RIGHT, ZERO?
OH
WHAT?
YEAH...
I THOUGHT YOU GUYS WOULD FORGET.
THE CLASS THAT SCORES THE LOWEST IN THE EXAMS...
...MUST WORK AT THE BALL.
?!
YUKI CROSS, I'M WORRIED.
DOIK
YOU'RE ALWAYS LOWERING OUR CLASS AVERAGE.
PRESIDENT, THAT'S RATHER MEAN...

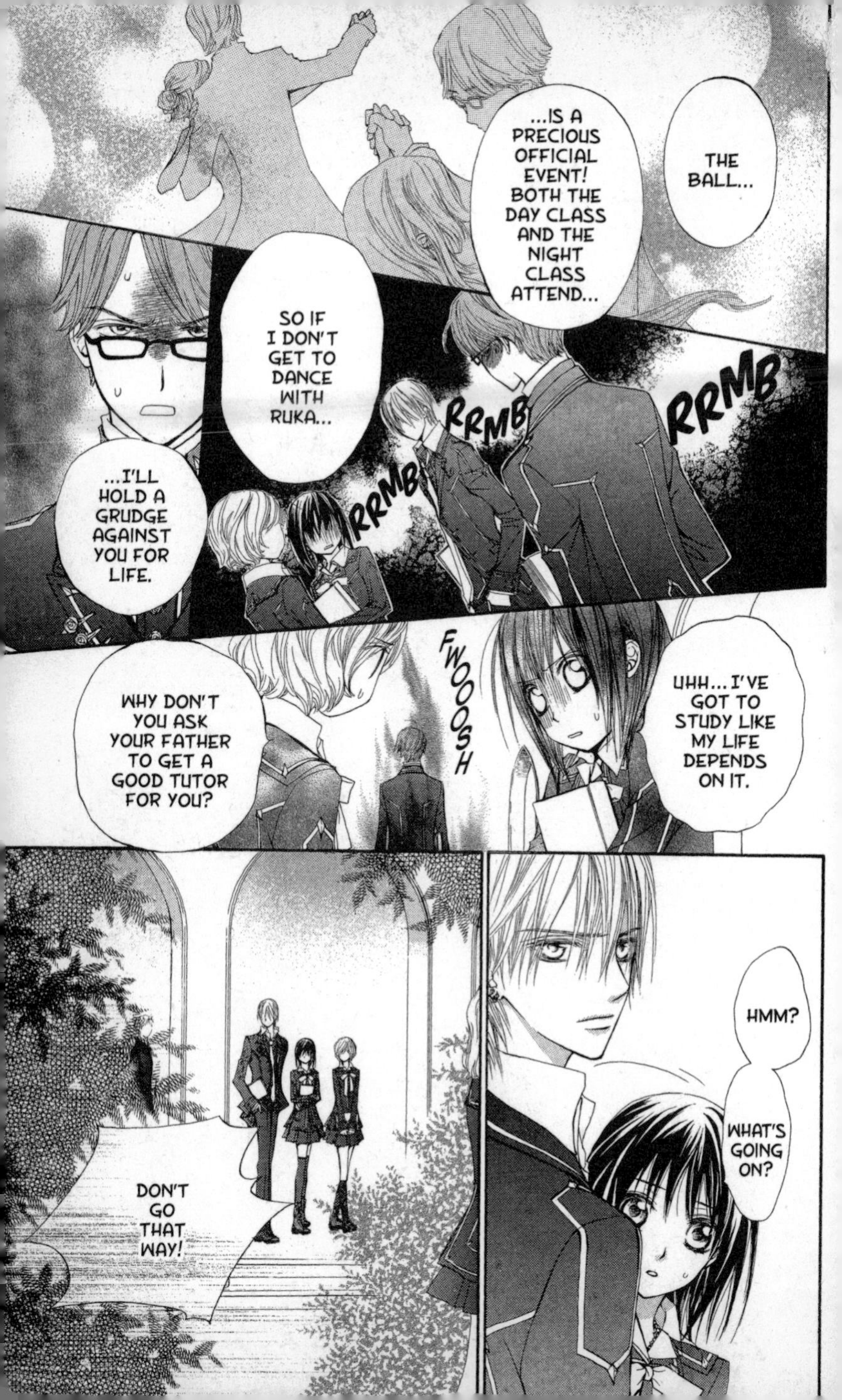
THE BALL...
...IS A PRECIOUS OFFICIAL EVENT! BOTH THE DAY CLASS AND THE NIGHT CLASS ATTEND...
RRMB
RRMB
SO IF I DON'T GET TO DANCE WITH RUKA...
RRMB
...I'LL HOLD A GRUDGE AGAINST YOU FOR LIFE.
UHH... I'VE GOT TO STUDY LIKE MY LIFE DEPENDS ON IT.
FWOOOSH
WHY DON'T YOU ASK YOUR FATHER TO GET A GOOD TUTOR FOR YOU?
HMM?
WHAT'S GOING ON?
DON'T GO THAT WAY!

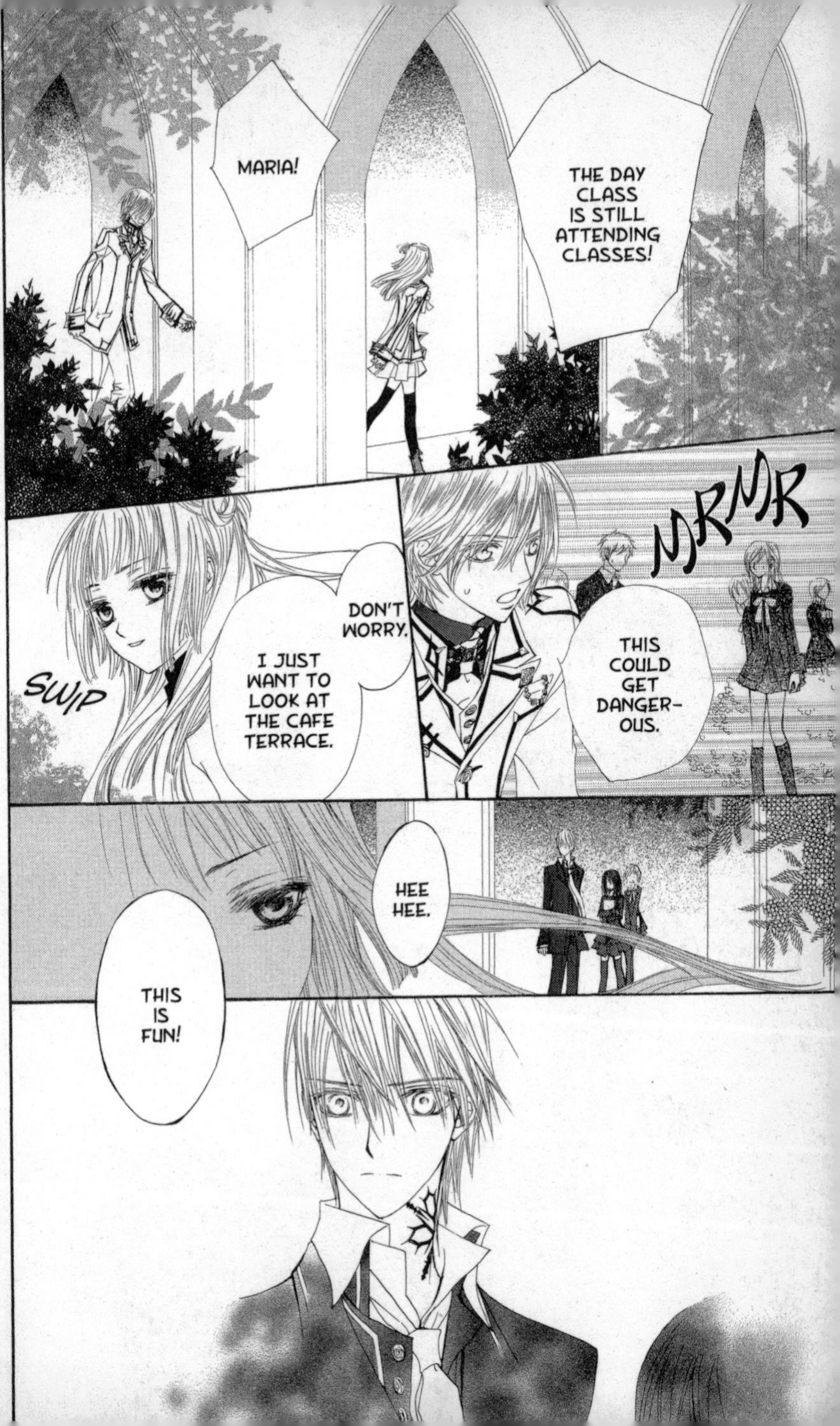
THE DAY CLASS IS STILL ATTENDING CLASSES!
MARIA!
MRMR
THIS COULD GET DANGER-OUS.
DON'T WORRY.
I JUST WANT TO LOOK AT THE CAFE TERRACE.
SWIP
HEE HEE.
THIS IS FUN!

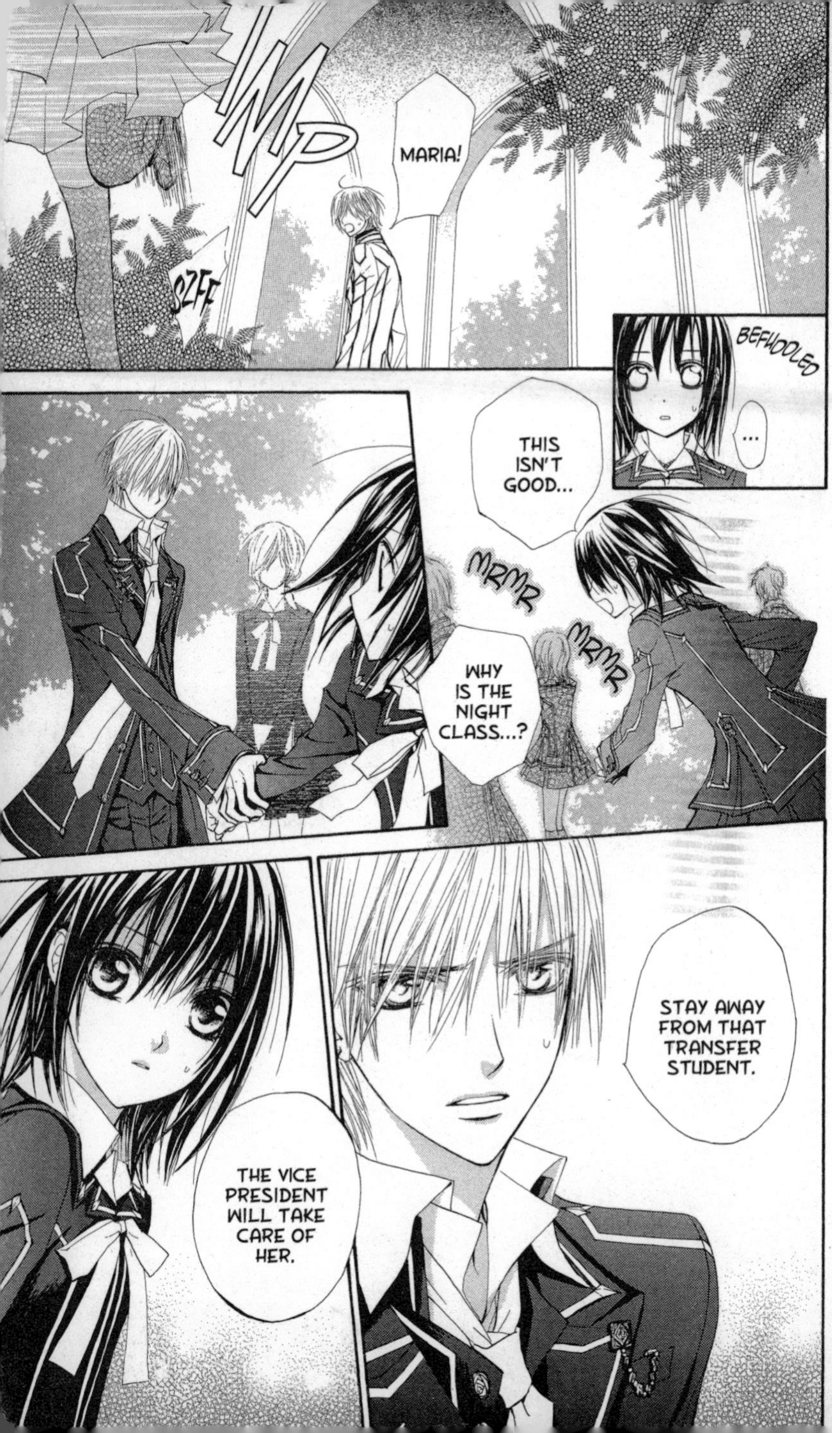
WMP
MARIA!
SZFF
BEFUDDLED
...
THIS ISN'T GOOD...
MRMR
MRMR
WHY IS THE NIGHT CLASS...?
STAY AWAY FROM THAT TRANSFER STUDENT.
THE VICE PRESIDENT WILL TAKE CARE OF HER.

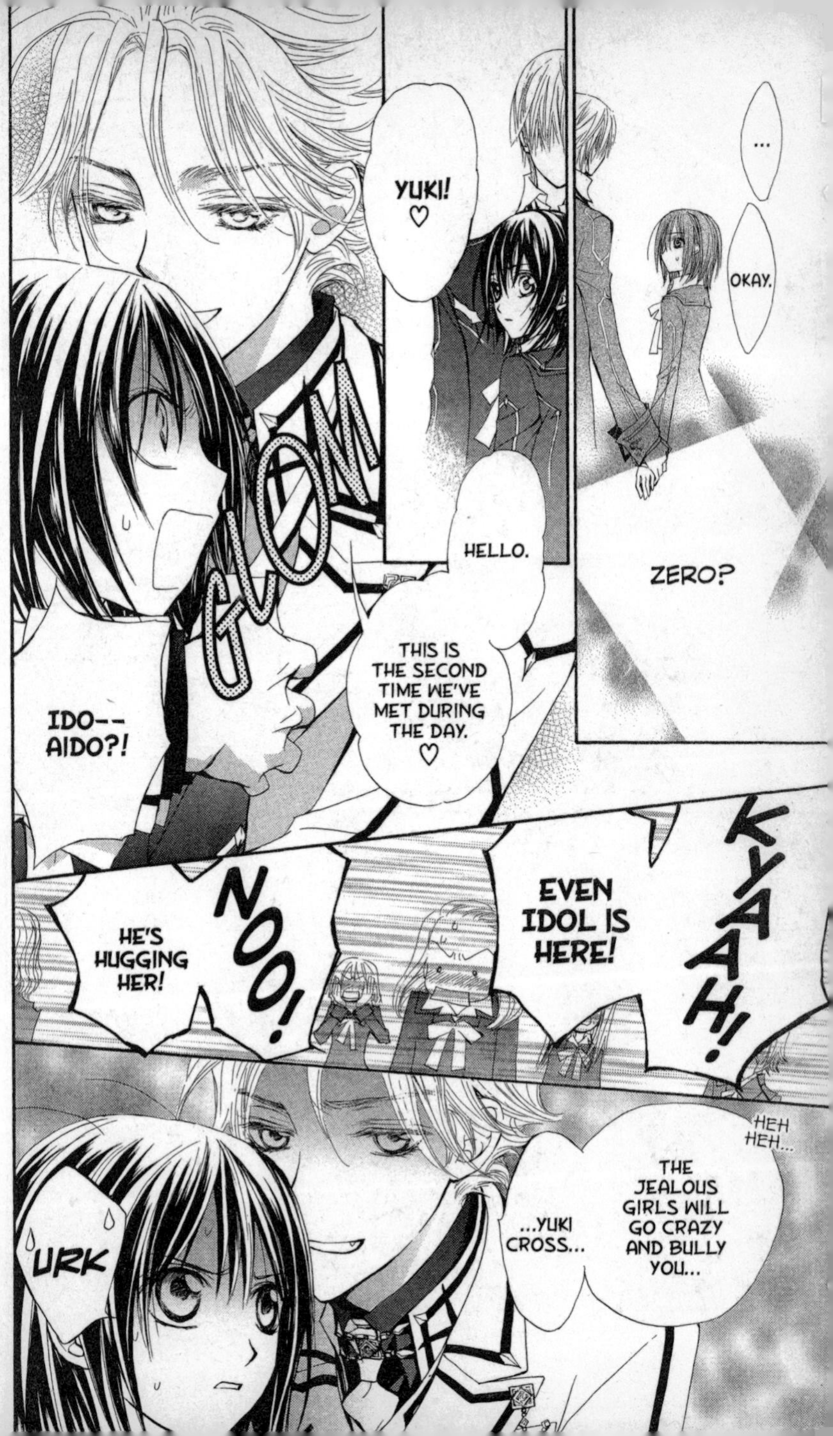
...
OKAY.
ZERO?
YUKI! ♡
HELLO.
THIS IS THE SECOND TIME WE'VE MET DURING THE DAY. ♡
GLOM
IDO-- AIDO?!
KYAAH!
EVEN IDOL IS HERE!
NOO!
HE'S HUGGING HER!
HEH HEH...
THE JEALOUS GIRLS WILL GO CRAZY AND BULLY YOU...
...YUKI CROSS...
URK

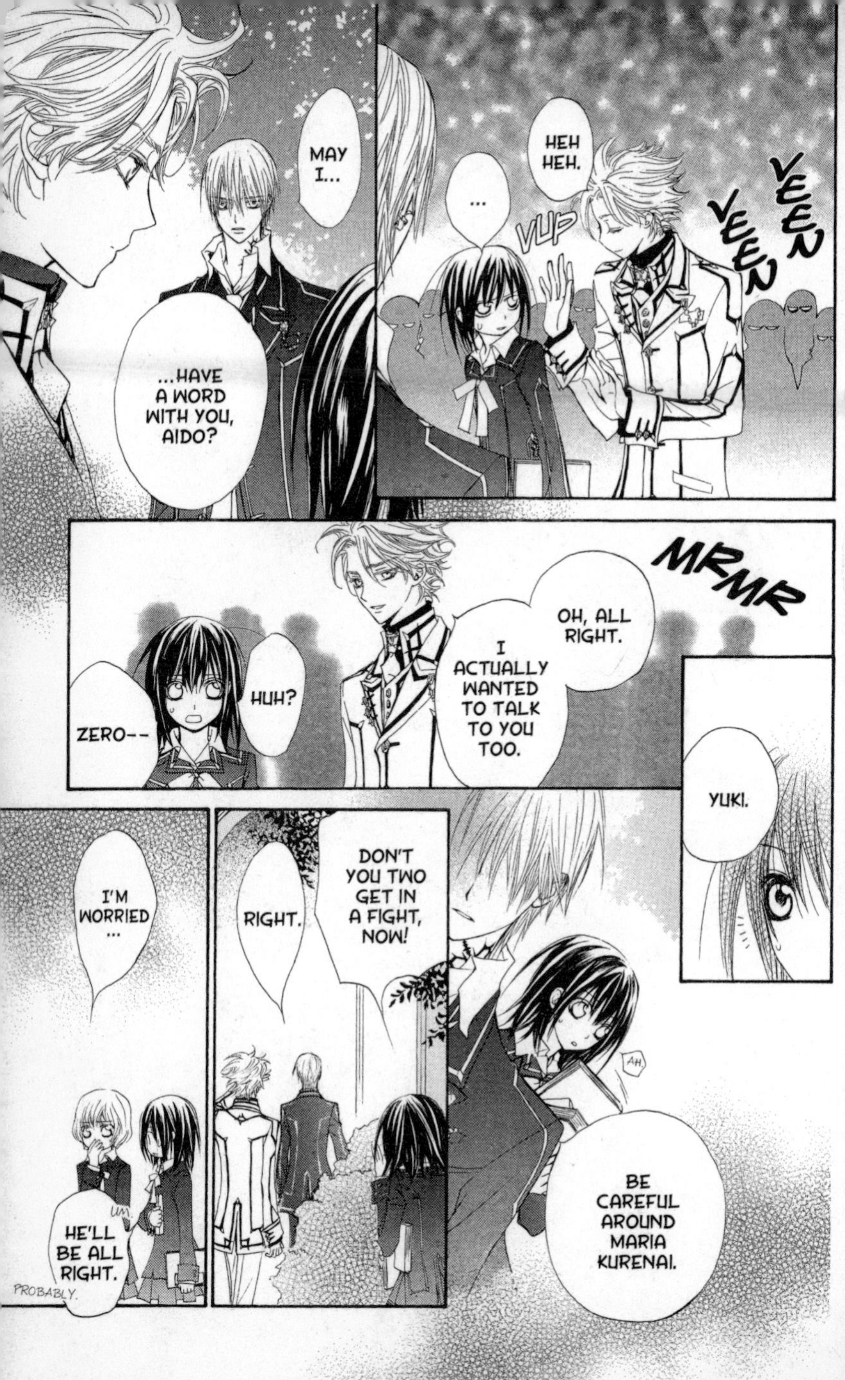

VEEN VEEN
HEH HEH.
...
VUP
MAY I...
...HAVE A WORD WITH YOU, AIDO?
MRMR
OH, ALL RIGHT.
I ACTUALLY WANTED TO TALK TO YOU TOO.
HUH?
ZERO--
YUKI.
AH.
BE CAREFUL AROUND MARIA KURENAI.
DON'T YOU TWO GET IN A FIGHT, NOW!
RIGHT.
I'M WORRIED ...
UM
HE'LL BE ALL RIGHT.
PROBABLY.

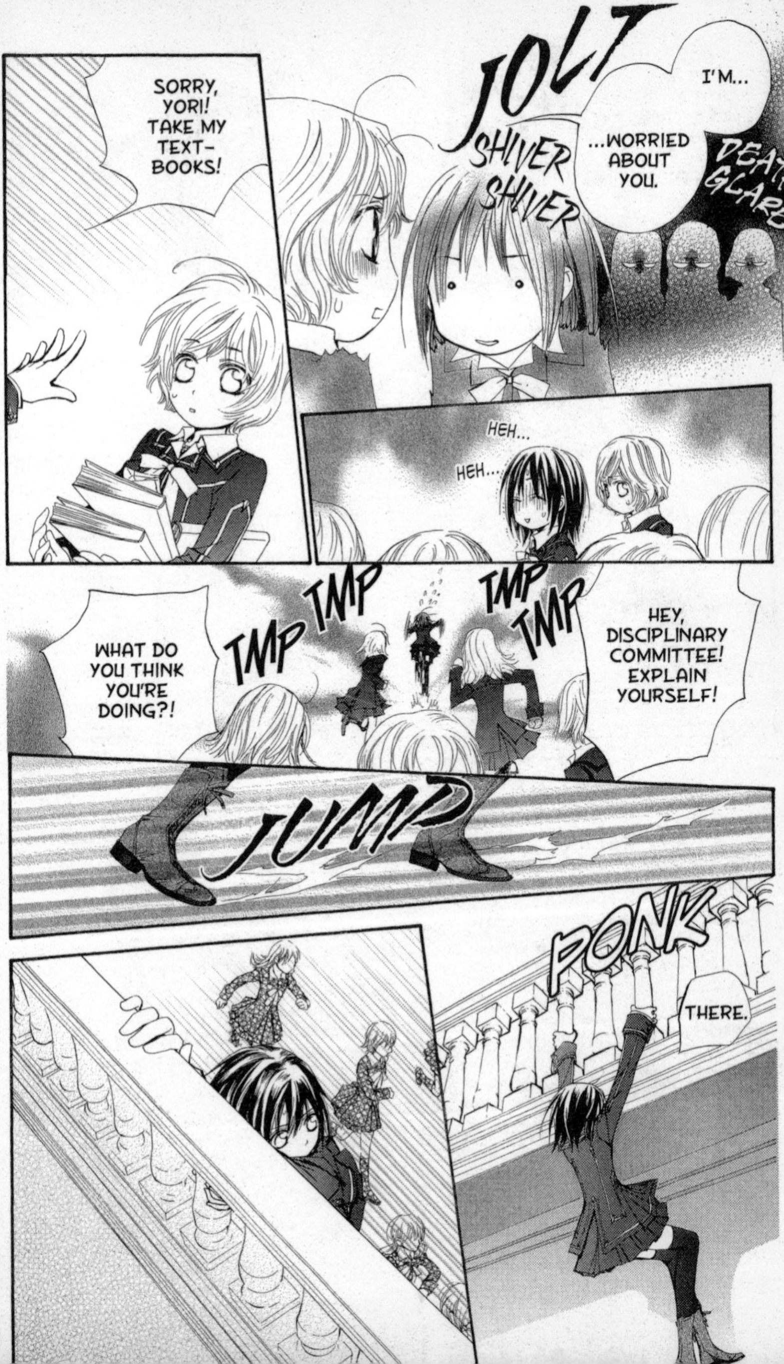

I'M...
...WORRIED ABOUT YOU.
JOLT
SHIVER SHIVER
DEATH GLARE
HEH...
HEH...
SORRY, YORI! TAKE MY TEXT-BOOKS!
HEY, DISCIPLINARY COMMITTEE! EXPLAIN YOURSELF!
TMP TMP
TMP TMP
WHAT DO YOU THINK YOU'RE DOING?!
JUMP
PONK
THERE.

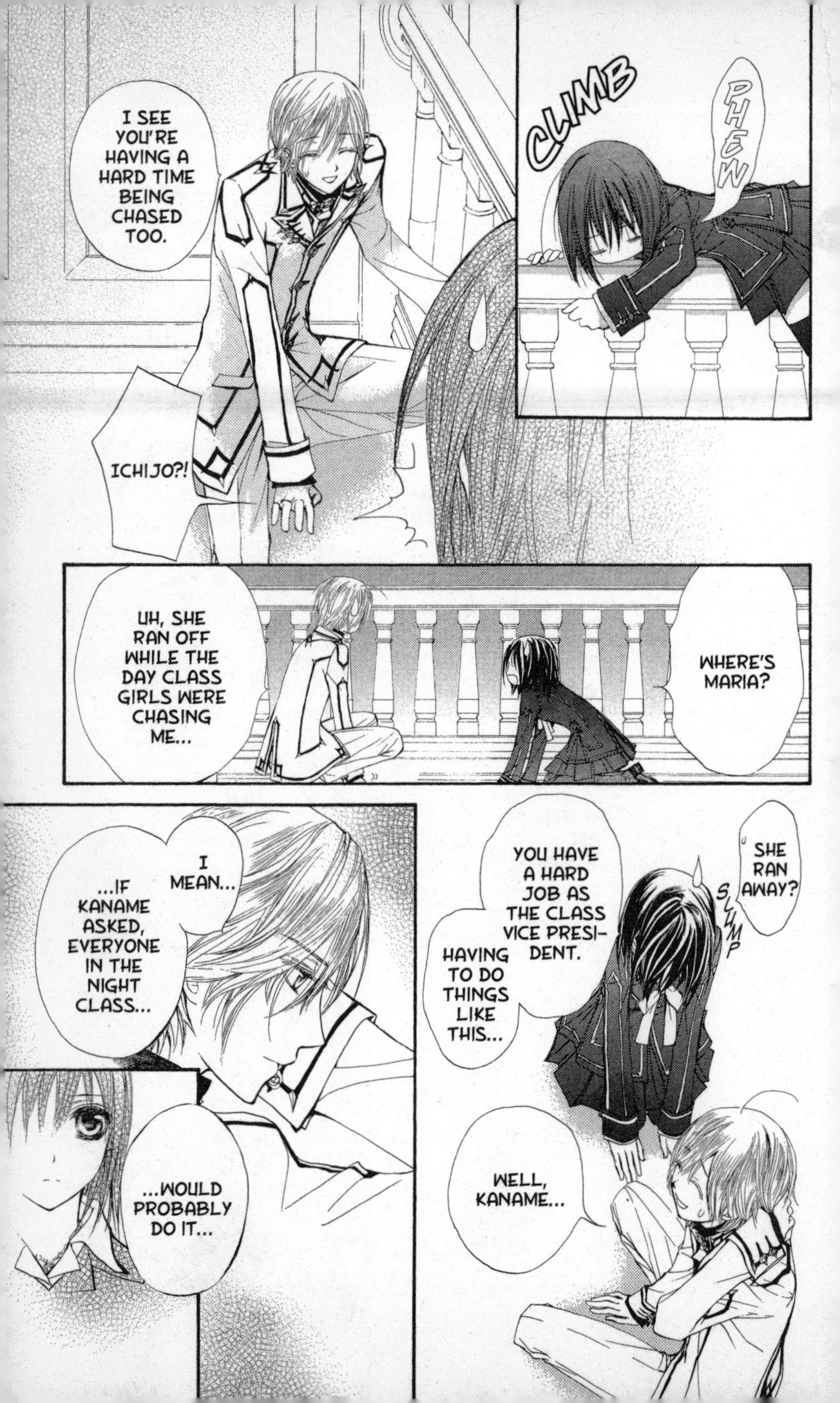
CLIMB
PHEW
I SEE YOU'RE HAVING A HARD TIME BEING CHASED TOO.
ICHIJO?!
WHERE'S MARIA?
UH, SHE RAN OFF WHILE THE DAY CLASS GIRLS WERE CHASING ME...
SHE RAN AWAY?
SLUMP
YOU HAVE A HARD JOB AS THE CLASS VICE PRESI-DENT.
HAVING TO DO THINGS LIKE THIS...
WELL, KANAME...
I MEAN...
...IF KANAME ASKED, EVERYONE IN THE NIGHT CLASS...
...WOULD PROBABLY DO IT...

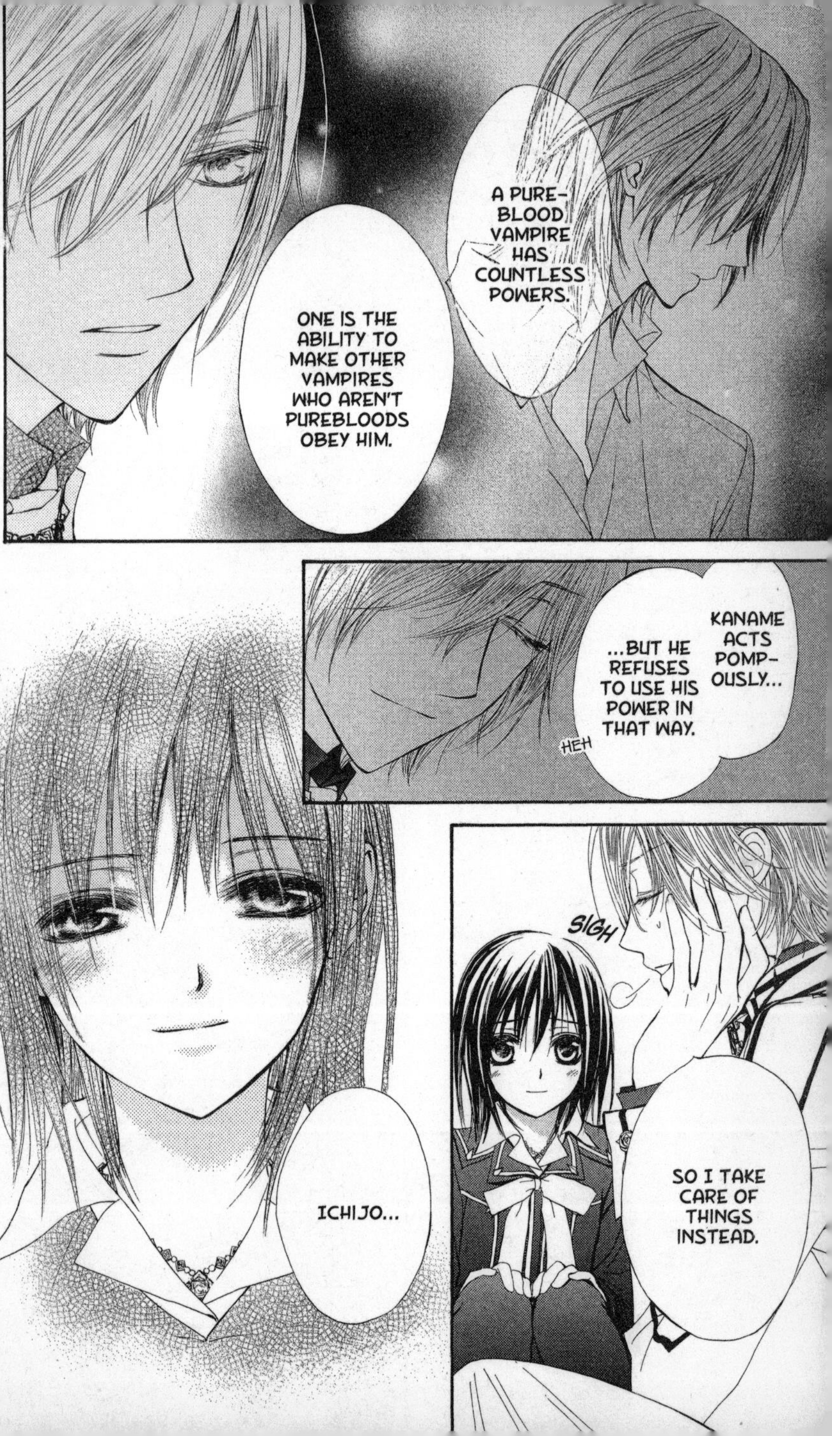
A PURE-BLOOD VAMPIRE HAS COUNTLESS POWERS.
ONE IS THE ABILITY TO MAKE OTHER VAMPIRES WHO AREN'T PUREBLOODS OBEY HIM.
KANAME ACTS POMP-OUSLY...
...BUT HE REFUSES TO USE HIS POWER IN THAT WAY.
HEH
SIGH
SO I TAKE CARE OF THINGS INSTEAD.
ICHIJO...

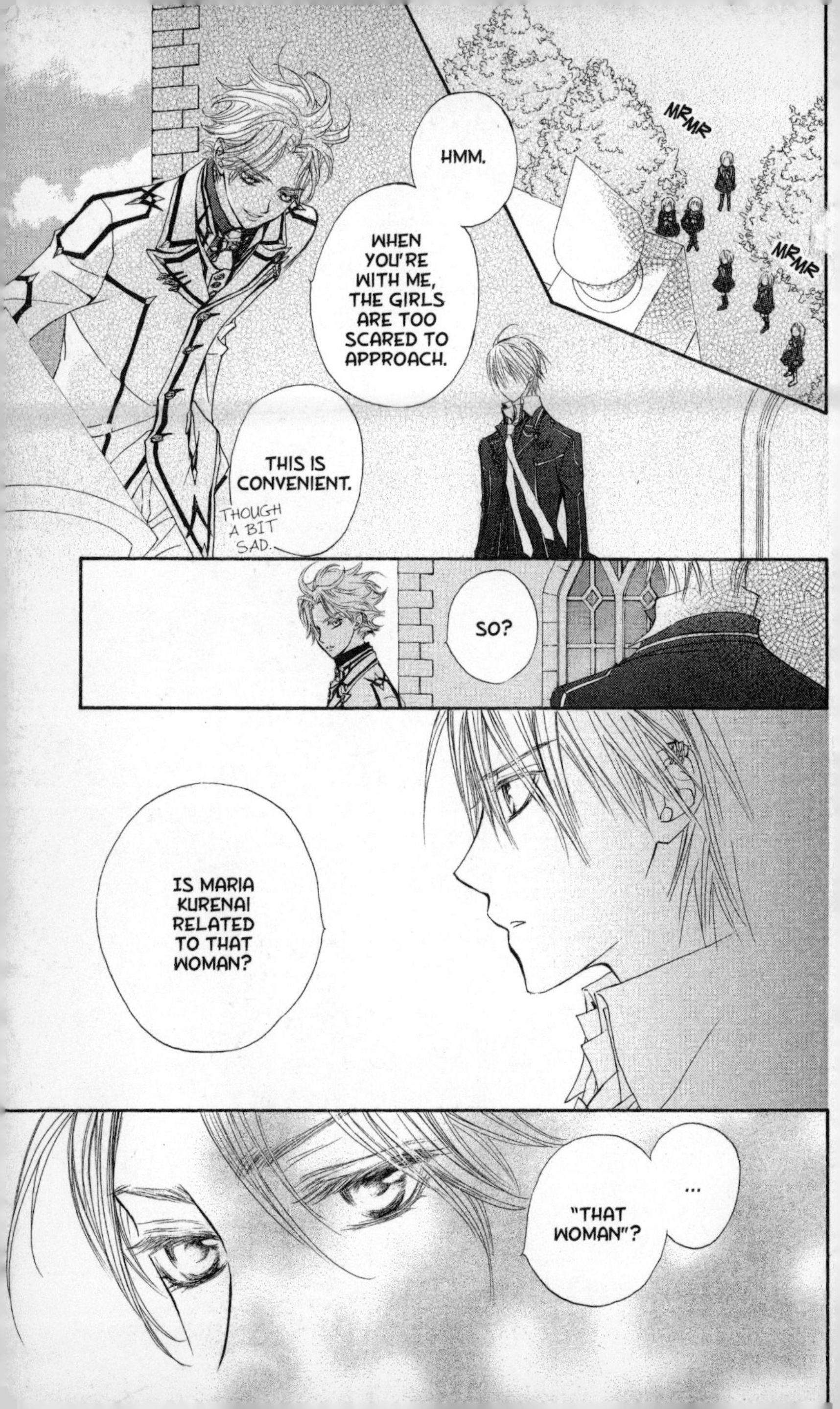
MRMR
MRMR
HMM.
WHEN YOU'RE WITH ME, THE GIRLS ARE TOO SCARED TO APPROACH.
THIS IS CONVENIENT.
THOUGH A BIT SAD.
SO?
IS MARIA KURENAI RELATED TO THAT WOMAN?
...
"THAT WOMAN"?

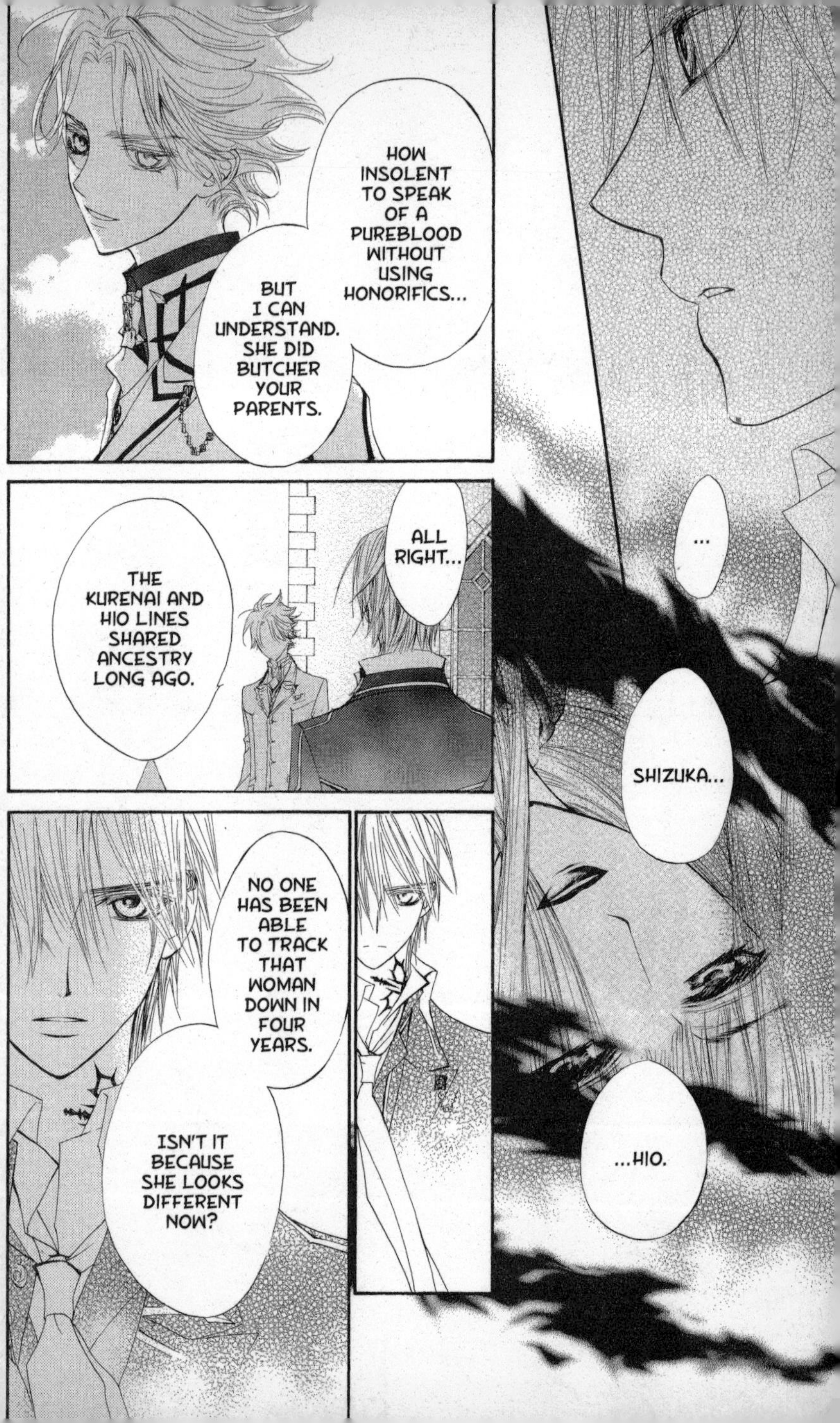
...
SHIZUKA...
...HIO.
HOW INSOLENT TO SPEAK OF A PUREBLOOD WITHOUT USING HONORIFICS...
BUT I CAN UNDERSTAND. SHE DID BUTCHER YOUR PARENTS.
ALL RIGHT...
THE KURENAI AND HIO LINES SHARED ANCESTRY LONG AGO.
NO ONE HAS BEEN ABLE TO TRACK THAT WOMAN DOWN IN FOUR YEARS.
ISN'T IT BECAUSE SHE LOOKS DIFFERENT NOW?

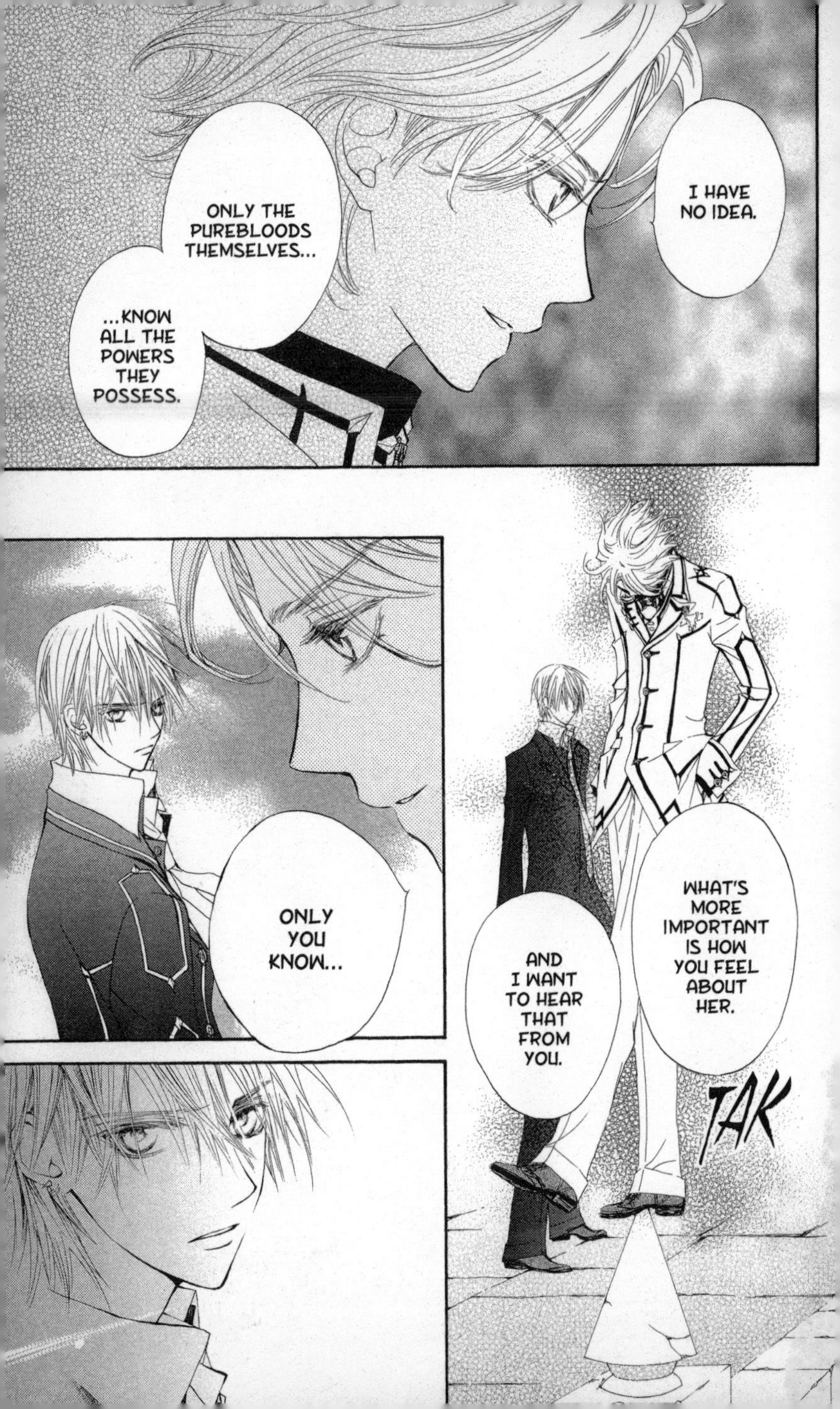
I HAVE NO IDEA.
ONLY THE PUREBLOODS THEMSELVES...
...KNOW ALL THE POWERS THEY POSSESS.
WHAT'S MORE IMPORTANT IS HOW YOU FEEL ABOUT HER.
AND I WANT TO HEAR THAT FROM YOU.
TAK
ONLY YOU KNOW...

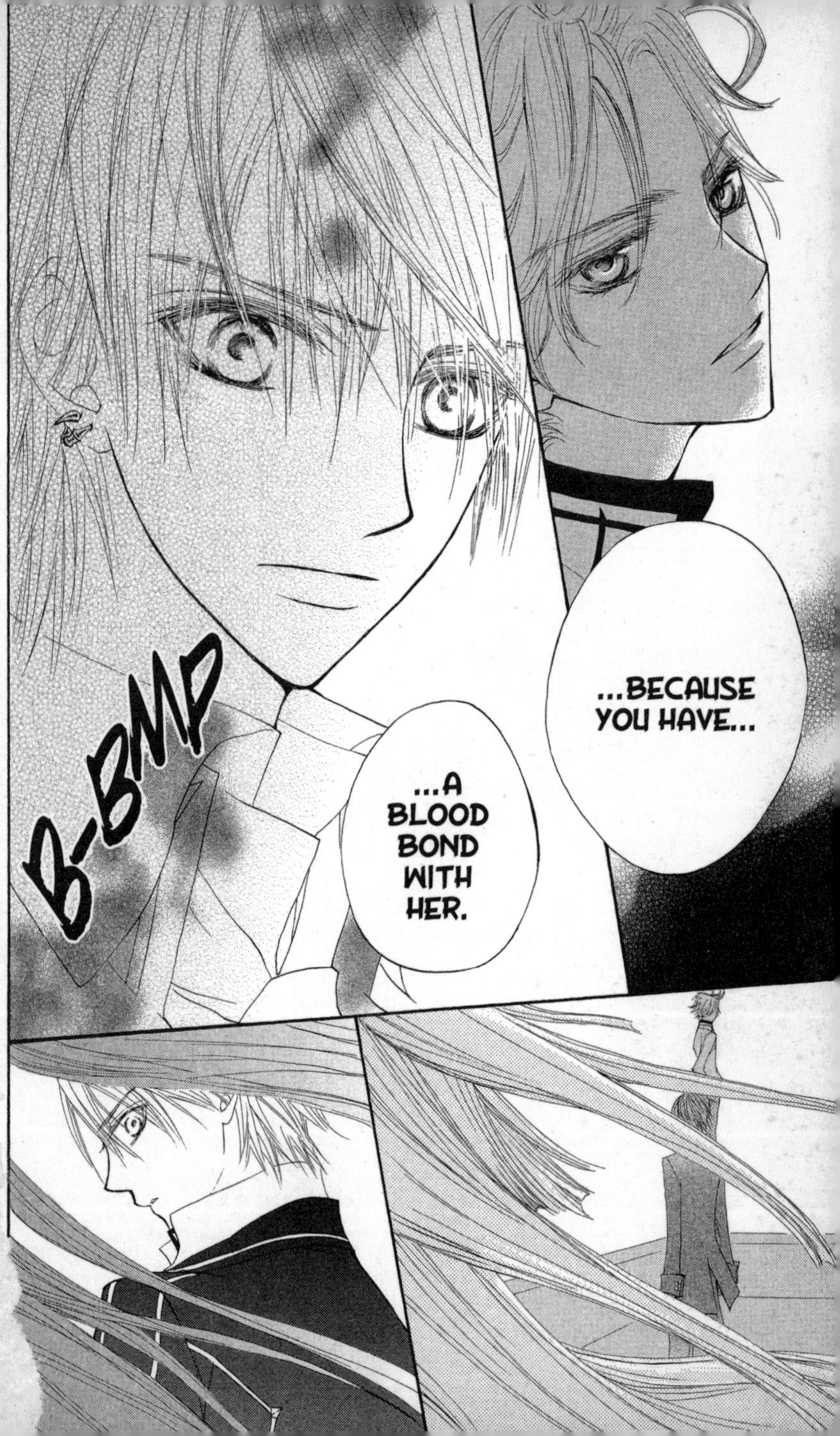
...BECAUSE YOU HAVE...
...A BLOOD BOND WITH HER.
B-BMP

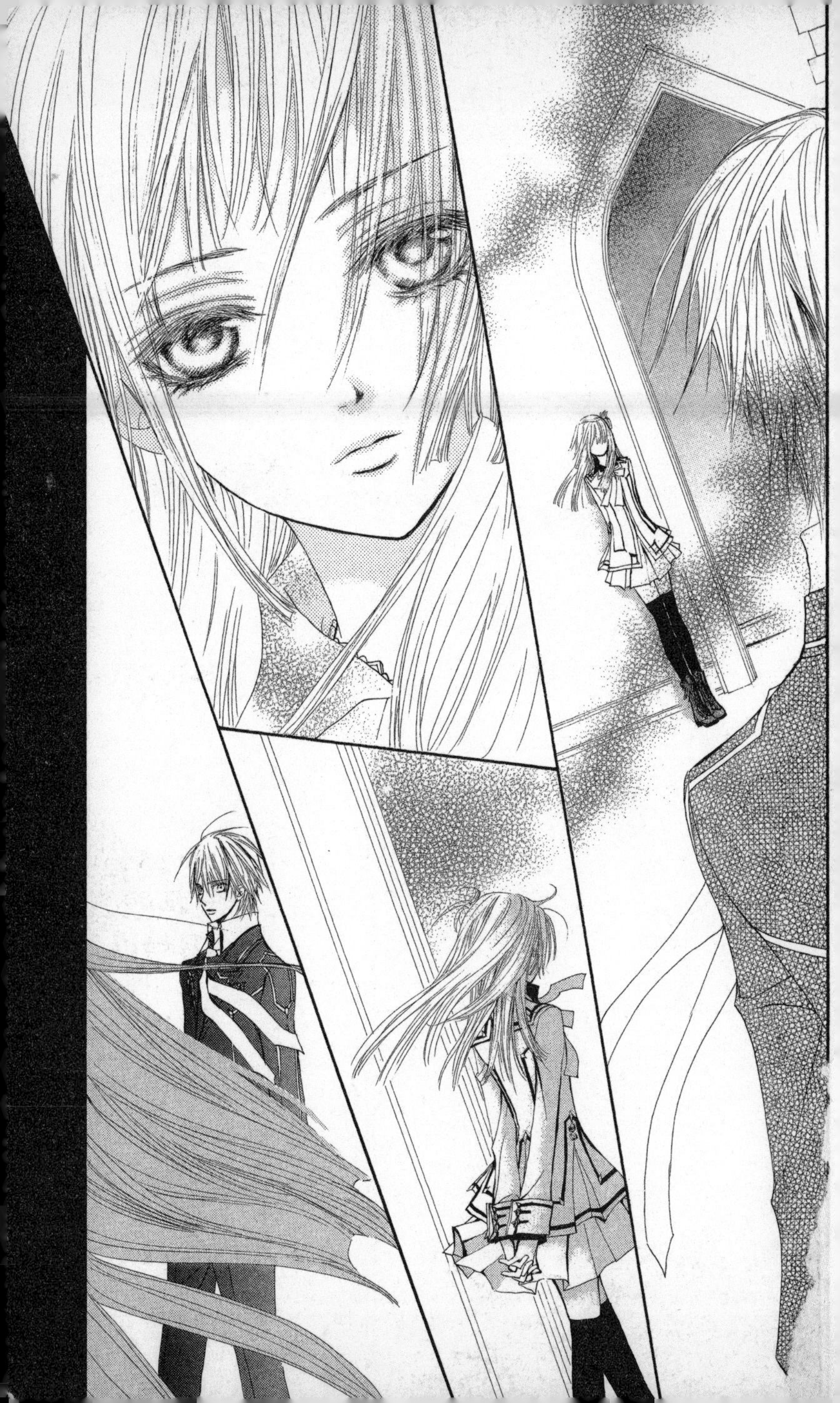

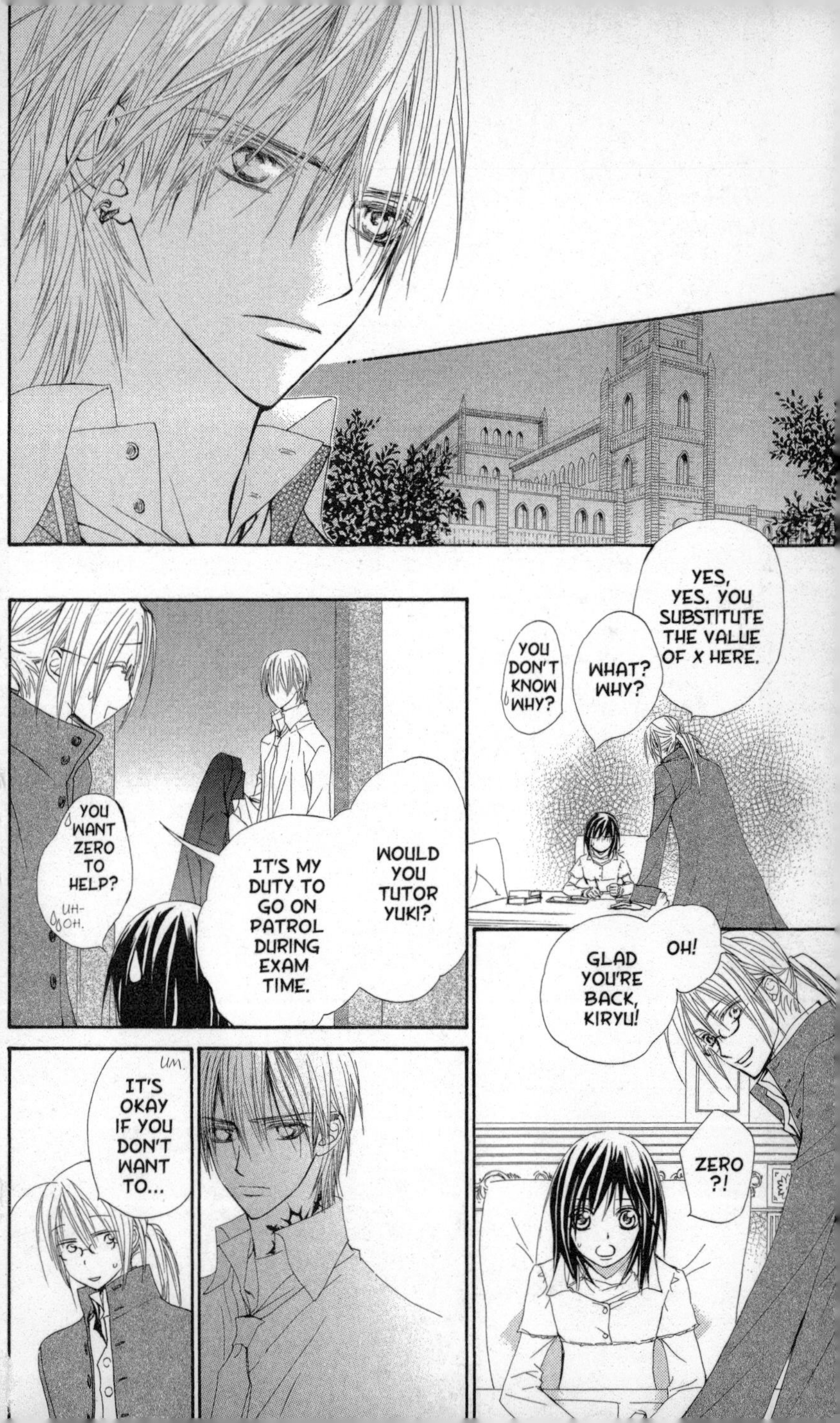

YES, YES. YOU SUBSTITUTE THE VALUE OF X HERE.
WHAT? WHY?
YOU DON'T KNOW WHY?
OH!
GLAD YOU'RE BACK, KIRYU!
ZERO?!
WOULD YOU TUTOR YUKI?
IT'S MY DUTY TO GO ON PATROL DURING EXAM TIME.
YOU WANT ZERO TO HELP?
UH-OH.
UM.
IT'S OKAY IF YOU DON'T WANT TO...

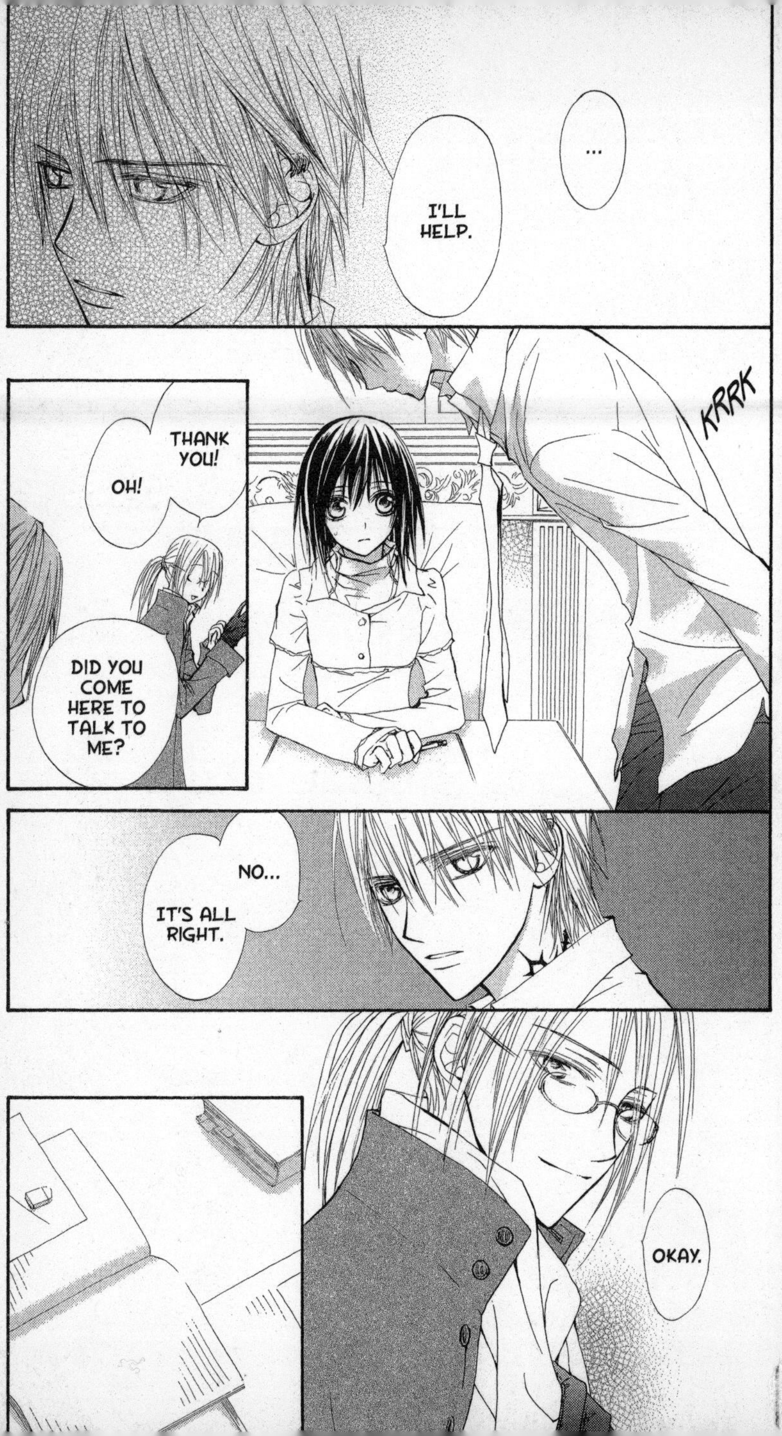
...
I'LL HELP.
KRRK
THANK YOU!
OH!
DID YOU COME HERE TO TALK TO ME?
NO...
IT'S ALL RIGHT.
OKAY.

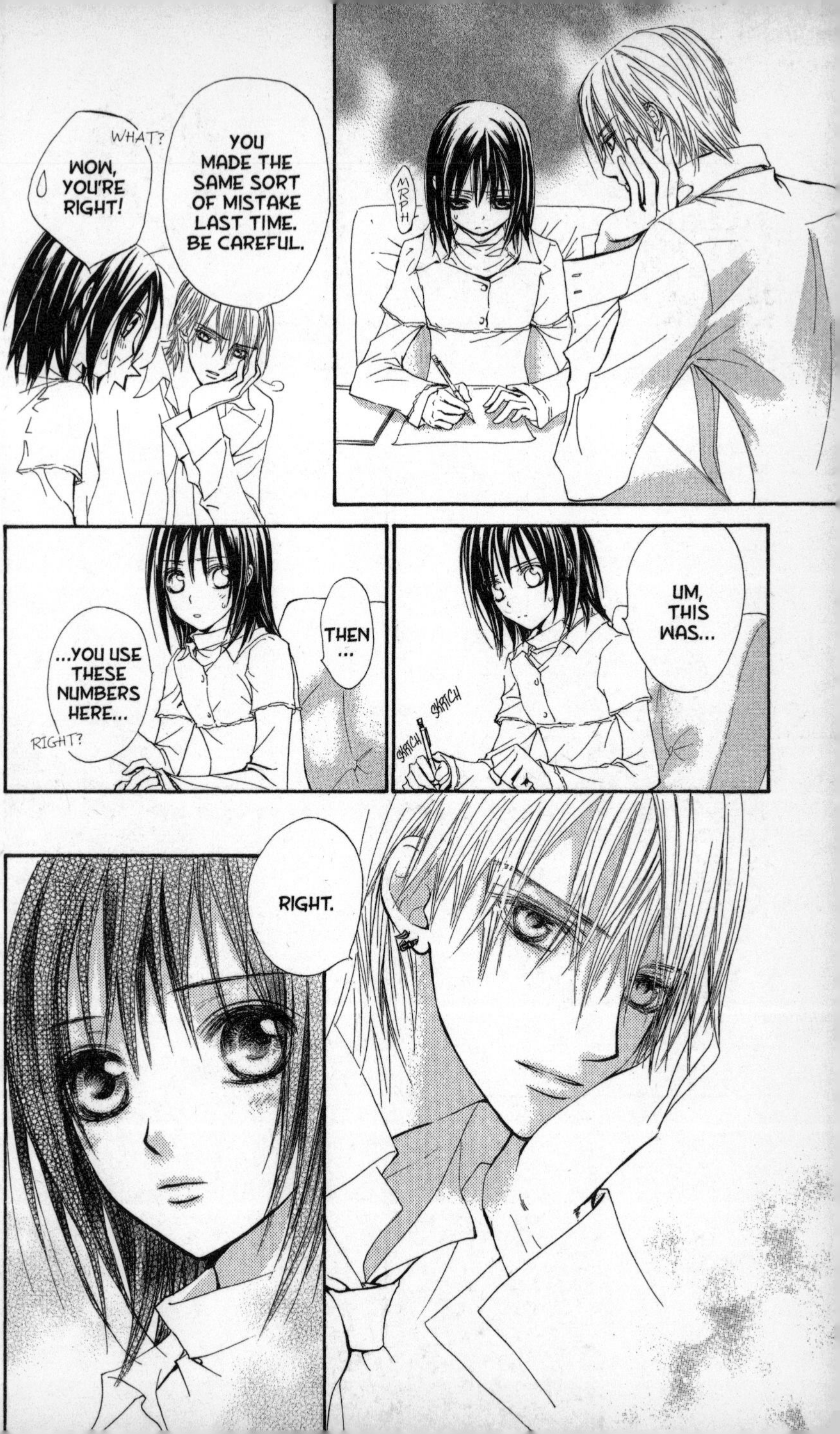
MRPH
YOU MADE THE SAME SORT OF MISTAKE LAST TIME. BE CAREFUL.
WHAT?
WOW, YOU'RE RIGHT!
UM, THIS WAS...
SKRTCH
SKRTCH
THEN...
...YOU USE THESE NUMBERS HERE...
RIGHT?
RIGHT.

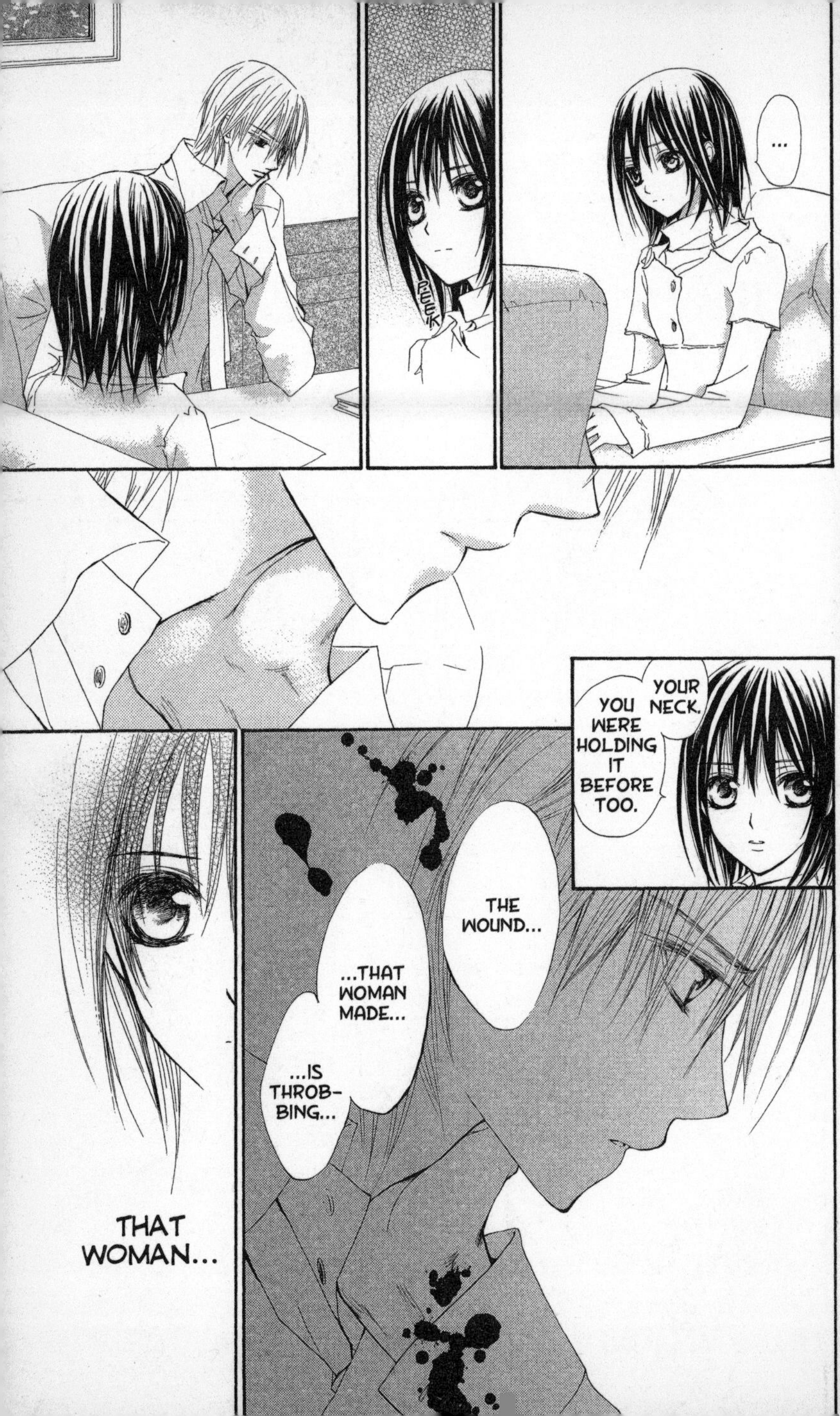
...
PEEK
YOUR NECK.
YOU WERE HOLDING IT BEFORE TOO.
THE WOUND...
...THAT WOMAN MADE...
...IS THROB-BING...
THAT WOMAN...

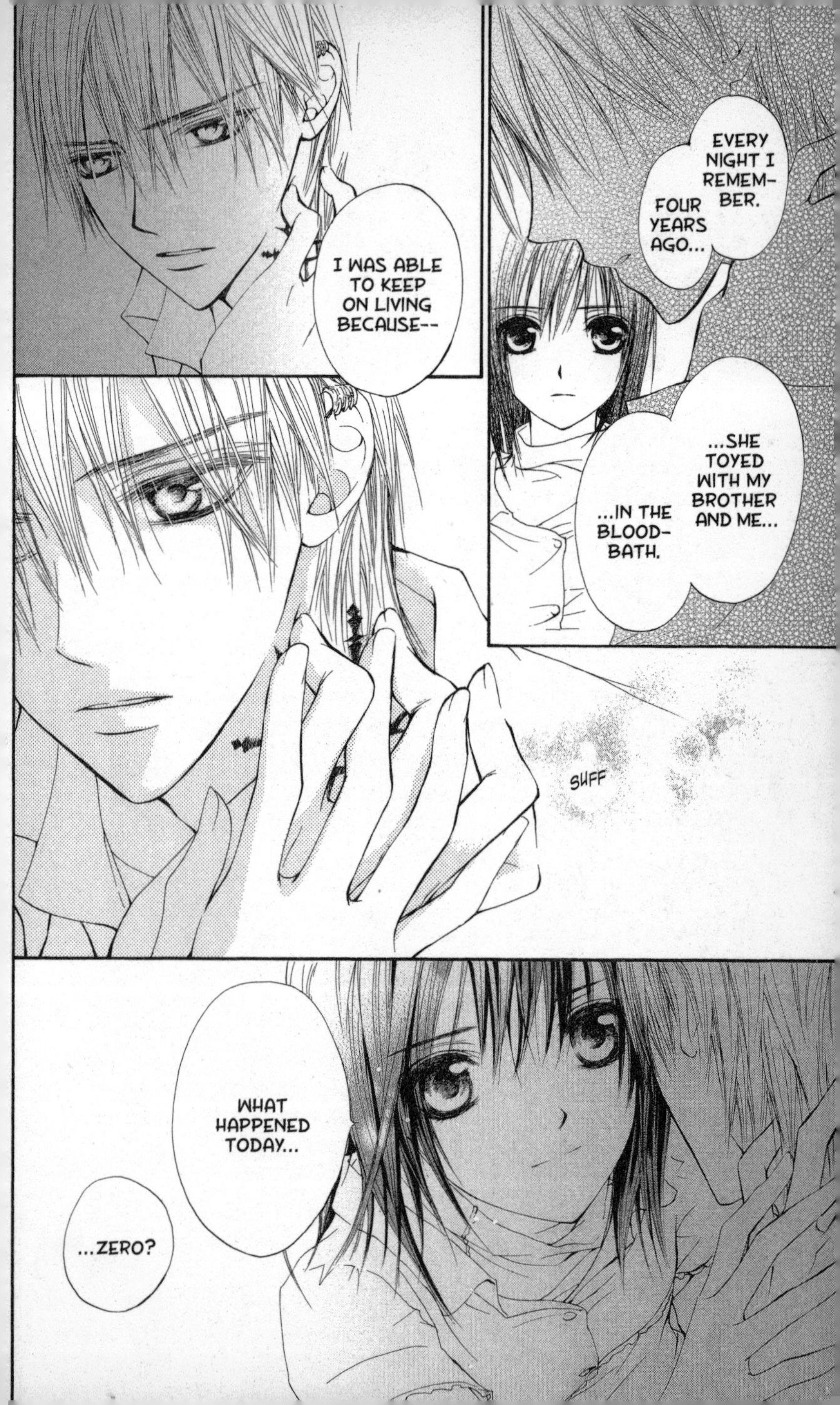
EVERY NIGHT I REMEMBER.
FOUR YEARS AGO...
...SHE TOYED WITH MY BROTHER AND ME...
...IN THE BLOOD-BATH.
I WAS ABLE TO KEEP ON LIVING BECAUSE--
SUFF
WHAT HAPPENED TODAY...
...ZERO?

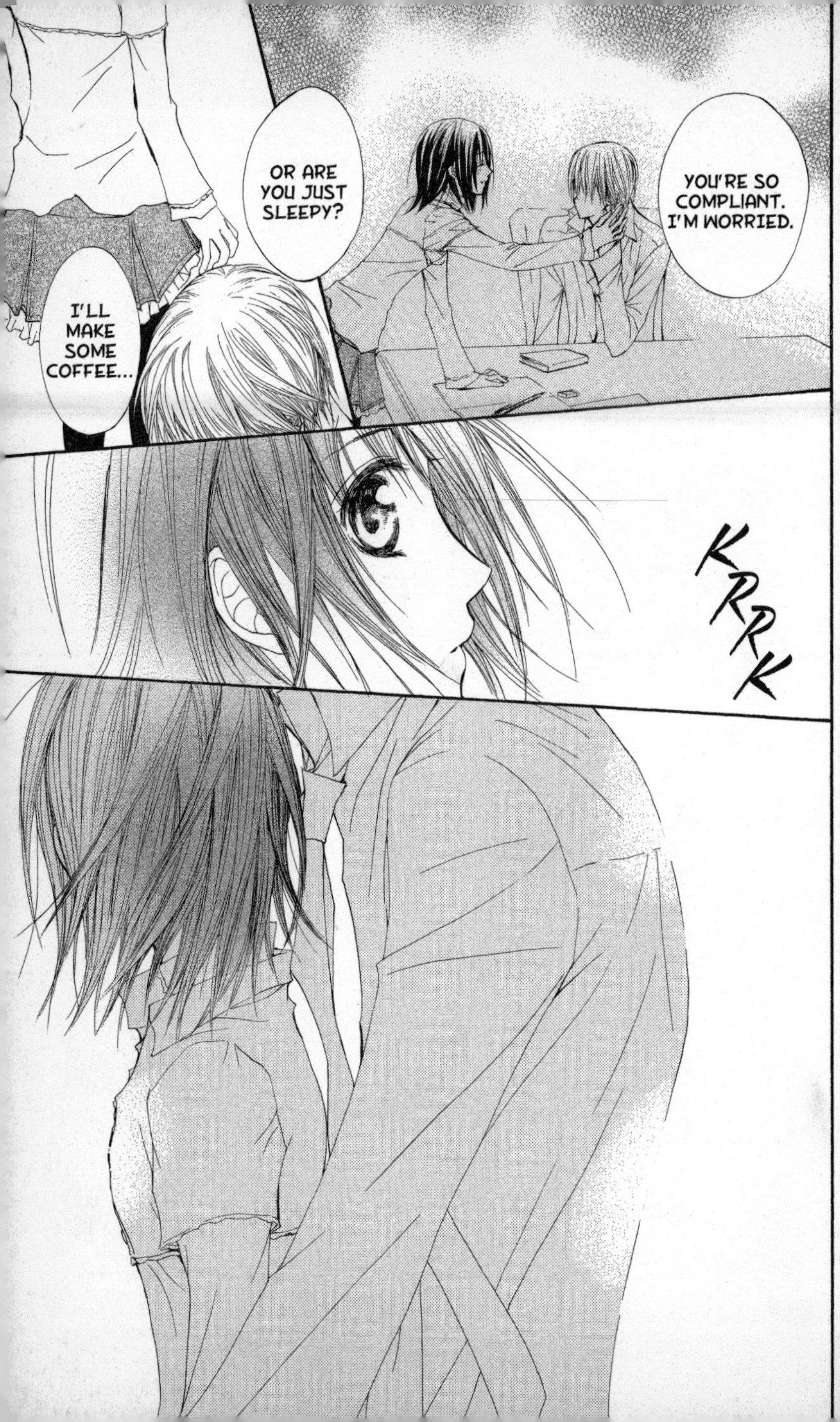
YOU'RE SO COMPLIANT. I'M WORRIED.
OR ARE YOU JUST SLEEPY?
I'LL MAKE SOME COFFEE...
KRRK

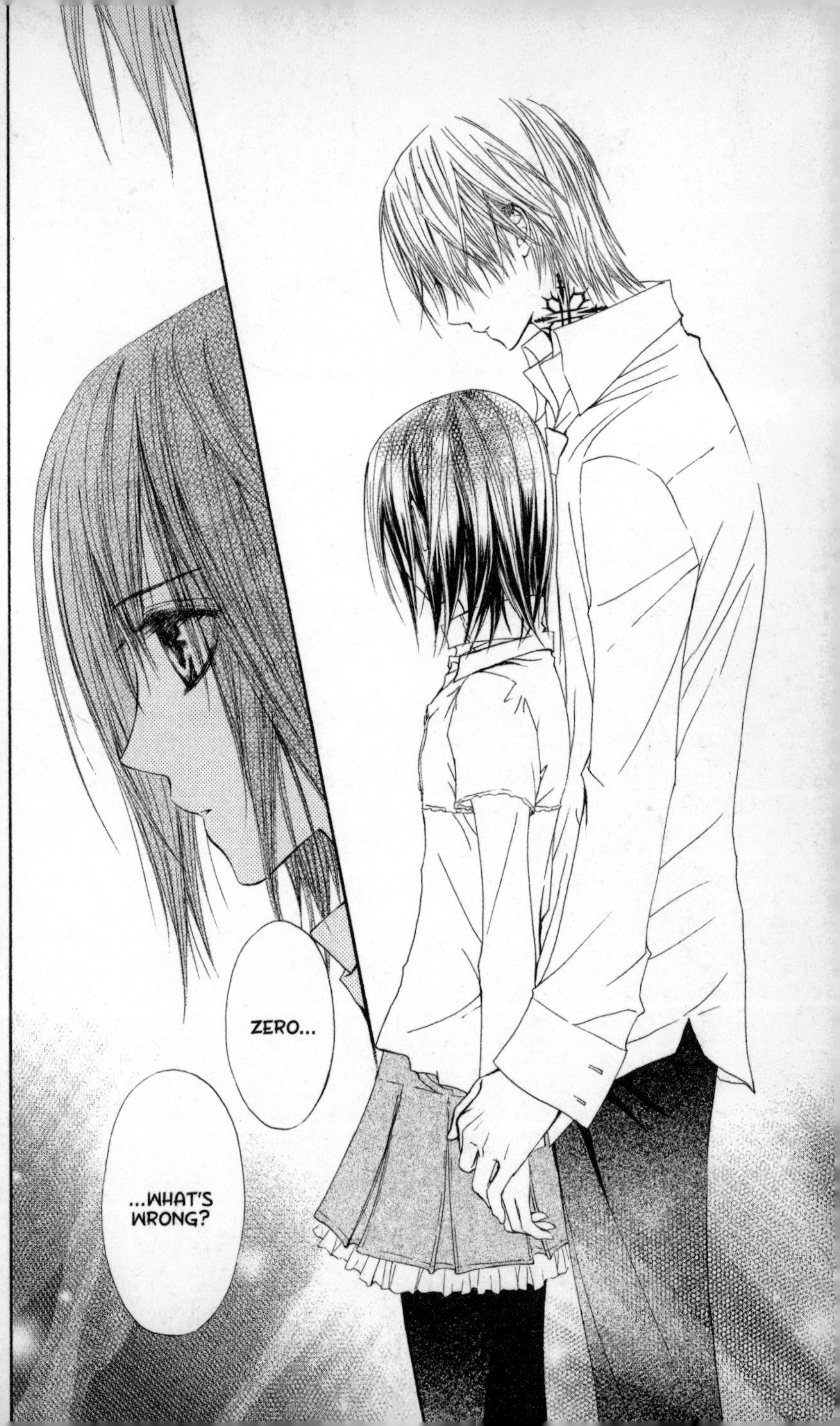
ZERO...
...WHAT'S WRONG?

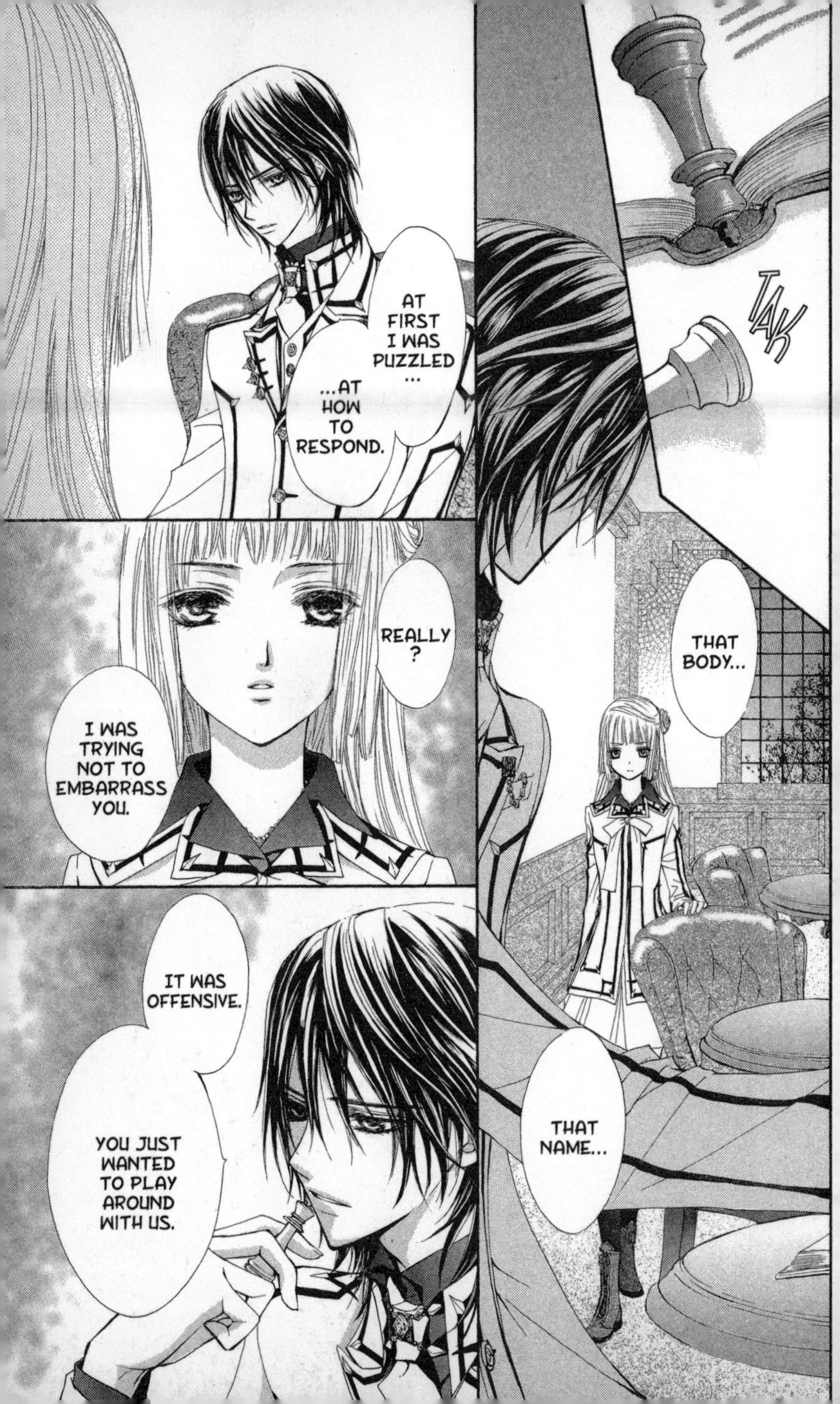
TAK
THAT BODY...
THAT NAME...
AT FIRST I WAS PUZZLED...
...AT HOW TO RESPOND.
REALLY?
I WAS TRYING NOT TO EMBARRASS YOU.
IT WAS OFFENSIVE.
YOU JUST WANTED TO PLAY AROUND WITH US.

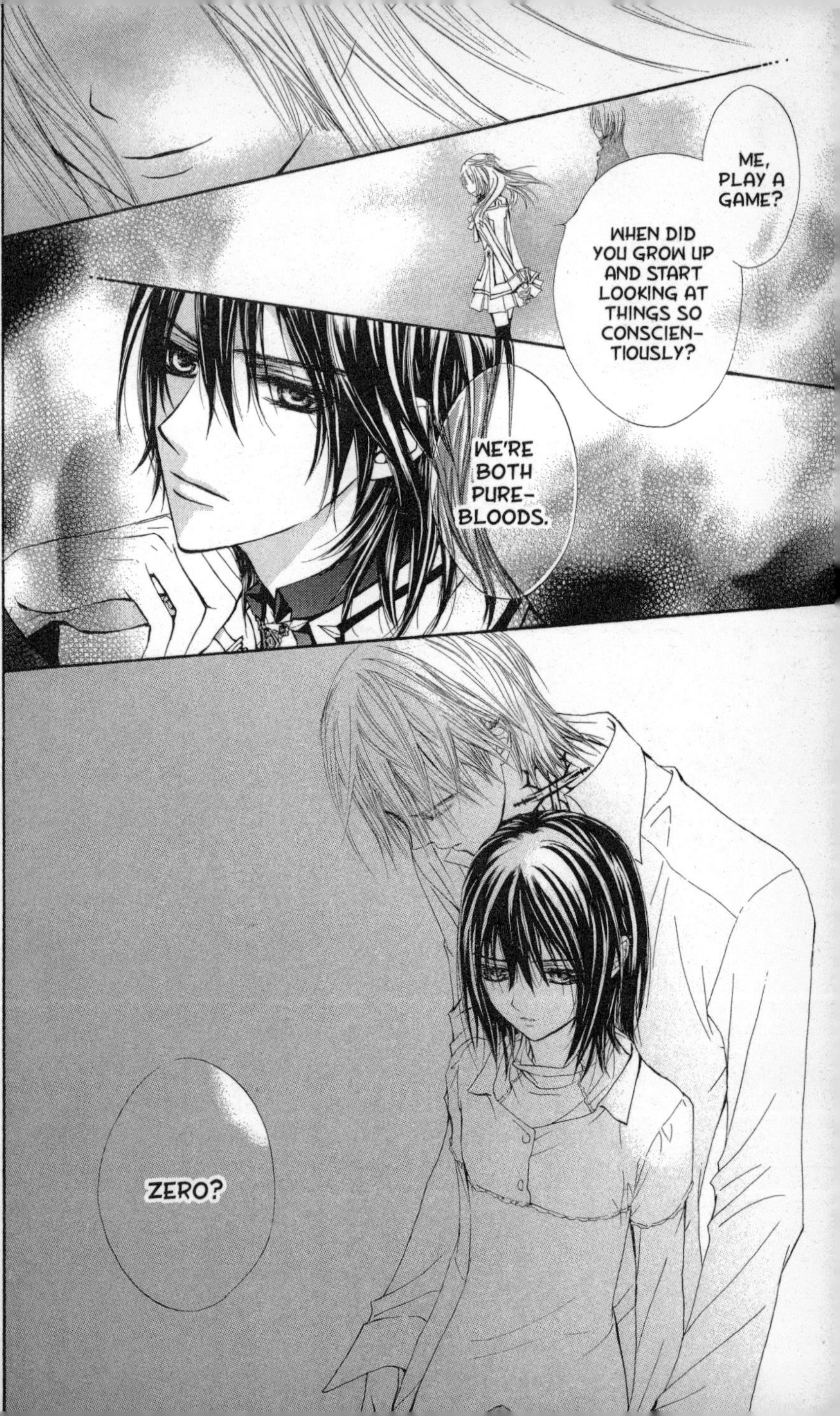
ME, PLAY A GAME?
WHEN DID YOU GROW UP AND START LOOKING AT THINGS SO CONSCIEN-TIOUSLY?
WE'RE BOTH PURE-BLOODS.
ZERO?

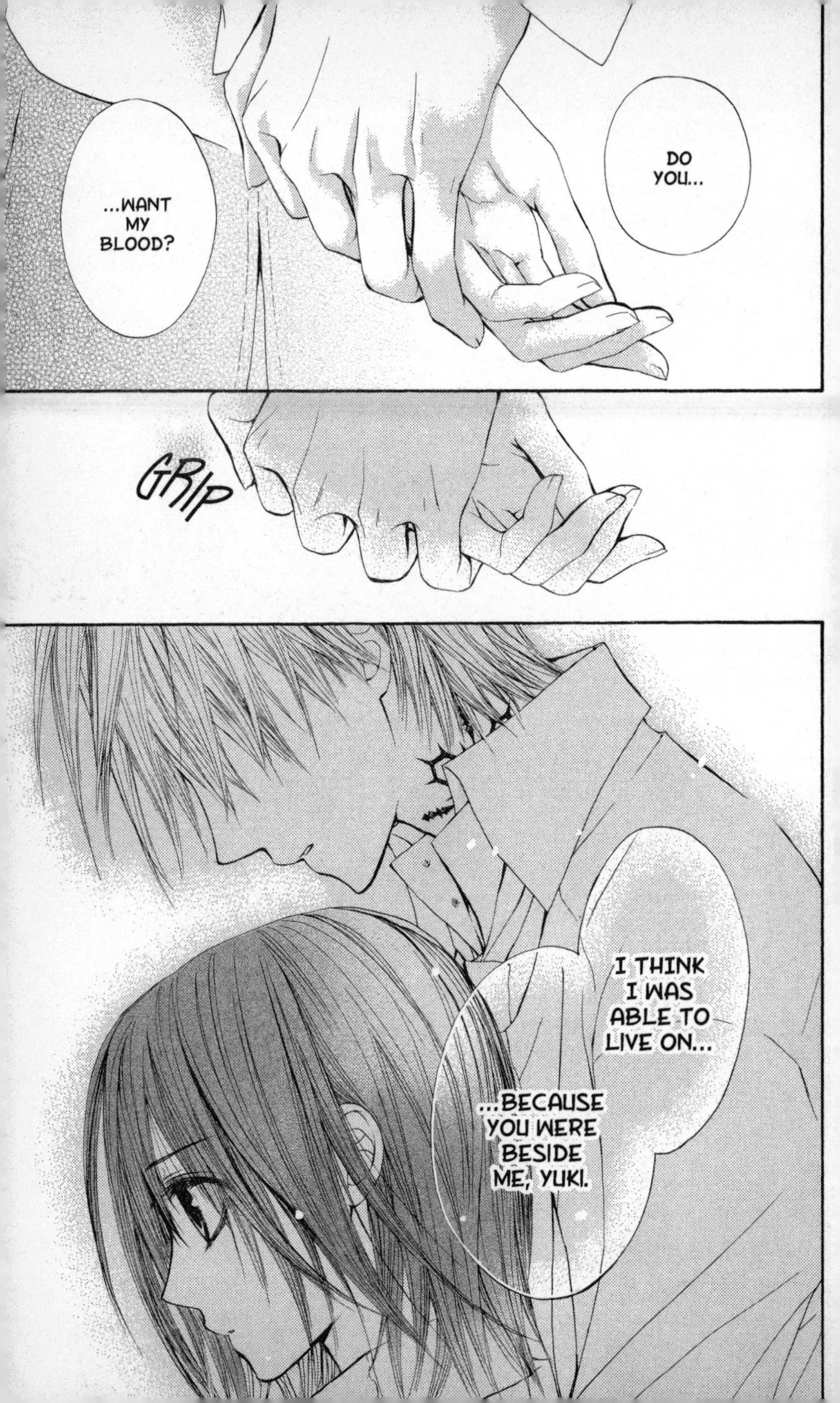
DO YOU...
...WANT MY BLOOD?
GRIP
I THINK I WAS ABLE TO LIVE ON...
...BECAUSE YOU WERE BESIDE ME, YUKI.

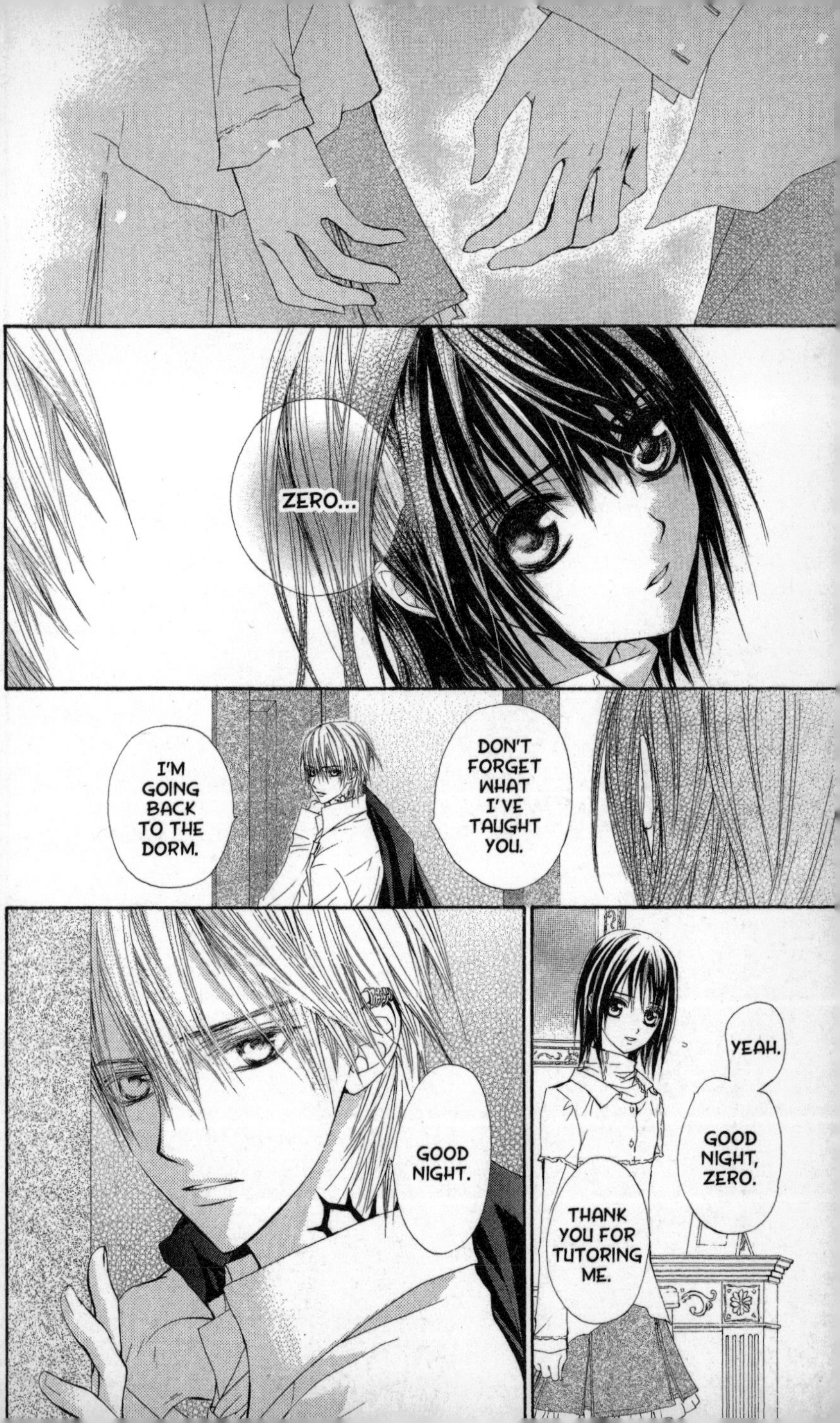
ZERO...
DON'T FORGET WHAT I'VE TAUGHT YOU.
I'M GOING BACK TO THE DORM.
YEAH.
GOOD NIGHT, ZERO.
THANK YOU FOR TUTORING ME.
GOOD NIGHT.

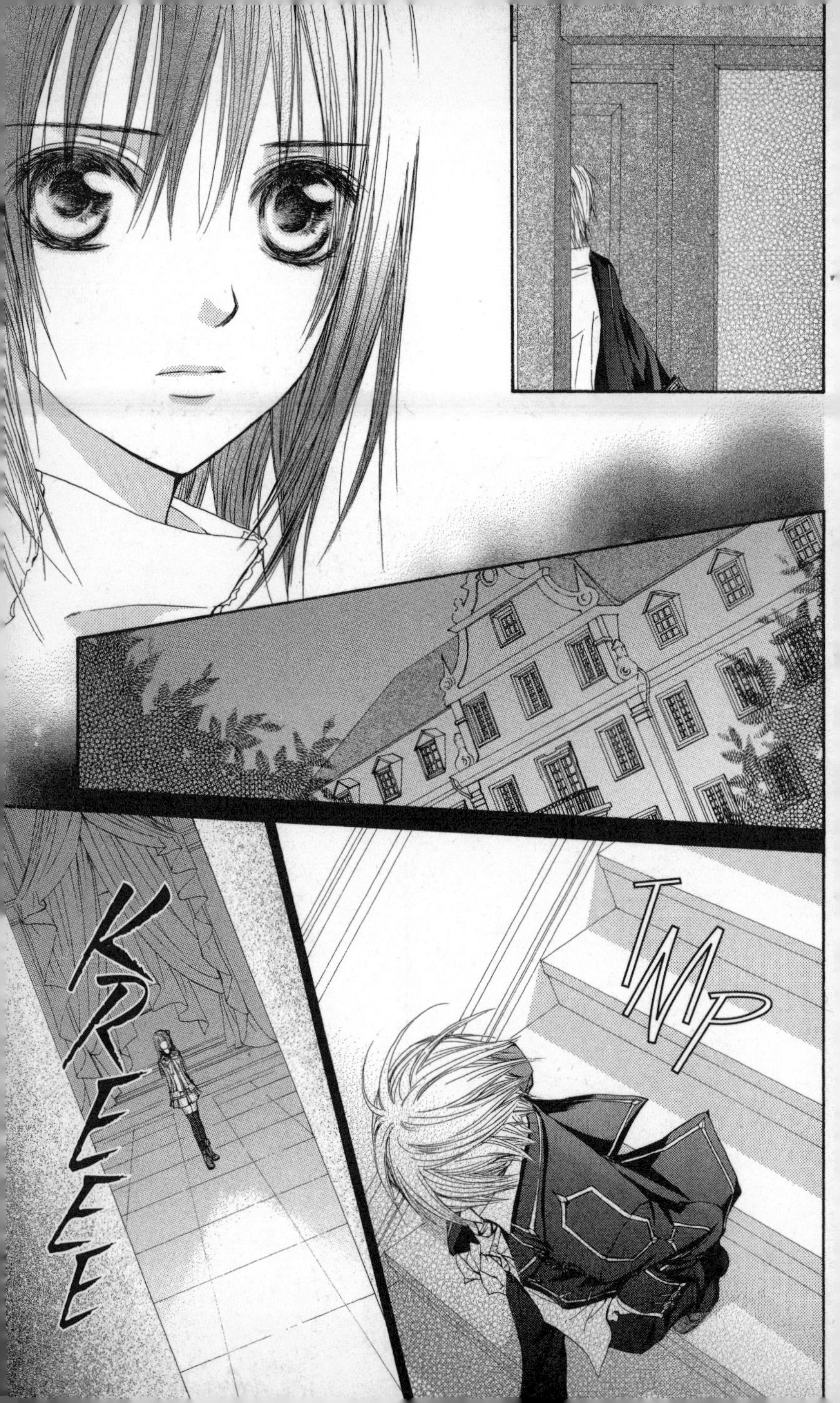
TMP
KREEEE

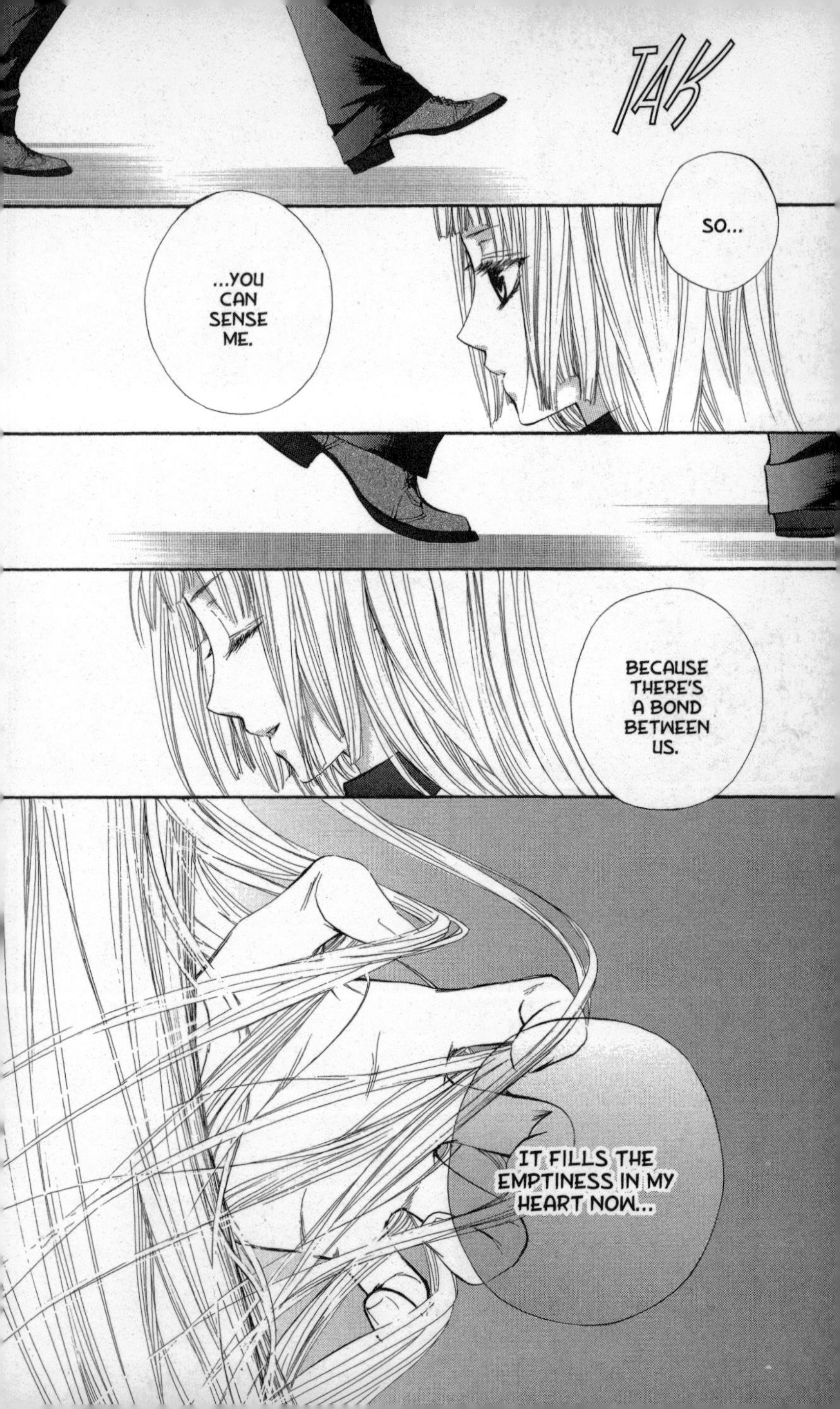
TAK
SO...
...YOU CAN SENSE ME.
BECAUSE THERE'S A BOND BETWEEN US.
IT FILLS THE EMPTINESS IN MY HEART NOW...

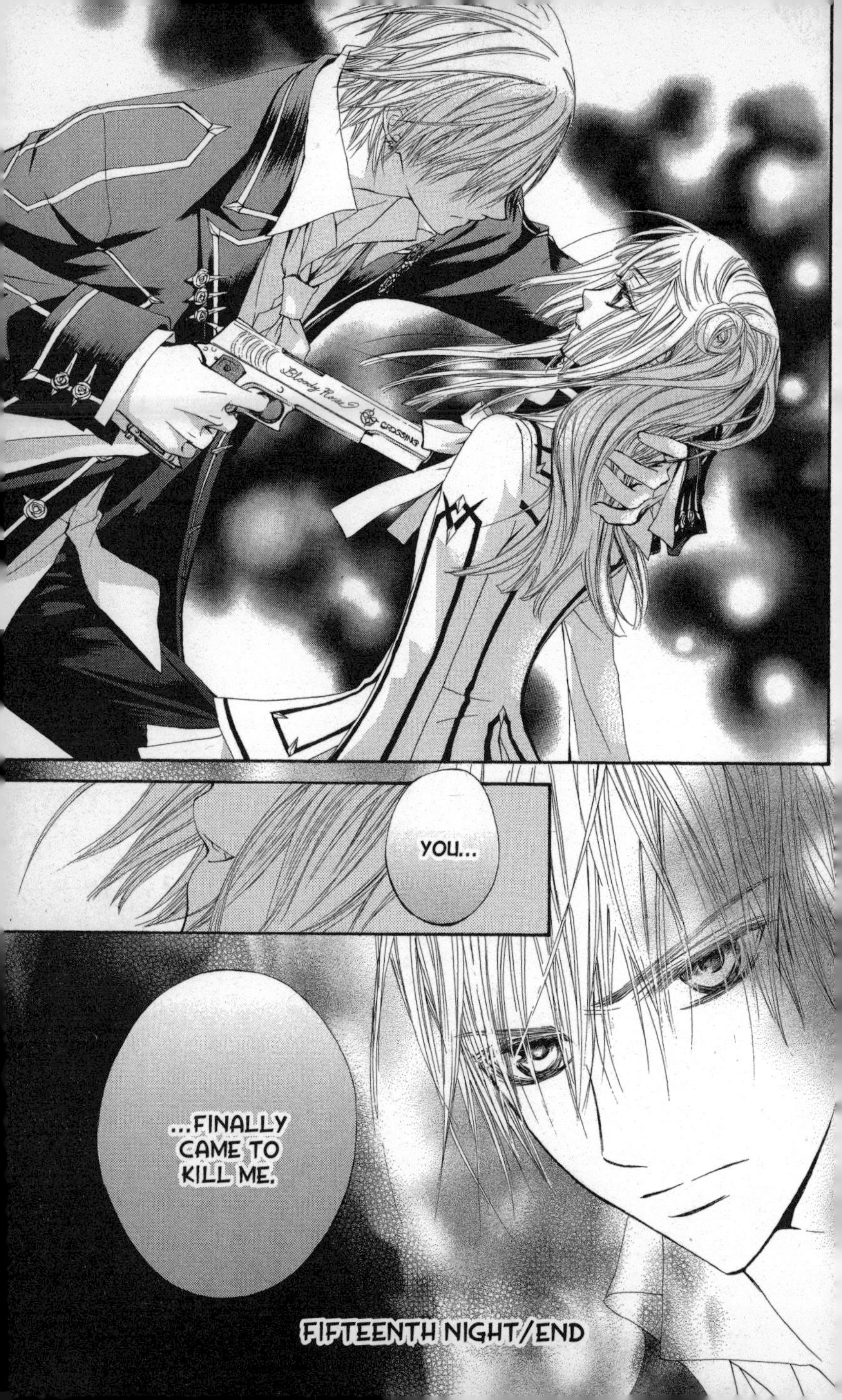
Bloody Rose
CROSSING
YOU...
...FINALLY CAME TO KILL ME.
FIFTEENTH NIGHT/END

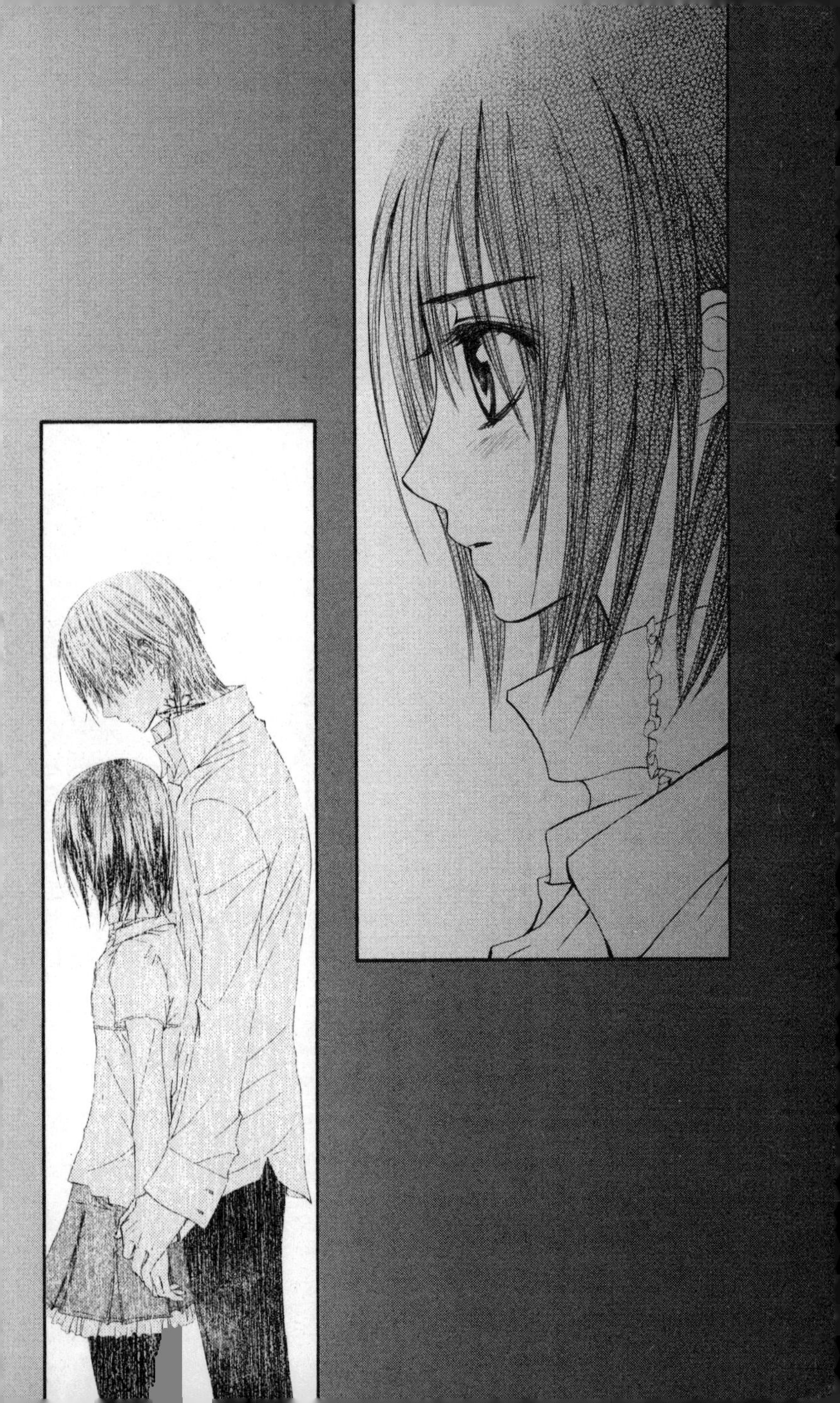

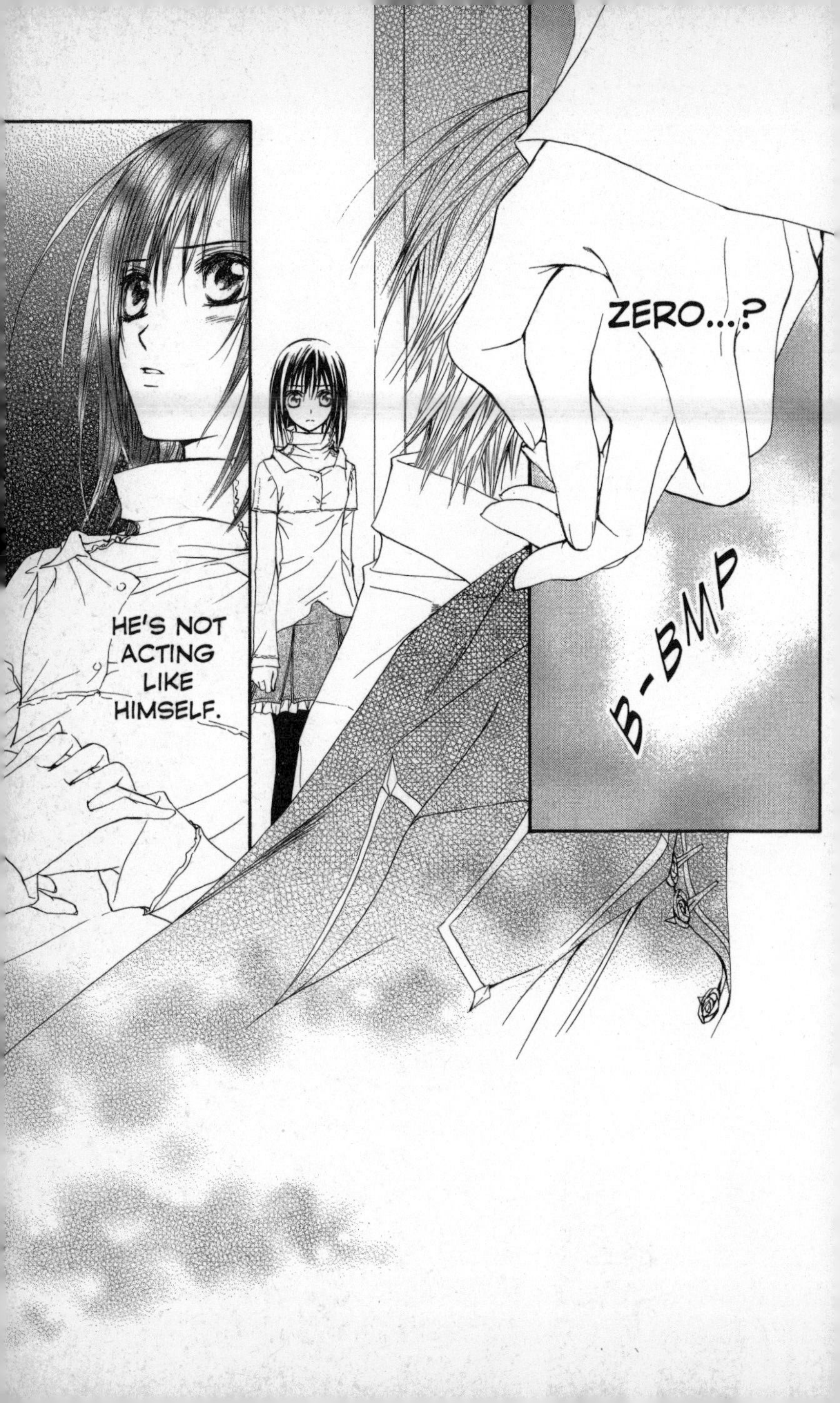
ZERO...?
B-BMP
HE'S NOT ACTING LIKE HIMSELF.

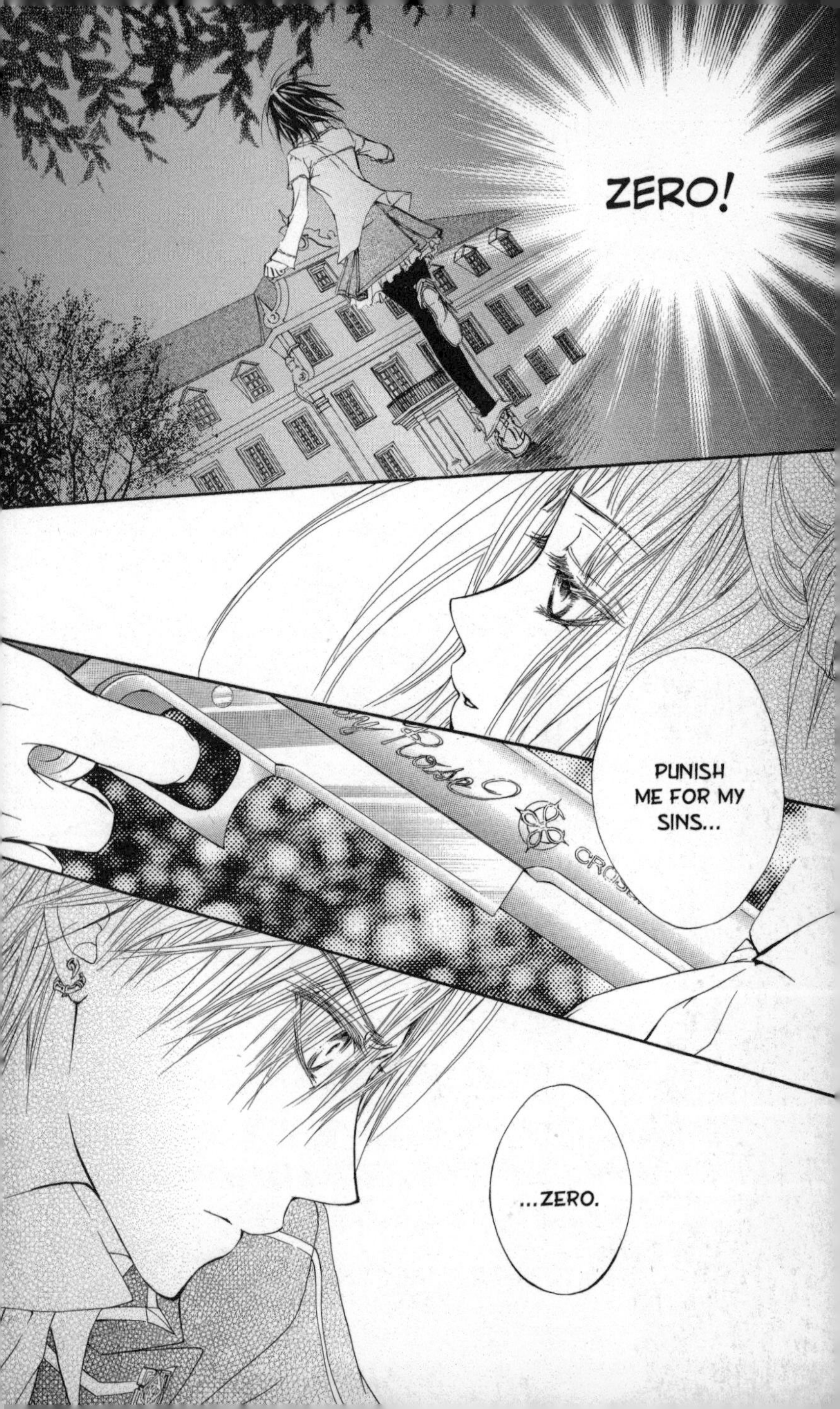
ZERO!
PUNISH ME FOR MY SINS...
...ZERO.

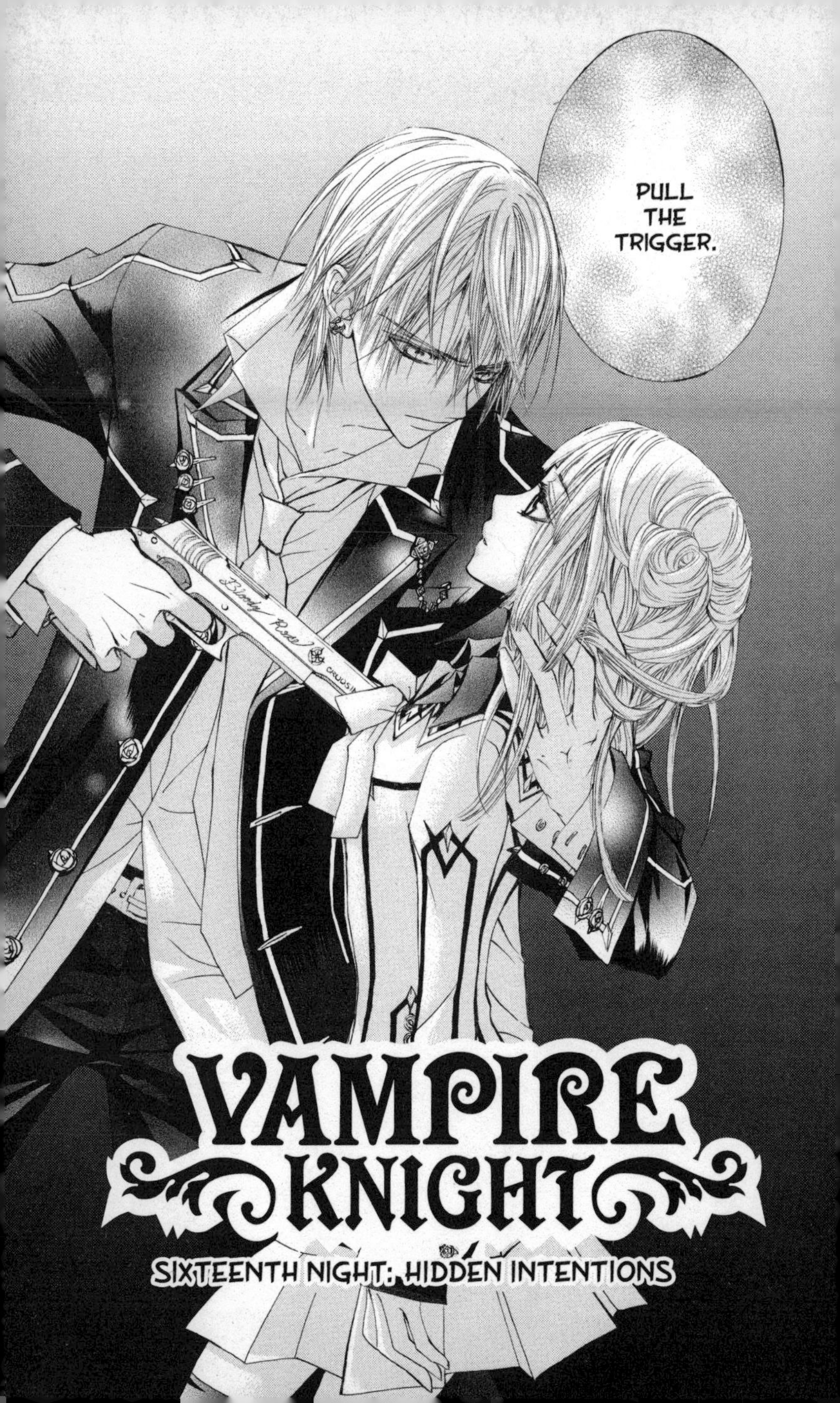
PULL THE TRIGGER.
VAMPIRE KNIGHT
SIXTEENTH NIGHT: HIDDEN INTENTIONS

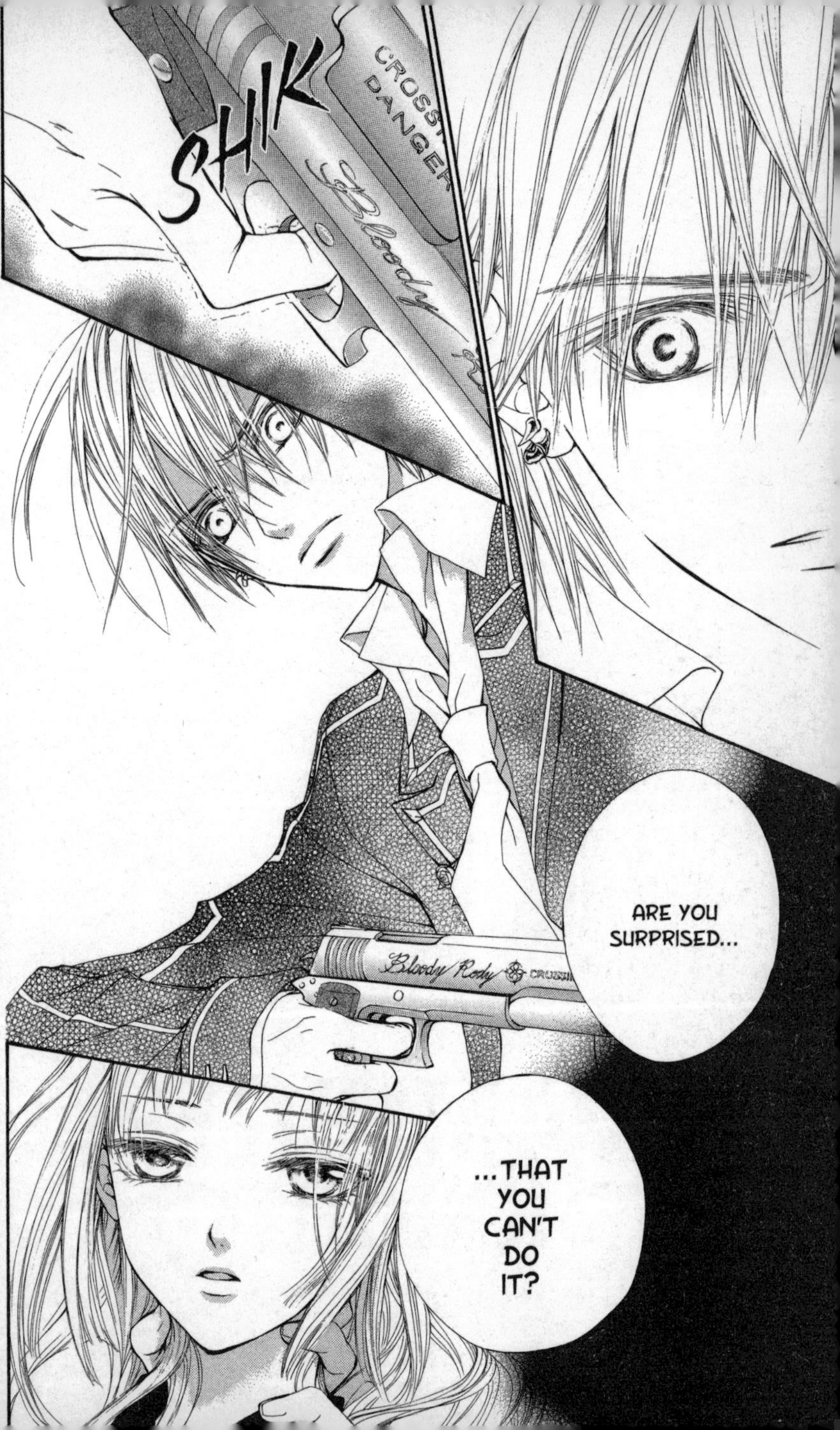
SHIK
CROSS
DANGER
Bloody
Bloody Rody
CROSS
ARE YOU SURPRISED...
...THAT YOU CAN'T DO IT?

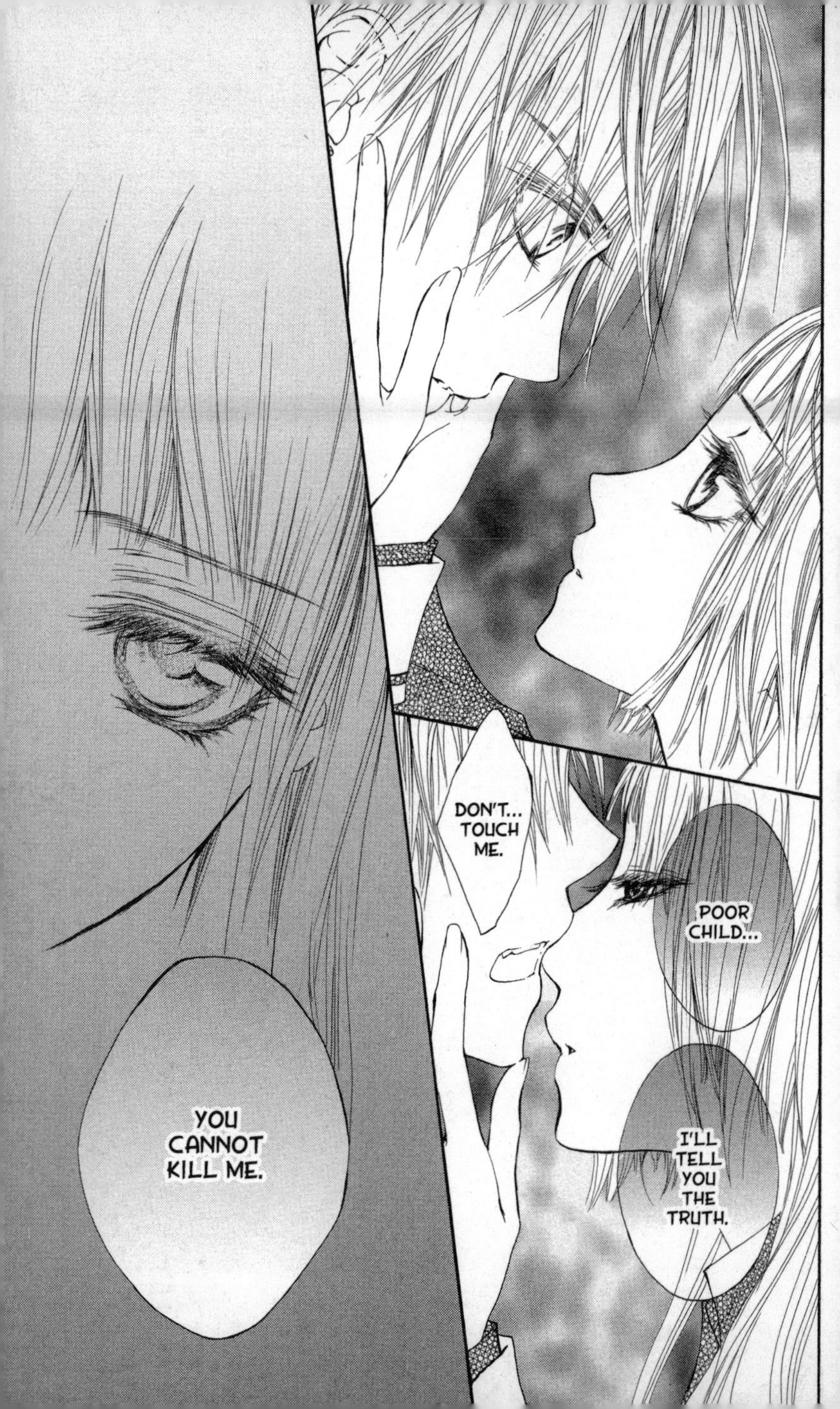
DON'T... TOUCH ME.
POOR CHILD...
I'LL TELL YOU THE TRUTH.
YOU CANNOT KILL ME.

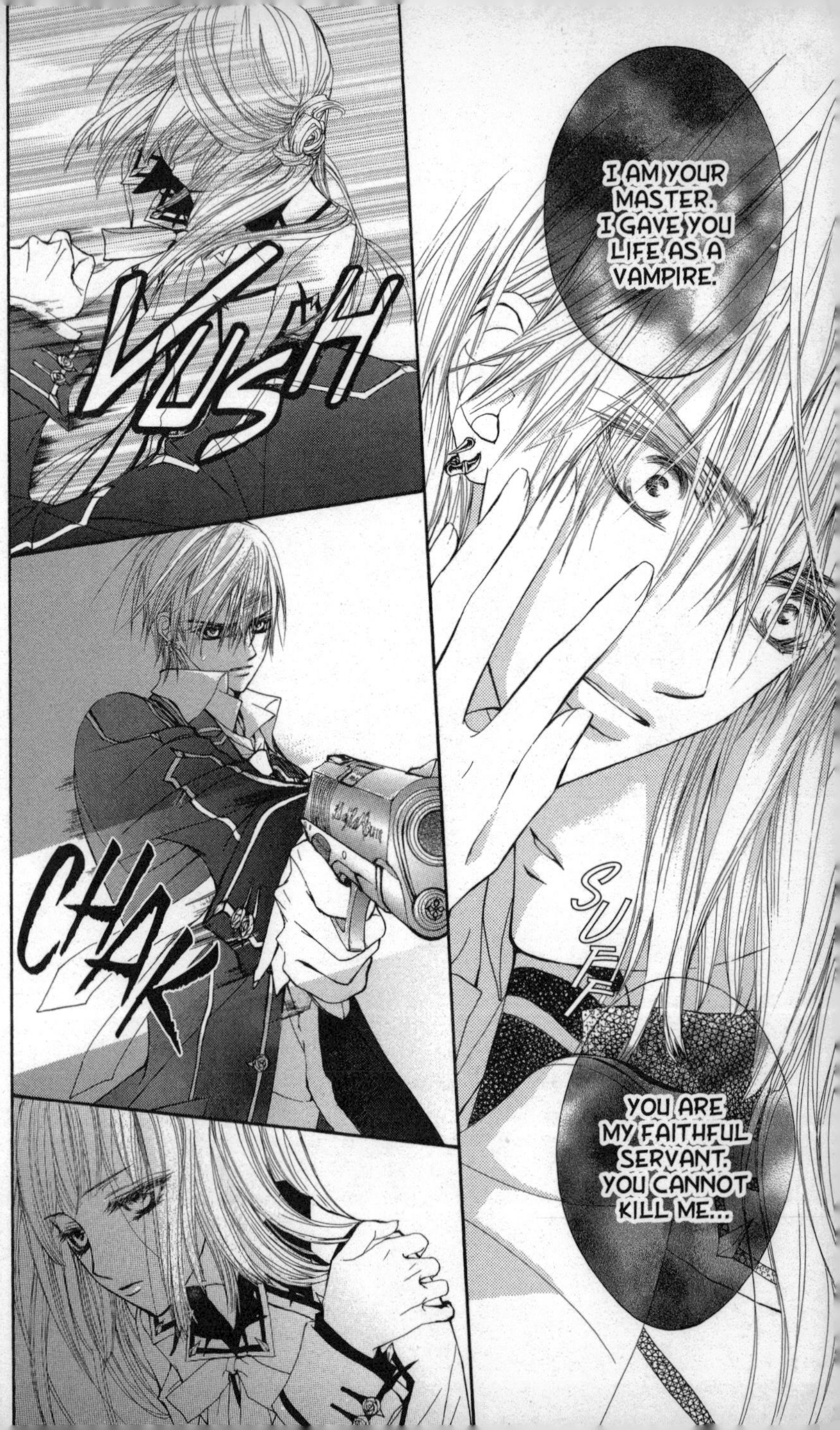
I AM YOUR MASTER. I GAVE YOU LIFE AS A VAMPIRE.
SUFF
YOU ARE MY FAITHFUL SERVANT. YOU CANNOT KILL ME...
VUSH
CHAK

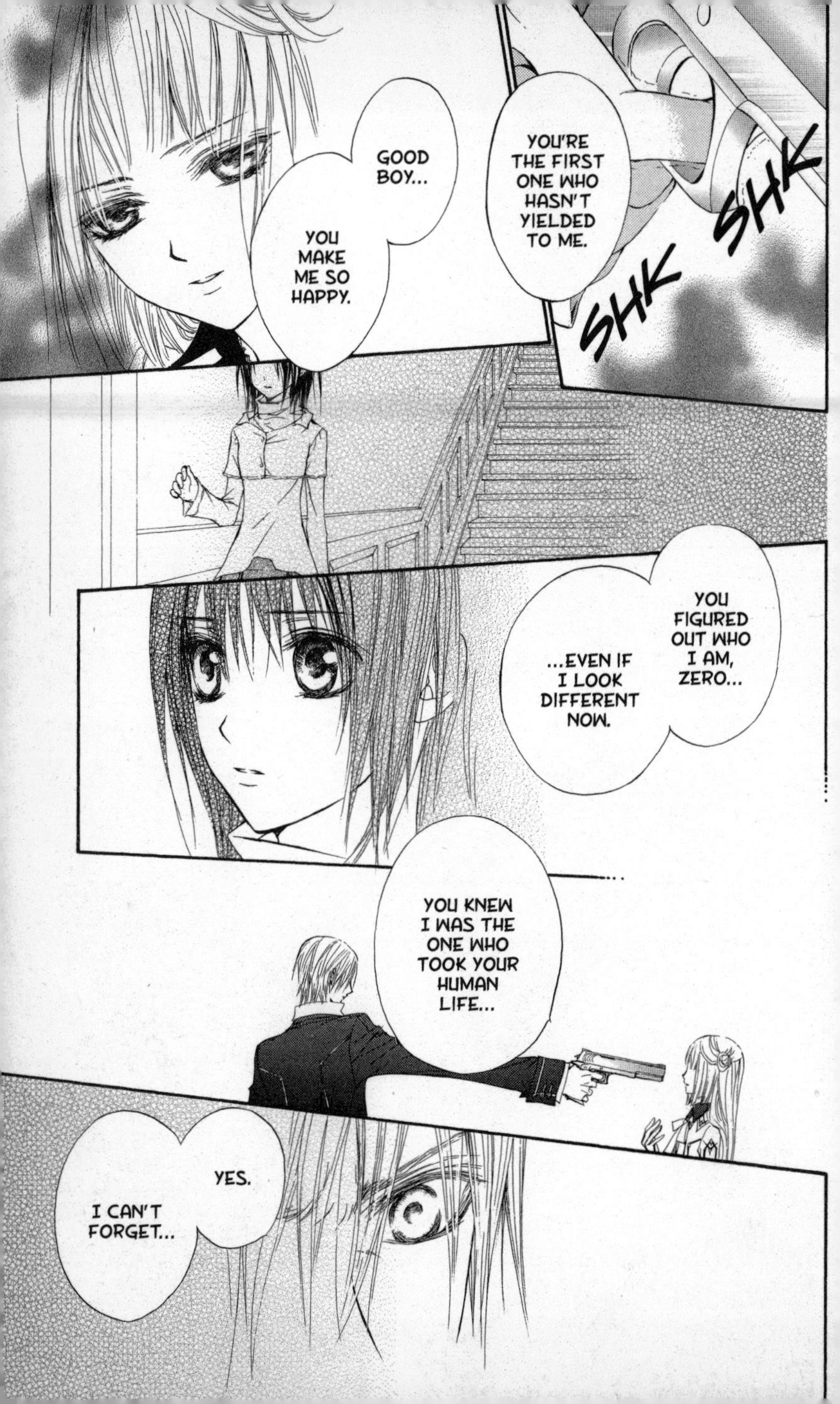
YOU'RE THE FIRST ONE WHO HASN'T YIELDED TO ME.
SHK SHK
GOOD BOY...
YOU MAKE ME SO HAPPY.
YOU FIGURED OUT WHO I AM, ZERO...
...EVEN IF I LOOK DIFFERENT NOW.
YOU KNEW I WAS THE ONE WHO TOOK YOUR HUMAN LIFE...
YES.
I CAN'T FORGET...

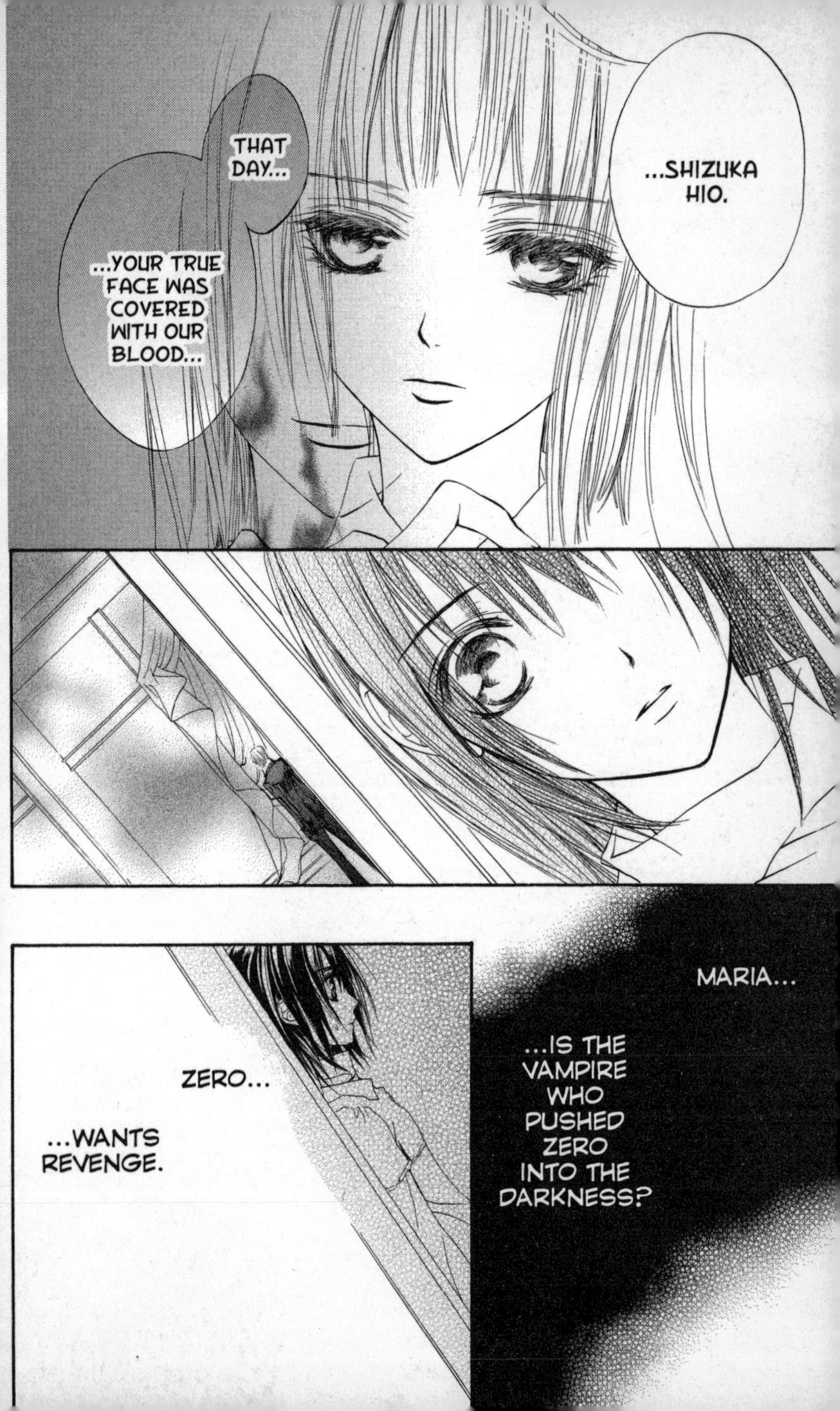
...SHIZUKA HIO.
THAT DAY...
...YOUR TRUE FACE WAS COVERED WITH OUR BLOOD...
MARIA...
...IS THE VAMPIRE WHO PUSHED ZERO INTO THE DARKNESS?
ZERO...
...WANTS REVENGE.

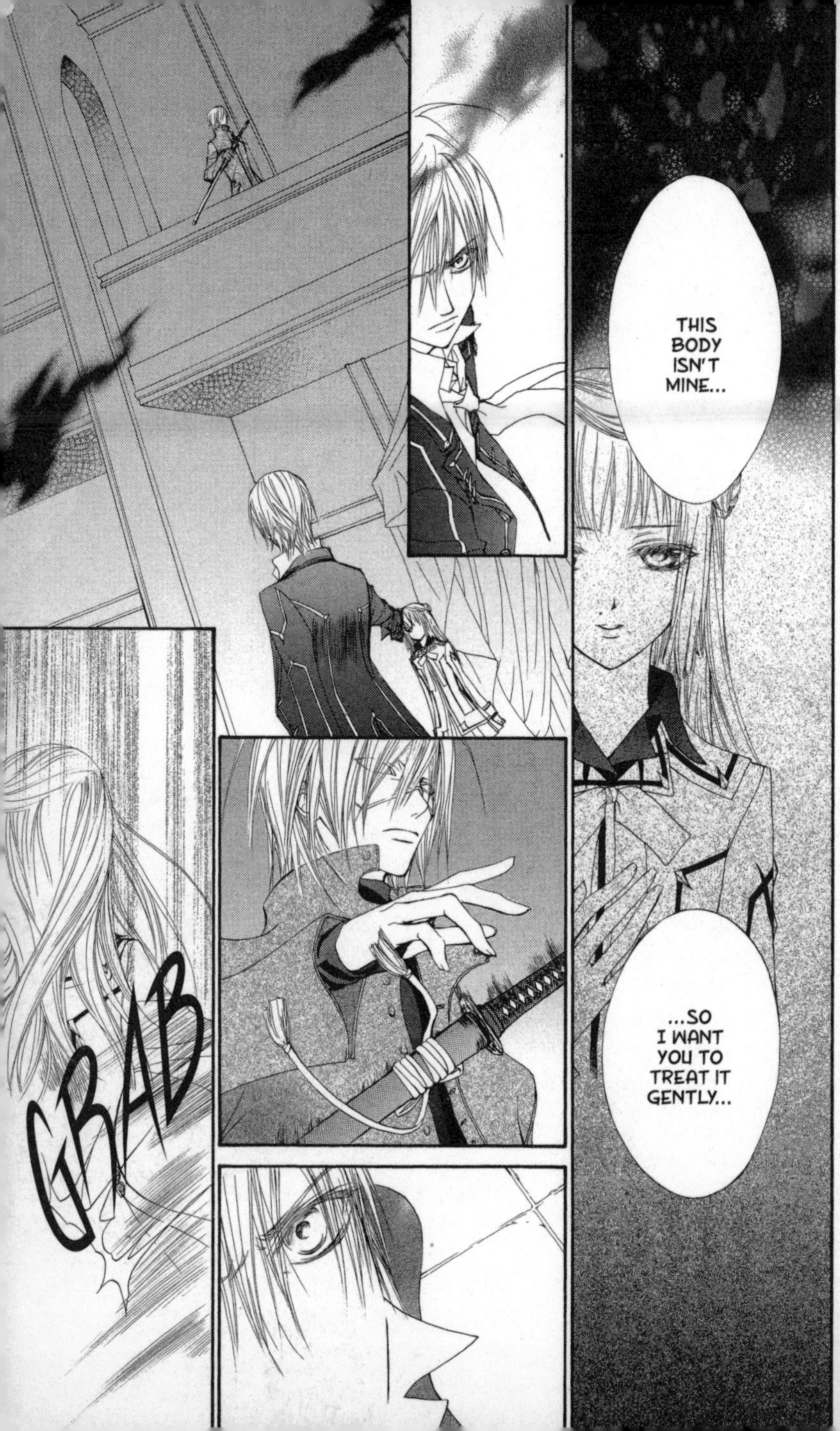
THIS BODY ISN'T MINE...
...SO I WANT YOU TO TREAT IT GENTLY...
GRAB

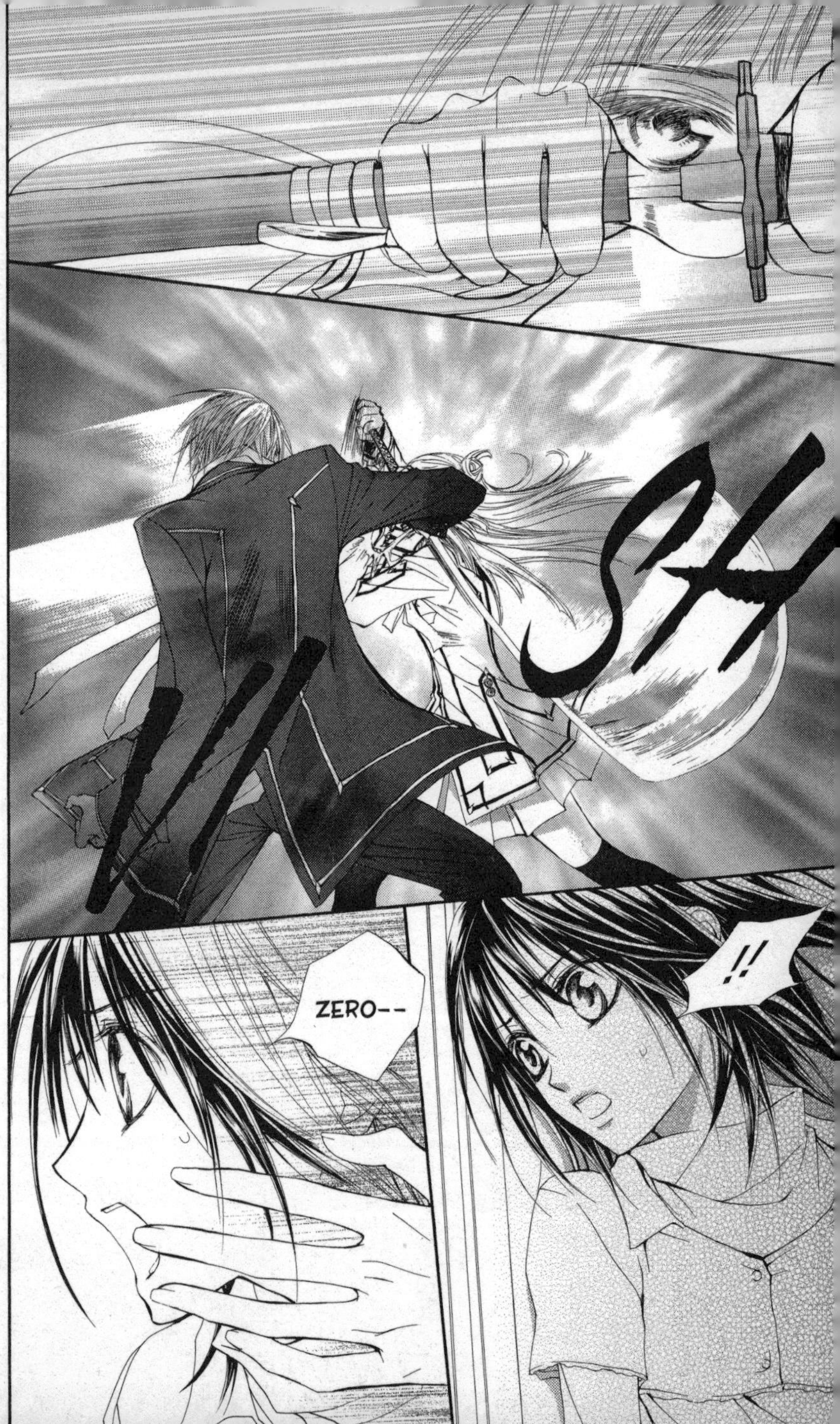
SH
!!
ZERO--

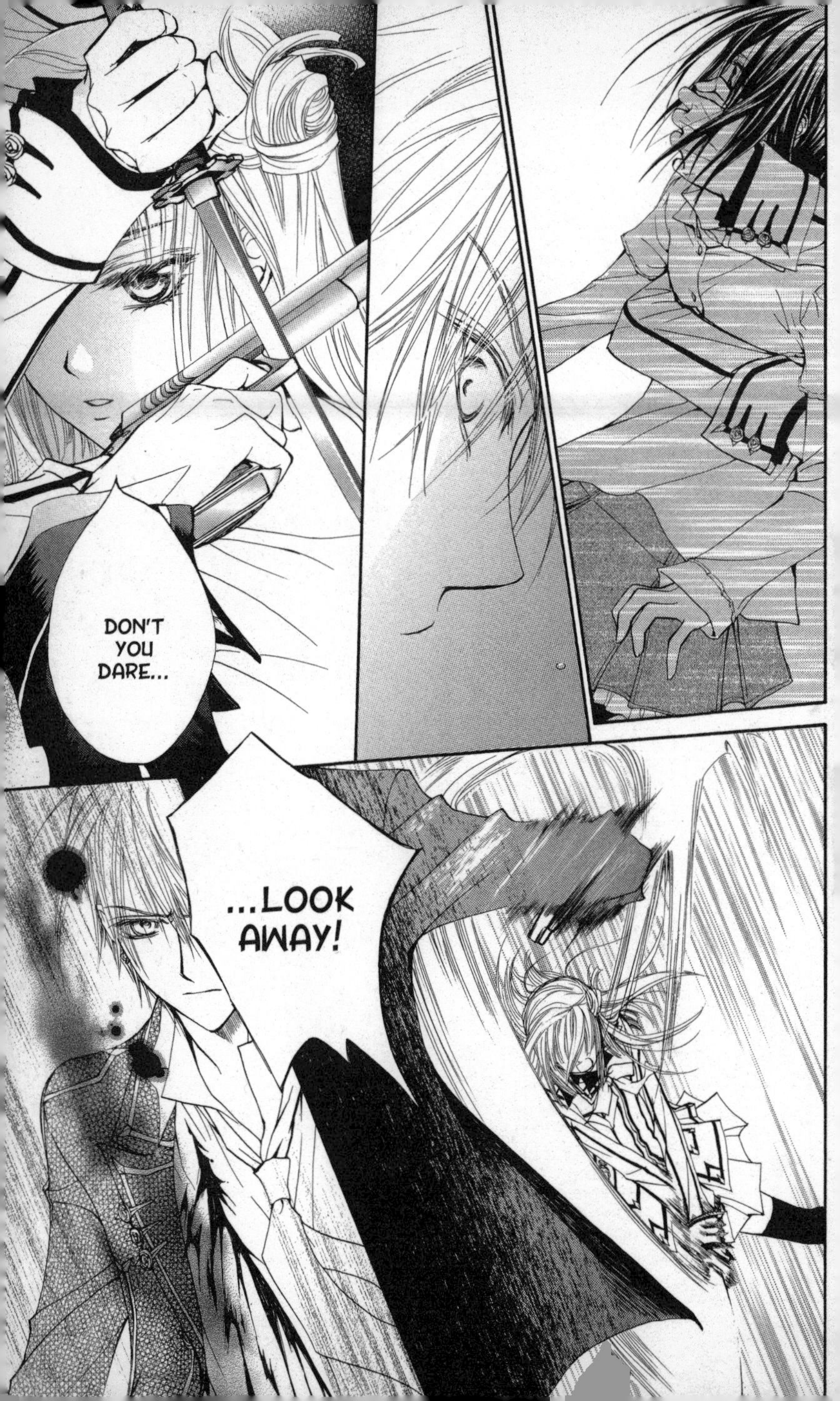
DON'T YOU DARE...
...LOOK AWAY!

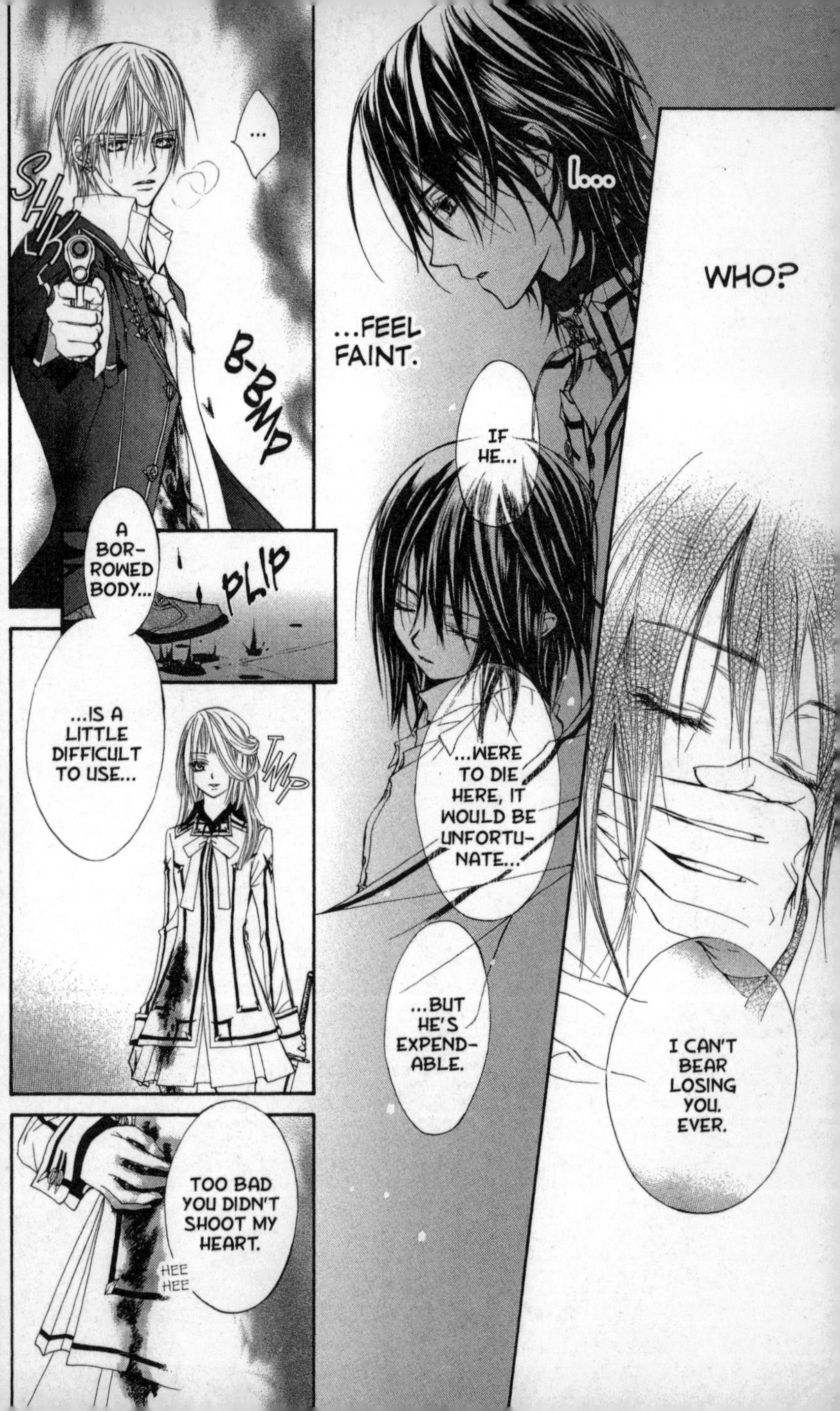
WHO?
I...
...FEEL FAINT.
IF HE...
...WERE TO DIE HERE, IT WOULD BE UNFORTUNATE...
...BUT HE'S EXPENDABLE.
I CAN'T BEAR LOSING YOU. EVER.
...
SHK
B-BMP
A BORROWED BODY...
PLIP
...IS A LITTLE DIFFICULT TO USE...
TMP
TOO BAD YOU DIDN'T SHOOT MY HEART.
HEE HEE

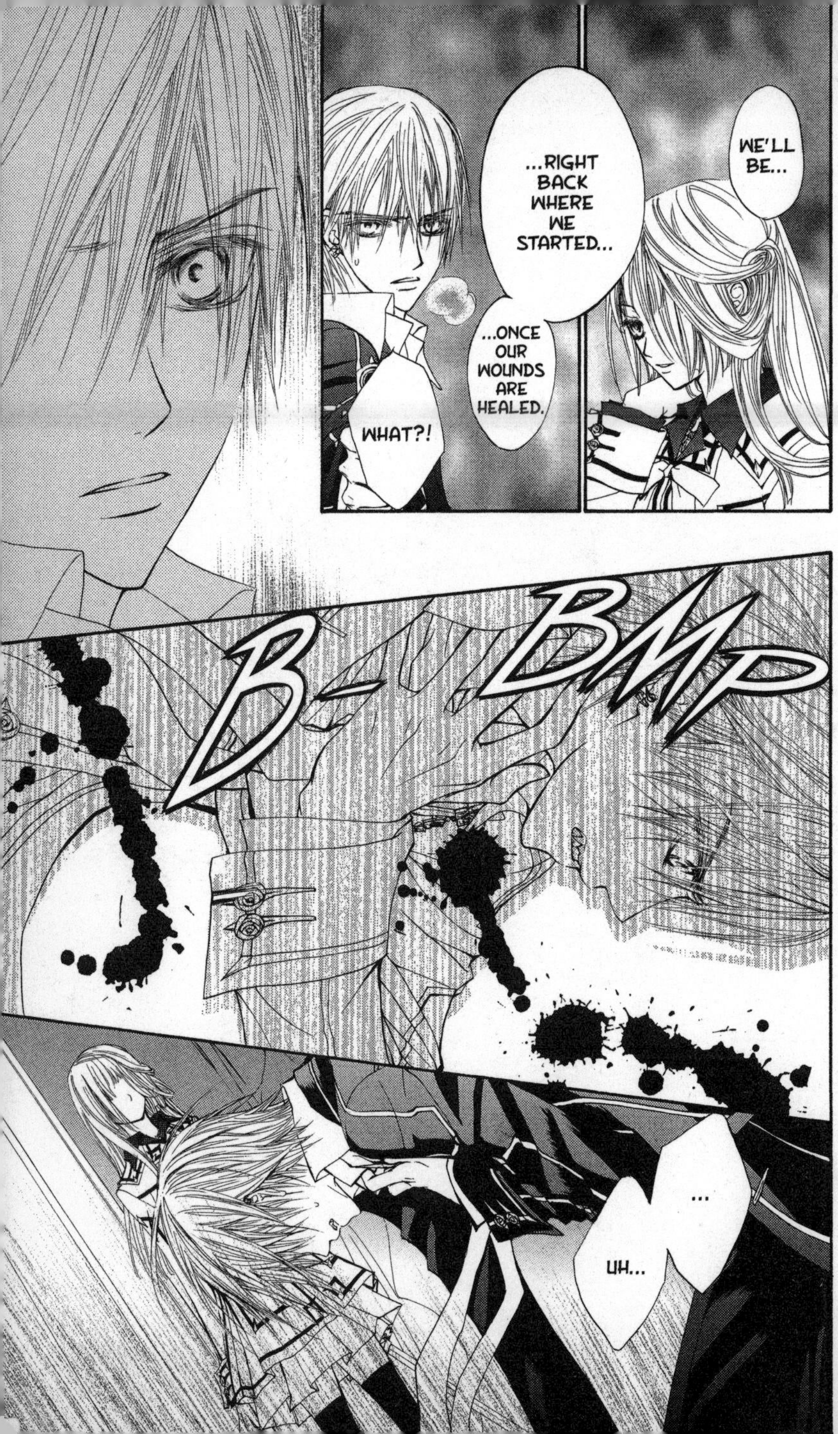
WE'LL BE...
...RIGHT BACK WHERE WE STARTED...
...ONCE OUR WOUNDS ARE HEALED.
WHAT?!
B-BMP
...
UH...

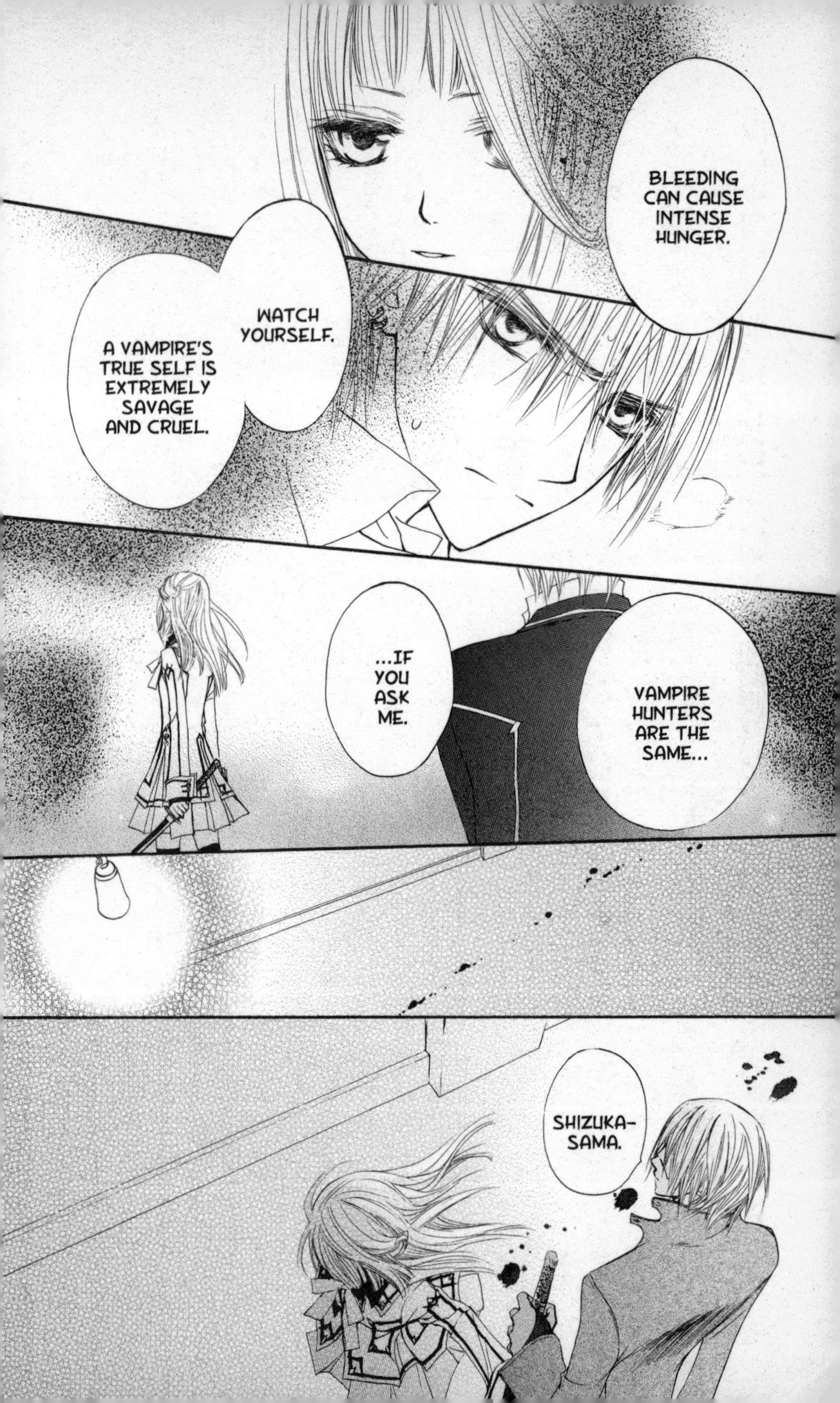
BLEEDING CAN CAUSE INTENSE HUNGER.
WATCH YOURSELF.
A VAMPIRE'S TRUE SELF IS EXTREMELY SAVAGE AND CRUEL.
VAMPIRE HUNTERS ARE THE SAME...
...IF YOU ASK ME.
SHIZUKA-SAMA.

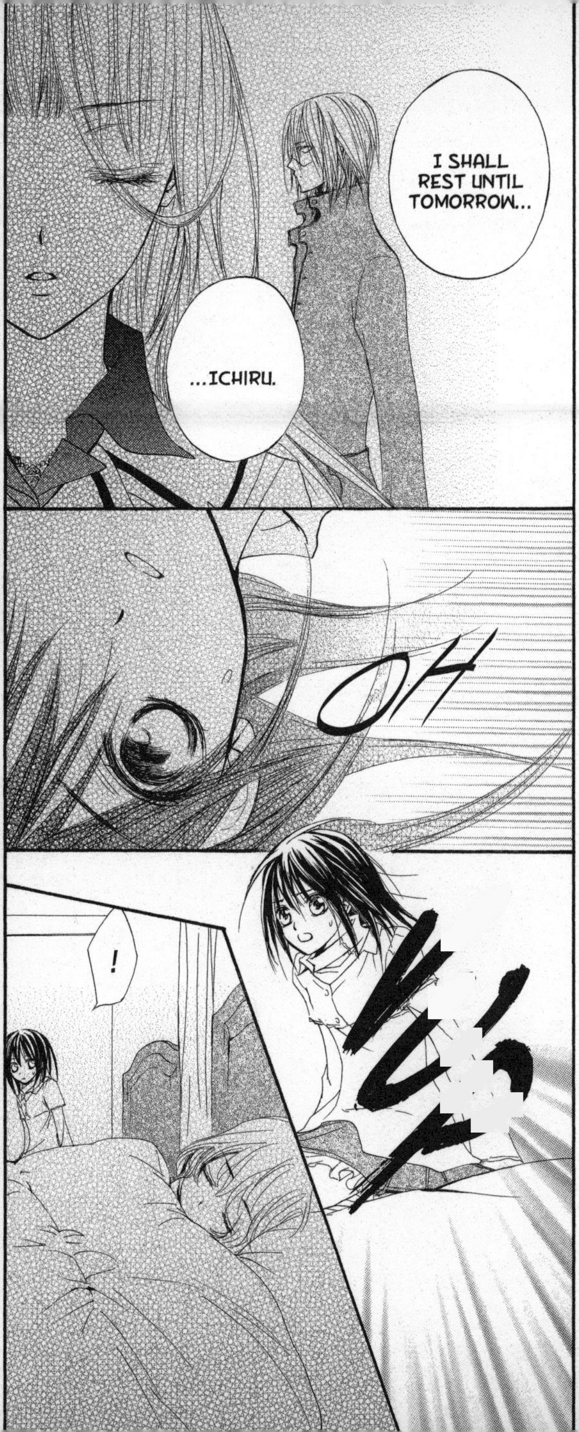
I SHALL REST UNTIL TOMORROW...
...ICHIRU.
OH
!

II

The summer before volume 4 went on sale, I was called to do several autograph sessions. This break allowed to me to refresh myself!

I was really happy to be able to meet my fans. I really thank the *LaLa* department for making these precious encounters possible. I also thank everybody who came when it was so hot outside. Woo! Now I can do my best!

The autograph sessions were part of *LaLa*'s 30th anniversary event, the *LaLa* Academy Summer Festival. I got to experience only a little of the "summer festival" atmosphere, but it looked really fun. I'm a *LaLa* reader myself, so I regret not being able to enjoy the festival fully.

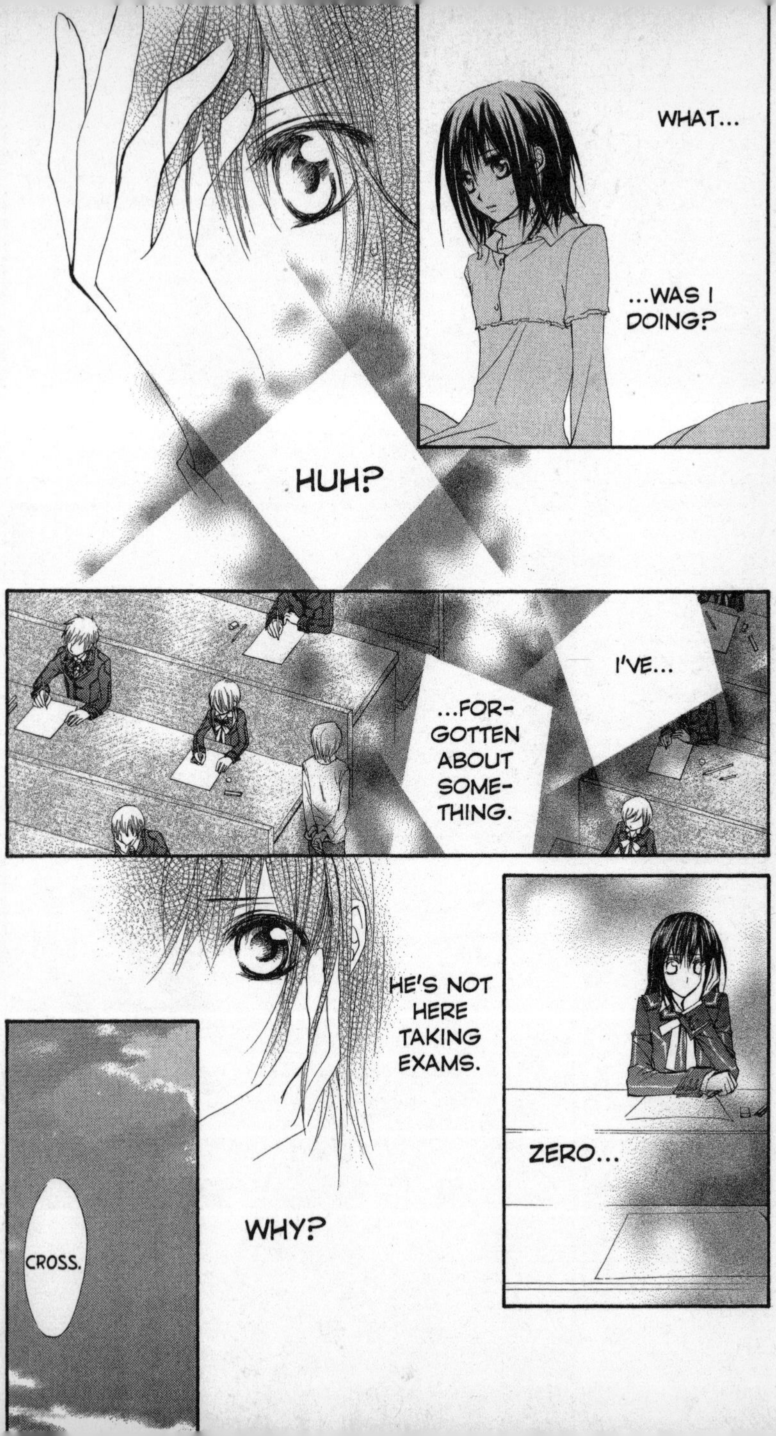
WHAT...
...WAS I DOING?
HUH?
I'VE...
...FOR-GOTTEN ABOUT SOME-THING.
ZERO...
HE'S NOT HERE TAKING EXAMS.
WHY?
CROSS.

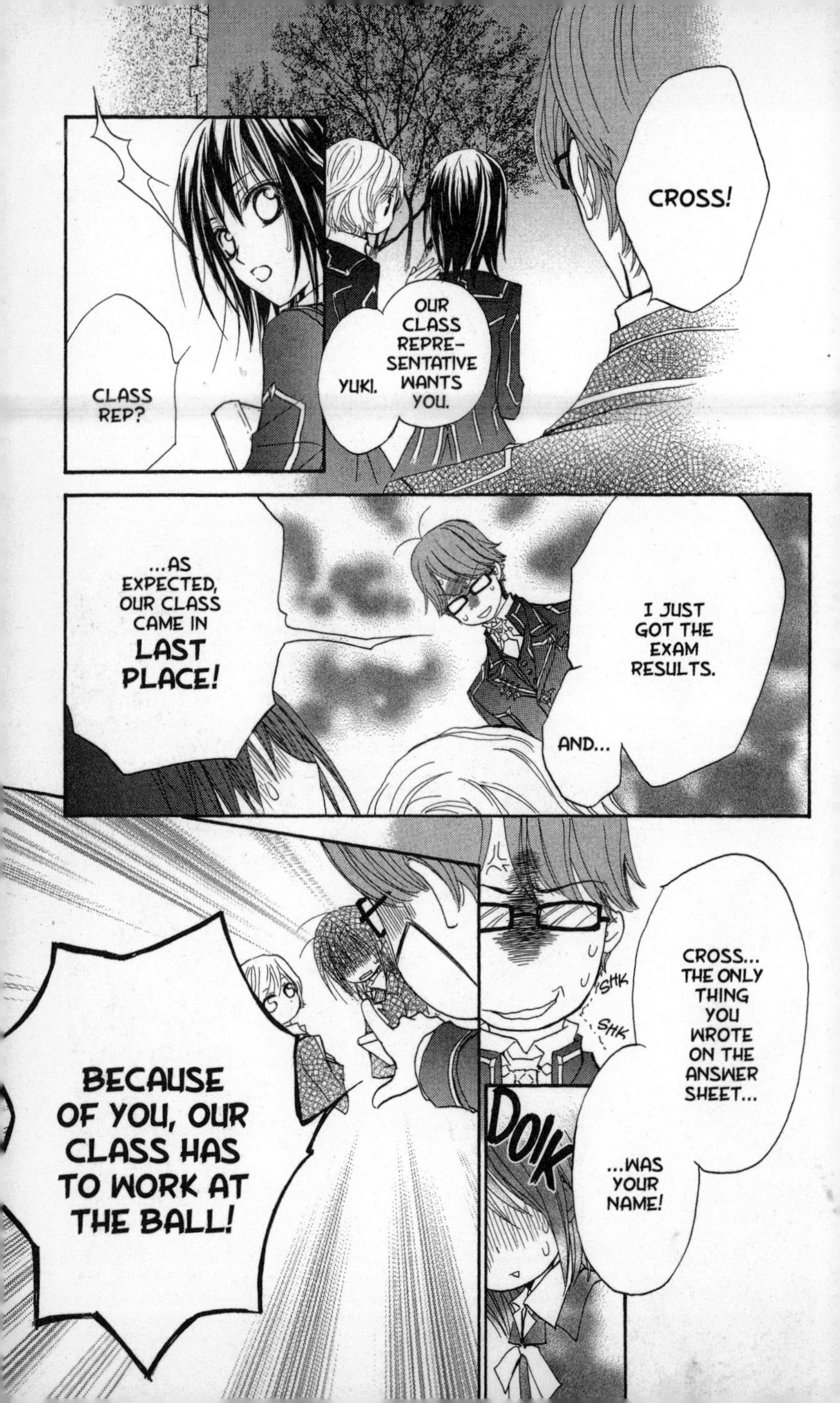
CROSS!
OUR CLASS REPRESENTATIVE WANTS YOU.
YUKI.
CLASS REP?
I JUST GOT THE EXAM RESULTS.
AND...
...AS EXPECTED, OUR CLASS CAME IN **LAST PLACE!**
CROSS... THE ONLY THING YOU WROTE ON THE ANSWER SHEET...
SHK
SHK
...WAS YOUR NAME!
DOIK
BECAUSE OF YOU, OUR CLASS HAS TO WORK AT THE BALL!

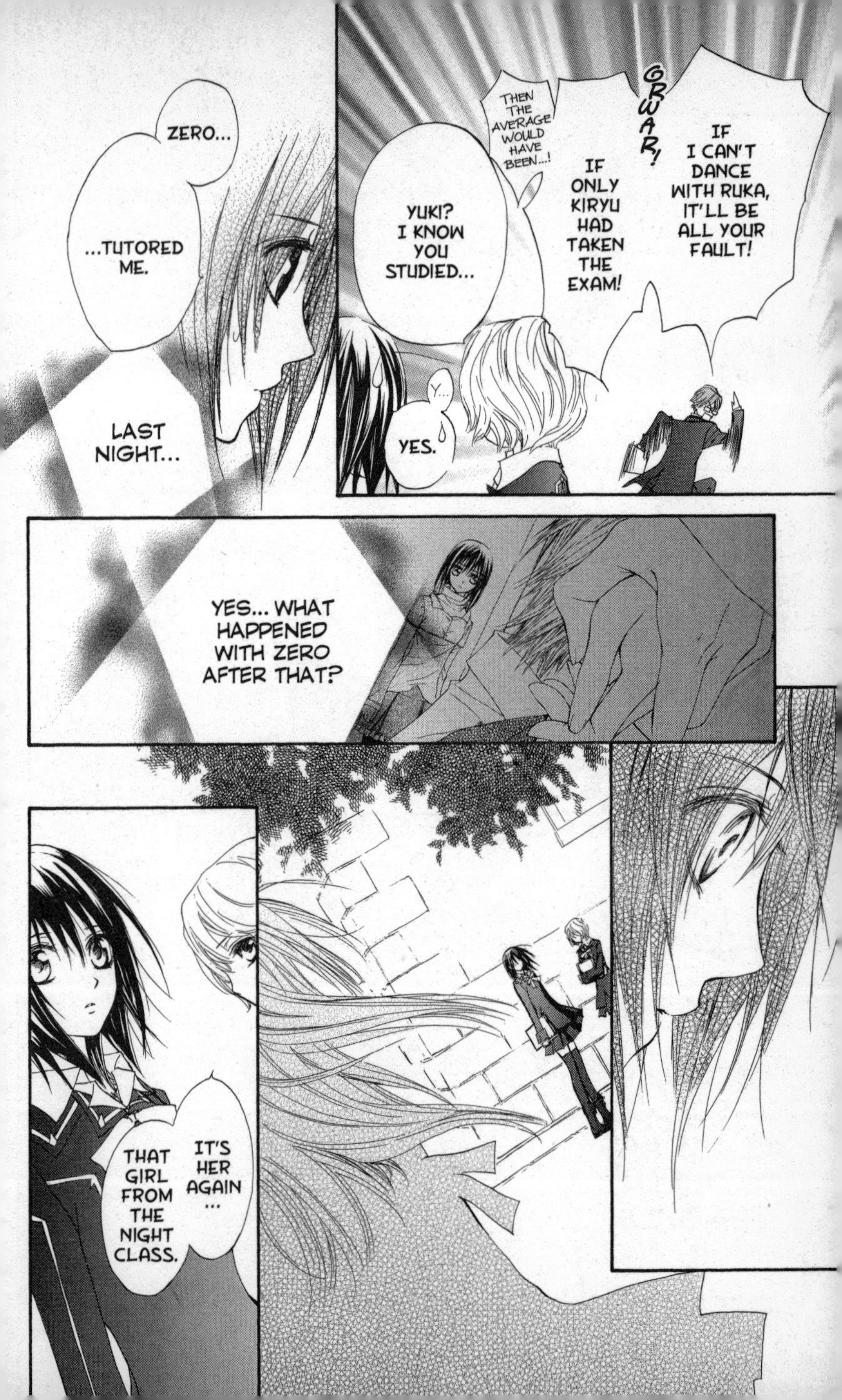
IF I CAN'T DANCE WITH RUKA, IT'LL BE ALL YOUR FAULT!
GRWAR!
IF ONLY KIRYU HAD TAKEN THE EXAM!
THEN THE AVERAGE WOULD HAVE BEEN...!
YUKI? I KNOW YOU STUDIED...
Y... YES.
ZERO... ...TUTORED ME.
LAST NIGHT...
YES... WHAT HAPPENED WITH ZERO AFTER THAT?
IT'S HER AGAIN ...
THAT GIRL FROM THE NIGHT CLASS.

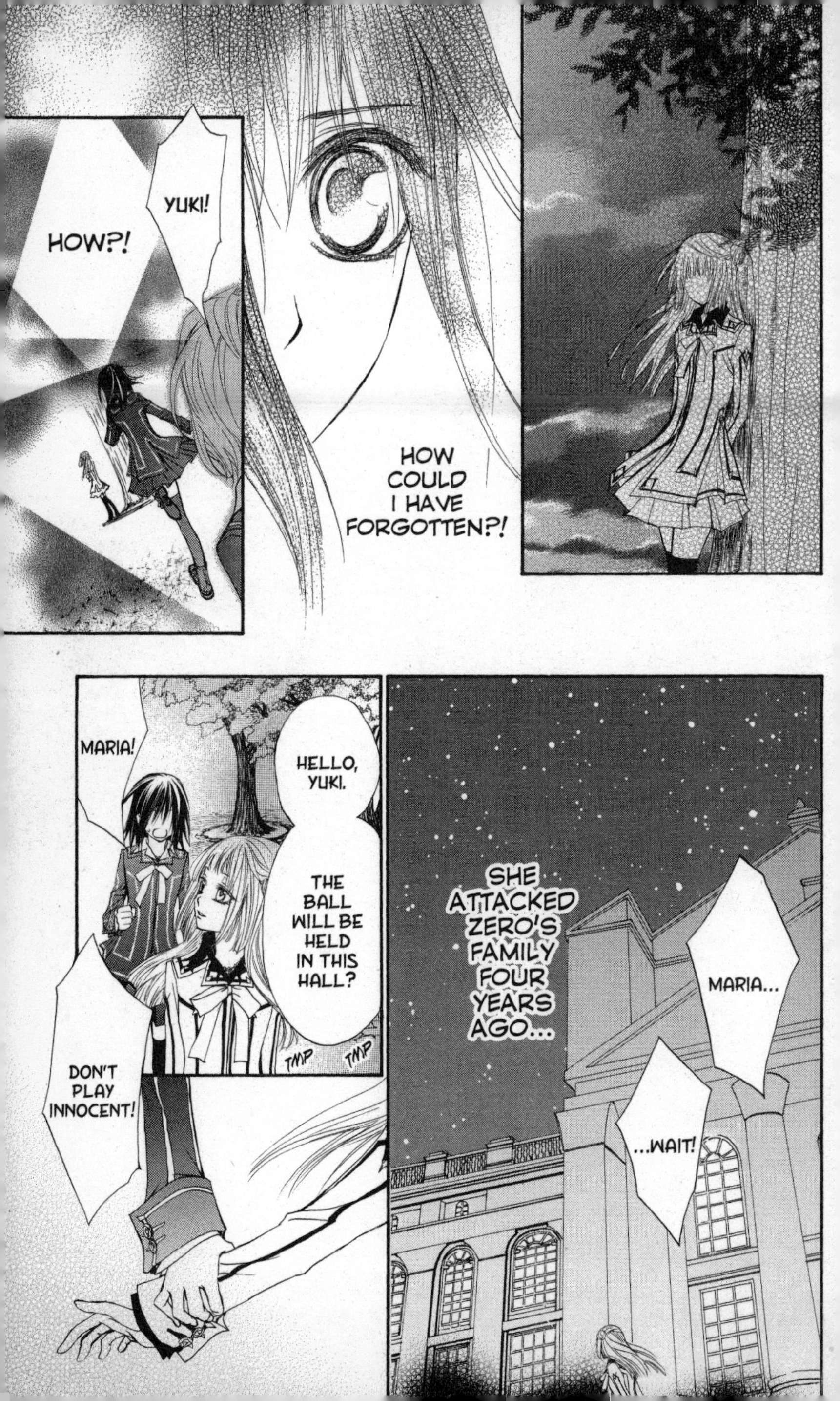
HOW COULD I HAVE FORGOTTEN?!
YUKI!
HOW?!
SHE ATTACKED ZERO'S FAMILY FOUR YEARS AGO...
MARIA...
...WAIT!
MARIA!
HELLO, YUKI.
THE BALL WILL BE HELD IN THIS HALL?
TMP
TMP
DON'T PLAY INNOCENT!

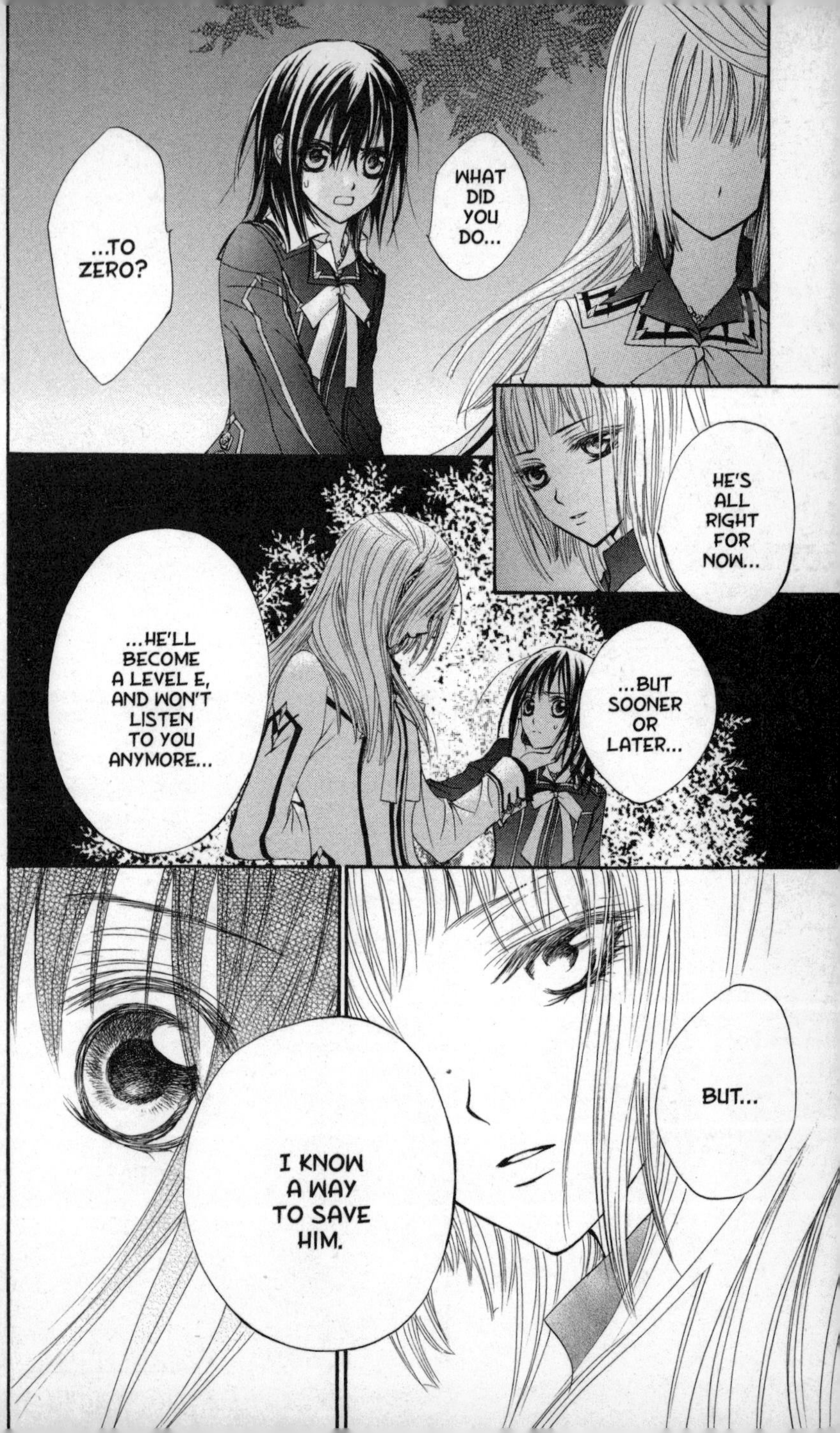
WHAT DID YOU DO...
...TO ZERO?
HE'S ALL RIGHT FOR NOW...
...BUT SOONER OR LATER...
...HE'LL BECOME A LEVEL E, AND WON'T LISTEN TO YOU ANYMORE...
BUT...
I KNOW A WAY TO SAVE HIM.

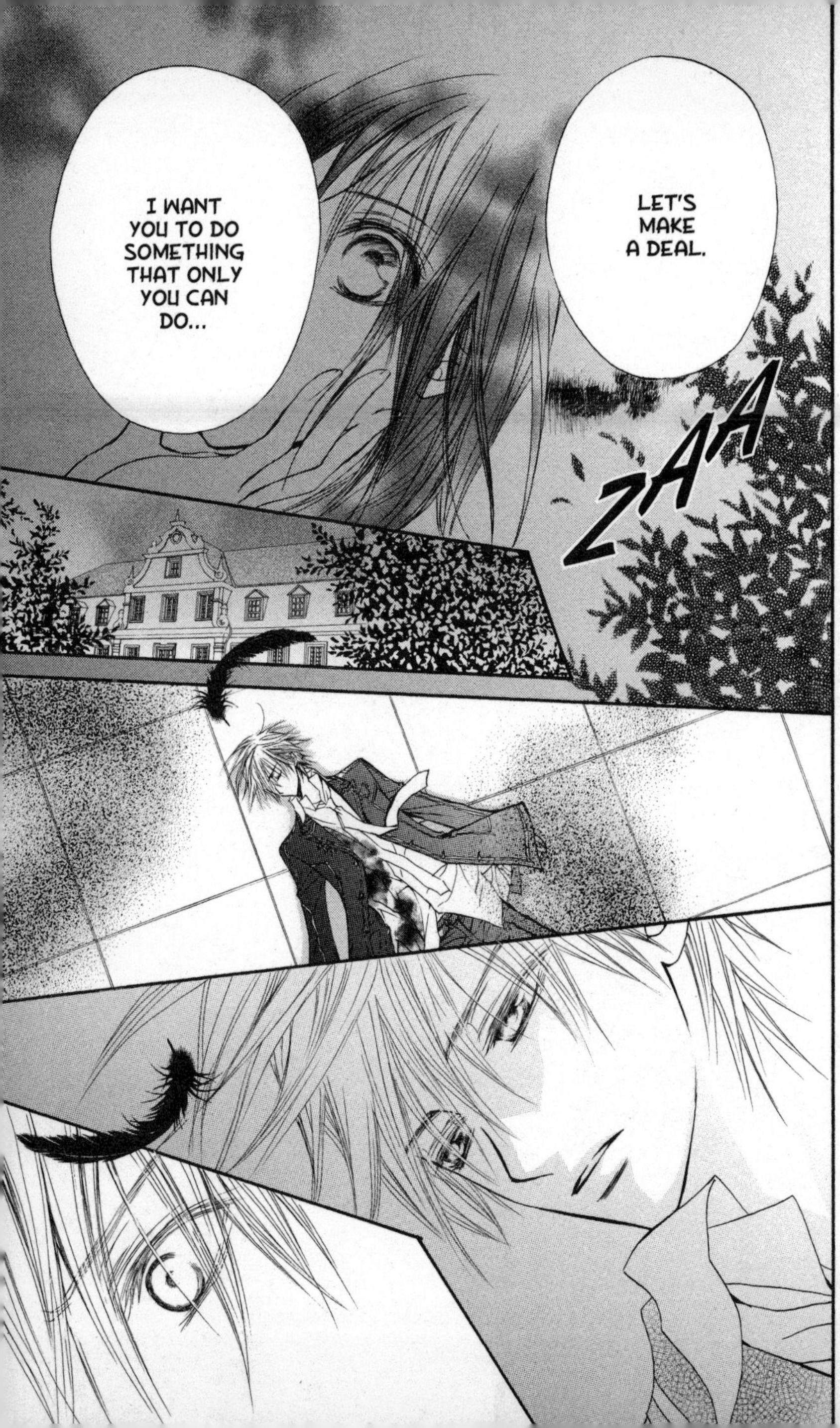
LET'S MAKE A DEAL.
I WANT YOU TO DO SOMETHING THAT ONLY YOU CAN DO...
ZAA

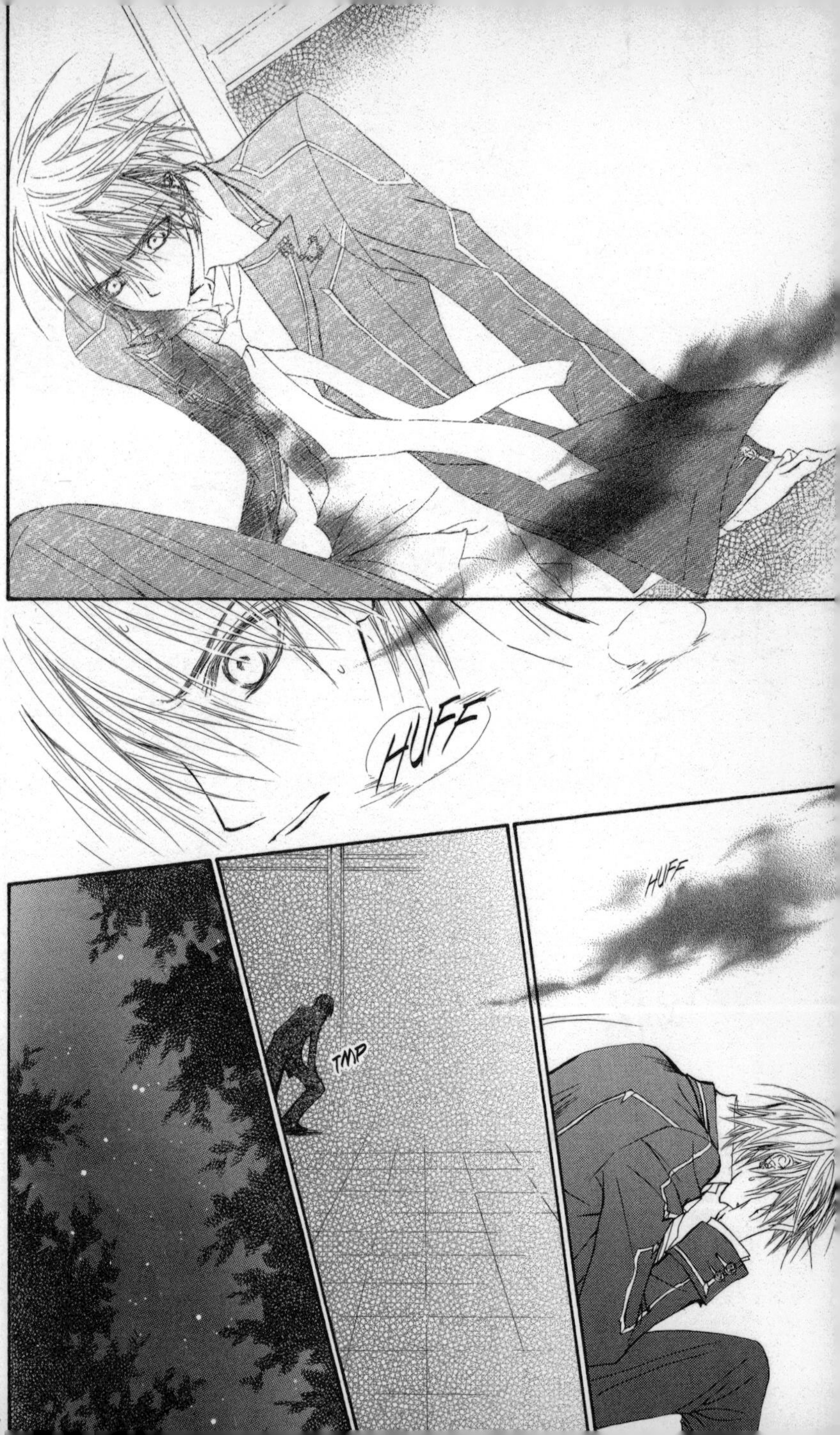
HUFF
HUFF
TMP

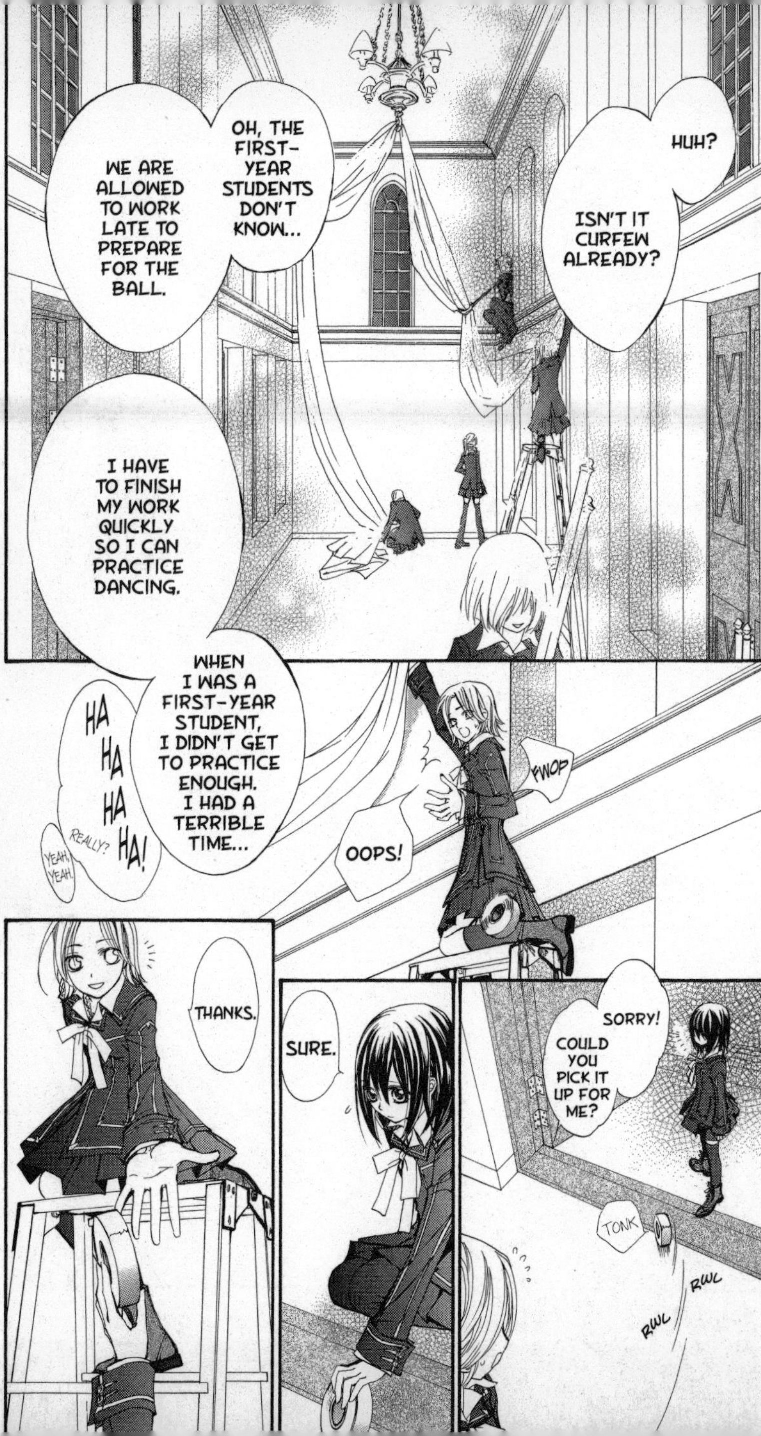

HUH?
ISN'T IT CURFEW ALREADY?
OH, THE FIRST-YEAR STUDENTS DON'T KNOW...
WE ARE ALLOWED TO WORK LATE TO PREPARE FOR THE BALL.
I HAVE TO FINISH MY WORK QUICKLY SO I CAN PRACTICE DANCING.
FWOP
OOPS!
WHEN I WAS A FIRST-YEAR STUDENT, I DIDN'T GET TO PRACTICE ENOUGH. I HAD A TERRIBLE TIME...
HA HA HA HA!
REALLY?
YEAH, YEAH.
SORRY!
COULD YOU PICK IT UP FOR ME?
TONK
RWL
RWL
SURE.
THANKS.

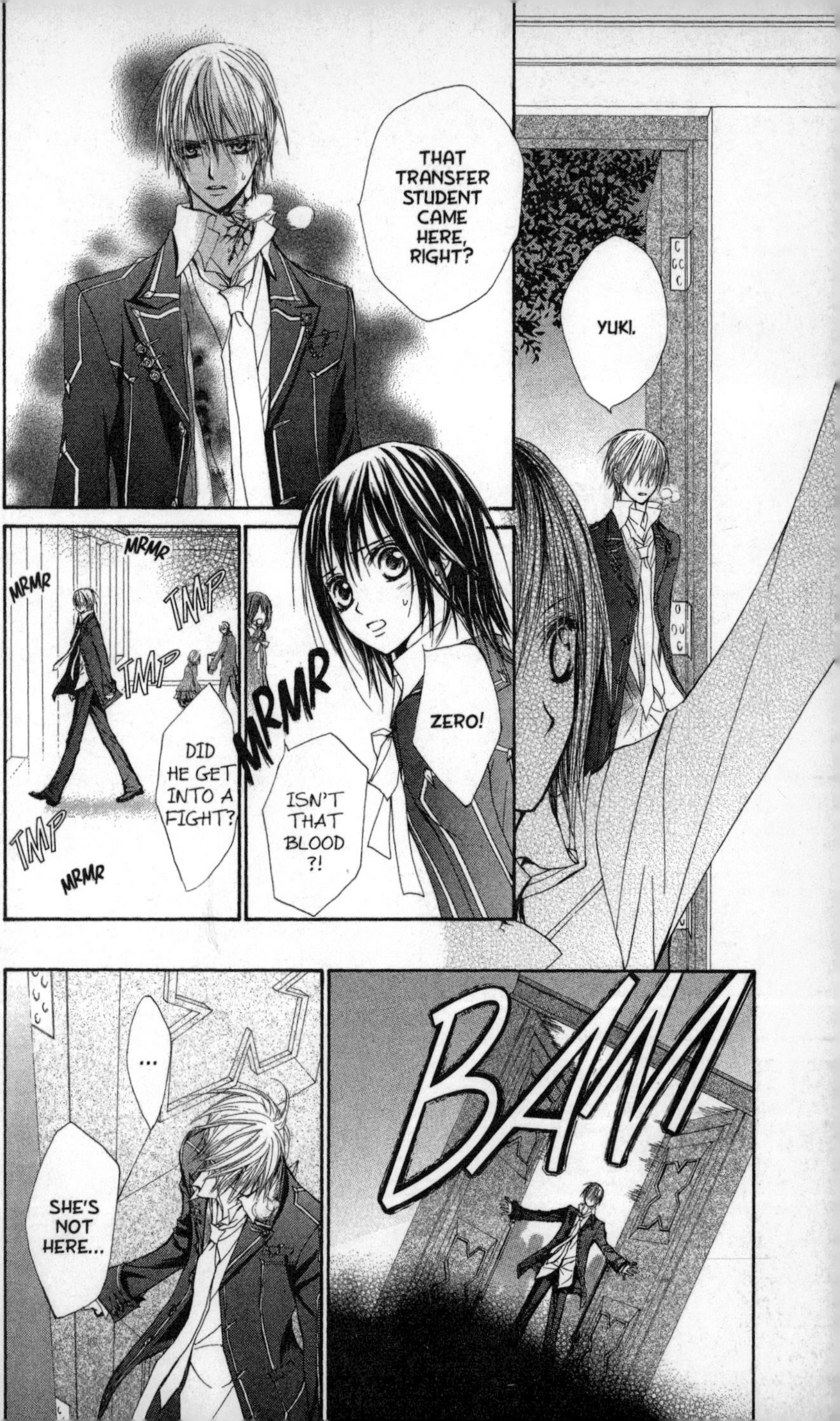
YUKI.
THAT TRANSFER STUDENT CAME HERE, RIGHT?
ZERO!
MRMR
ISN'T THAT BLOOD ?!
MRMR
TMP
TMP
MRMR
DID HE GET INTO A FIGHT?
TMP
MRMR
BAM
...
SHE'S NOT HERE...

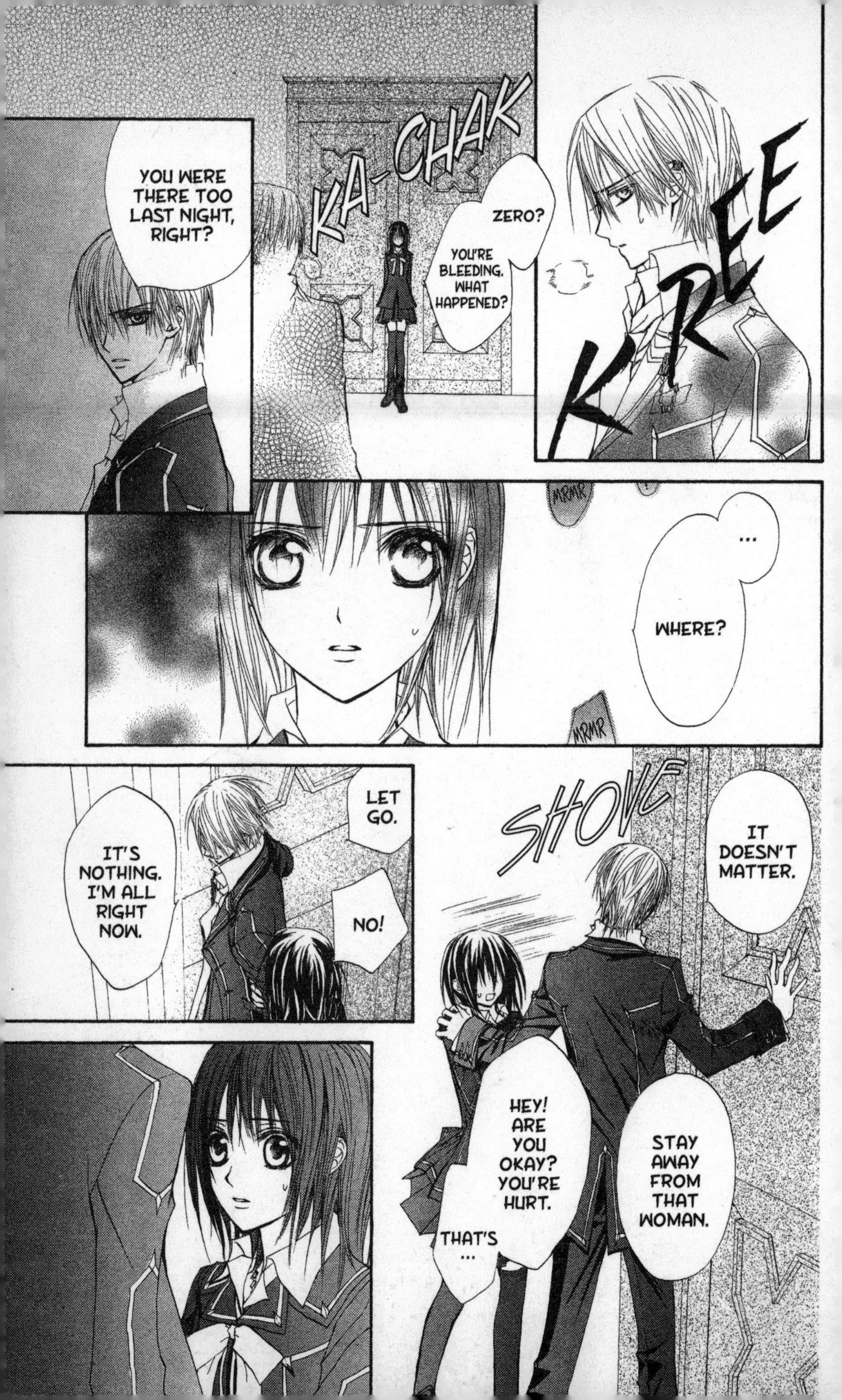
KREE
KA-CHAK
ZERO?
YOU'RE BLEEDING. WHAT HAPPENED?
YOU WERE THERE TOO LAST NIGHT, RIGHT?
MRMR
...
WHERE?
MRMR
SHOVE
IT DOESN'T MATTER.
STAY AWAY FROM THAT WOMAN.
HEY! ARE YOU OKAY? YOU'RE HURT.
THAT'S ...
LET GO.
NO!
IT'S NOTHING. I'M ALL RIGHT NOW.

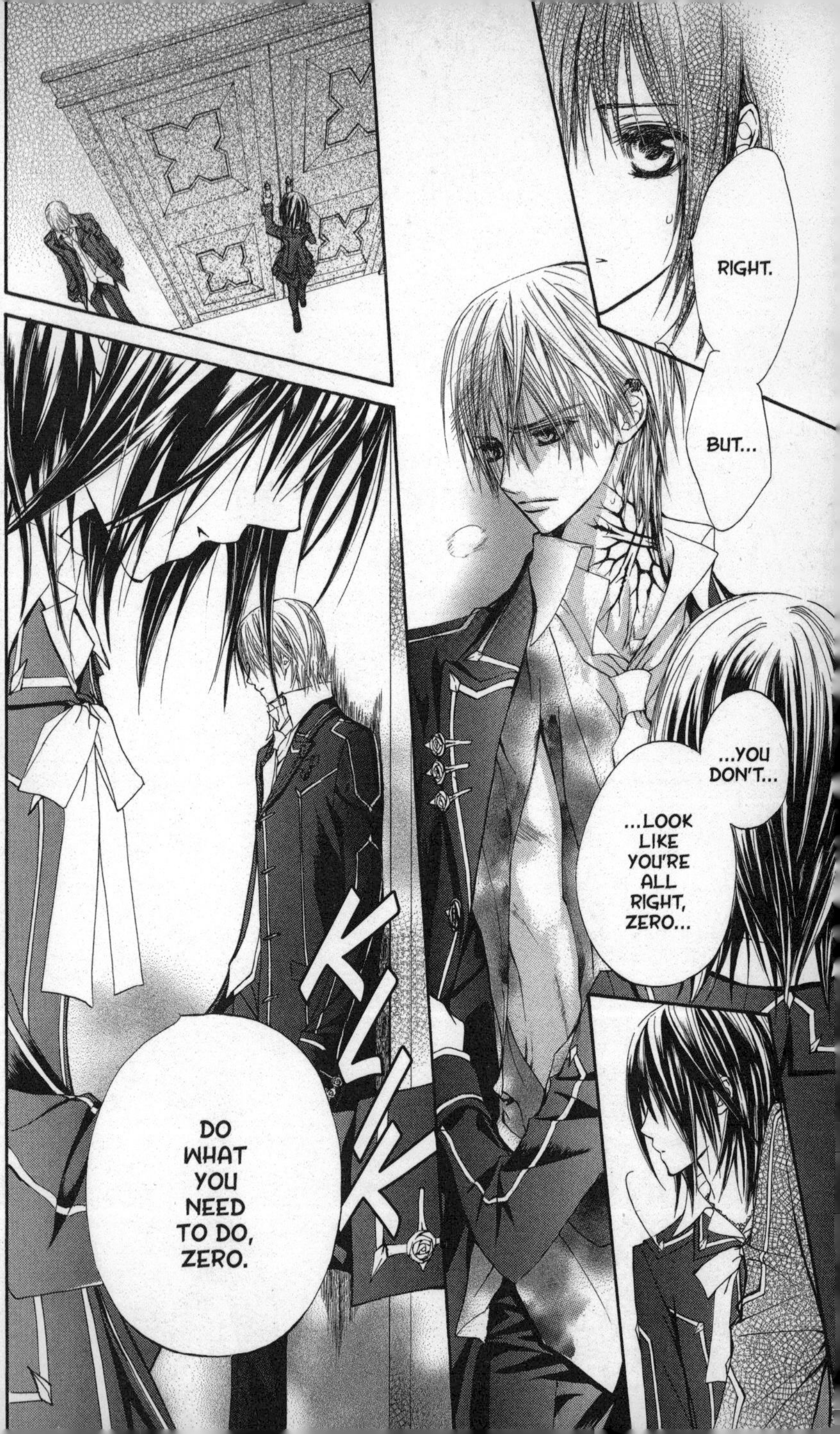
RIGHT.
BUT...
...YOU DON'T...
...LOOK LIKE YOU'RE ALL RIGHT, ZERO...
KLIK
DO WHAT YOU NEED TO DO, ZERO.

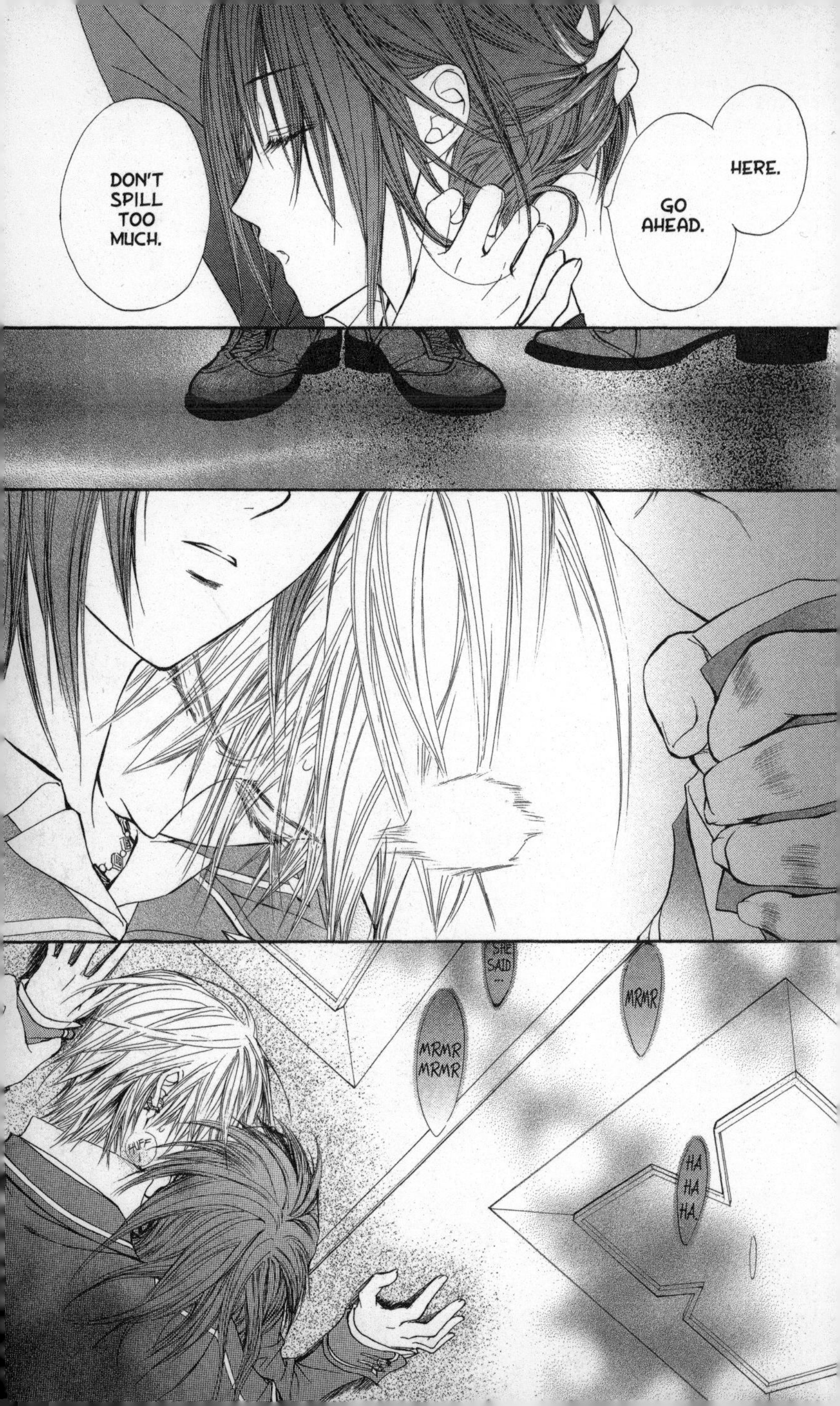
HERE.
GO AHEAD.
DON'T SPILL TOO MUCH.
MRMR
SHE SAID...
HA HA HA.
MRMR MRMR
HUFF

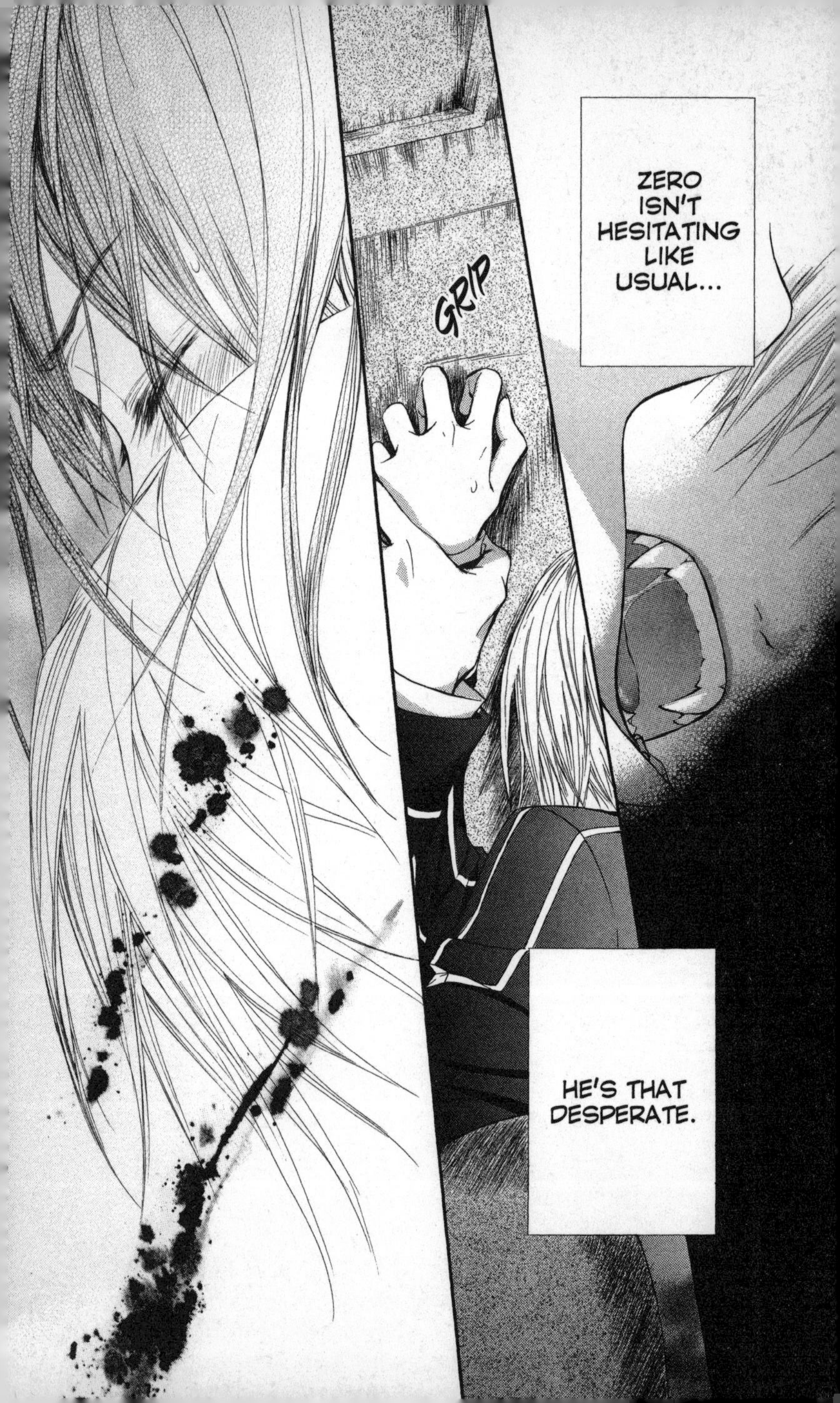
ZERO ISN'T HESITATING LIKE USUAL...
GRIP
HE'S THAT DESPERATE.

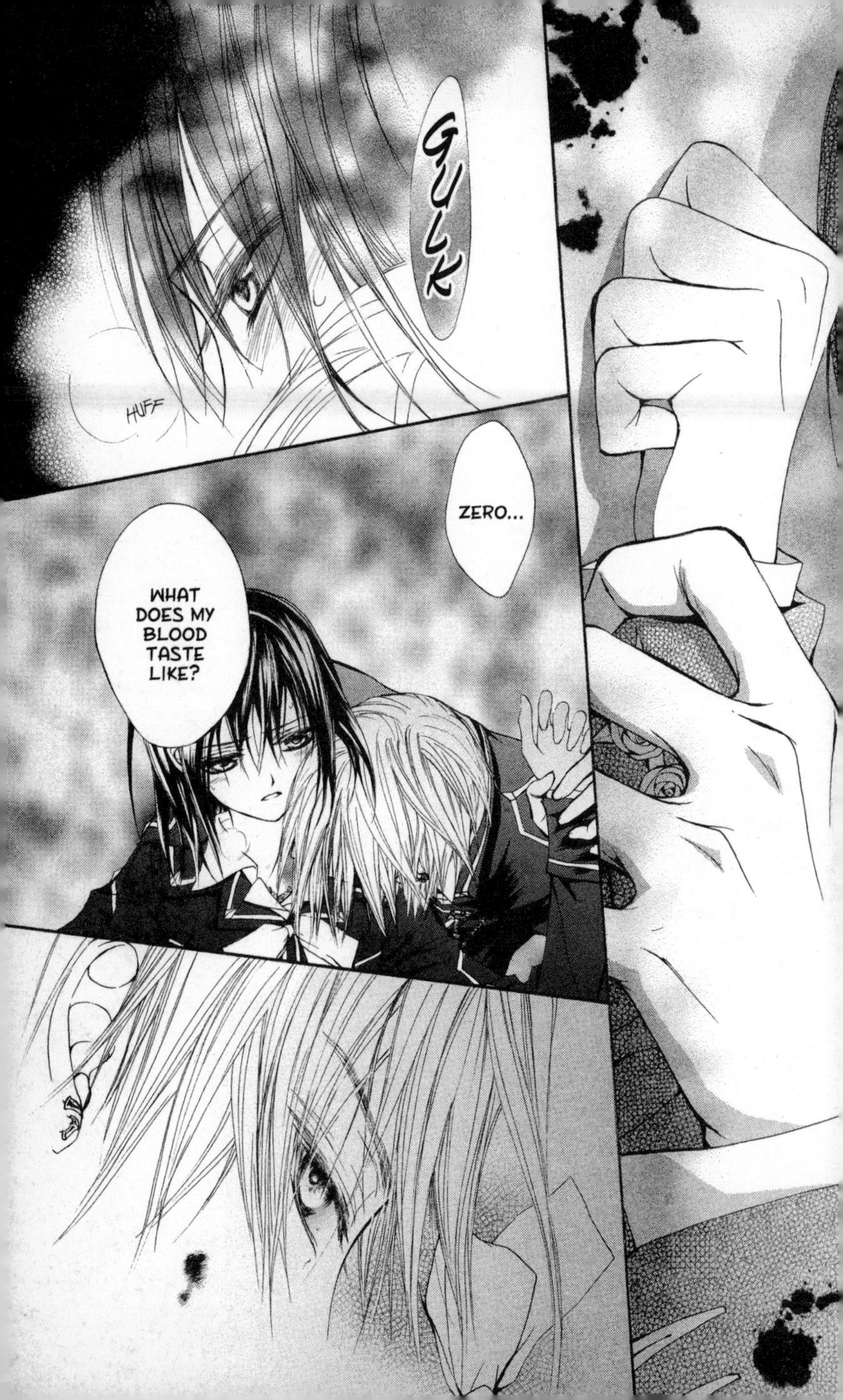
GULK
HUFF
ZERO...
WHAT DOES MY BLOOD TASTE LIKE?

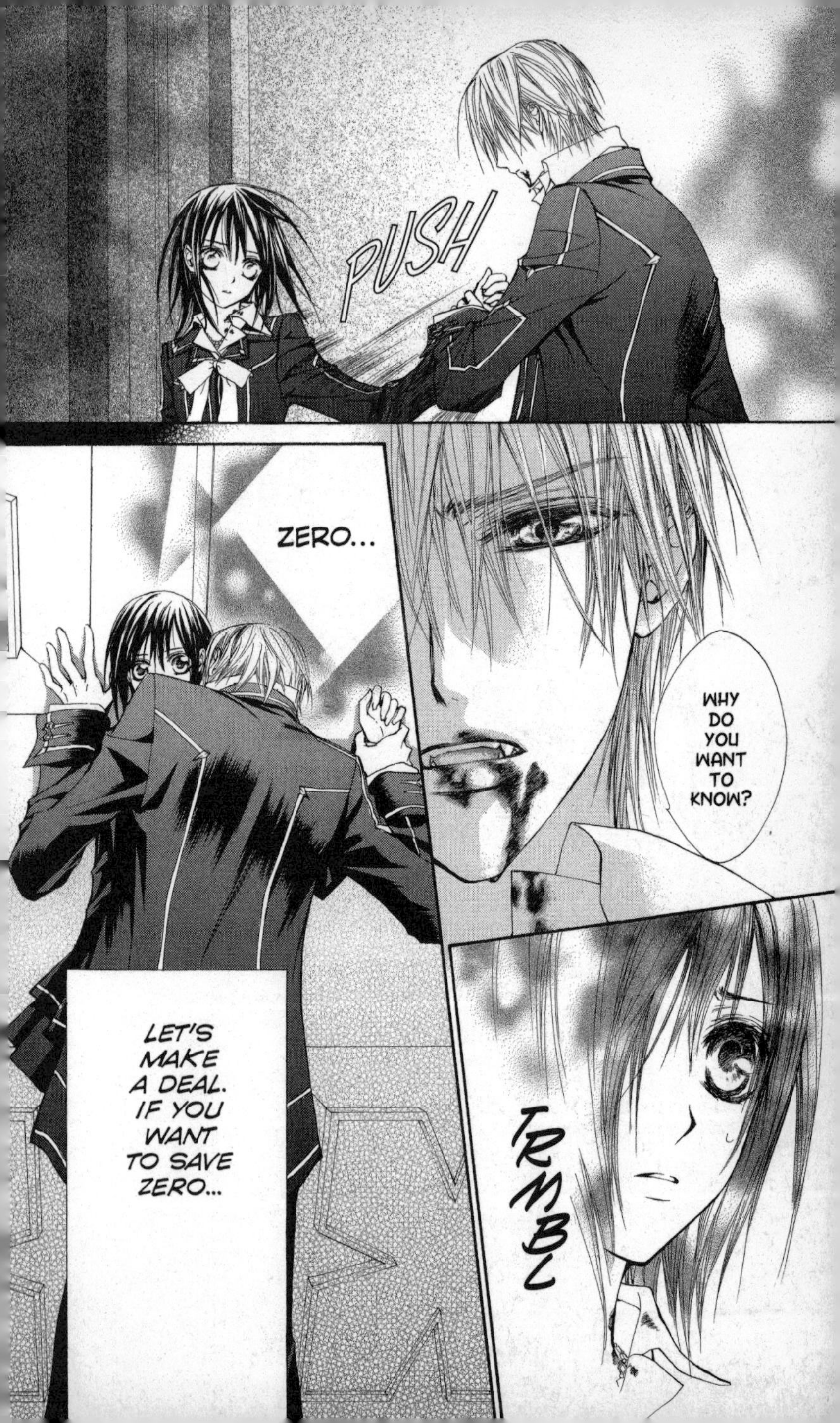
PUSH
WHY DO YOU WANT TO KNOW?
TRMBL
ZERO...
LET'S MAKE A DEAL. IF YOU WANT TO SAVE ZERO...

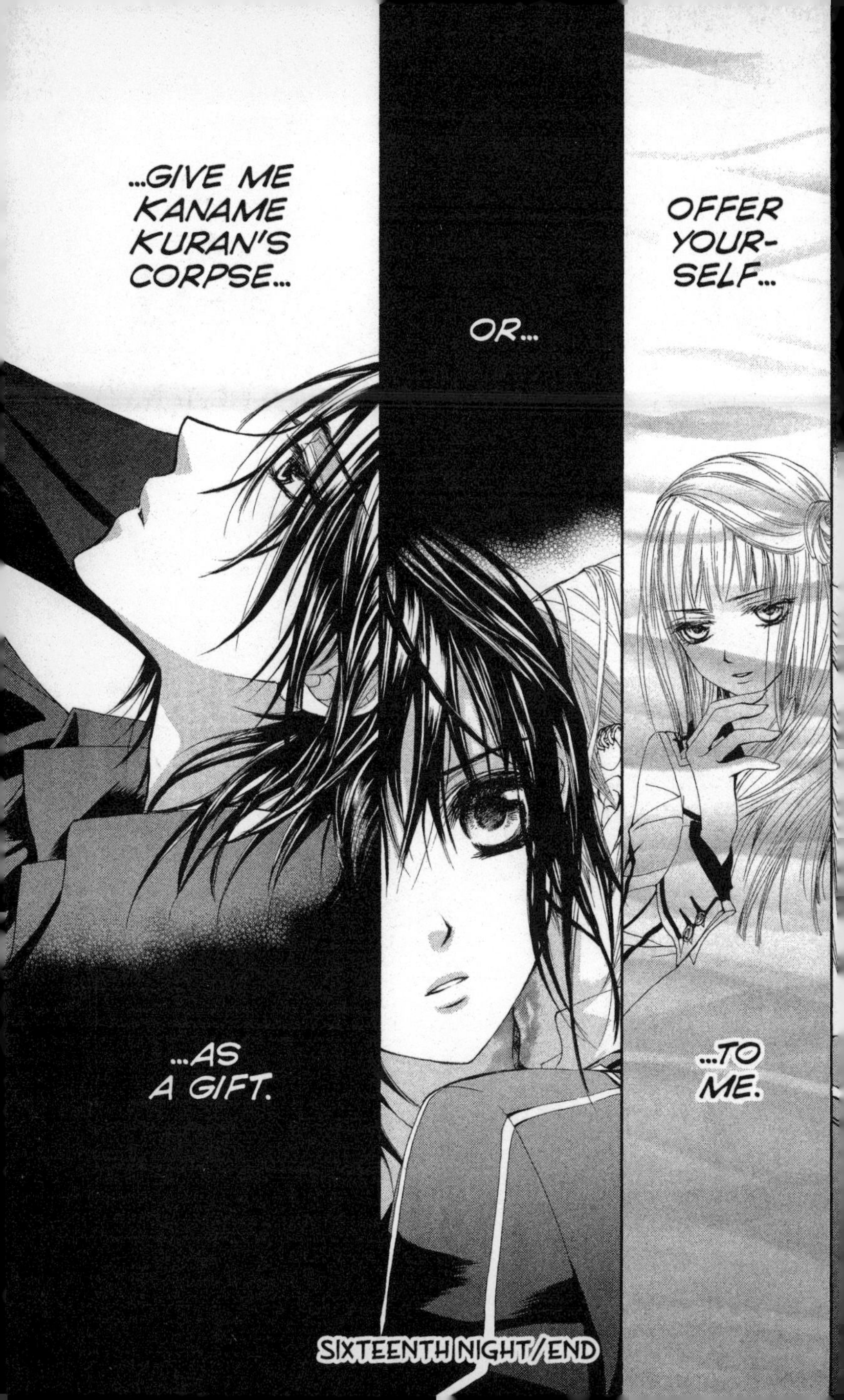
OFFER YOUR-SELF...
...TO ME.
OR...
...GIVE ME KANAME KURAN'S CORPSE...
...AS A GIFT.
SIXTEENTH NIGHT/END

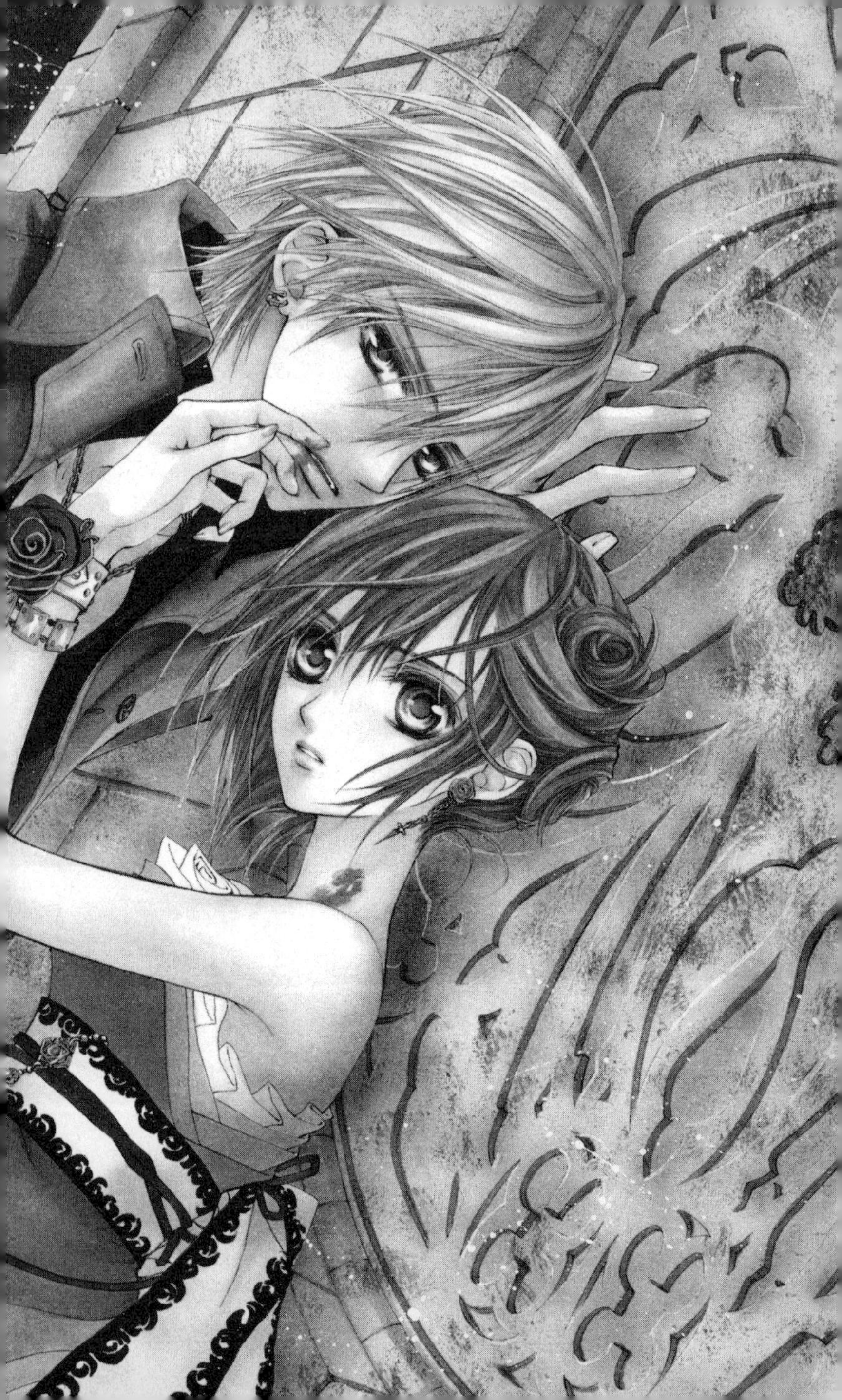

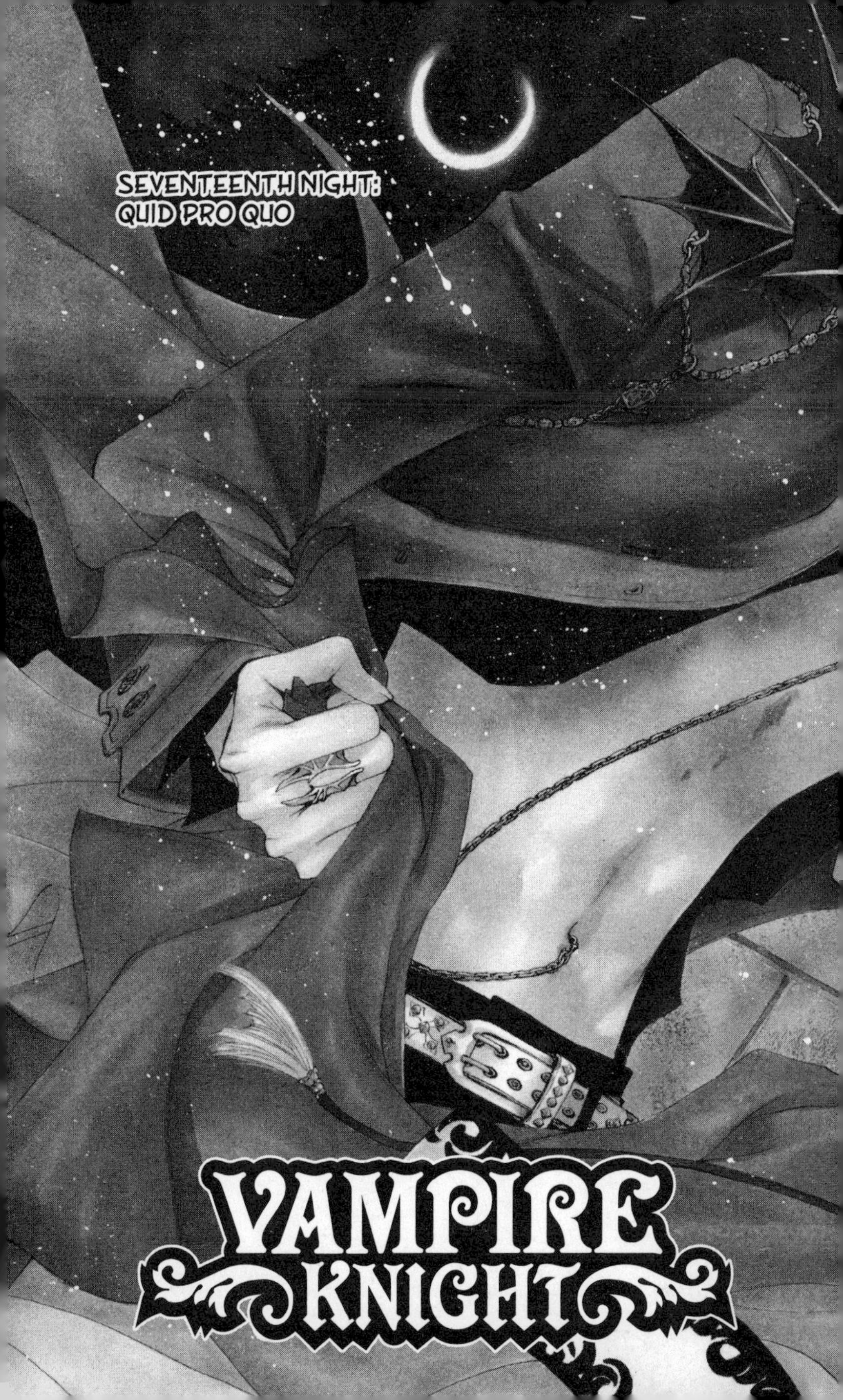
SEVENTEENTH NIGHT:
QUID PRO QUO
VAMPIRE KNIGHT

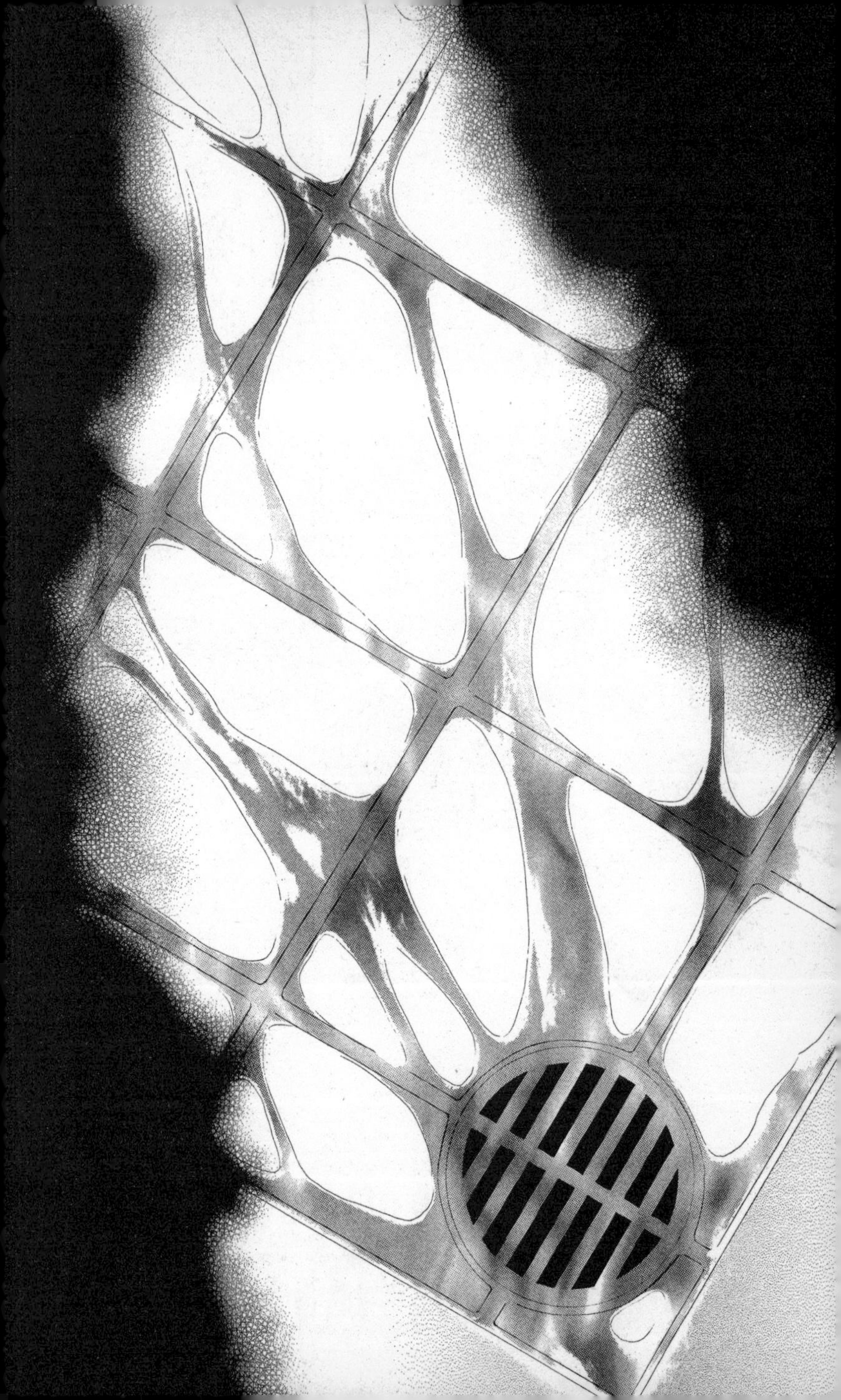

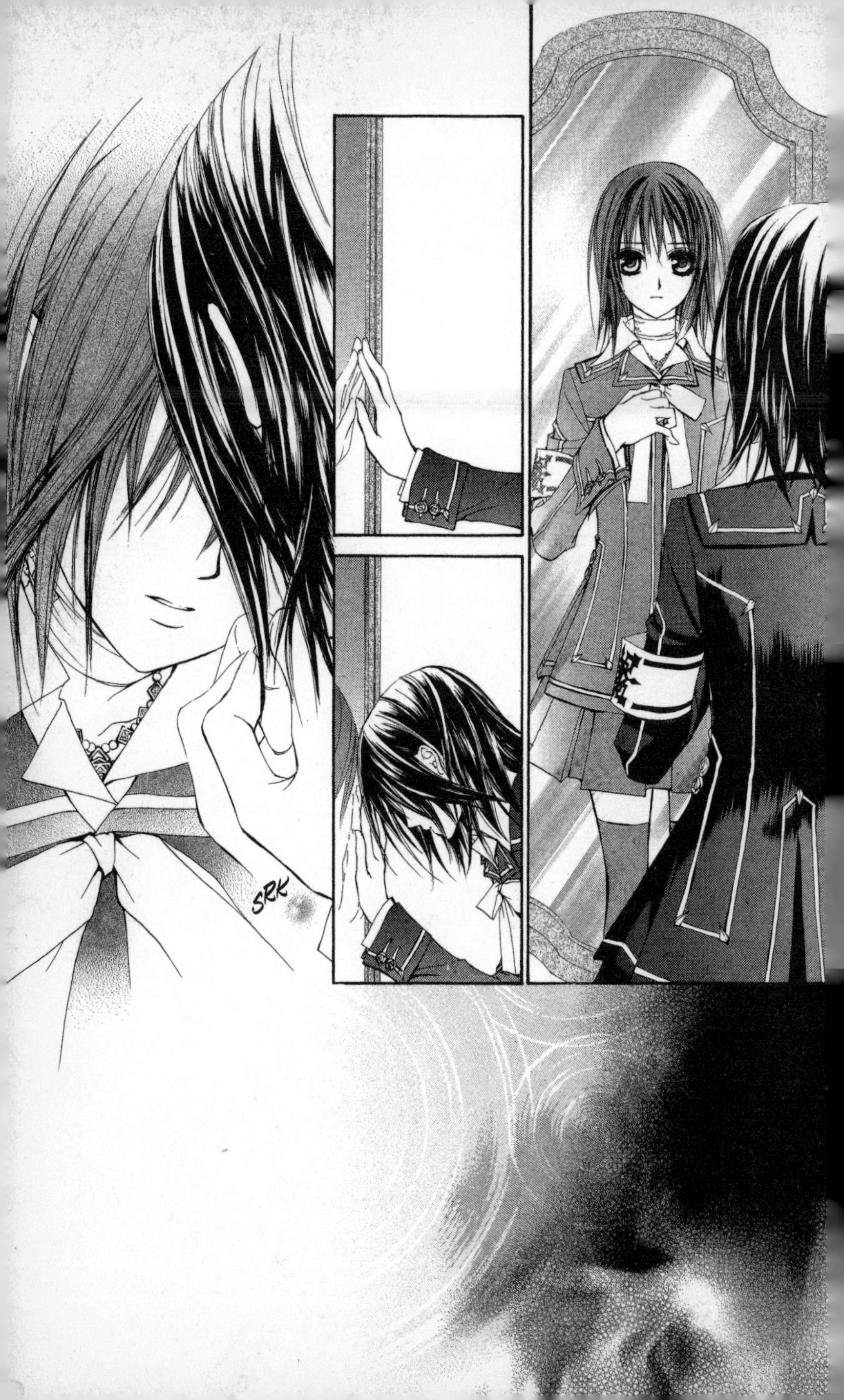
SRK

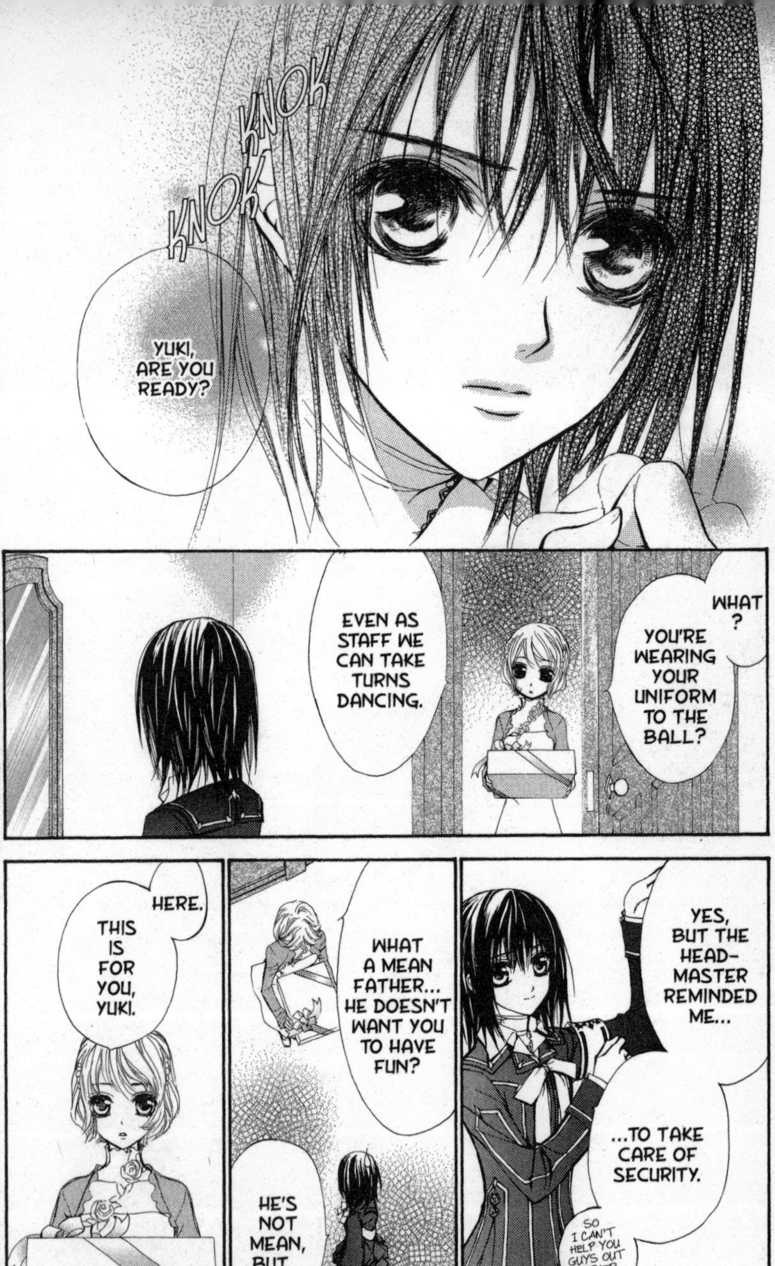
KNOK KNOK
YUKI, ARE YOU READY?
WHAT? YOU'RE WEARING YOUR UNIFORM TO THE BALL?
EVEN AS STAFF WE CAN TAKE TURNS DANCING.
YES, BUT THE HEAD-MASTER REMINDED ME...
...TO TAKE CARE OF SECURITY.
SO I CAN'T HELP YOU GUYS OUT EITHER.
WHAT A MEAN FATHER... HE DOESN'T WANT YOU TO HAVE FUN?
HE'S NOT MEAN, BUT...
HERE. THIS IS FOR YOU, YUKI.

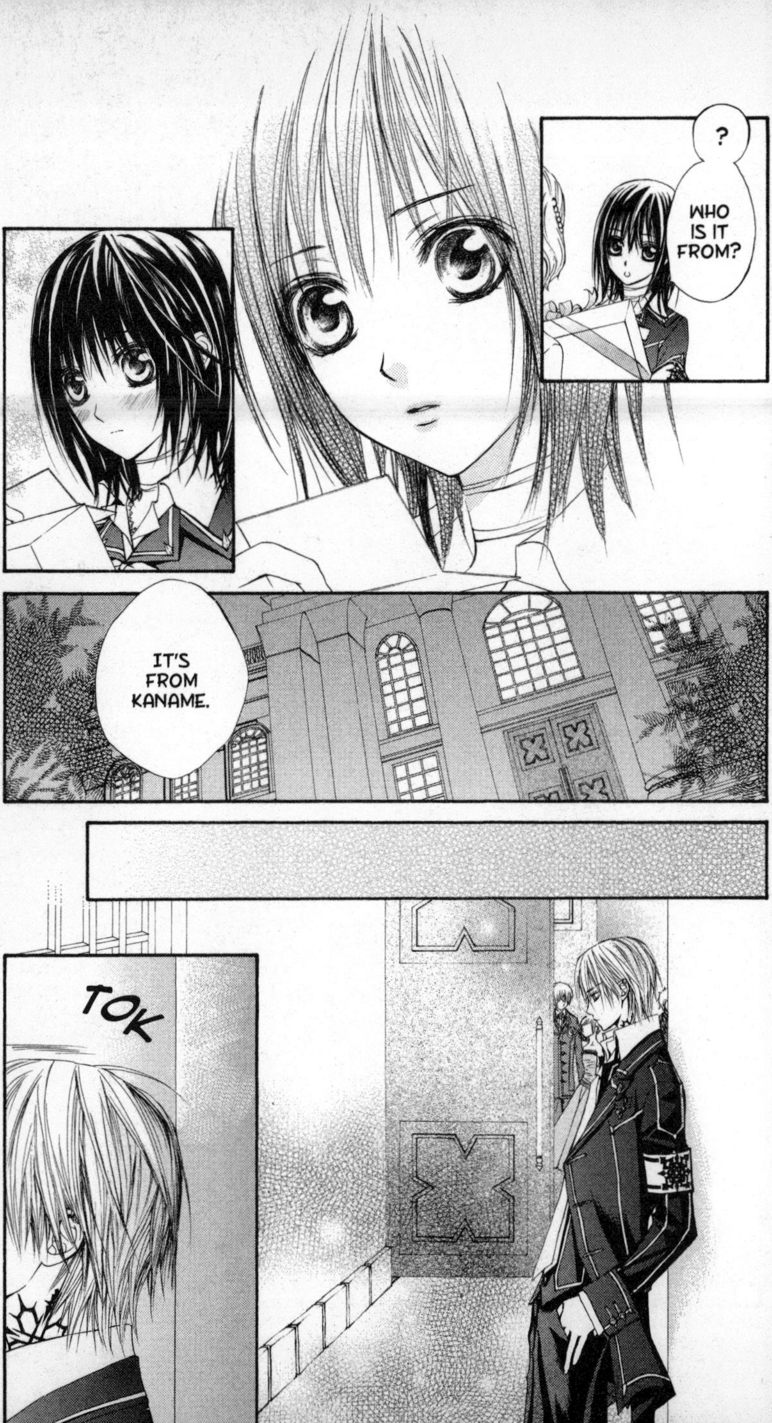
?
WHO IS IT FROM?
IT'S FROM KANAME.
TOK

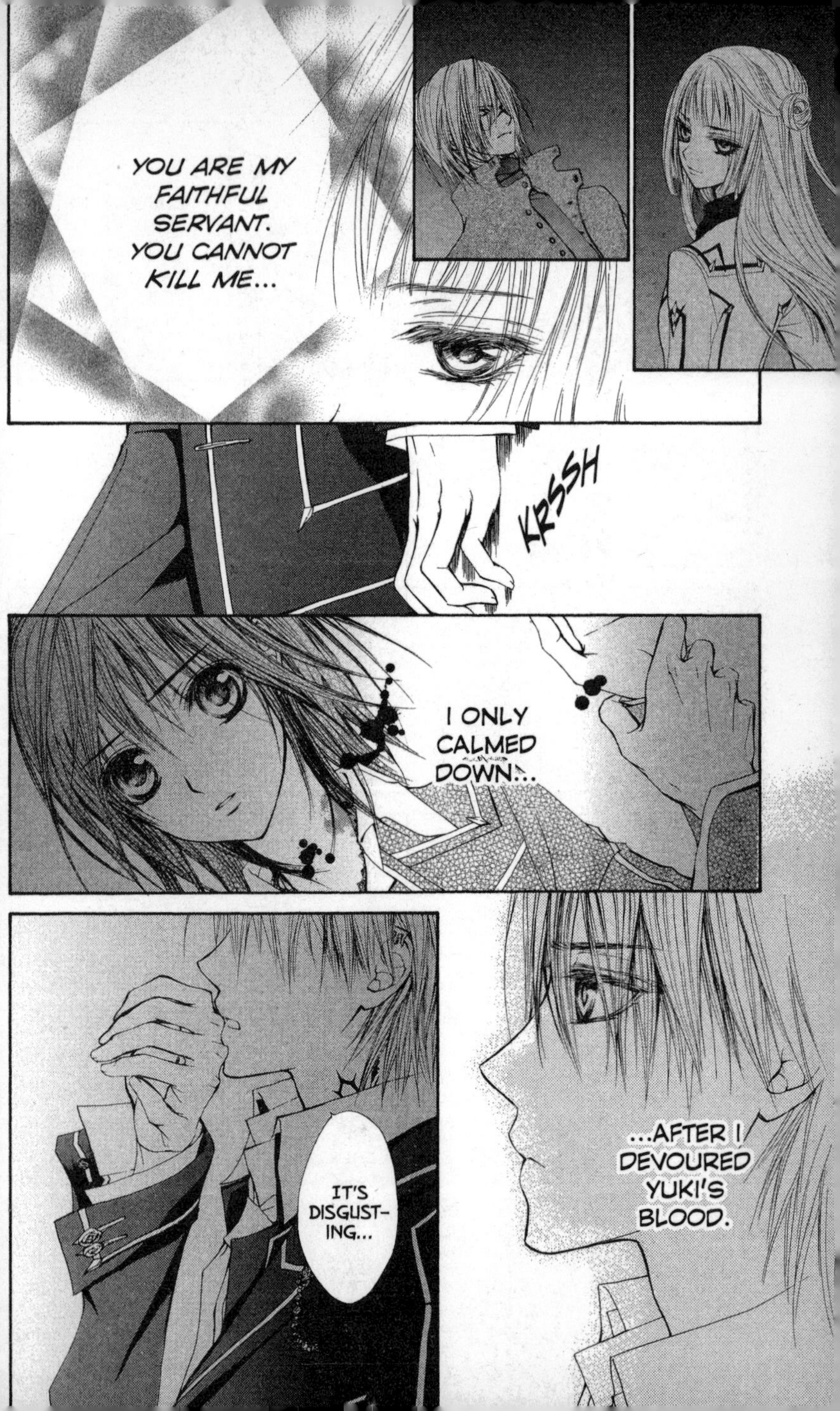
YOU ARE MY FAITHFUL SERVANT. YOU CANNOT KILL ME...
KRSSH
I ONLY CALMED DOWN...
...AFTER I DEVOURED YUKI'S BLOOD.
IT'S DISGUST-ING...

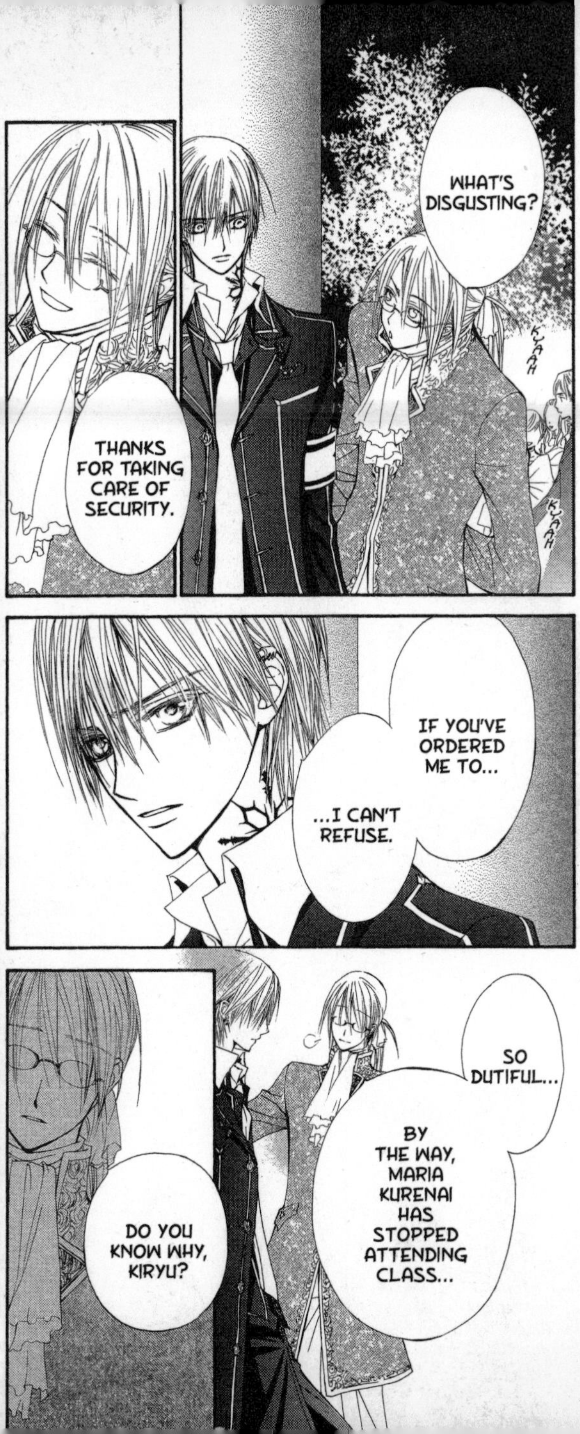
WHAT'S DISGUSTING?
KYAAH
KYAAH
THANKS FOR TAKING CARE OF SECURITY.
IF YOU'VE ORDERED ME TO...
...I CAN'T REFUSE.
SO DUTIFUL...
BY THE WAY, MARIA KURENAI HAS STOPPED ATTENDING CLASS...
DO YOU KNOW WHY, KIRYU?

III

Nowadays readers ask in their letters, "Don't you have a blog?"

I am interested in having one, but I don't know what to write in it, so I can't do it.

I'm someone who agonizes enough over how to fill these sidebars.

Yes...I don't know how much I should write. I write too much, and my editor says no. It happens every time. (It's because Hino can't learn.)

I want to put more comedy in my manga, but I chicken out after thinking about it...

Oh, in the bonus story at the end of this volume, I should have had Shiki lean on Rima. It's difficult to develop love relationships in this manga.

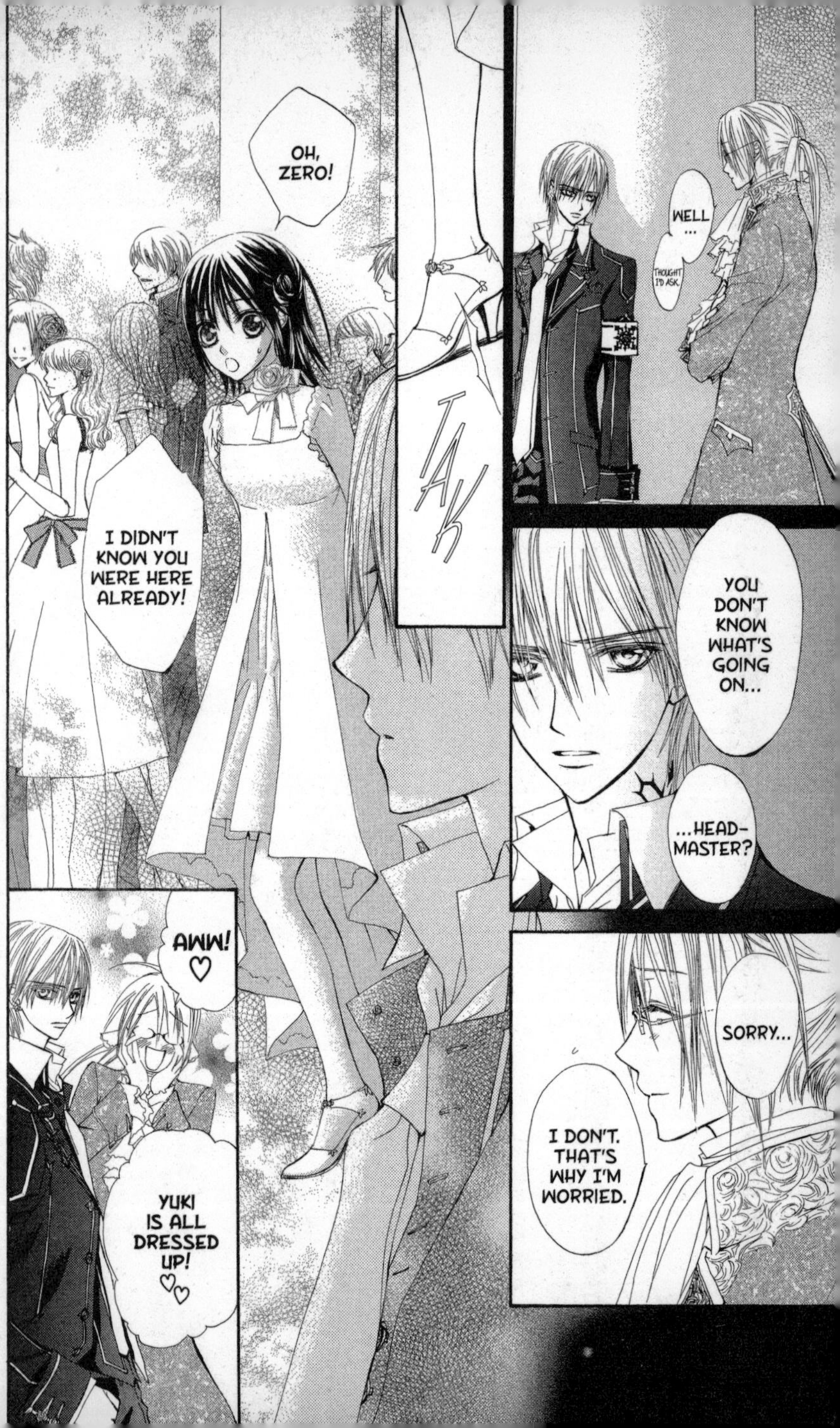
WELL ...
THOUGHT I'D ASK.
YOU DON'T KNOW WHAT'S GOING ON...
...HEAD-MASTER?
SORRY...
I DON'T. THAT'S WHY I'M WORRIED.
TAK
OH, ZERO!
I DIDN'T KNOW YOU WERE HERE ALREADY!
AWW! ♡
YUKI IS ALL DRESSED UP! ♡♡

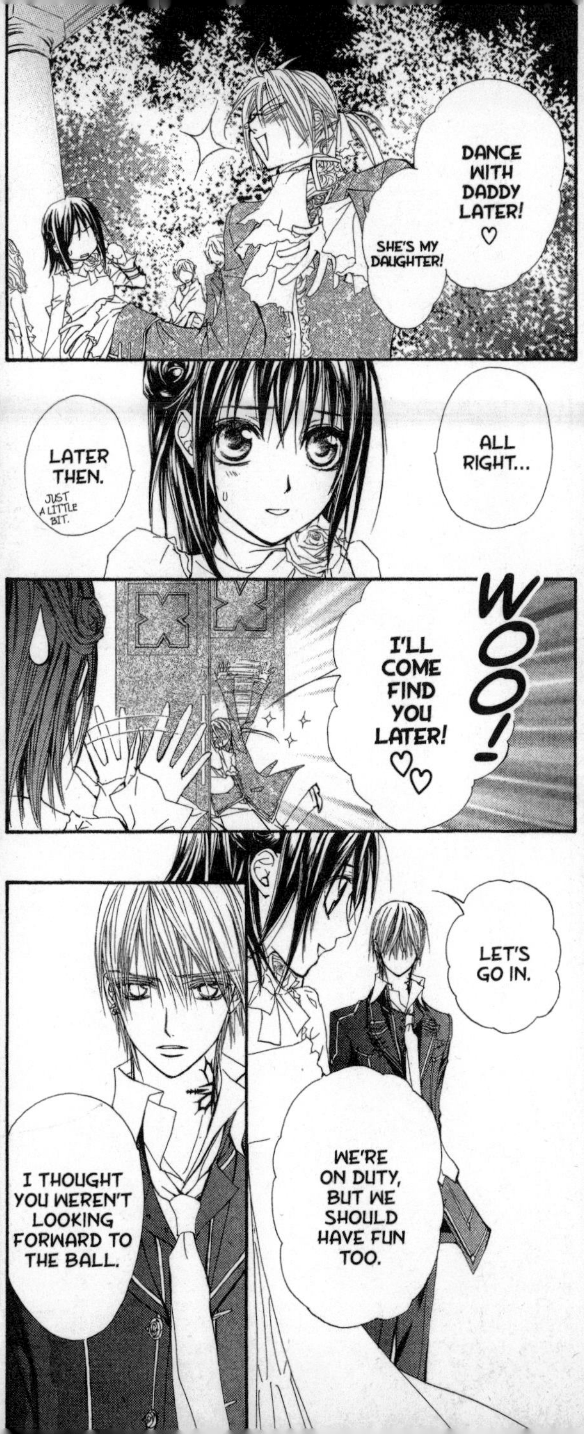
DANCE WITH DADDY LATER! ♡
SHE'S MY DAUGHTER!
ALL RIGHT...
LATER THEN.
JUST A LITTLE BIT.
WOOO!
I'LL COME FIND YOU LATER! ♡♡
LET'S GO IN.
WE'RE ON DUTY, BUT WE SHOULD HAVE FUN TOO.
I THOUGHT YOU WEREN'T LOOKING FORWARD TO THE BALL.

IV

The Shizuka arc isn't finished yet, so I can't talk too much about it, and that's hard. ♢

I started this series by first deciding how it would end (this is the first time I've done that). However, sometimes I've changed things as I've gone along, so I am keeping myself in suspense. (smile) ♢ It looks like those changes won't affect the ending for now.

It is really difficult to draw a series by creating a highlight scene in every chapter--I battle with my lack of ability. Every month. Ha ha ha... ♢

I had originally planned to end the Shizuka arc in volume 4. But that would have meant not delving into all the parts that need to be drawn thoroughly. ↓

(continues)

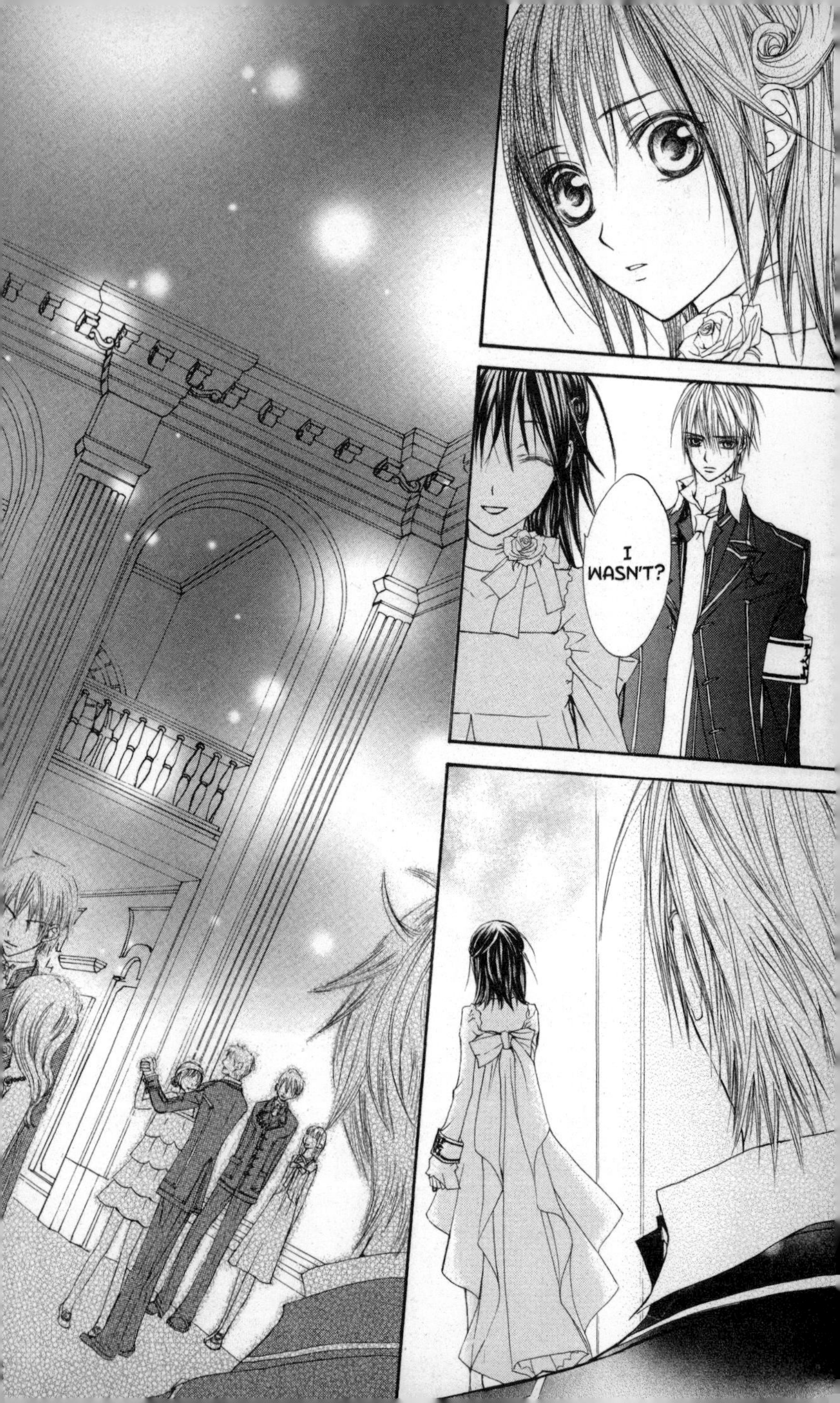
I WASN'T?

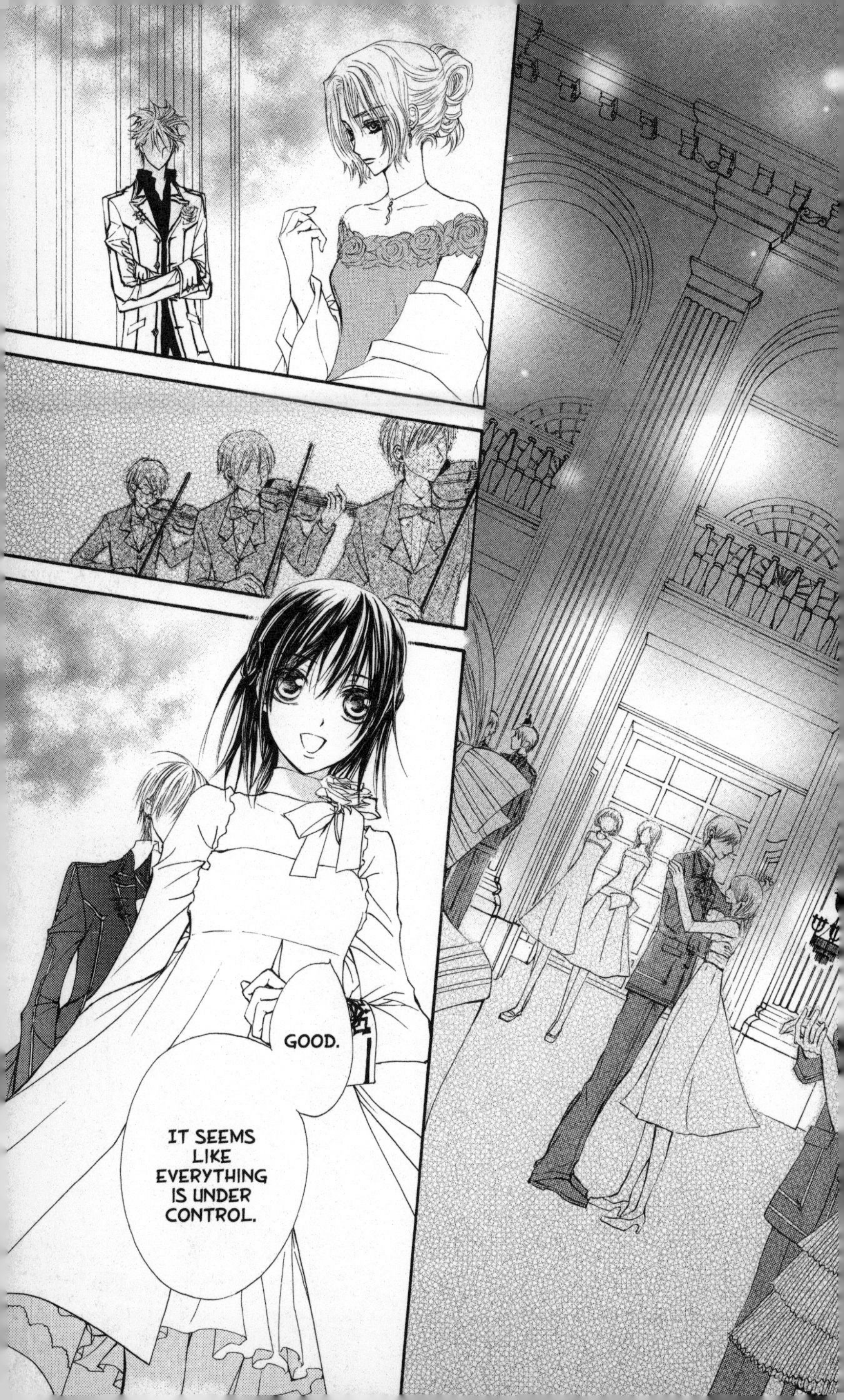
GOOD.
IT SEEMS LIKE EVERYTHING IS UNDER CONTROL.

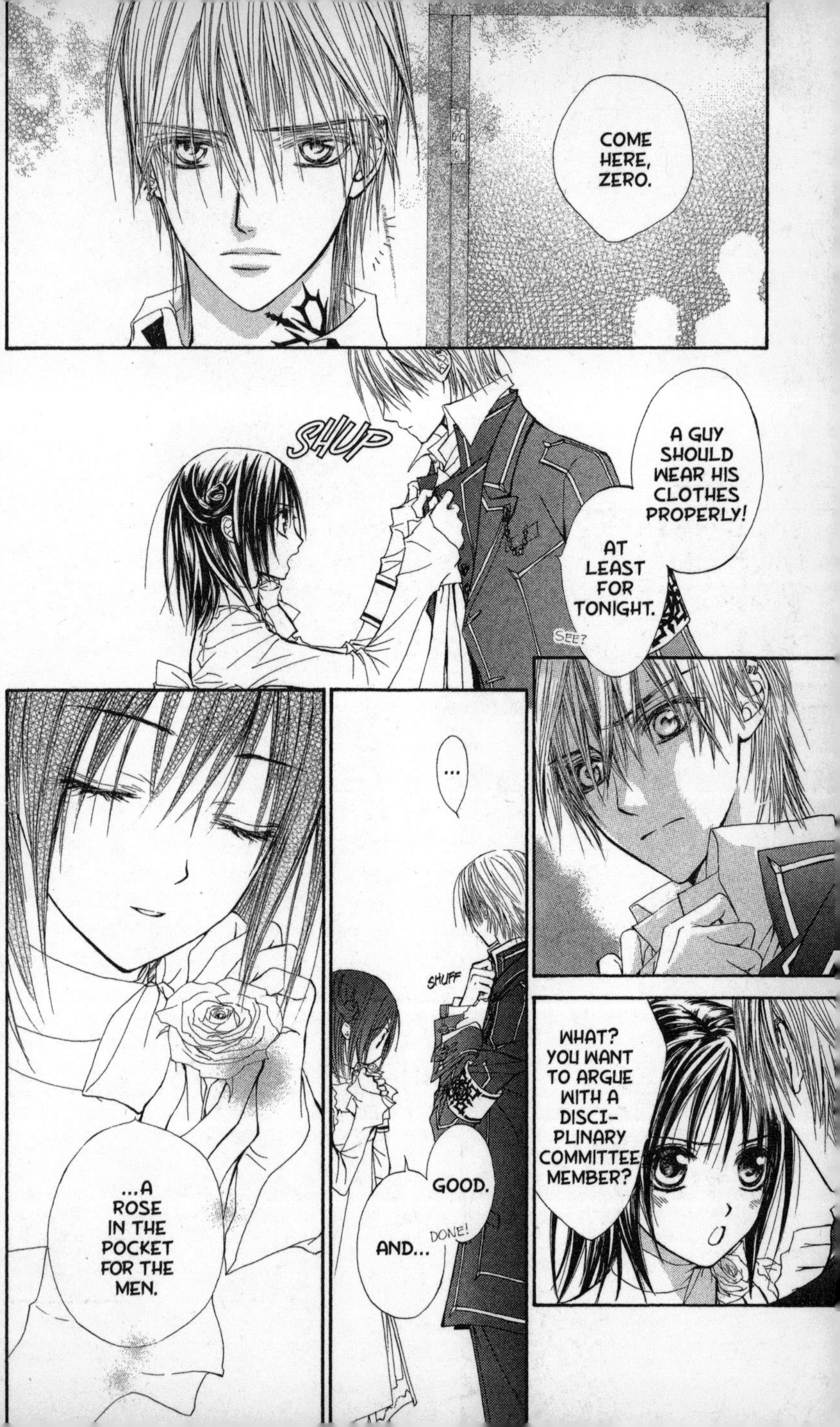
COME HERE, ZERO.
SHUP
A GUY SHOULD WEAR HIS CLOTHES PROPERLY!
AT LEAST FOR TONIGHT.
SEE?
WHAT? YOU WANT TO ARGUE WITH A DISCI-PLINARY COMMITTEE MEMBER?
...
SHUFF
GOOD.
DONE!
AND...
...A ROSE IN THE POCKET FOR THE MEN.

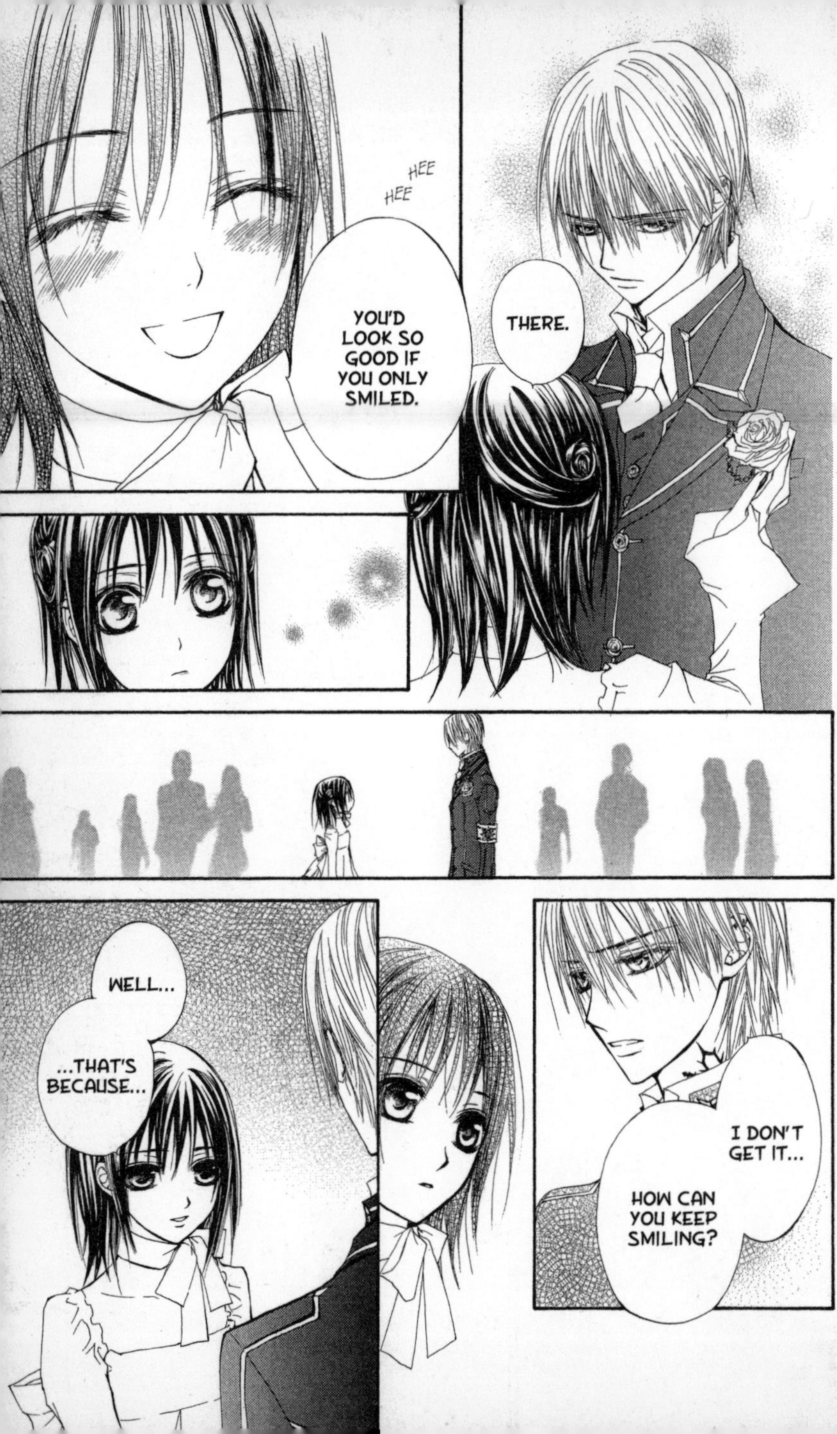
THERE.
HEE HEE
YOU'D LOOK SO GOOD IF YOU ONLY SMILED.
I DON'T GET IT...
HOW CAN YOU KEEP SMILING?
WELL...
...THAT'S BECAUSE...

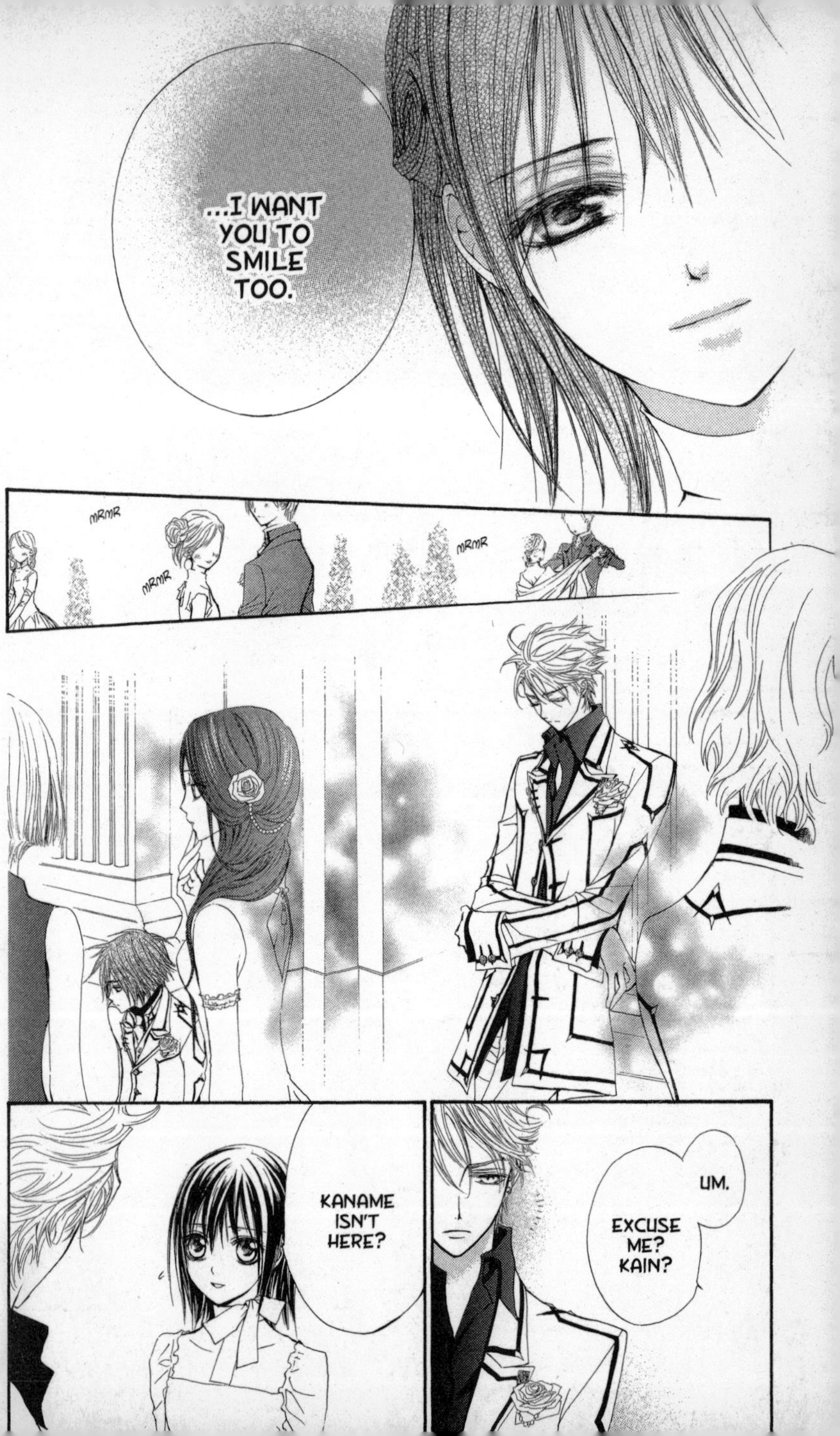
...I WANT YOU TO SMILE TOO.
MRMR
MRMR
MRMR
UM.
EXCUSE ME? KAIN?
KANAME ISN'T HERE?

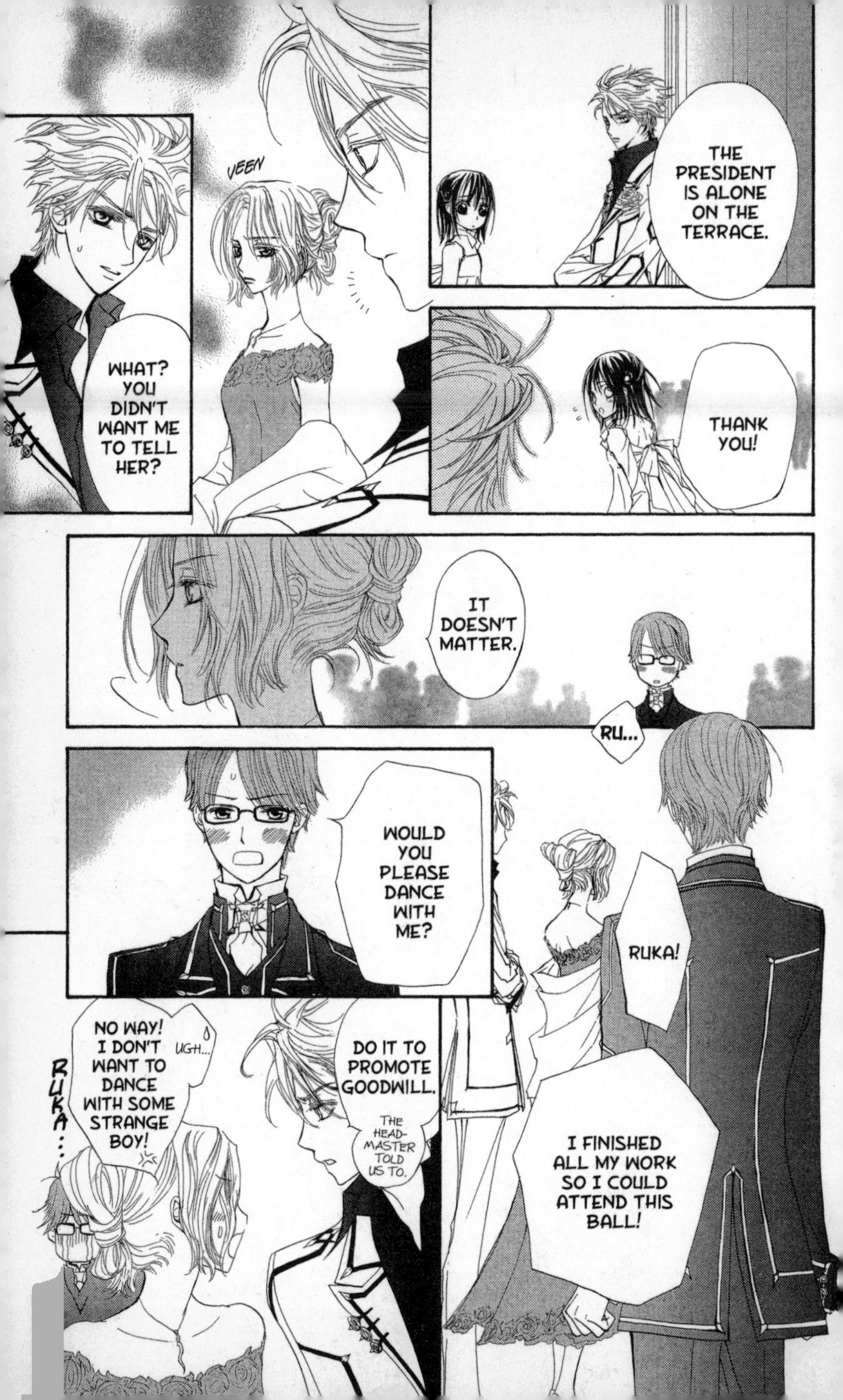
THE PRESIDENT IS ALONE ON THE TERRACE.
THANK YOU!
VEEN
WHAT? YOU DIDN'T WANT ME TO TELL HER?
IT DOESN'T MATTER.
RU...
RUKA!
I FINISHED ALL MY WORK SO I COULD ATTEND THIS BALL!
WOULD YOU PLEASE DANCE WITH ME?
DO IT TO PROMOTE GOODWILL.
THE HEAD-MASTER TOLD US TO.
NO WAY! I DON'T WANT TO DANCE WITH SOME STRANGE BOY!
UGH...
RUKA...

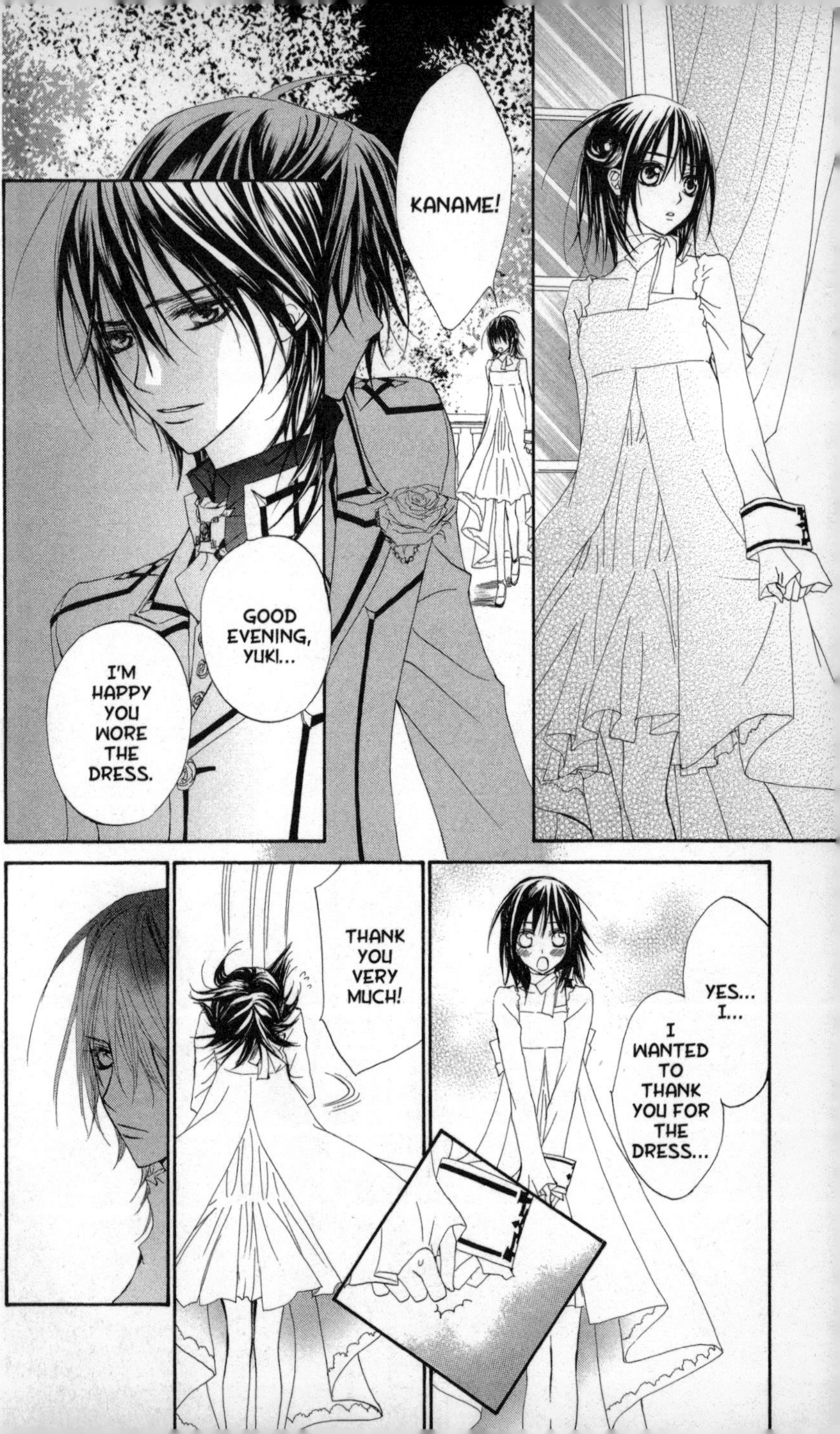
KANAME!
GOOD EVENING, YUKI...
I'M HAPPY YOU WORE THE DRESS.
YES... I... I WANTED TO THANK YOU FOR THE DRESS...
THANK YOU VERY MUCH!

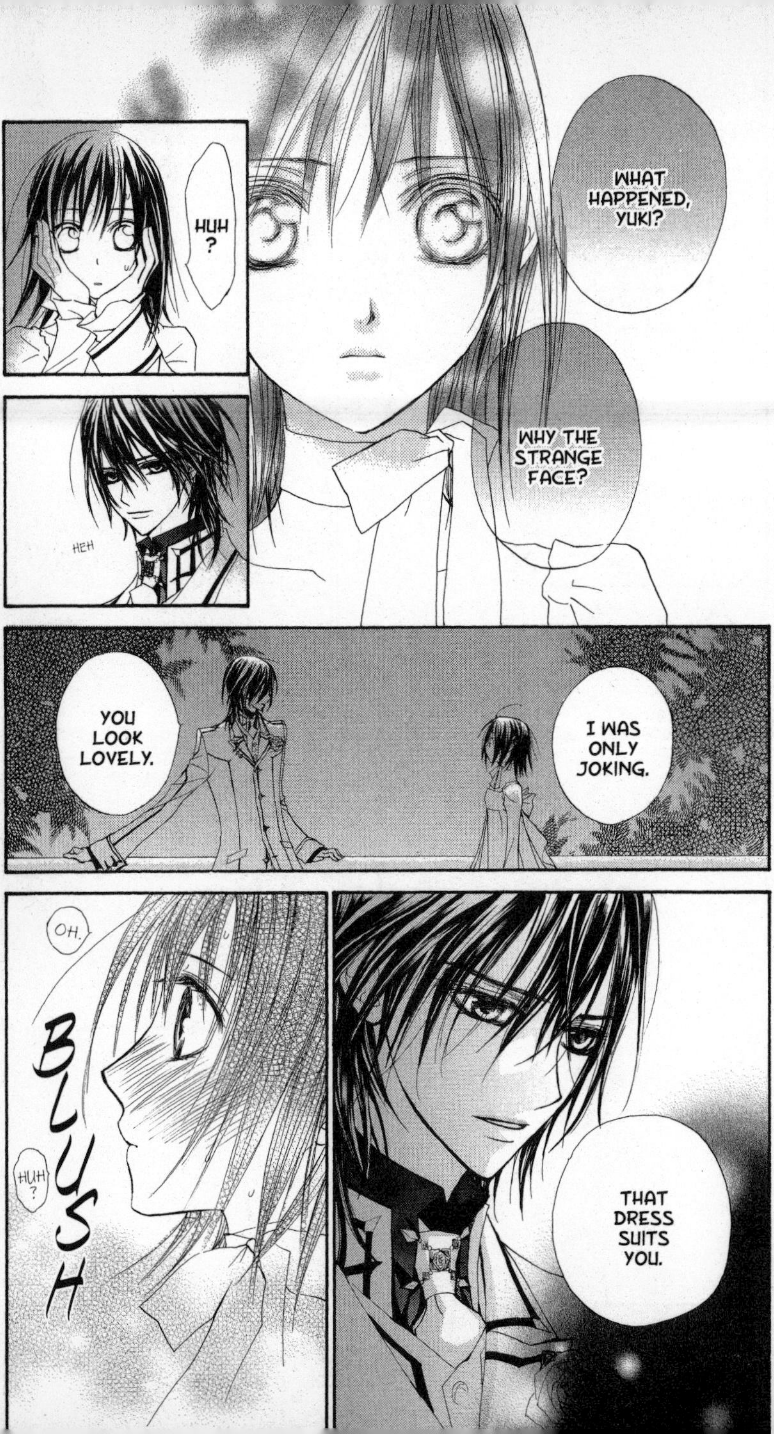
WHAT HAPPENED, YUKI?
WHY THE STRANGE FACE?
HUH?
HEH
I WAS ONLY JOKING.
YOU LOOK LOVELY.
THAT DRESS SUITS YOU.
OH.
BLUSH
HUH?

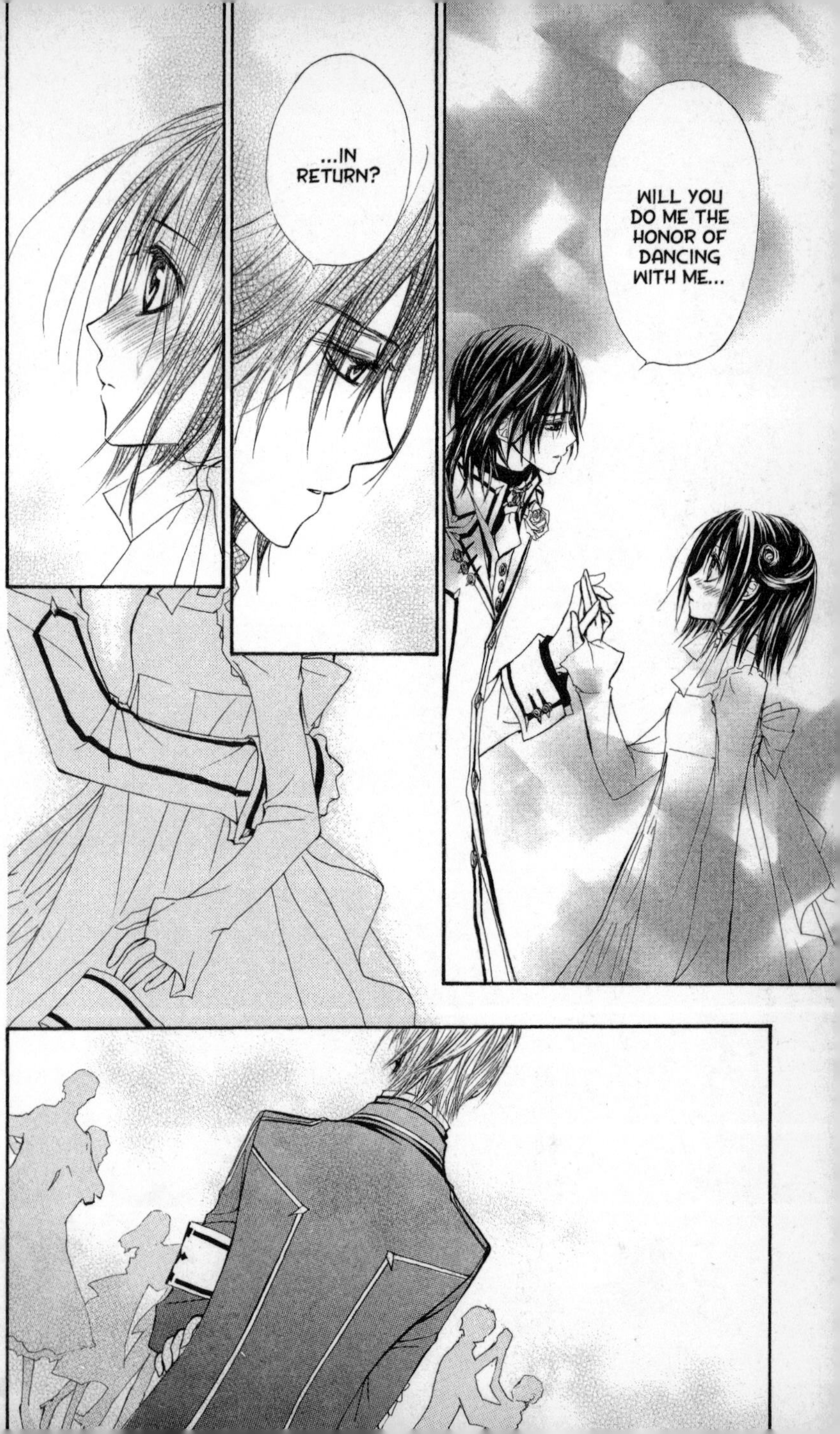
WILL YOU DO ME THE HONOR OF DANCING WITH ME...
...IN RETURN?

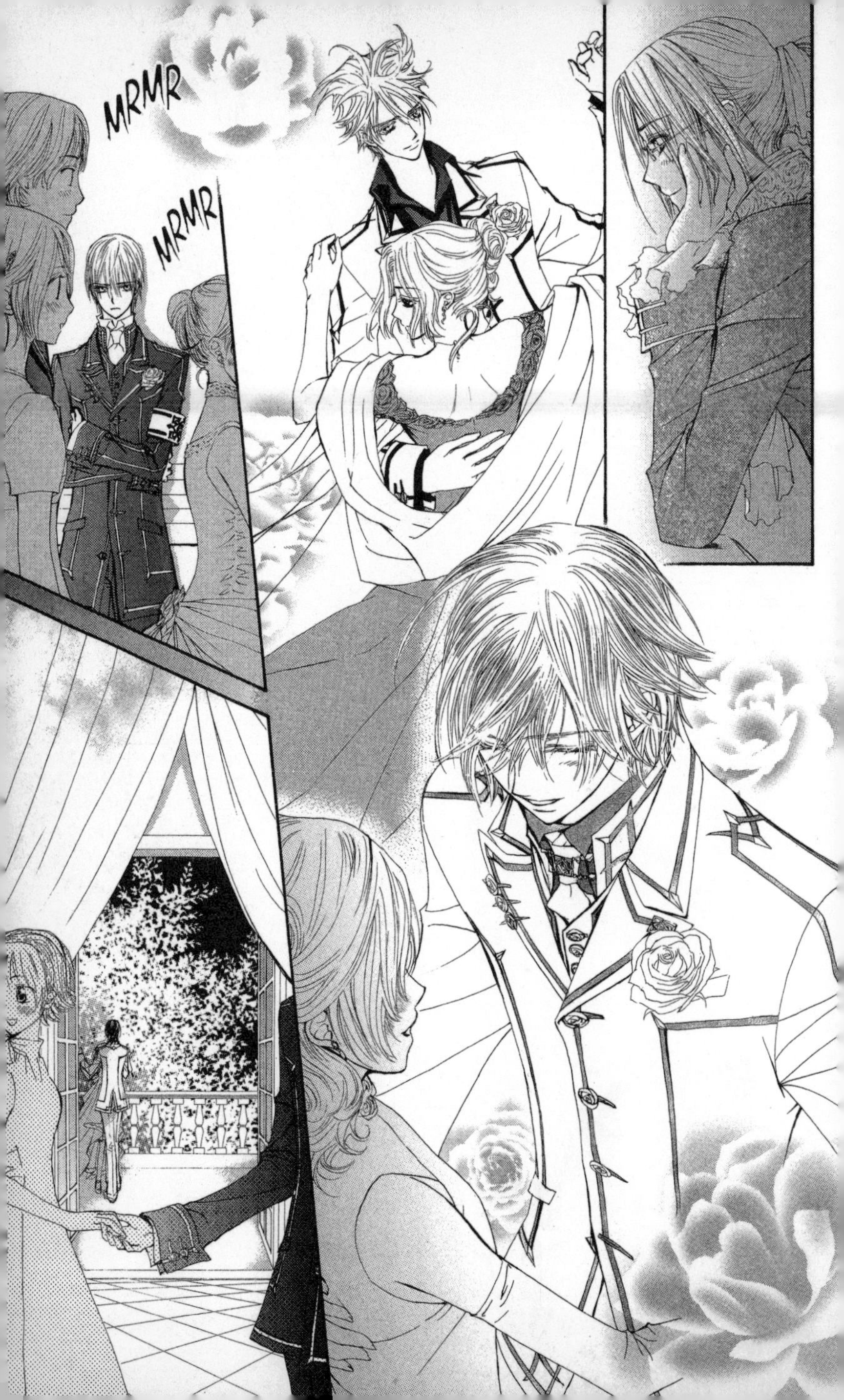
MRMR
MRMR

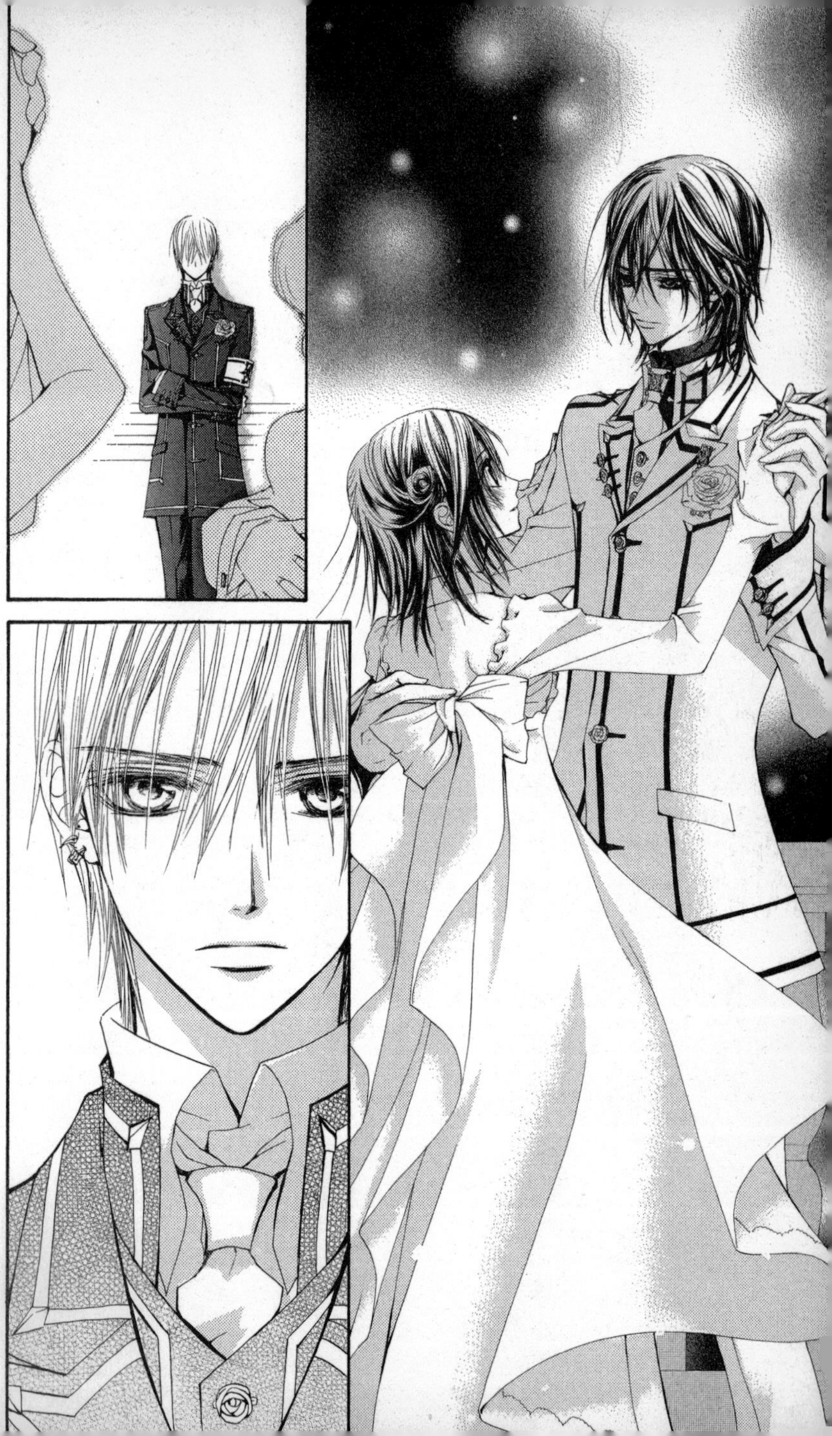

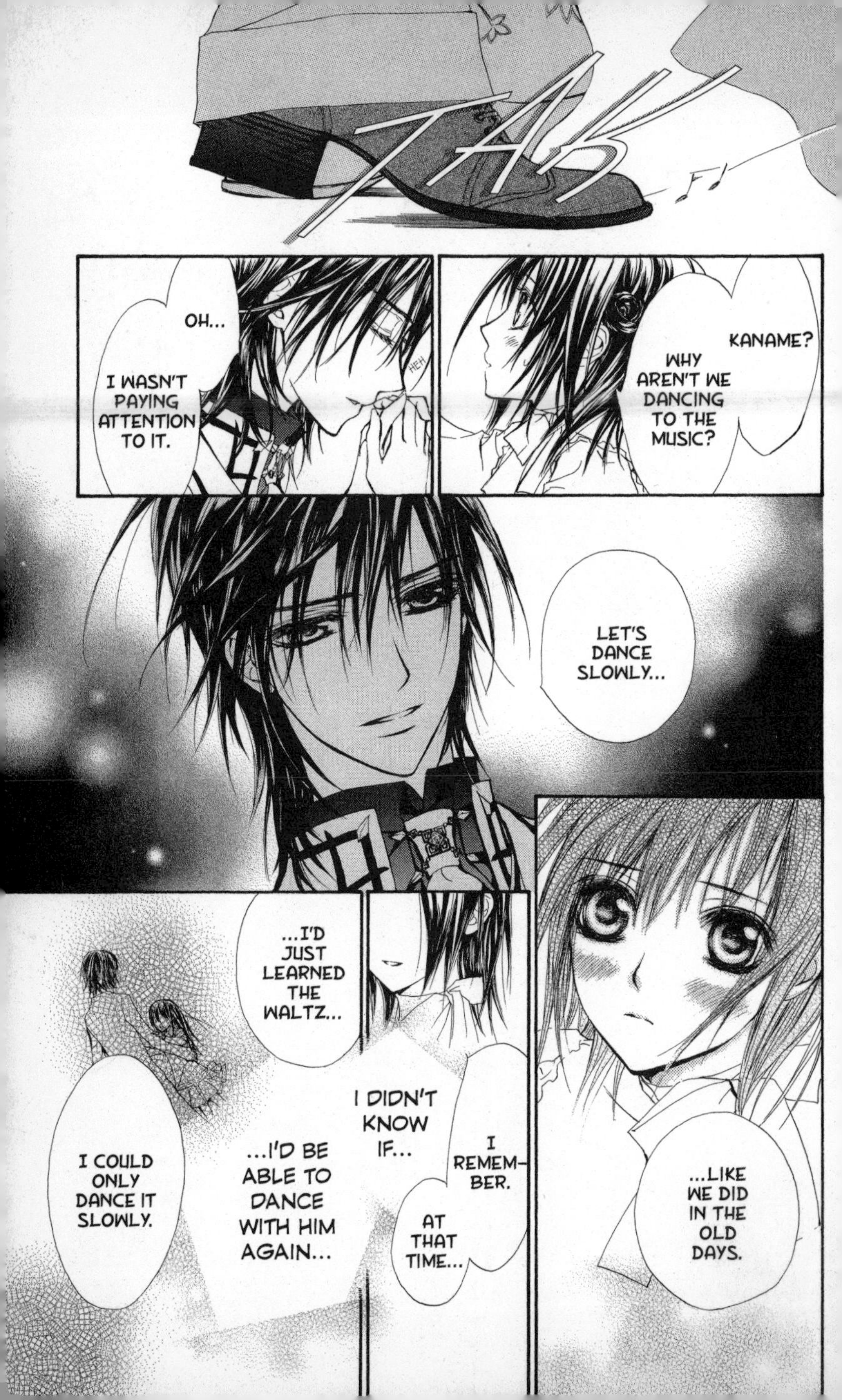
KANAME?
WHY AREN'T WE DANCING TO THE MUSIC?
HEH
OH...
I WASN'T PAYING ATTENTION TO IT.
LET'S DANCE SLOWLY...
...LIKE WE DID IN THE OLD DAYS.
I REMEMBER.
AT THAT TIME...
...I'D JUST LEARNED THE WALTZ...
I COULD ONLY DANCE IT SLOWLY.
I DIDN'T KNOW IF...
...I'D BE ABLE TO DANCE WITH HIM AGAIN...

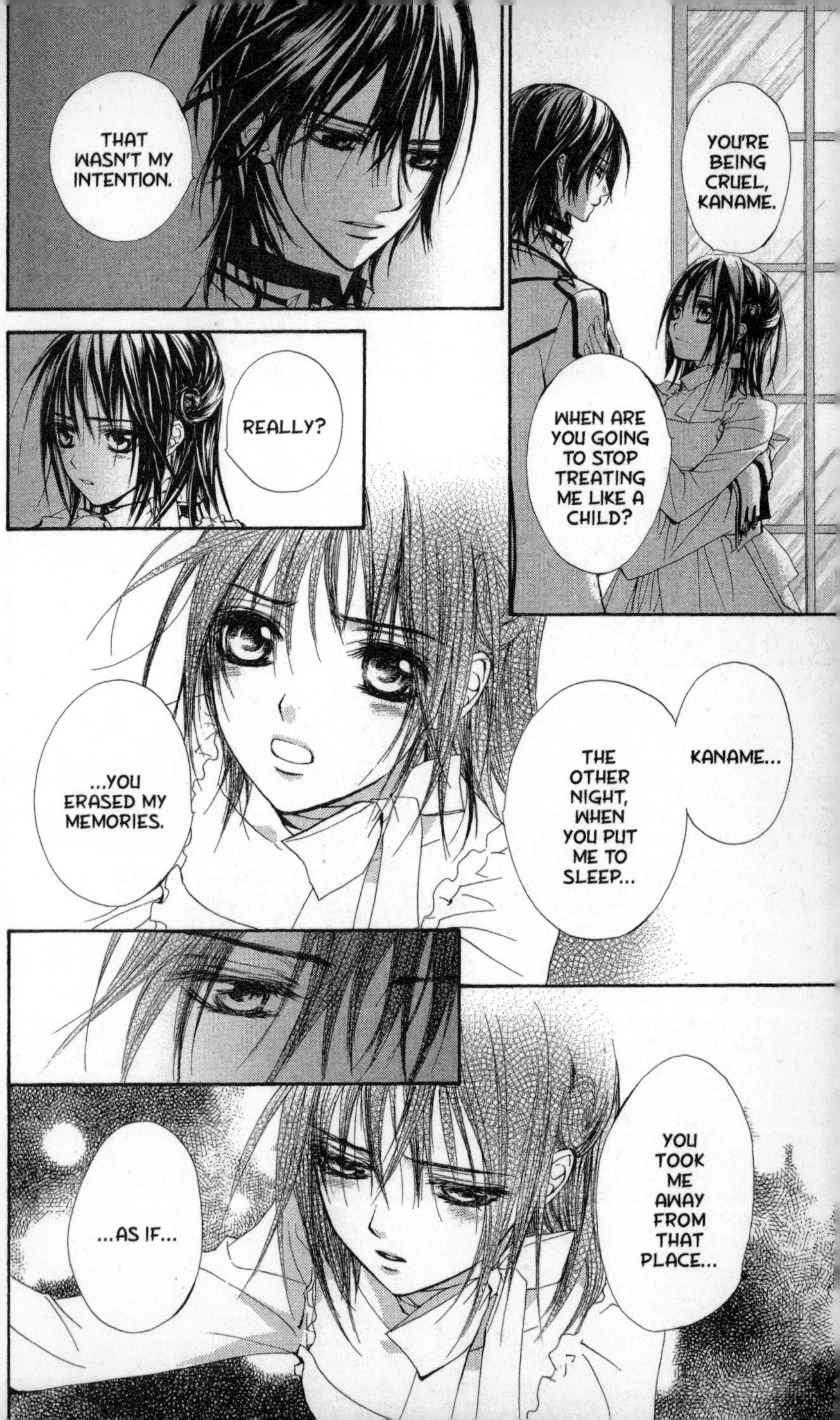
YOU'RE BEING CRUEL, KANAME.
WHEN ARE YOU GOING TO STOP TREATING ME LIKE A CHILD?
THAT WASN'T MY INTENTION.
REALLY?
KANAME...
THE OTHER NIGHT, WHEN YOU PUT ME TO SLEEP...
...YOU ERASED MY MEMORIES.
YOU TOOK ME AWAY FROM THAT PLACE...
...AS IF...

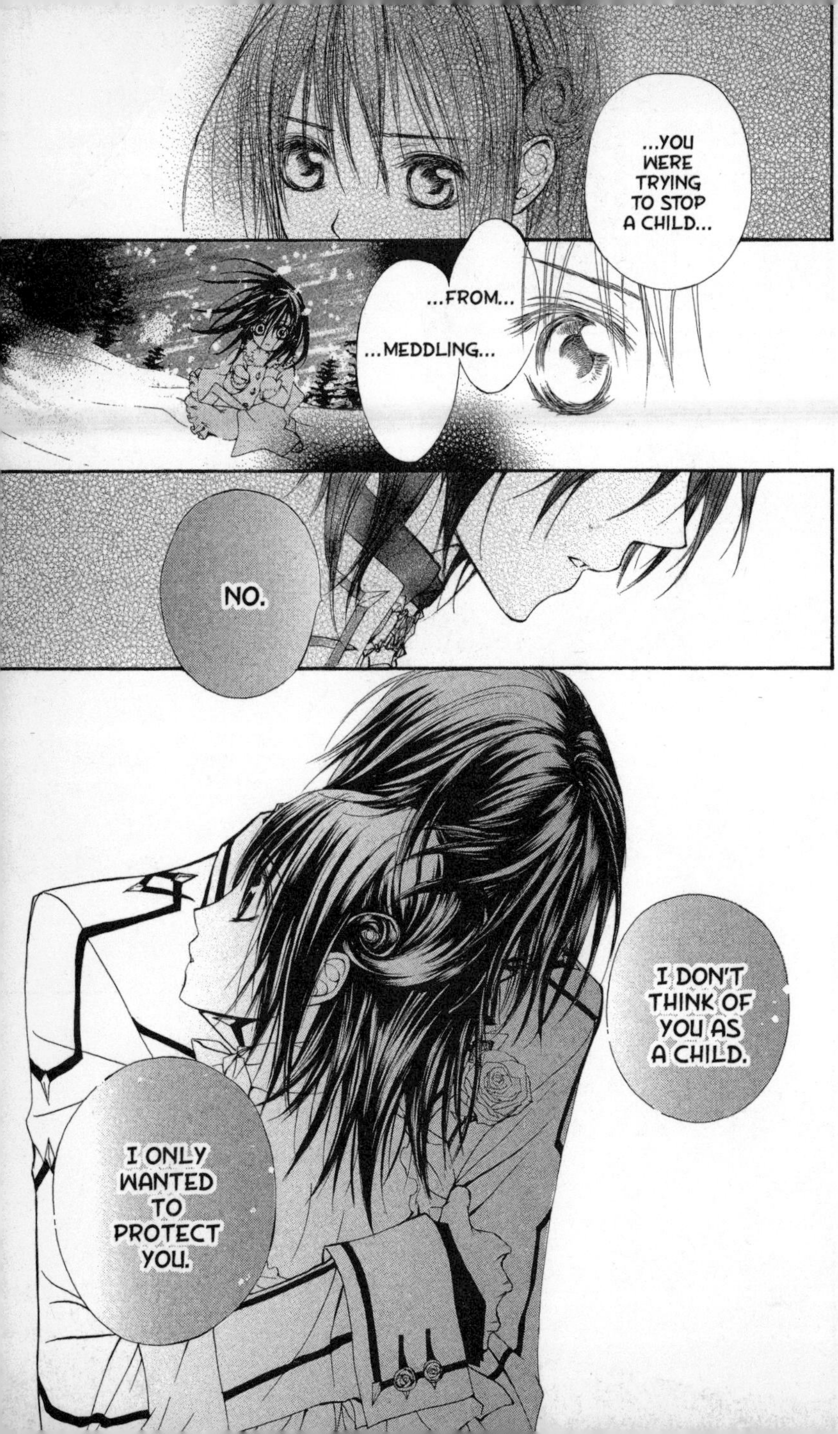
...YOU WERE TRYING TO STOP A CHILD...
...FROM...
...MEDDLING...
NO.
I DON'T THINK OF YOU AS A CHILD.
I ONLY WANTED TO PROTECT YOU.

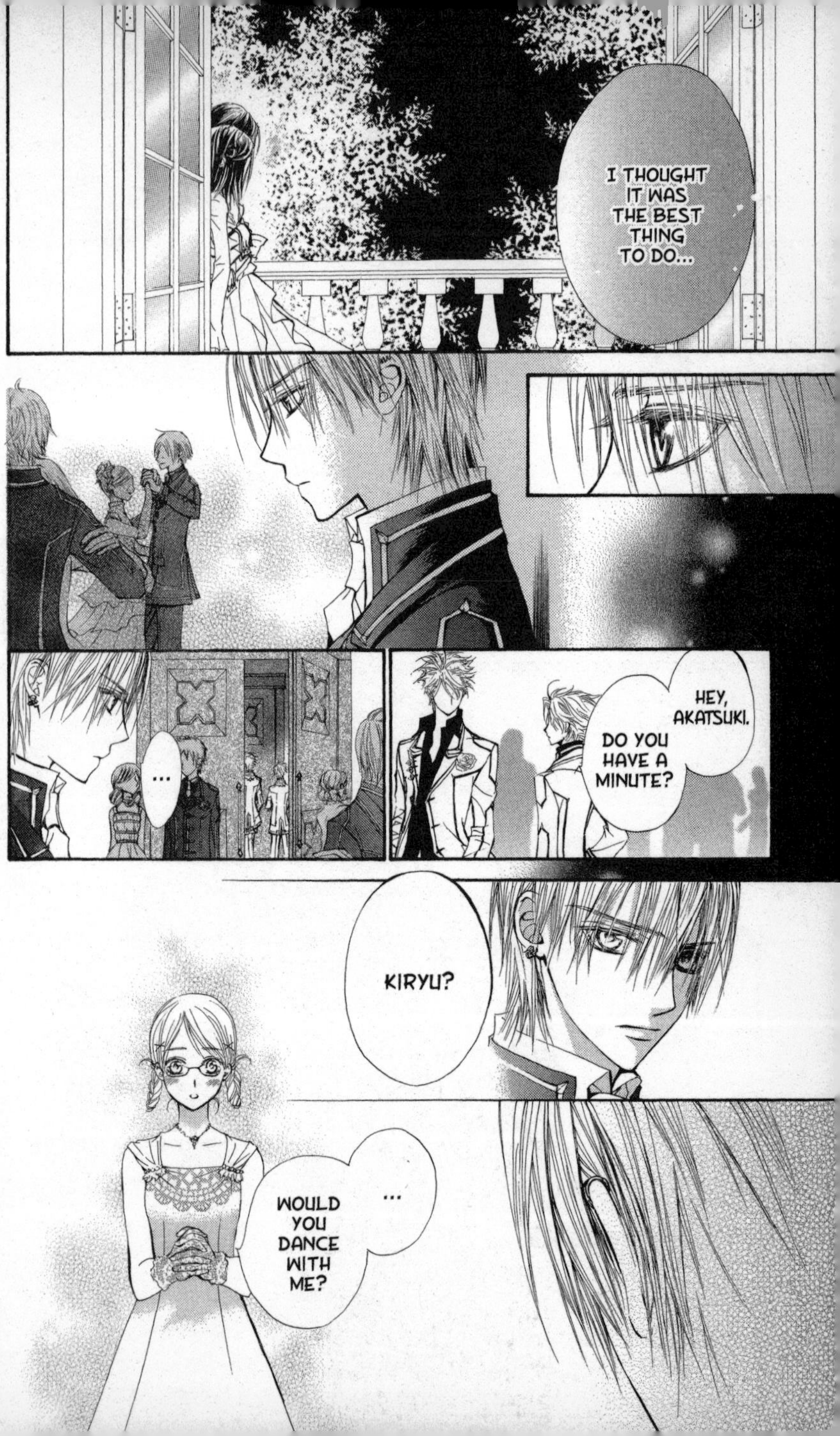

I THOUGHT IT WAS THE BEST THING TO DO...
HEY, AKATSUKI.
DO YOU HAVE A MINUTE?
...
KIRYU?
...
WOULD YOU DANCE WITH ME?

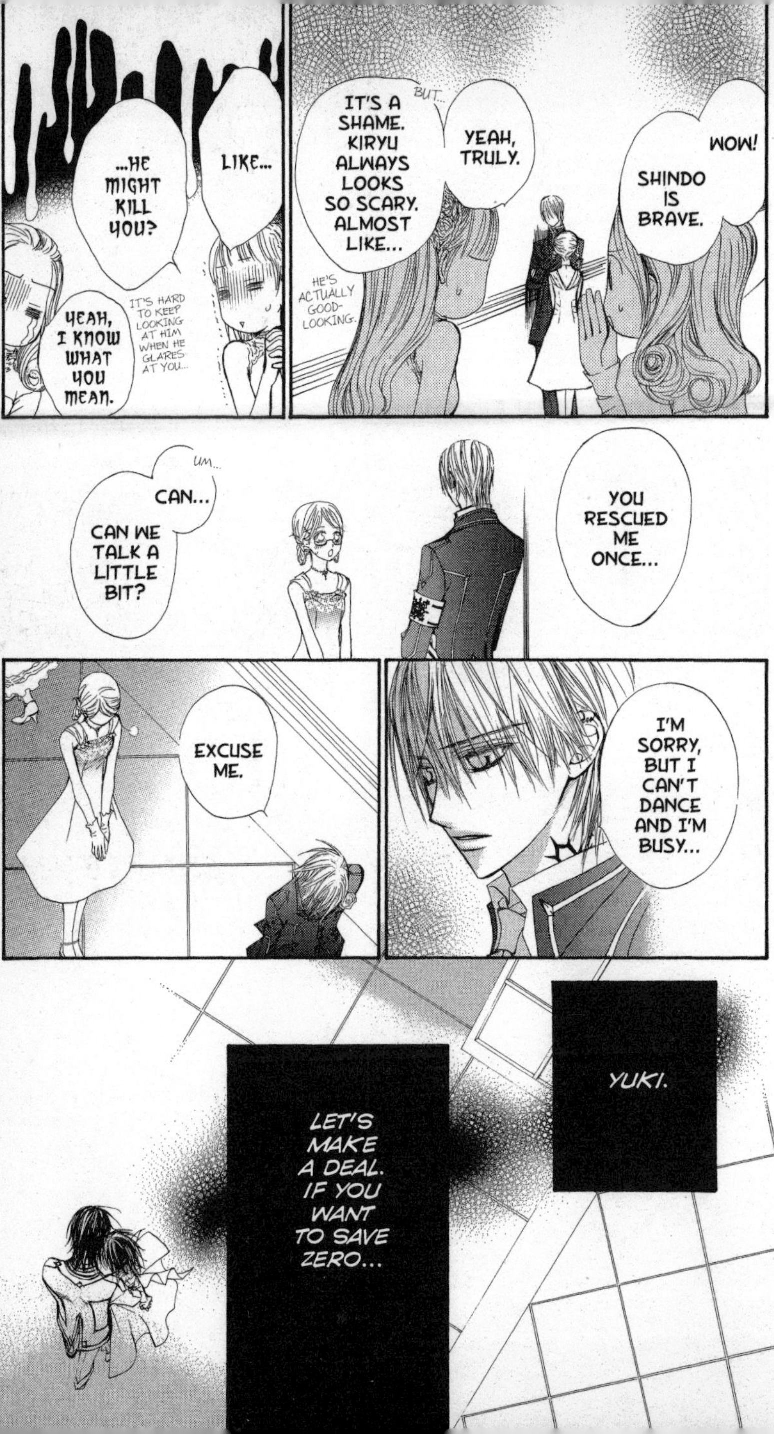
WOW!
SHINDO IS BRAVE.
YEAH, TRULY.
BUT...
IT'S A SHAME. KIRYU ALWAYS LOOKS SO SCARY. ALMOST LIKE...
HE'S ACTUALLY GOOD-LOOKING.
LIKE...
...HE MIGHT KILL YOU?
IT'S HARD TO KEEP LOOKING AT HIM WHEN HE GLARES AT YOU...
YEAH, I KNOW WHAT YOU MEAN.
YOU RESCUED ME ONCE...
UM...
CAN...
CAN WE TALK A LITTLE BIT?
I'M SORRY, BUT I CAN'T DANCE AND I'M BUSY...
EXCUSE ME.
YUKI.
LET'S MAKE A DEAL. IF YOU WANT TO SAVE ZERO...

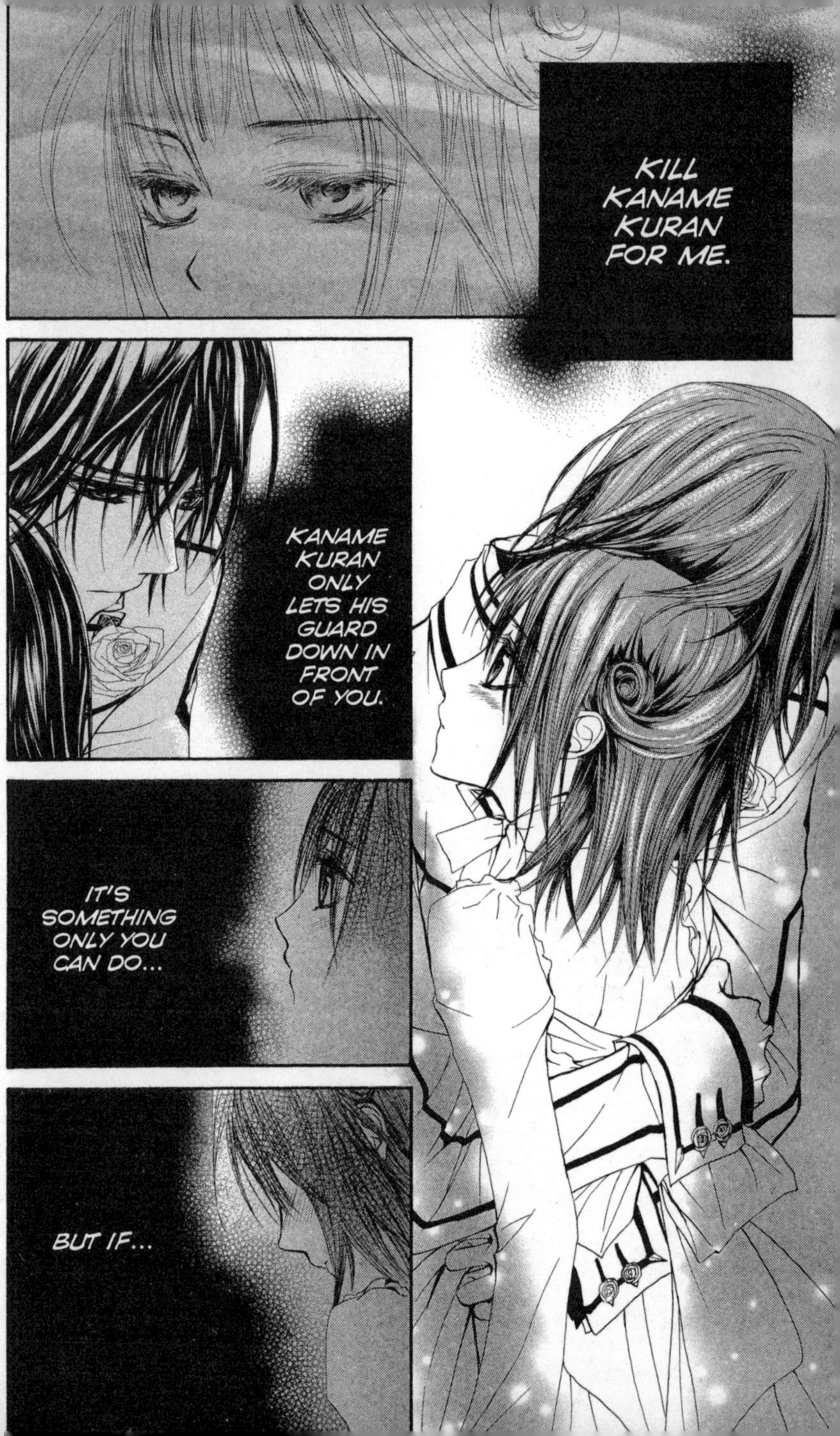
KILL KANAME KURAN FOR ME.
KANAME KURAN ONLY LETS HIS GUARD DOWN IN FRONT OF YOU.
IT'S SOMETHING ONLY YOU CAN DO...
BUT IF...

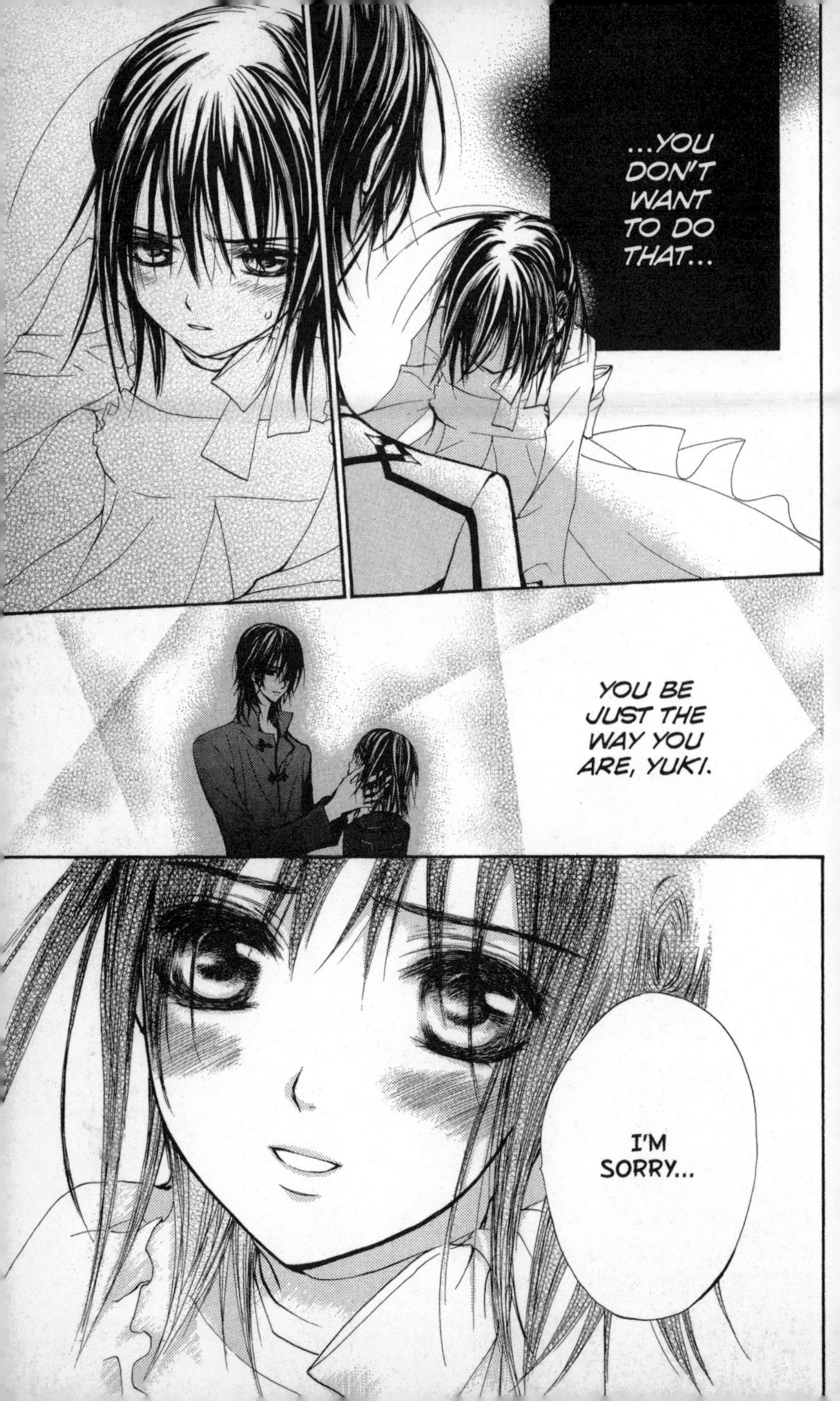
...YOU DON'T WANT TO DO THAT...
YOU BE JUST THE WAY YOU ARE, YUKI.
I'M SORRY...

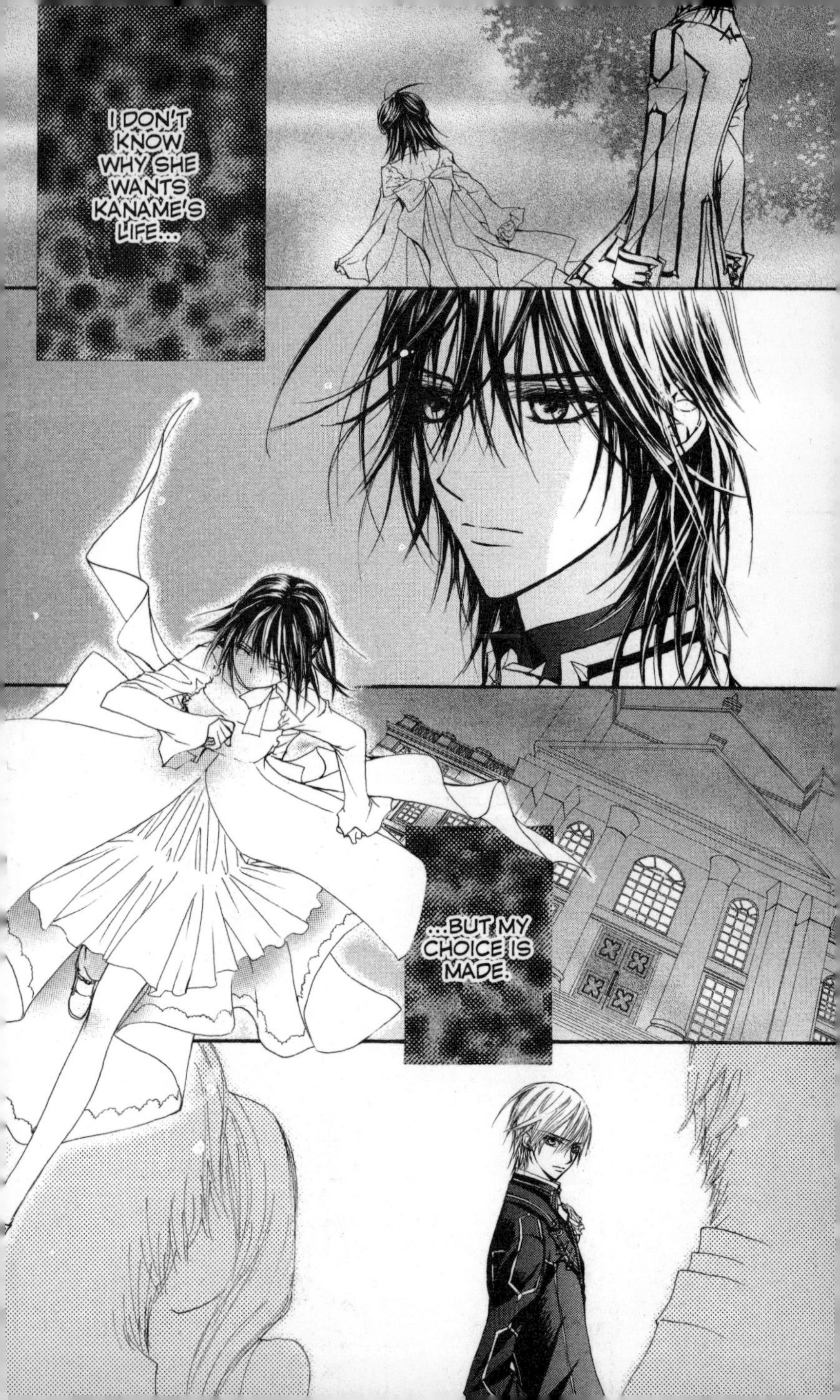
I DON'T KNOW WHY SHE WANTS KANAME'S LIFE...
...BUT MY CHOICE IS MADE.

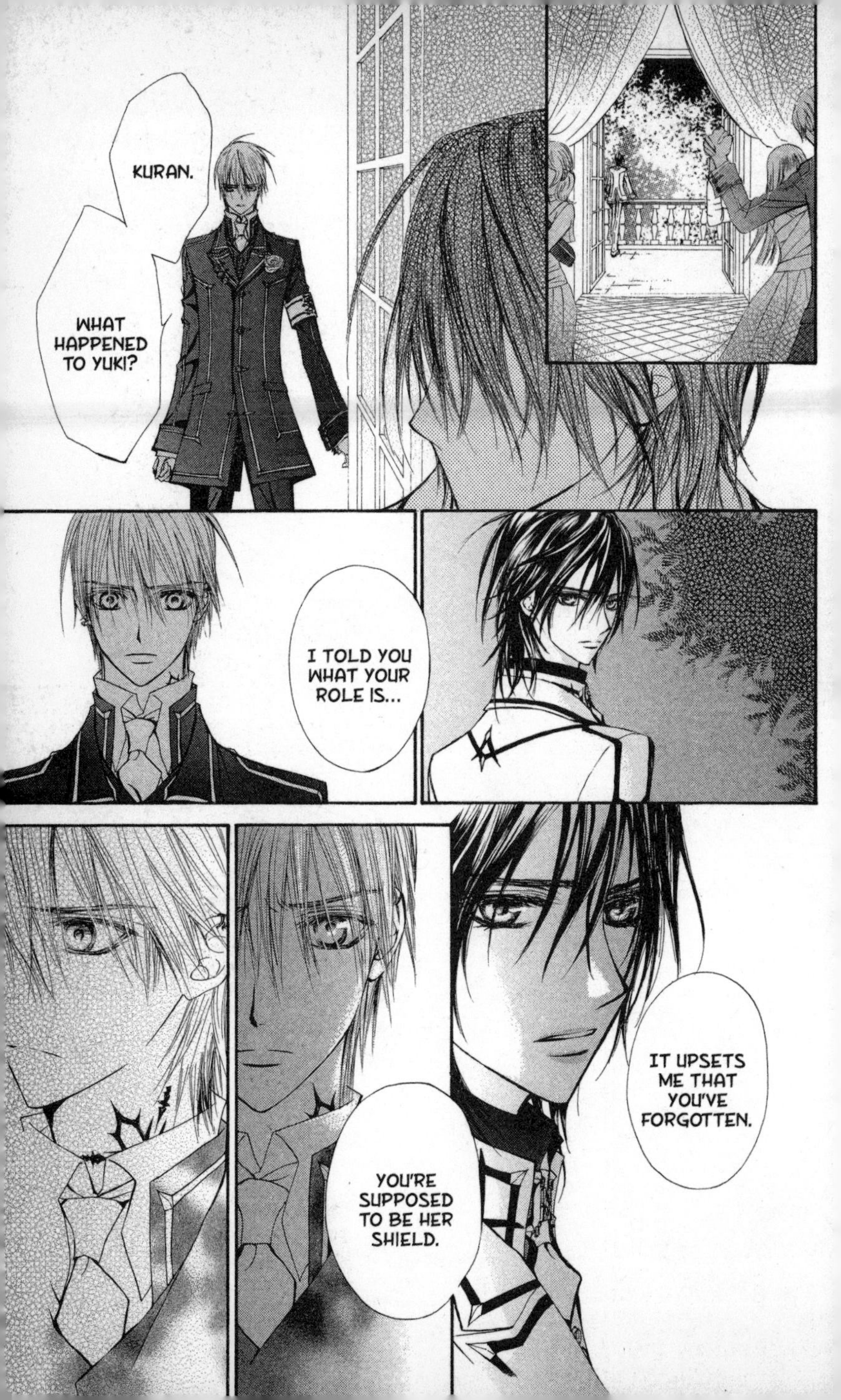
KURAN.
WHAT HAPPENED TO YUKI?
I TOLD YOU WHAT YOUR ROLE IS...
IT UPSETS ME THAT YOU'VE FORGOTTEN.
YOU'RE SUPPOSED TO BE HER SHIELD.

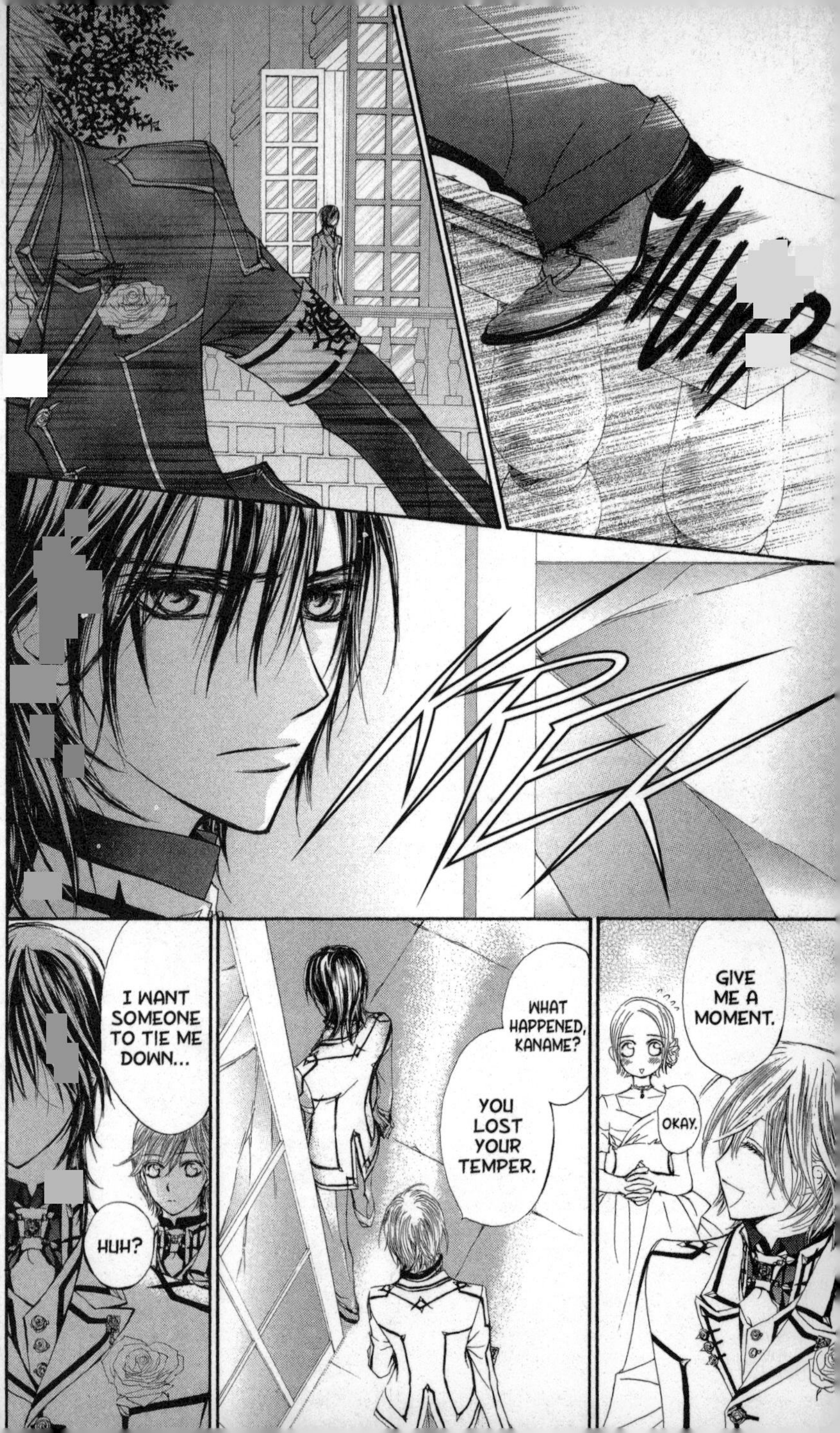
KRAK
GIVE ME A MOMENT.
OKAY.
WHAT HAPPENED, KANAME?
YOU LOST YOUR TEMPER.
I WANT SOMEONE TO TIE ME DOWN...
HUH?

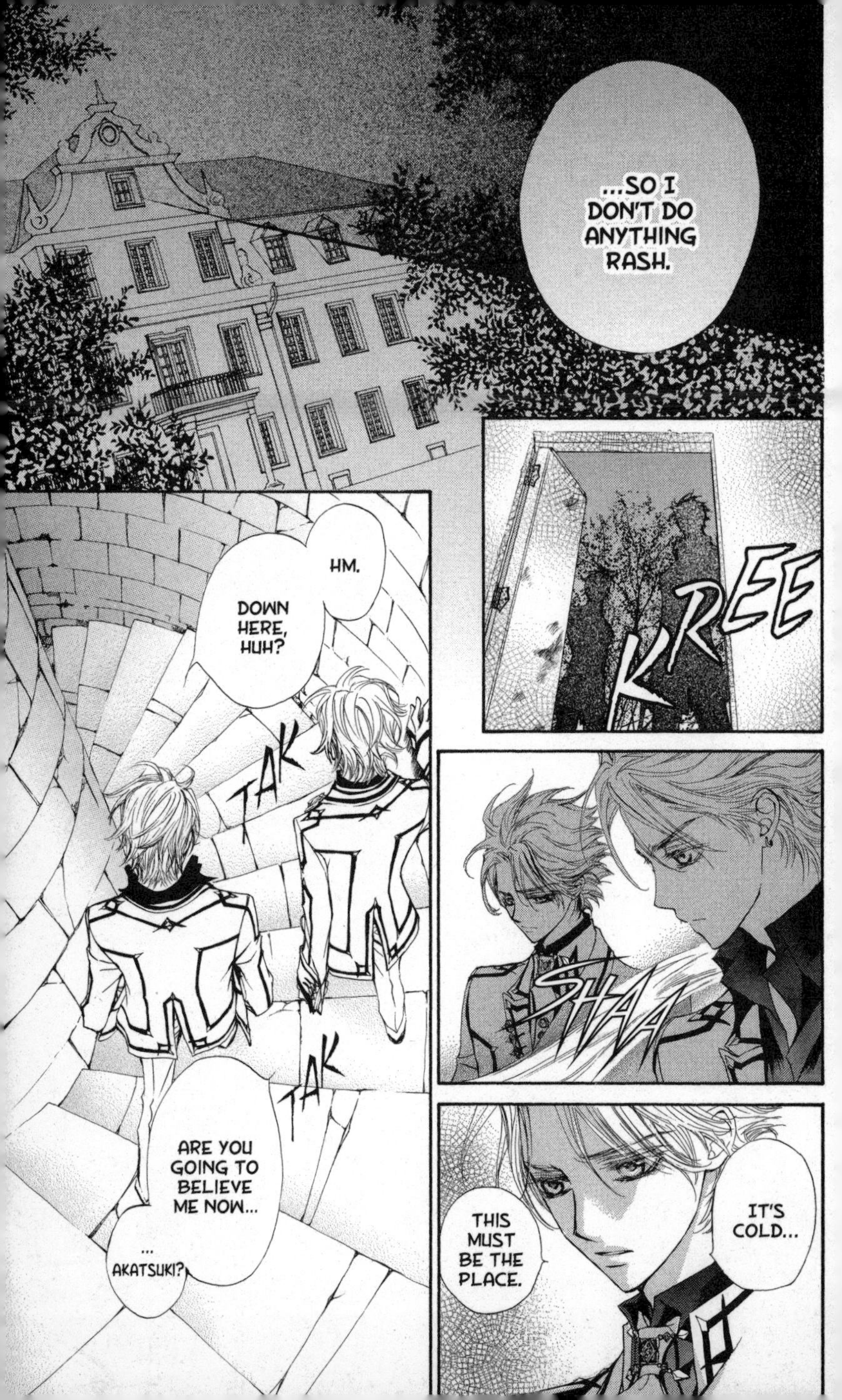
...SO I DON'T DO ANYTHING RASH.
KREEE
SHAA
IT'S COLD...
THIS MUST BE THE PLACE.
HM.
DOWN HERE, HUH?
TAK
TAK
ARE YOU GOING TO BELIEVE ME NOW...
...AKATSUKI?

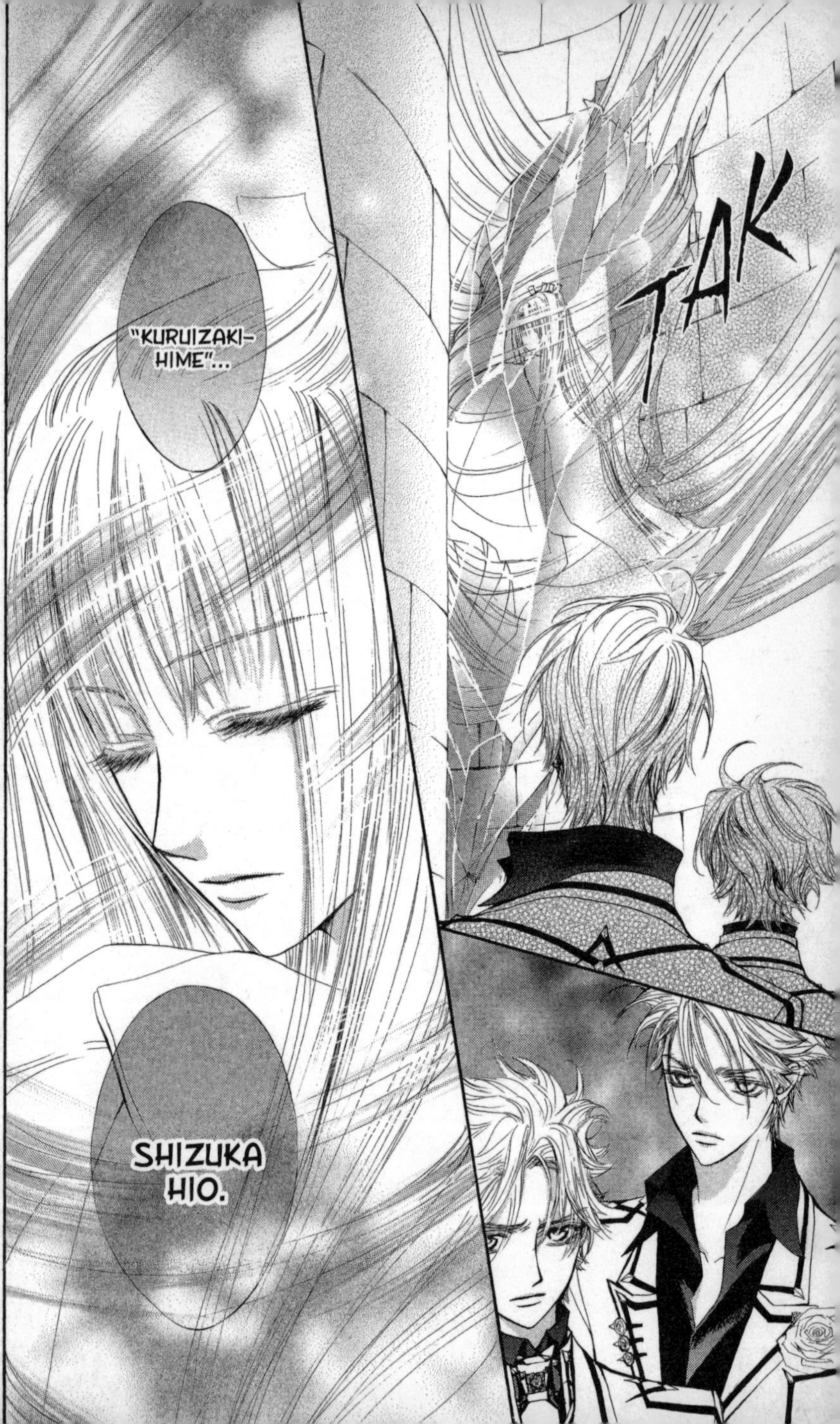
TAK
"KURUIZAKI-HIME"...
SHIZUKA HIO.

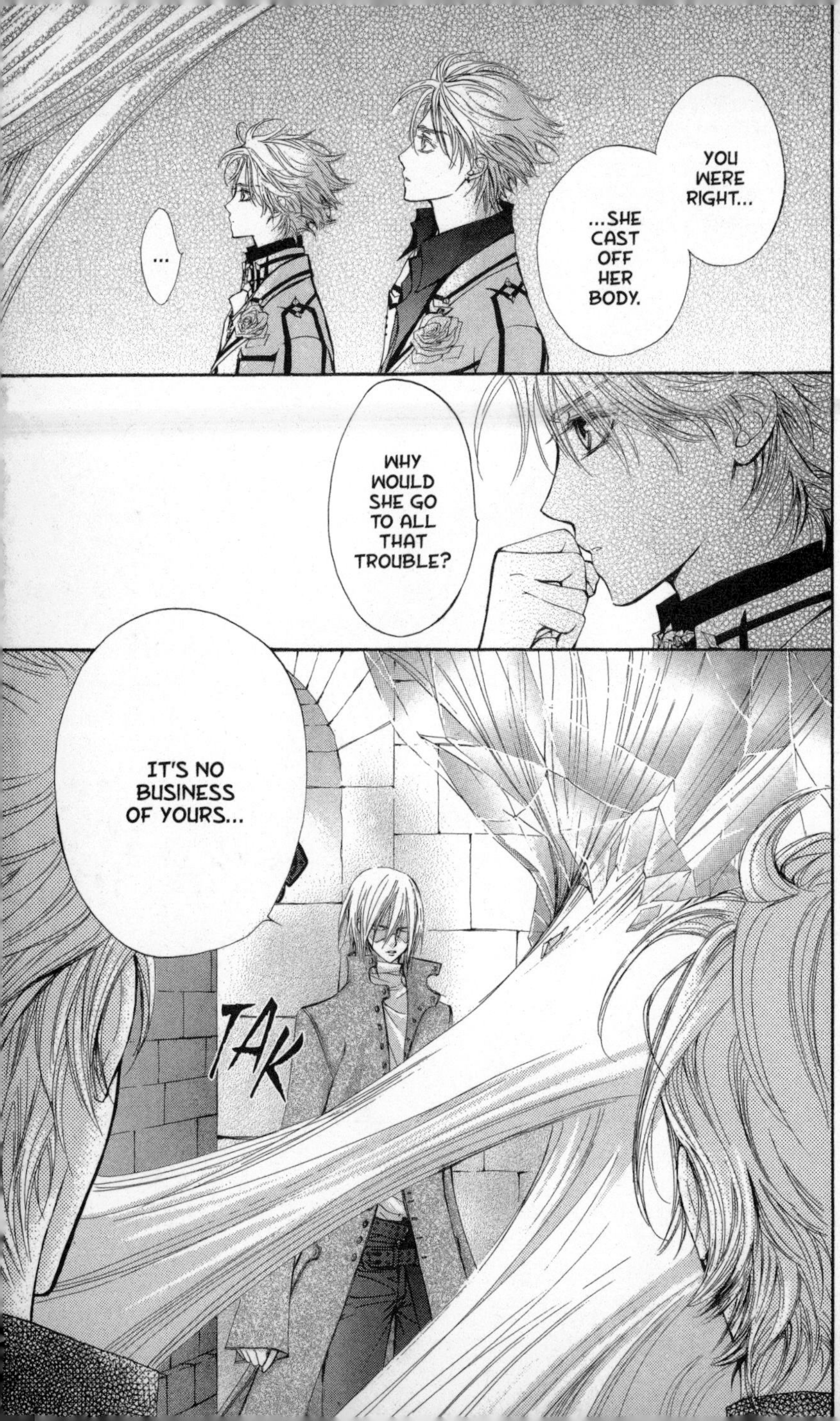
YOU WERE RIGHT...
...SHE CAST OFF HER BODY.
...
WHY WOULD SHE GO TO ALL THAT TROUBLE?
IT'S NO BUSINESS OF YOURS...
TAK

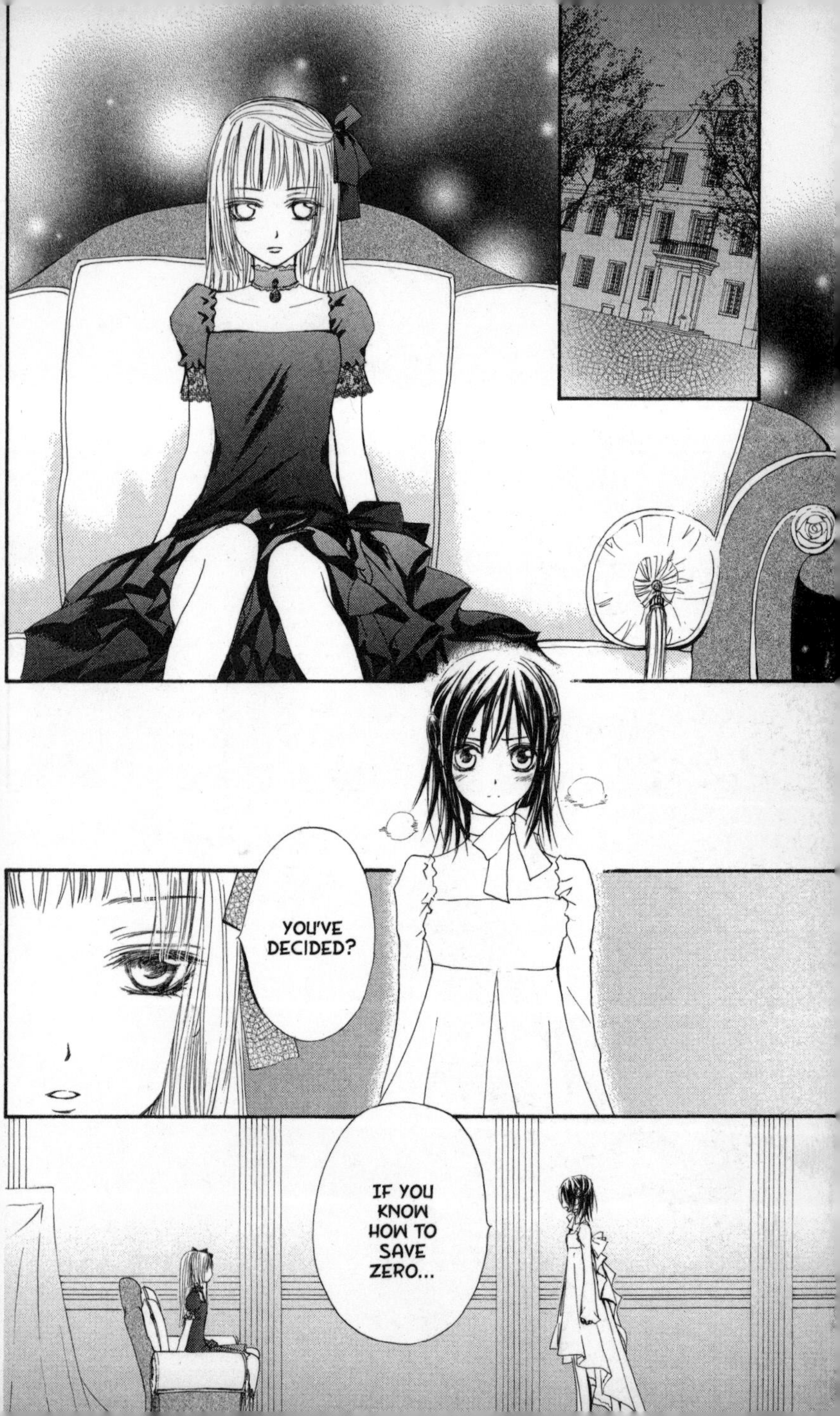
YOU'VE DECIDED?
IF YOU KNOW HOW TO SAVE ZERO...

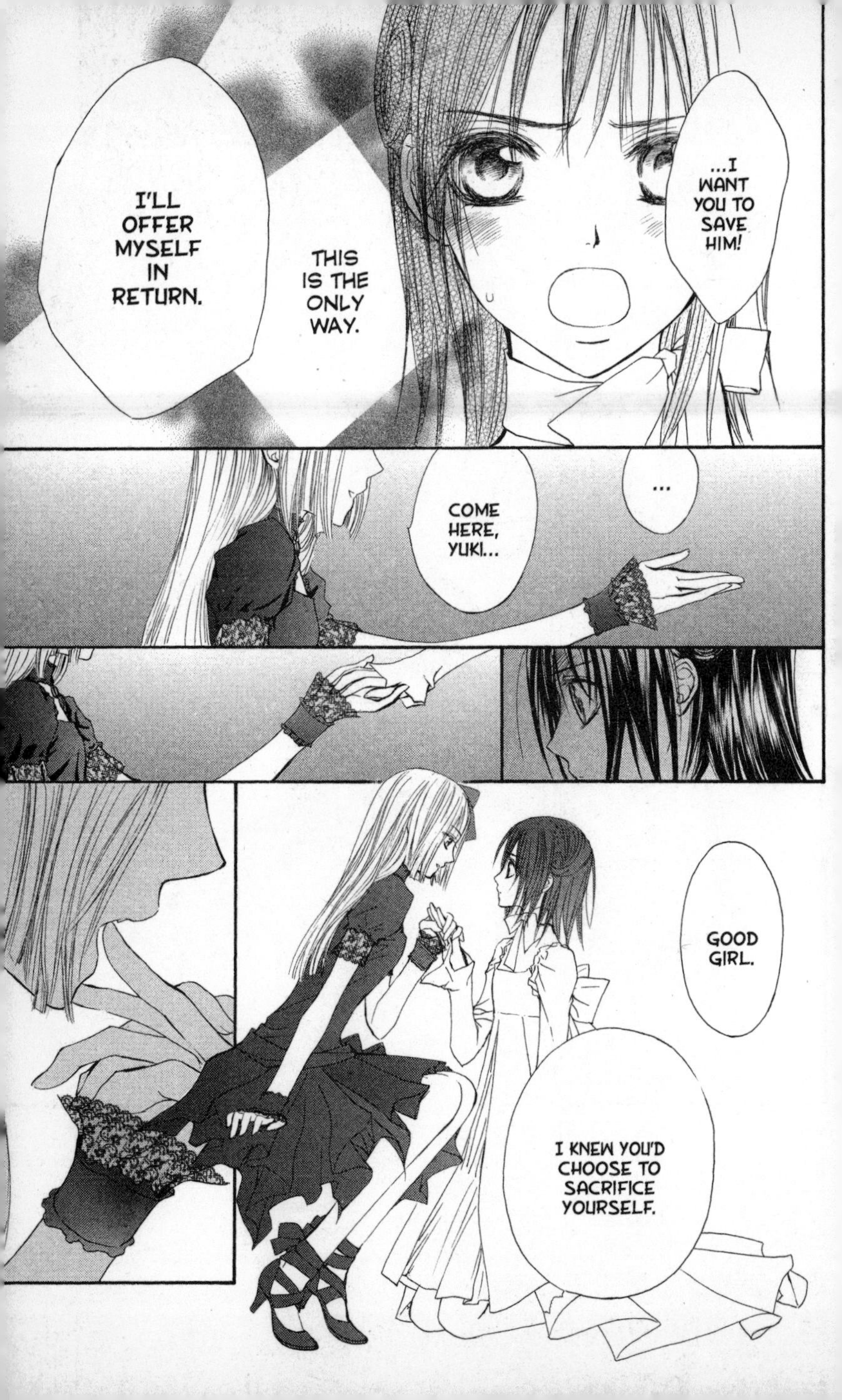
...I WANT YOU TO SAVE HIM!
THIS IS THE ONLY WAY.
I'LL OFFER MYSELF IN RETURN.
...
COME HERE, YUKI...
GOOD GIRL.
I KNEW YOU'D CHOOSE TO SACRIFICE YOURSELF.

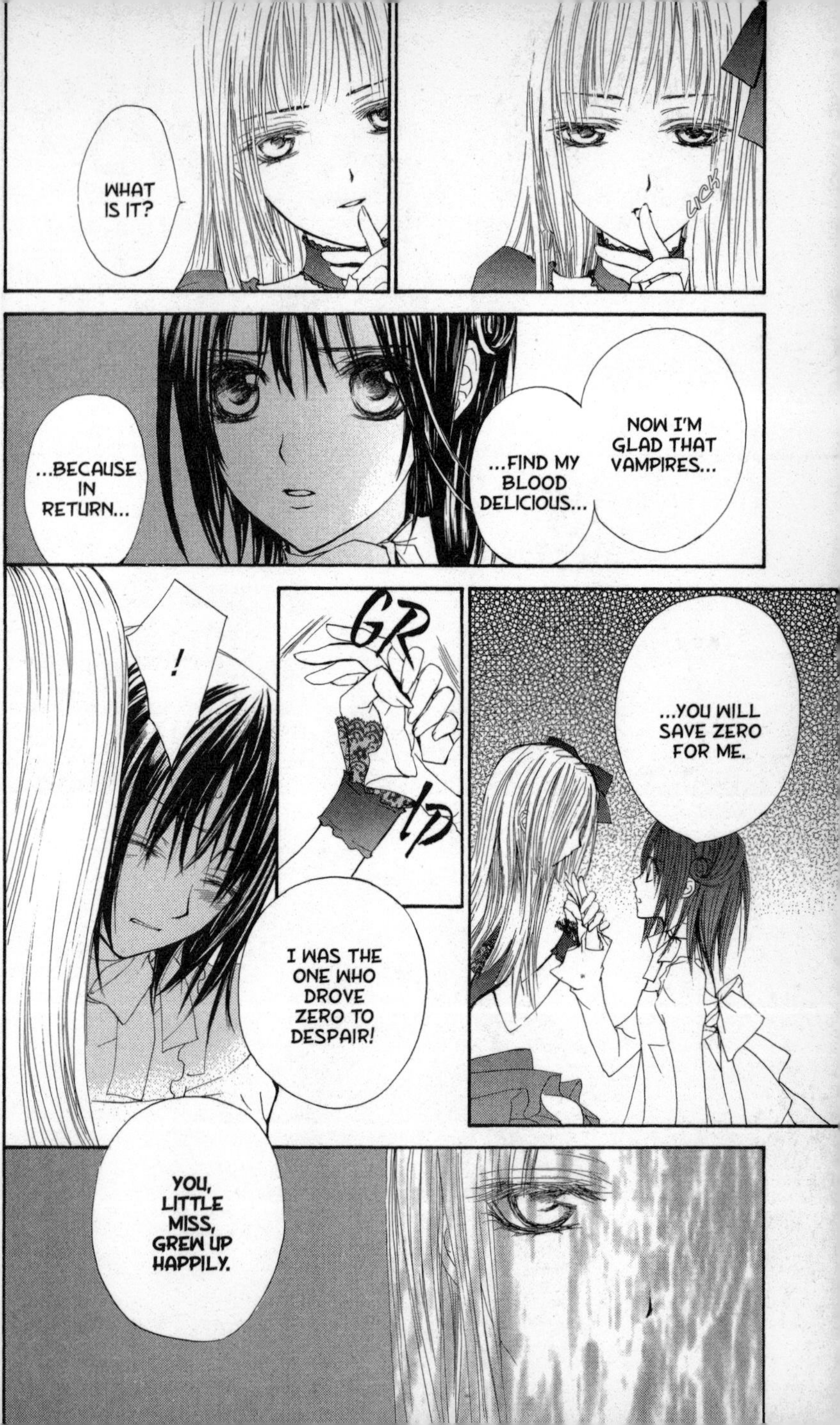
LICK
WHAT IS IT?
NOW I'M GLAD THAT VAMPIRES...
...FIND MY BLOOD DELICIOUS...
...BECAUSE IN RETURN...
...YOU WILL SAVE ZERO FOR ME.
GRIP
!
I WAS THE ONE WHO DROVE ZERO TO DESPAIR!
YOU, LITTLE MISS, GREW UP HAPPILY.

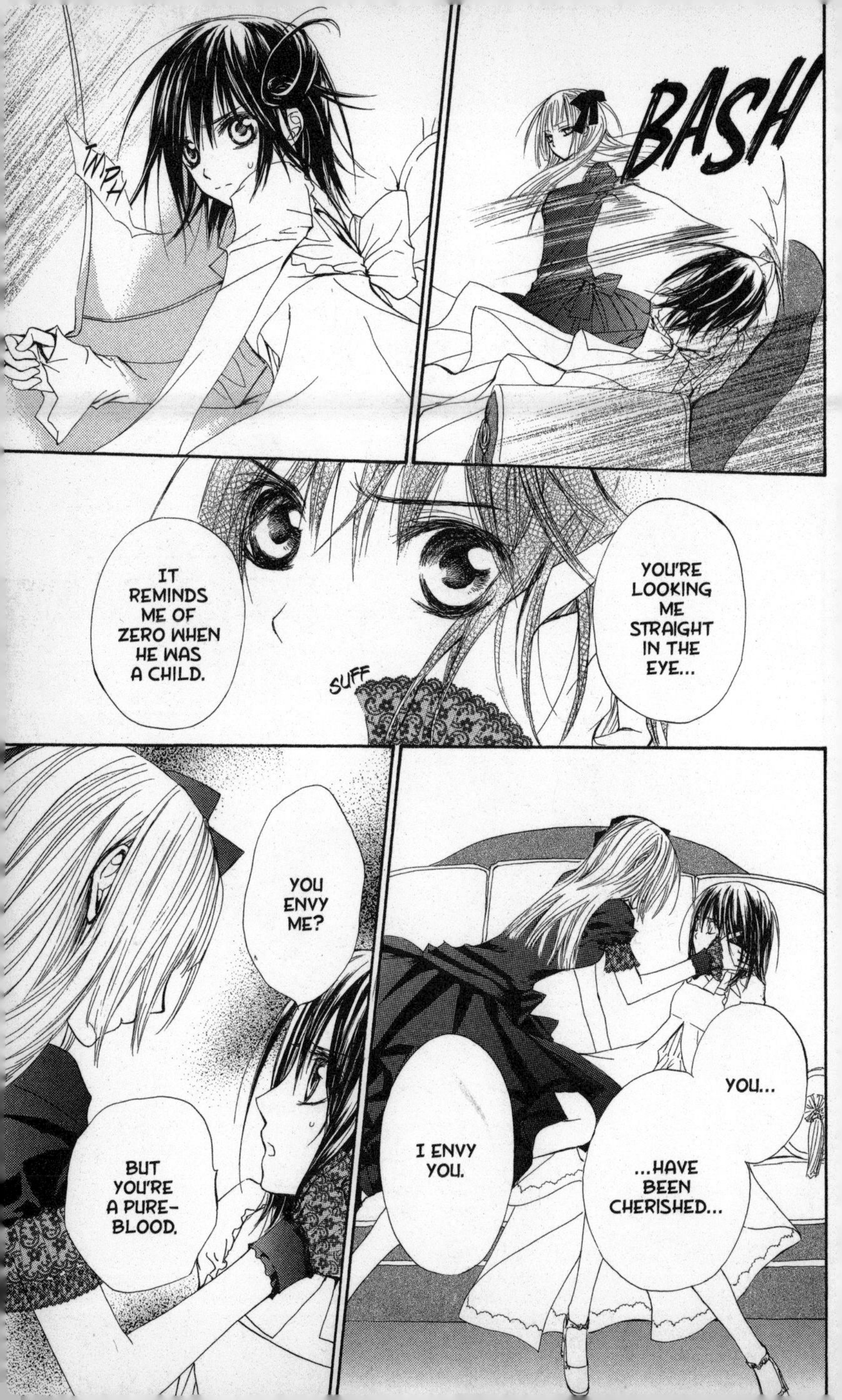
BASH
YOU'RE LOOKING ME STRAIGHT IN THE EYE...
SUFF
IT REMINDS ME OF ZERO WHEN HE WAS A CHILD.
YOU...
...HAVE BEEN CHERISHED...
I ENVY YOU.
YOU ENVY ME?
BUT YOU'RE A PURE-BLOOD.

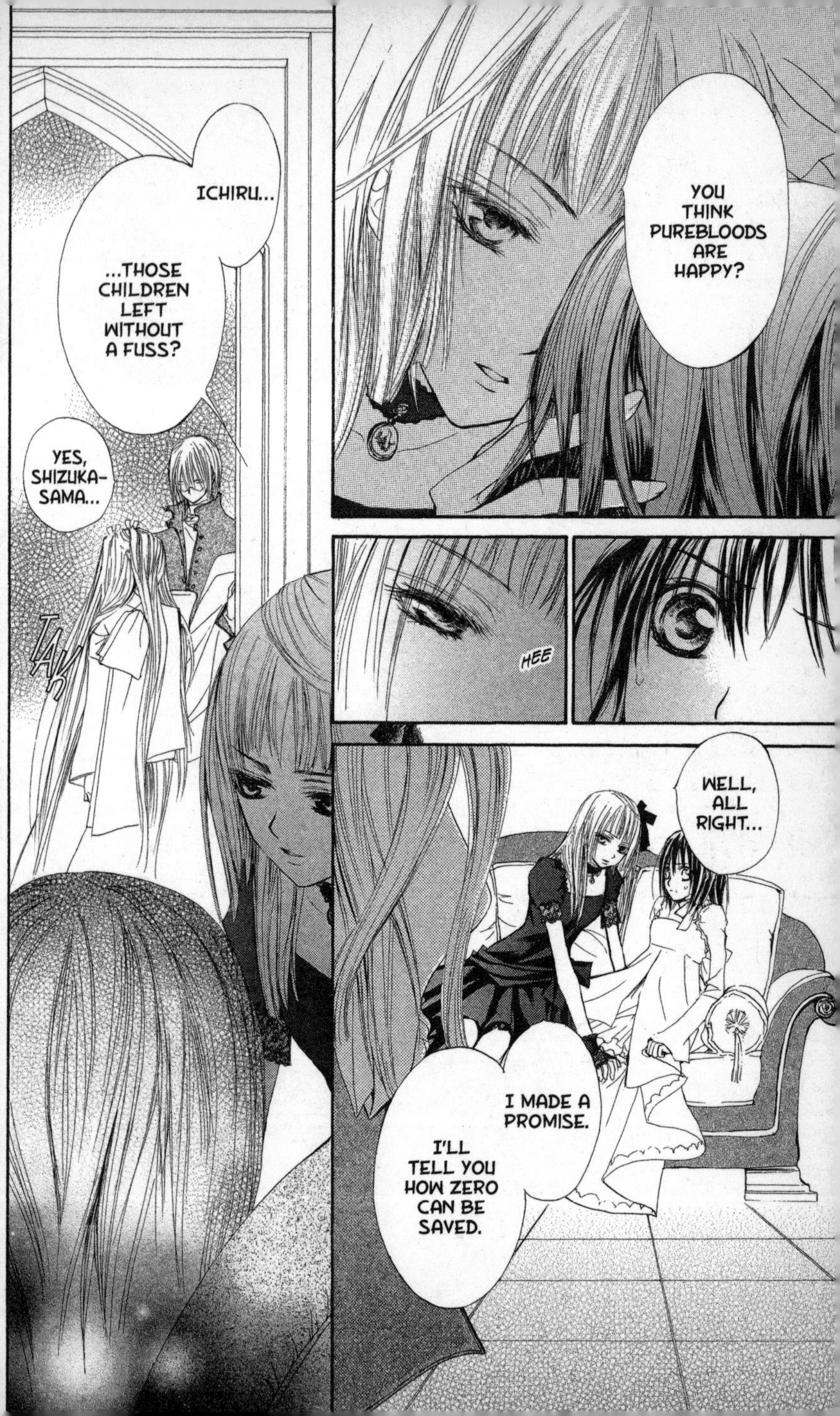
YOU THINK PUREBLOODS ARE HAPPY?
HEE
WELL, ALL RIGHT...
I MADE A PROMISE.
I'LL TELL YOU HOW ZERO CAN BE SAVED.
ICHIRU...
...THOSE CHILDREN LEFT WITHOUT A FUSS?
YES, SHIZUKA-SAMA...
TAK

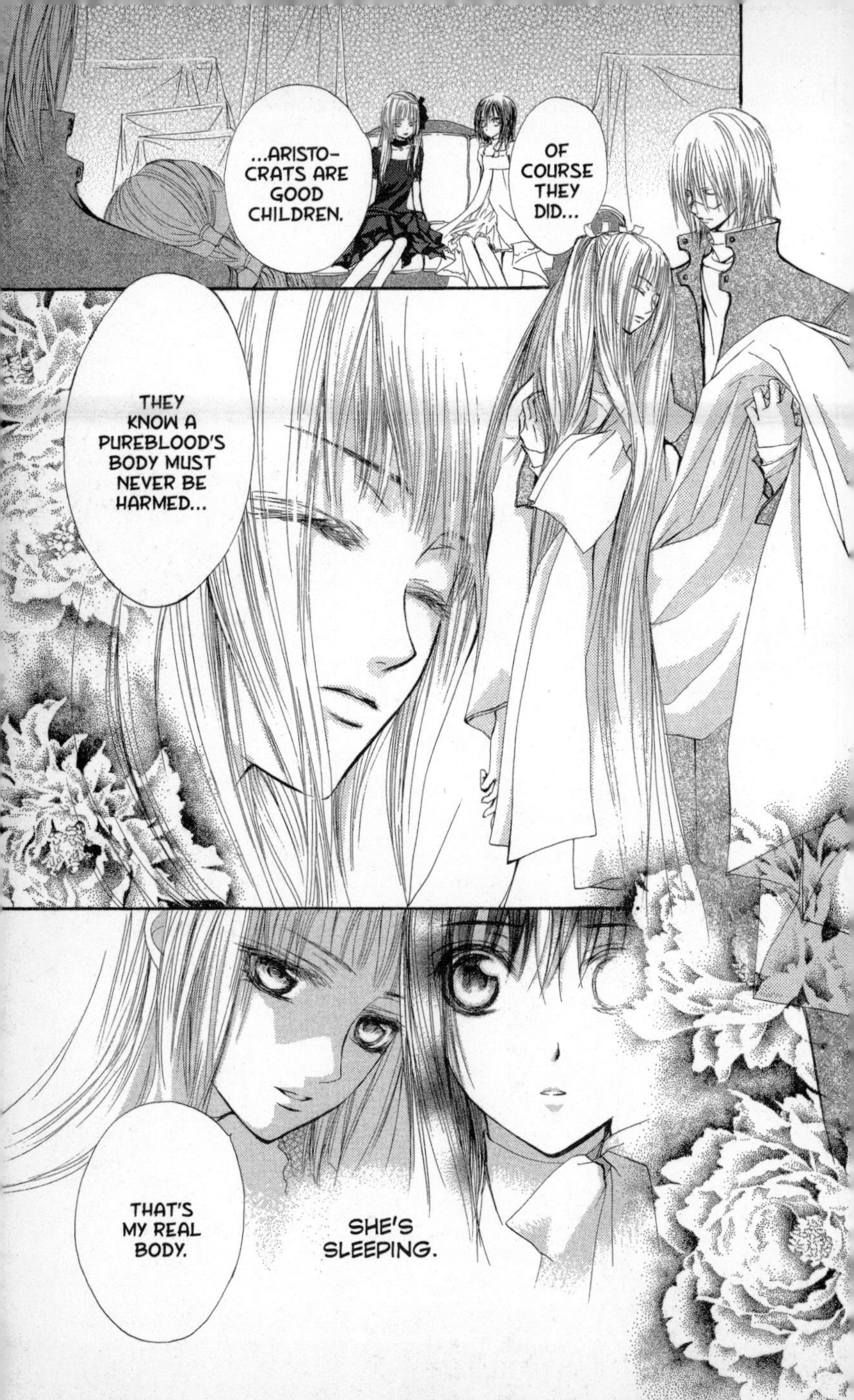
OF COURSE THEY DID...
...ARISTO-CRATS ARE GOOD CHILDREN.
THEY KNOW A PUREBLOOD'S BODY MUST NEVER BE HARMED...
SHE'S SLEEPING.
THAT'S MY REAL BODY.

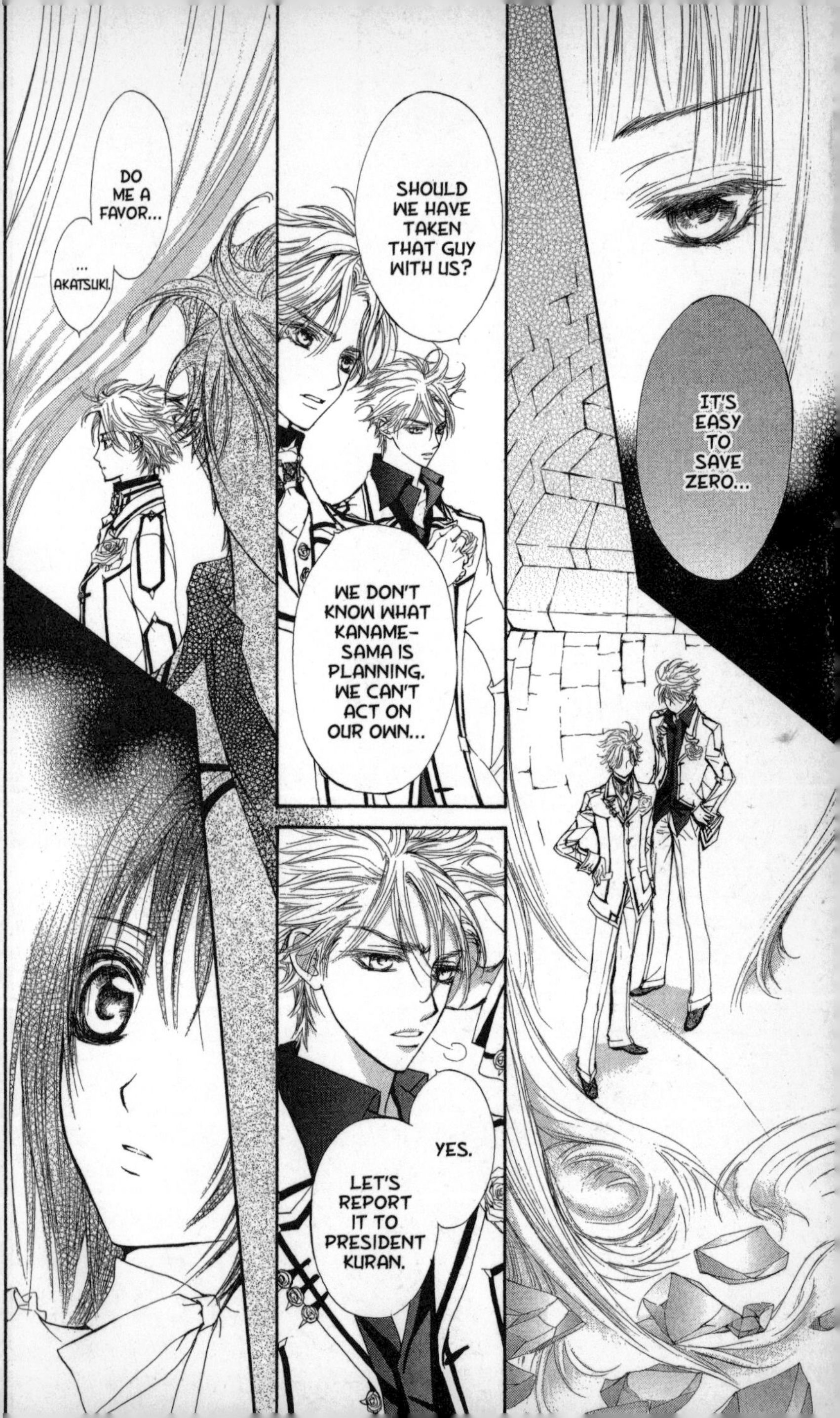
IT'S EASY TO SAVE ZERO...
SHOULD WE HAVE TAKEN THAT GUY WITH US?
WE DON'T KNOW WHAT KANAME-SAMA IS PLANNING. WE CAN'T ACT ON OUR OWN...
YES.
LET'S REPORT IT TO PRESIDENT KURAN.
DO ME A FAVOR...
...AKATSUKI.

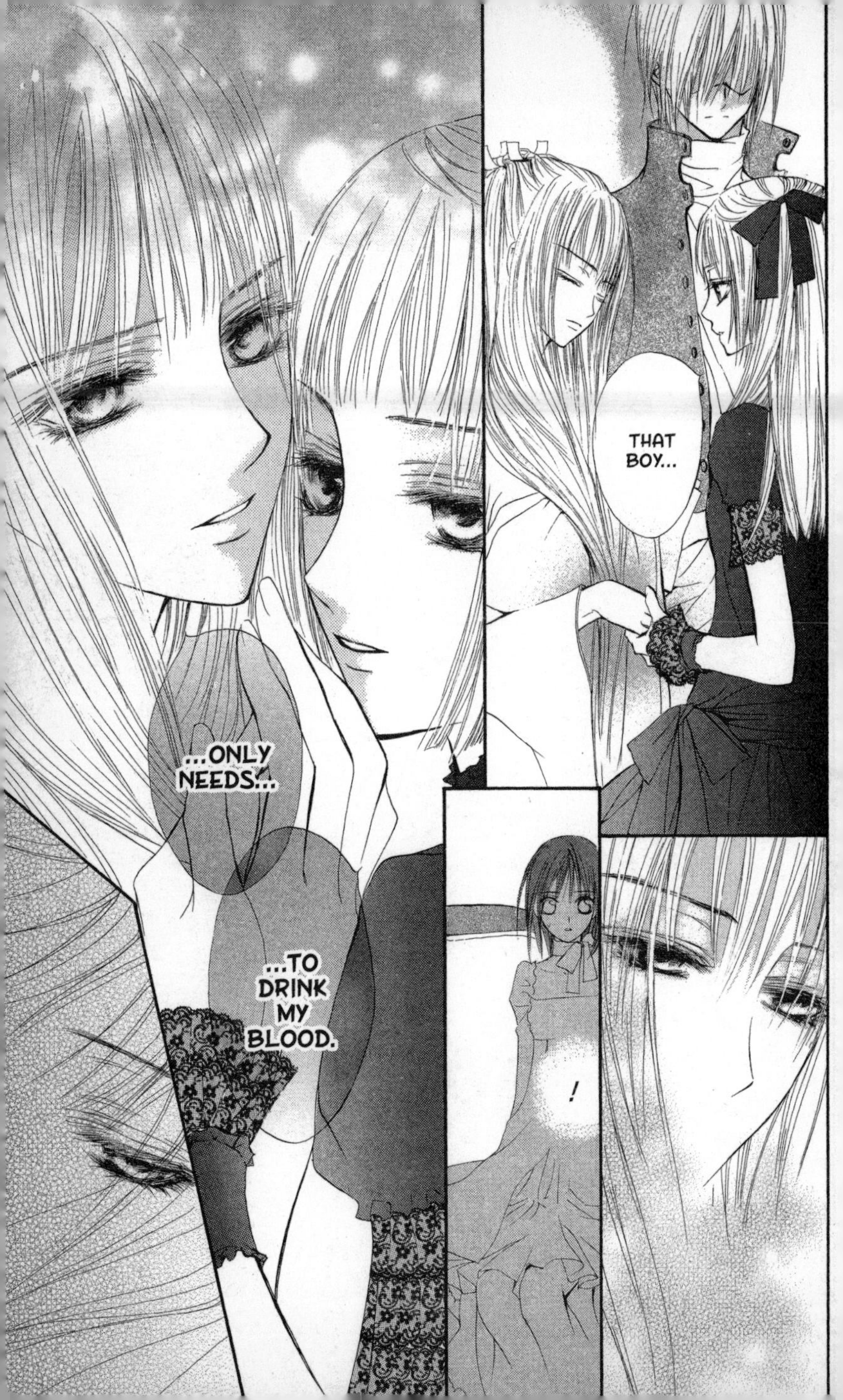

THAT BOY...
!
...ONLY NEEDS...
...TO DRINK MY BLOOD.

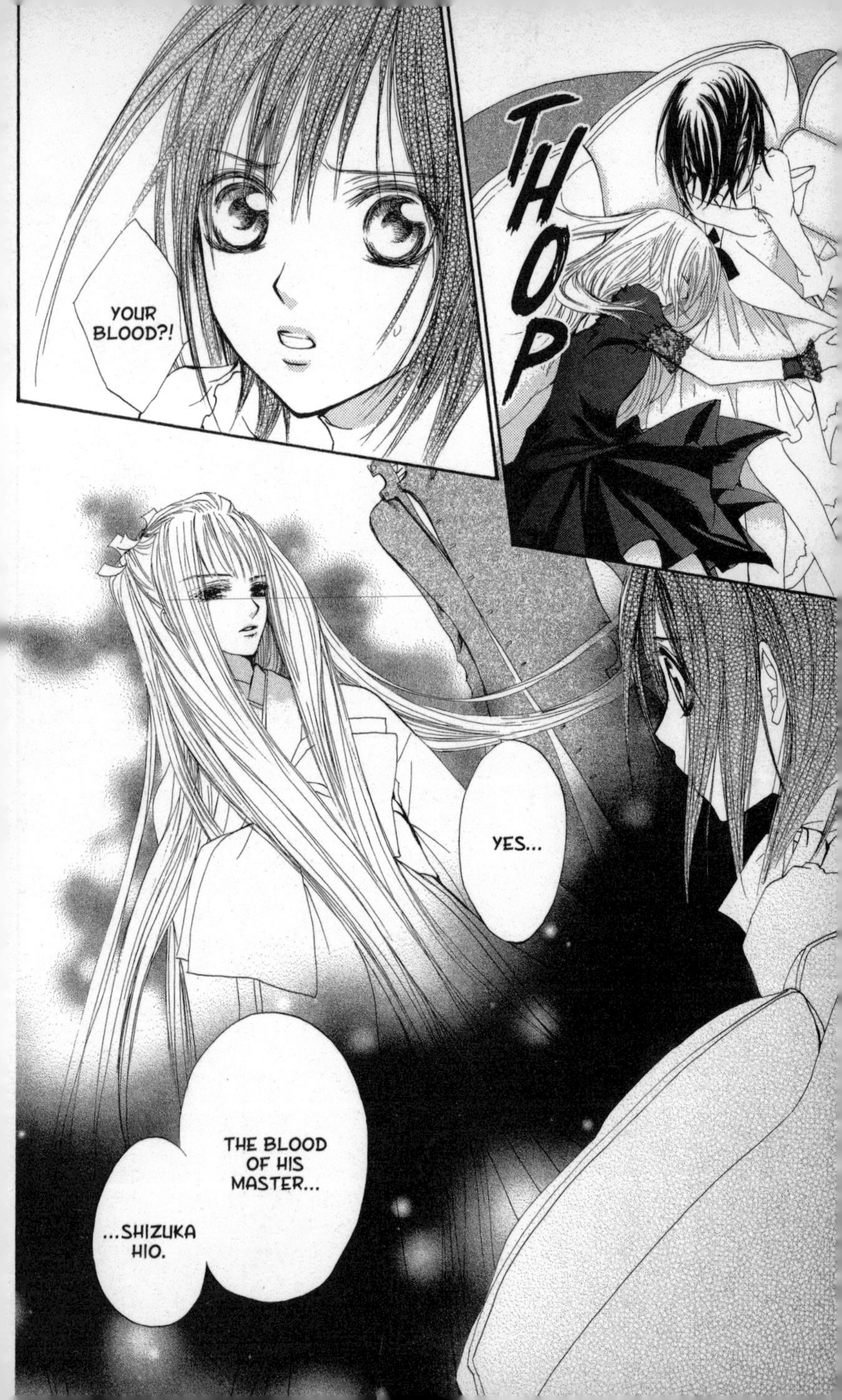
THOP
YOUR BLOOD?!
YES...
THE BLOOD OF HIS MASTER...
...SHIZUKA HIO.

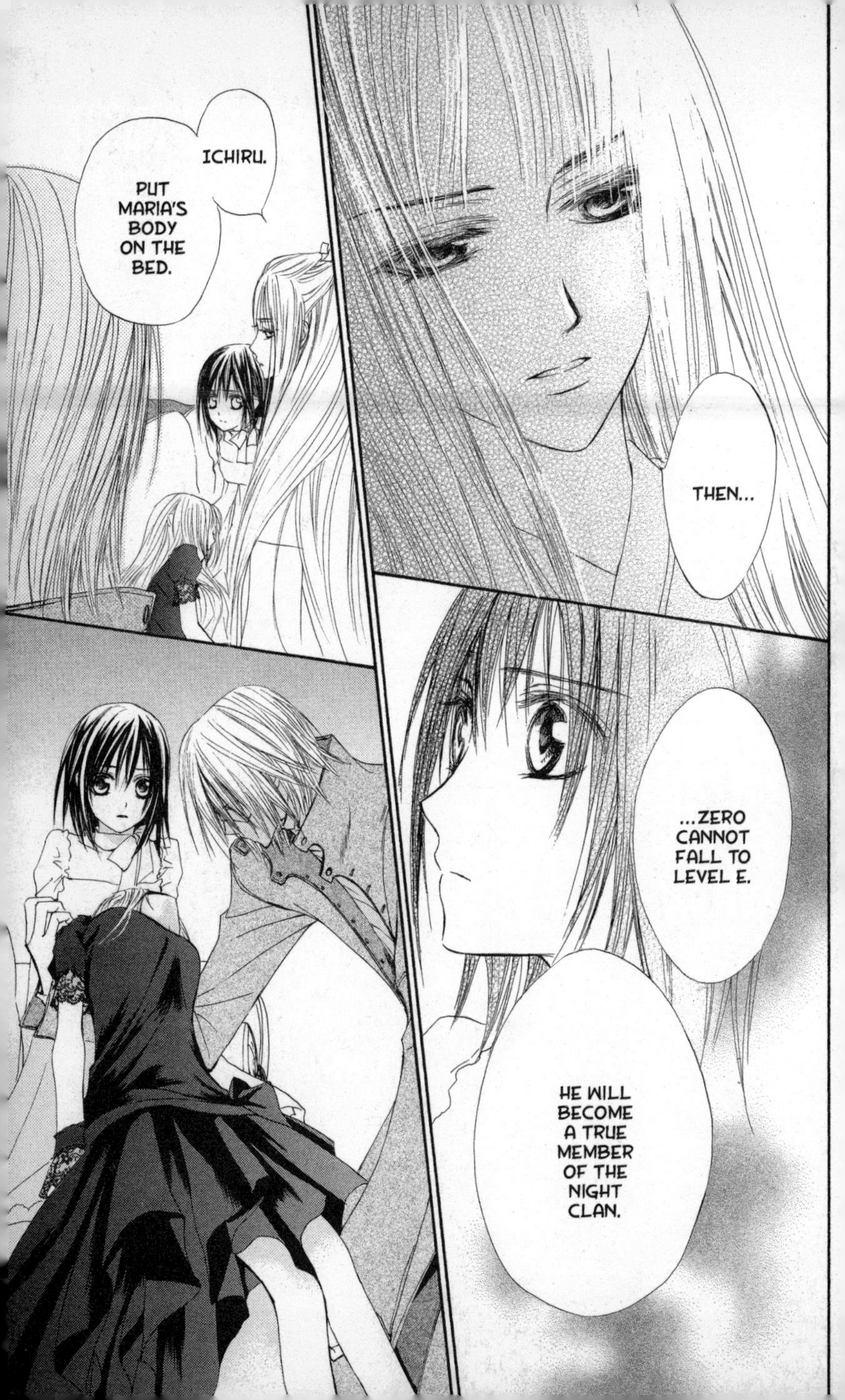
THEN...
ICHIRU.
PUT MARIA'S BODY ON THE BED.
...ZERO CANNOT FALL TO LEVEL E.
HE WILL BECOME A TRUE MEMBER OF THE NIGHT CLAN.

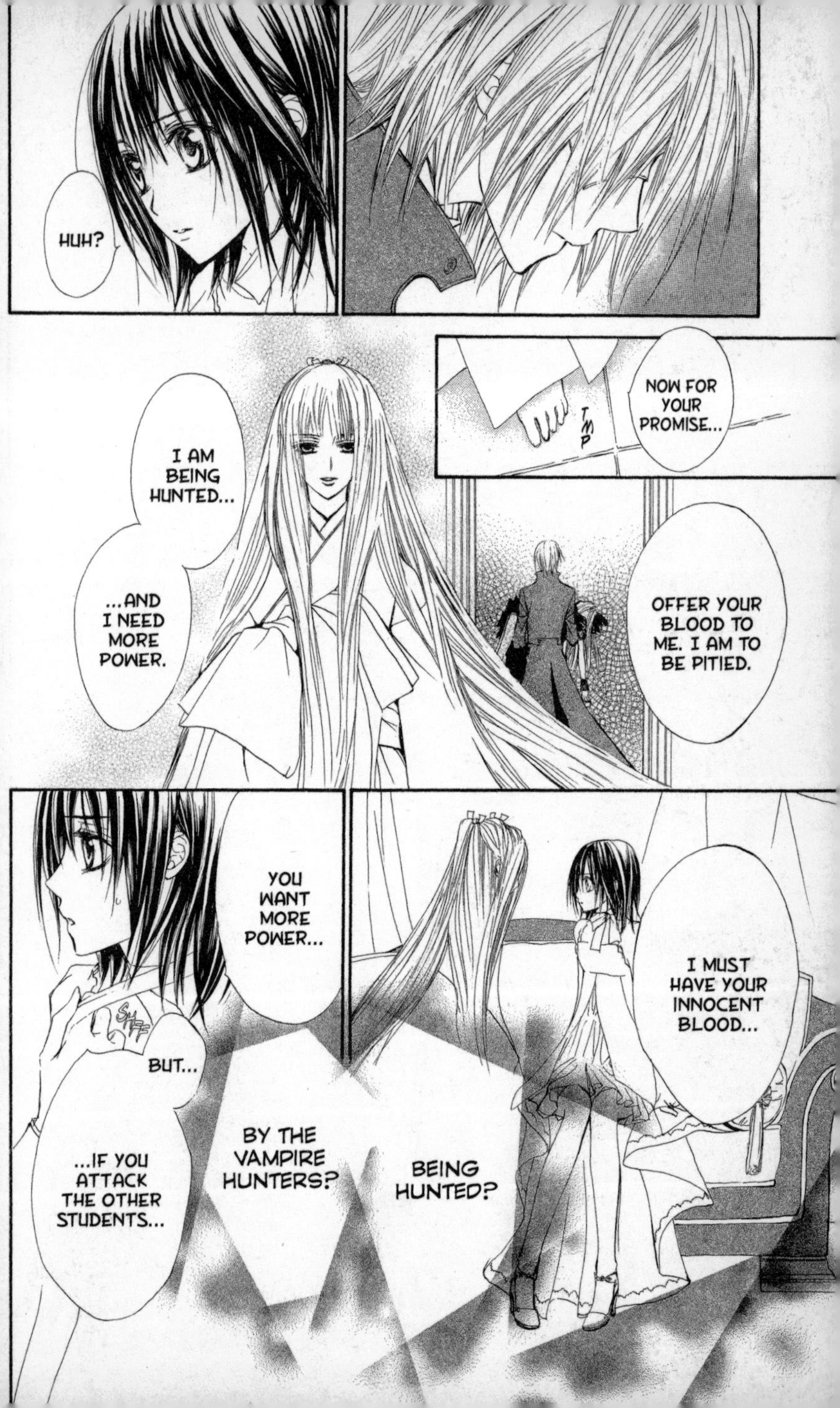

HUH?
TMP
NOW FOR YOUR PROMISE...
OFFER YOUR BLOOD TO ME. I AM TO BE PITIED.
I AM BEING HUNTED...
...AND I NEED MORE POWER.
I MUST HAVE YOUR INNOCENT BLOOD...
BEING HUNTED?
BY THE VAMPIRE HUNTERS?
YOU WANT MORE POWER...
SHFF
BUT...
...IF YOU ATTACK THE OTHER STUDENTS...

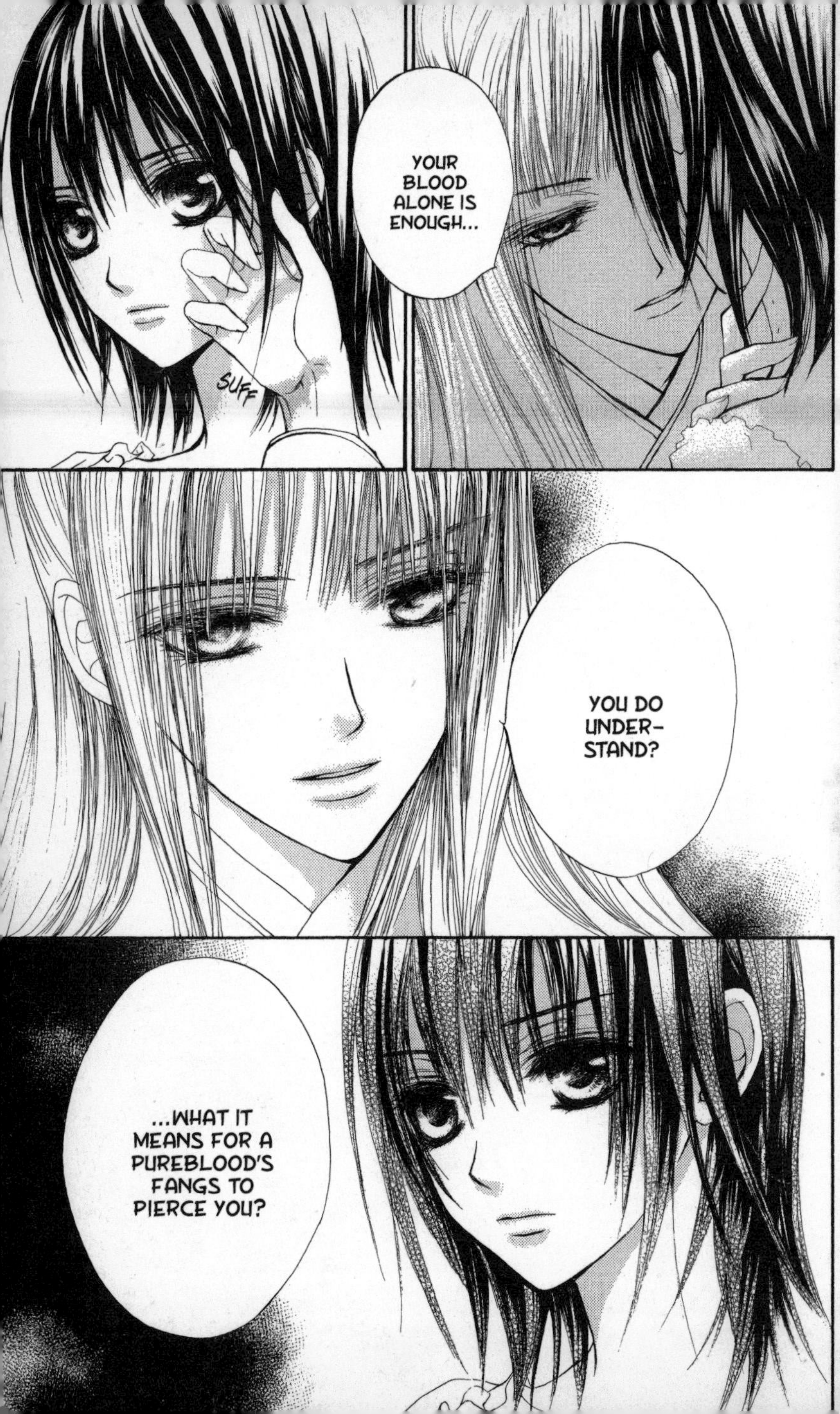
YOUR BLOOD ALONE IS ENOUGH...
SUFF
YOU DO UNDER-STAND?
...WHAT IT MEANS FOR A PUREBLOOD'S FANGS TO PIERCE YOU?

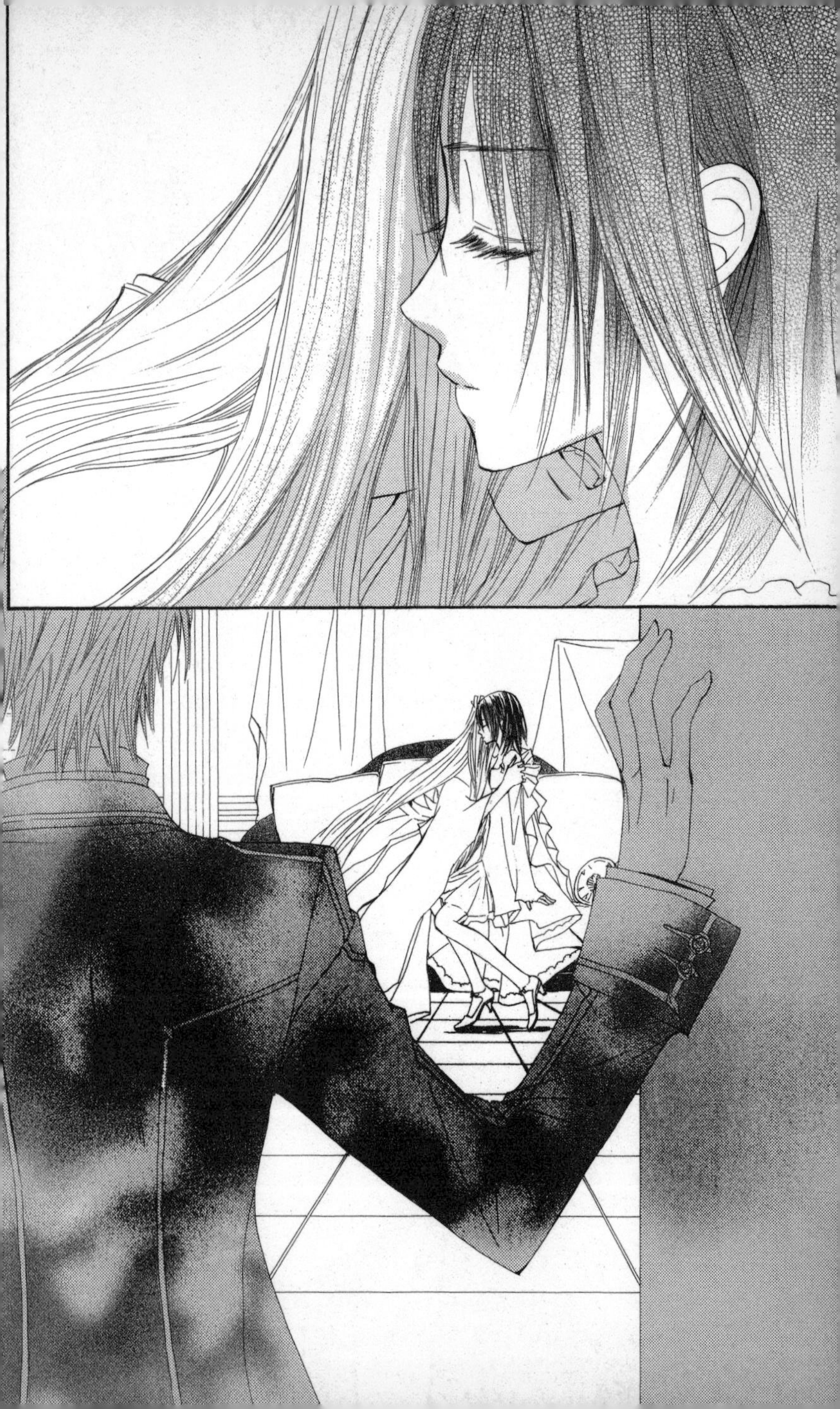

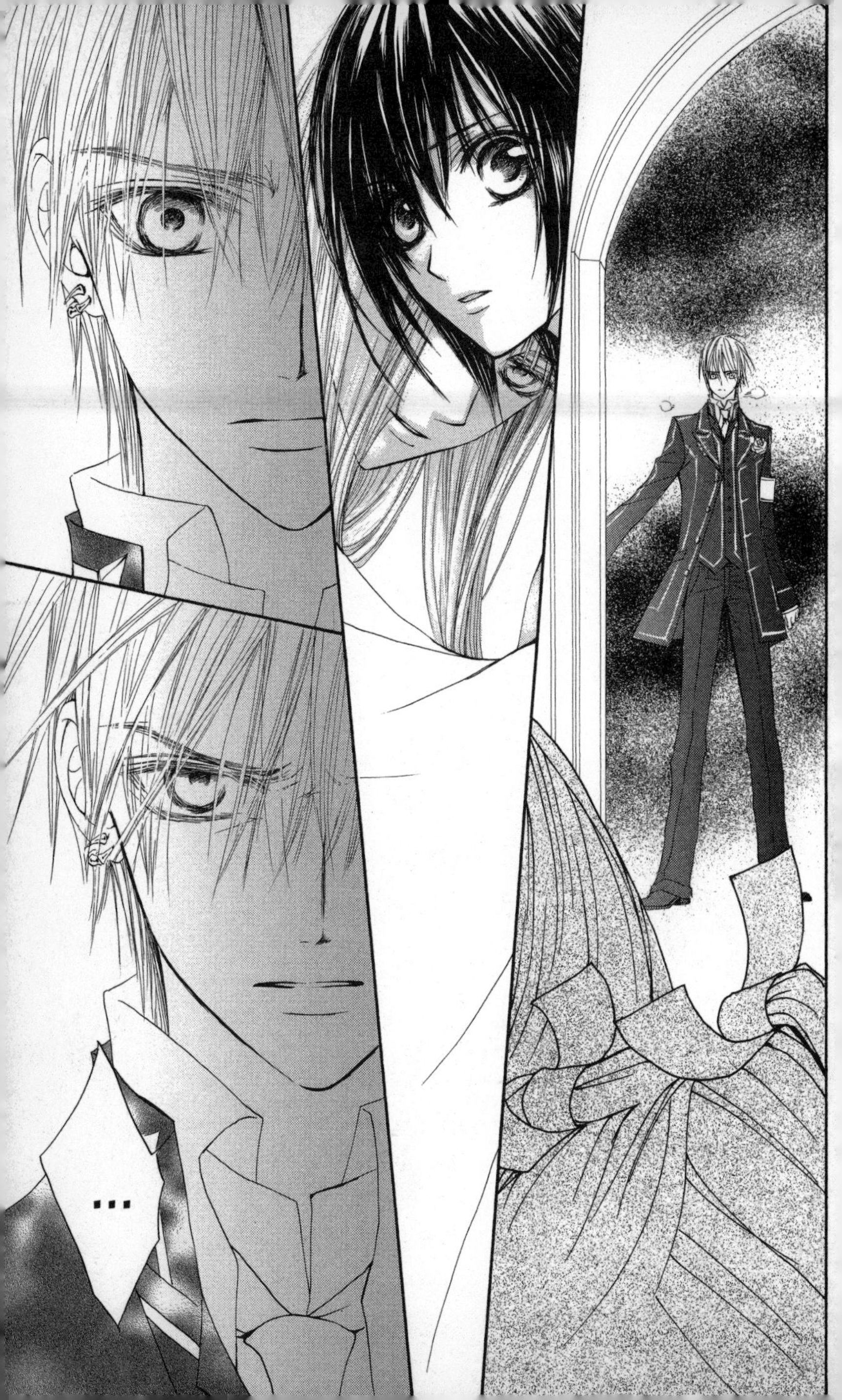
...

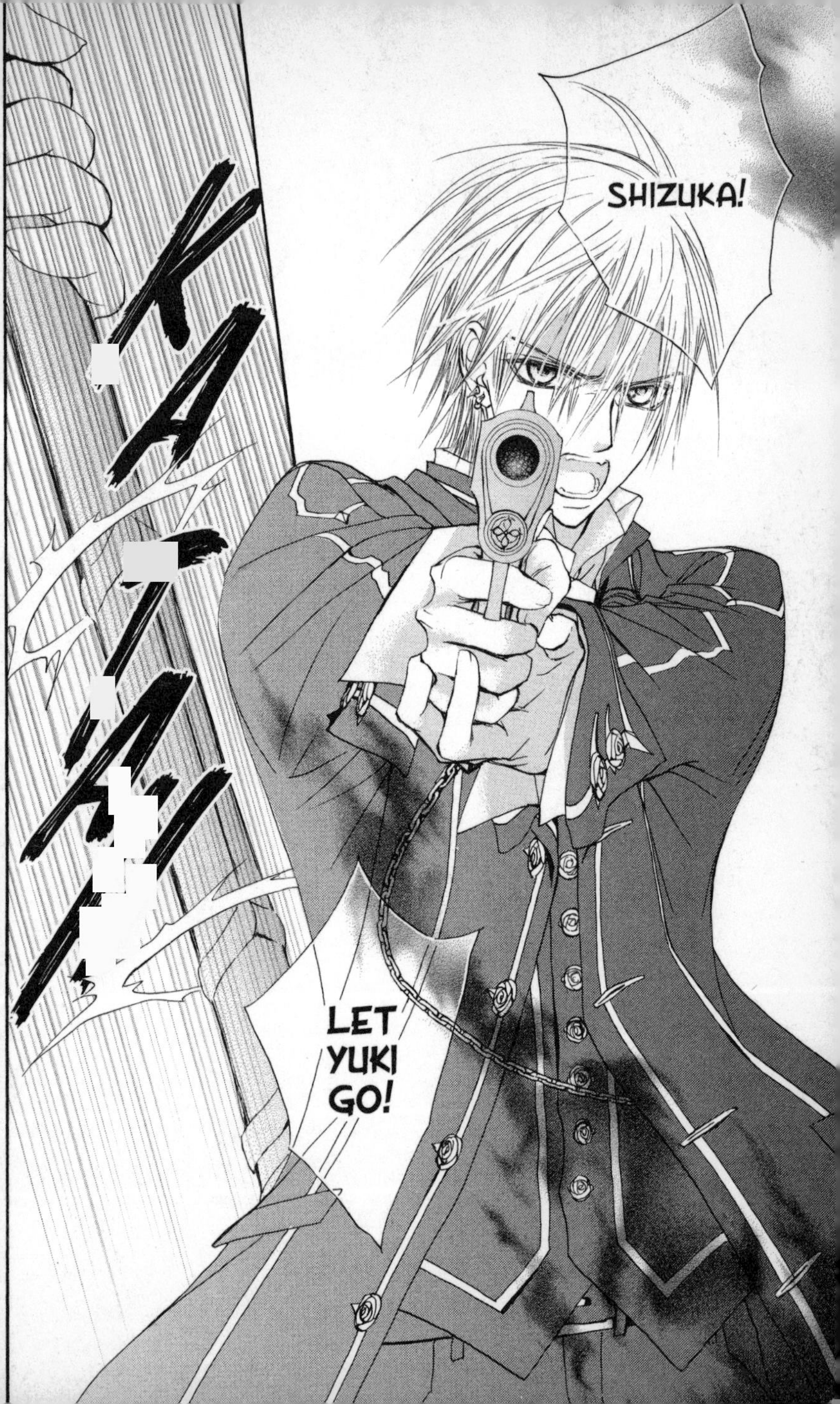
SHIZUKA!
LET YUKI GO!

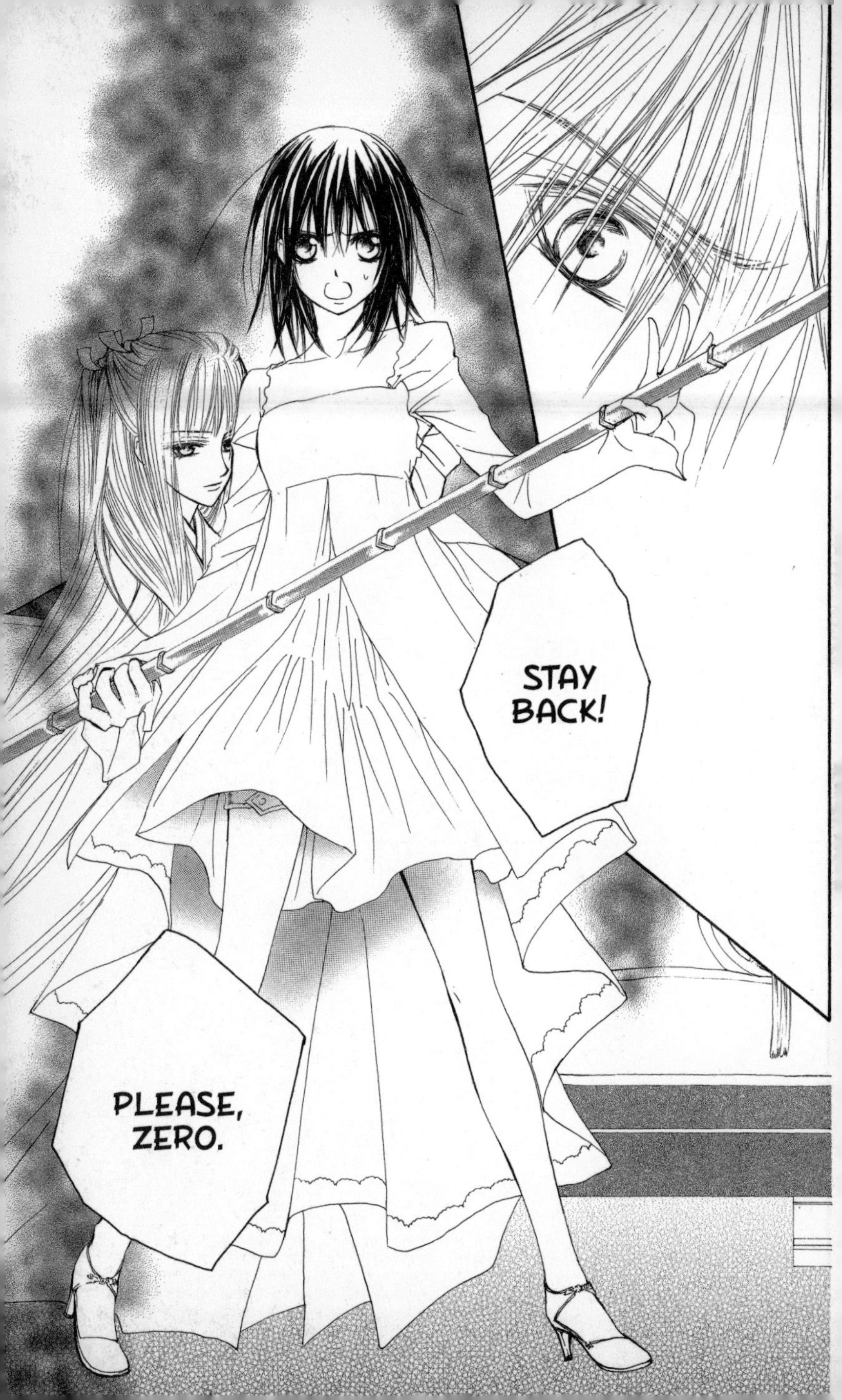
STAY BACK!
PLEASE, ZERO.

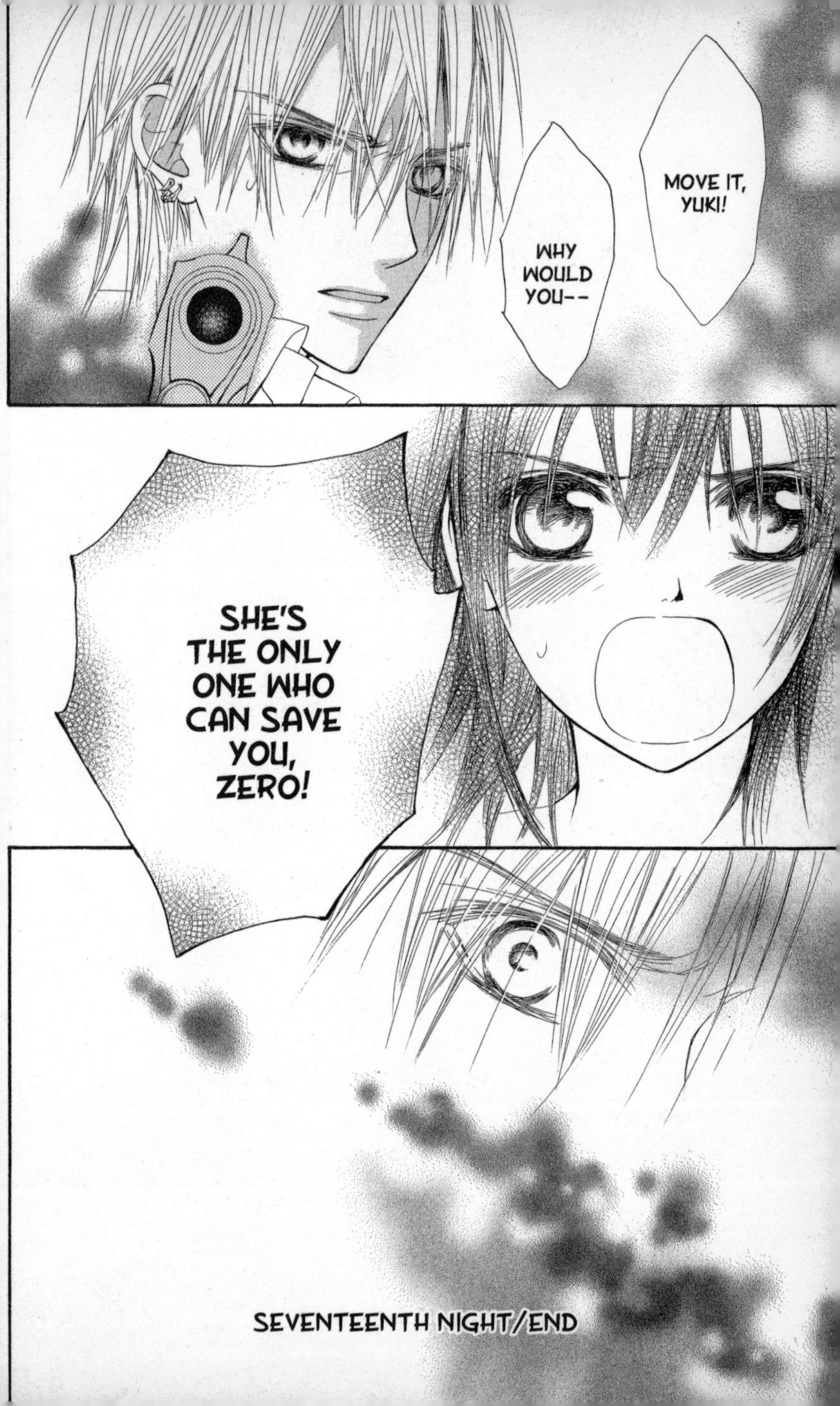
MOVE IT, YUKI!
WHY WOULD YOU--
SHE'S THE ONLY ONE WHO CAN SAVE YOU, ZERO!
SEVENTEENTH NIGHT/END

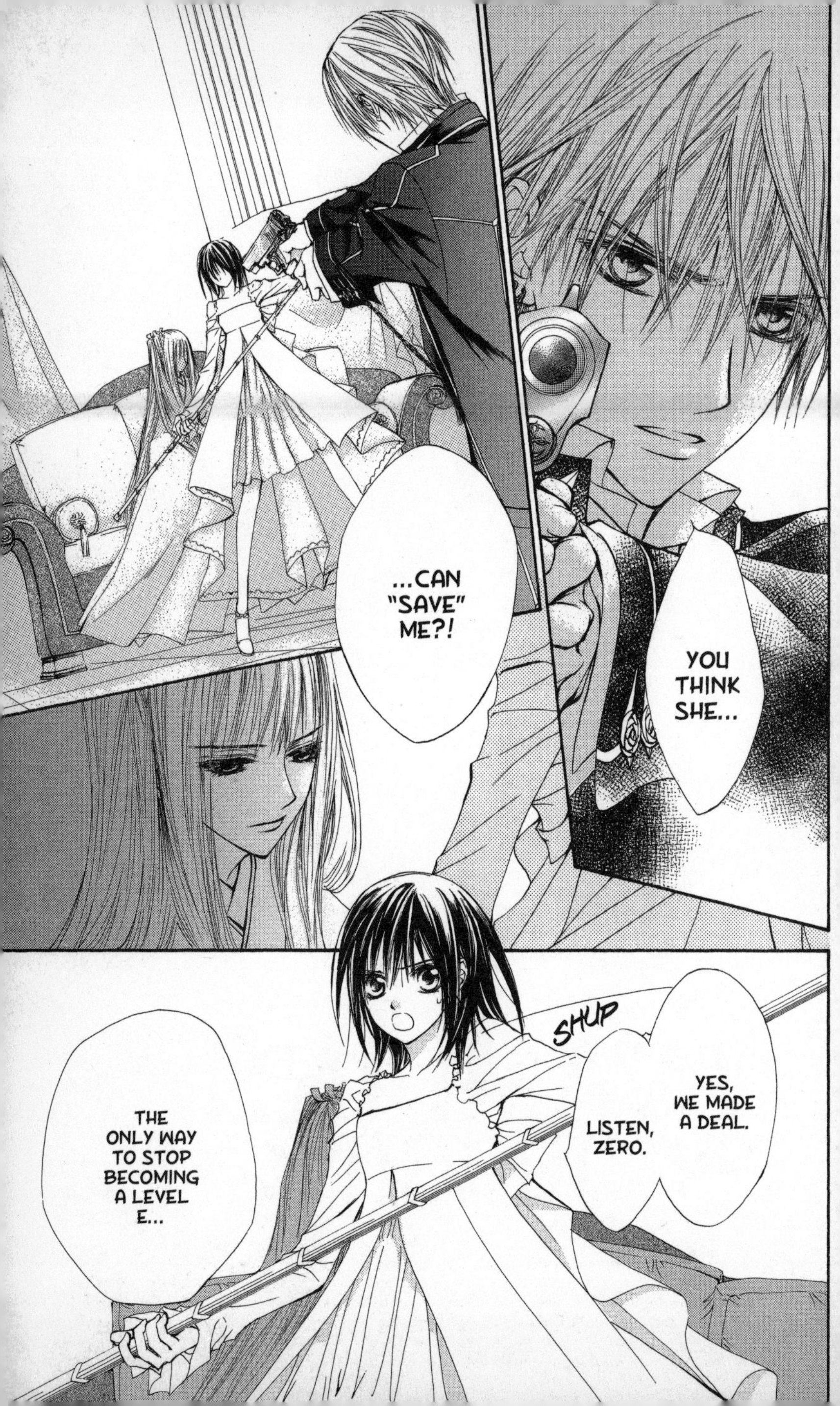
YOU THINK SHE...
...CAN "SAVE" ME?!
SHUP
YES, WE MADE A DEAL.
LISTEN, ZERO.
THE ONLY WAY TO STOP BECOMING A LEVEL E...

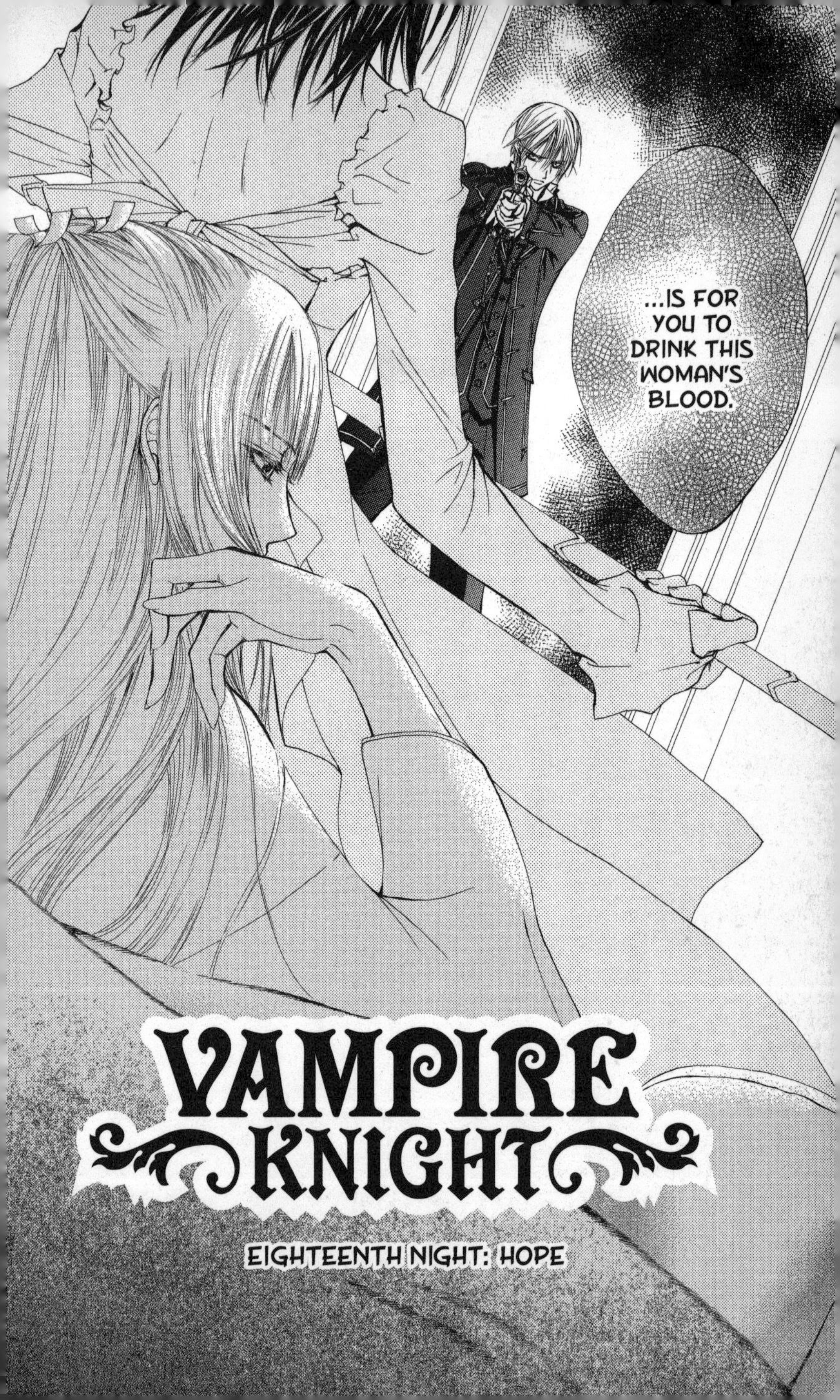
...IS FOR YOU TO DRINK THIS WOMAN'S BLOOD.
VAMPIRE KNIGHT
EIGHTEENTH NIGHT: HOPE

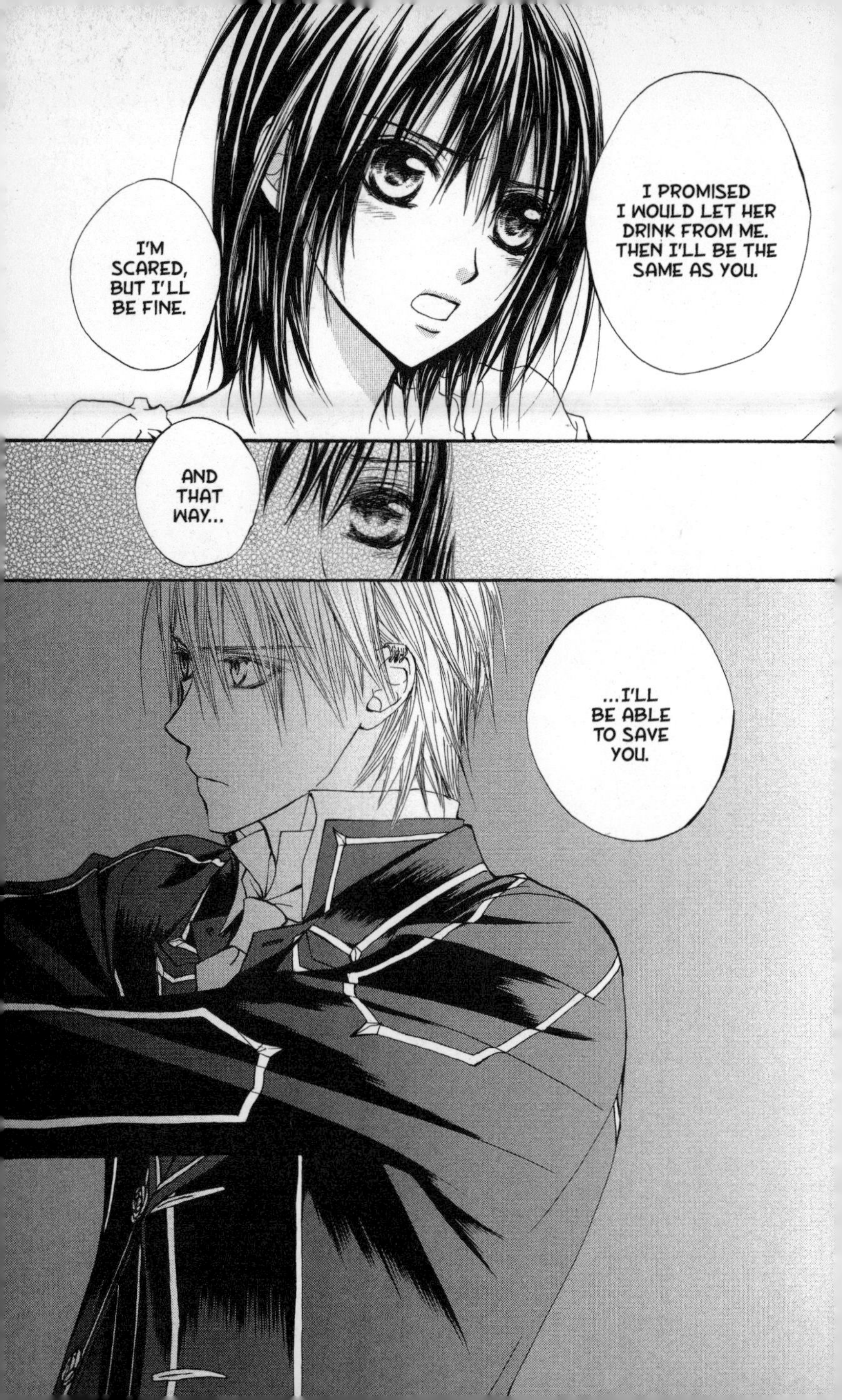
I PROMISED I WOULD LET HER DRINK FROM ME. THEN I'LL BE THE SAME AS YOU.
I'M SCARED, BUT I'LL BE FINE.
AND THAT WAY...
...I'LL BE ABLE TO SAVE YOU.

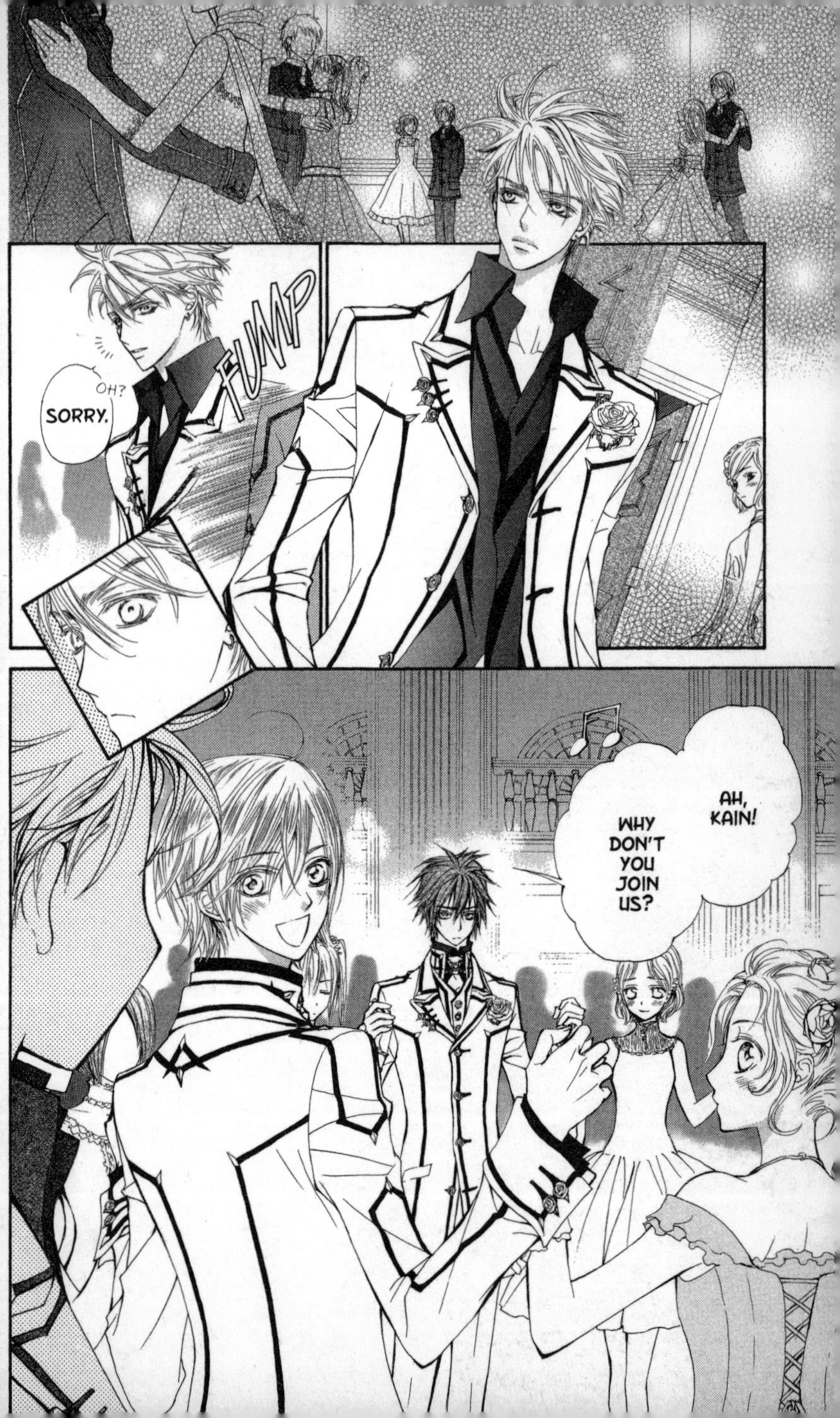
FUMP
OH?
SORRY.
AH, KAIN!
WHY DON'T YOU JOIN US?

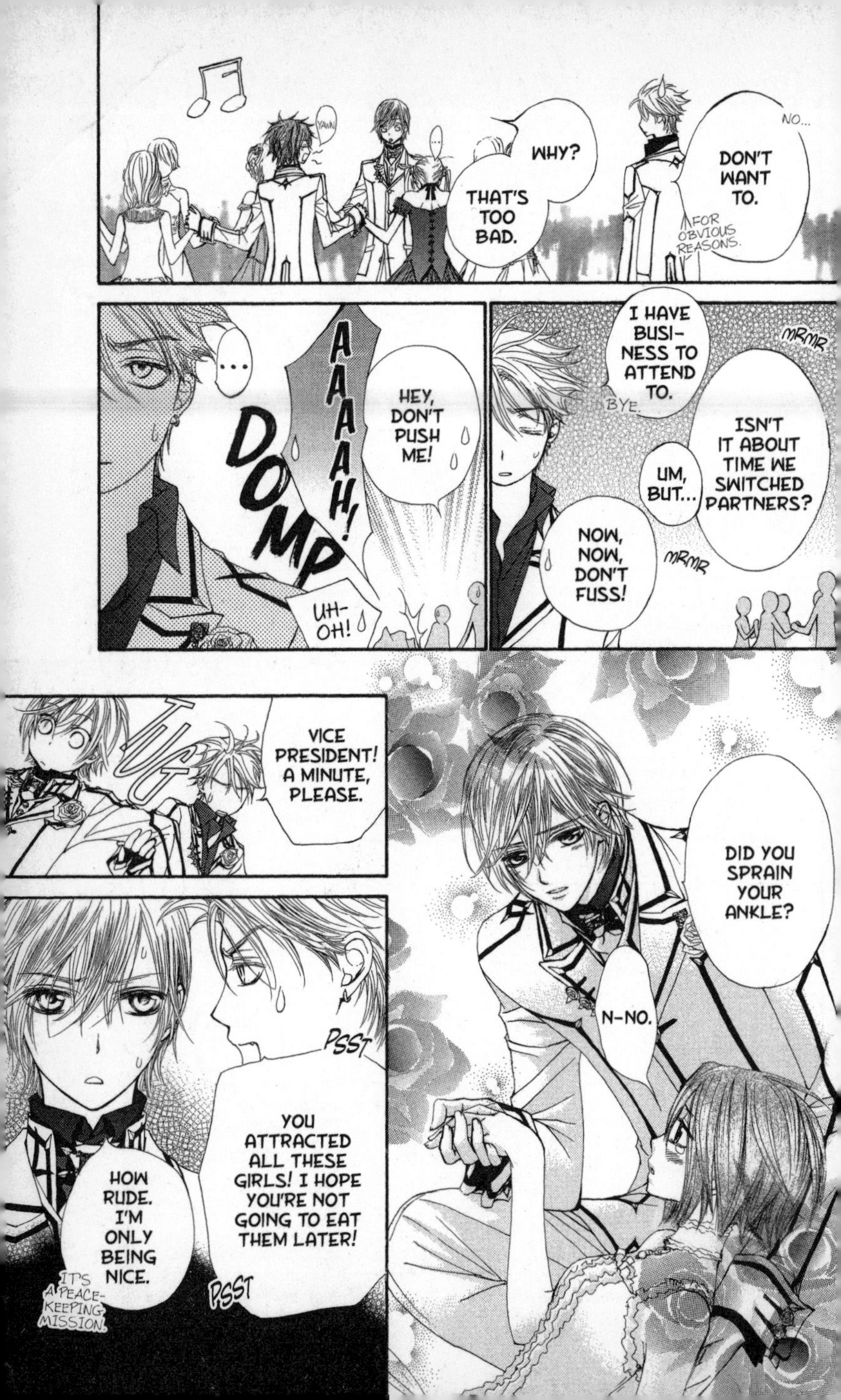
NO...
DON'T WANT TO.
FOR OBVIOUS REASONS.
WHY?
THAT'S TOO BAD.
...
YAWN
I HAVE BUSI-NESS TO ATTEND TO.
BYE.
MRMR
ISN'T IT ABOUT TIME WE SWITCHED PARTNERS?
UM, BUT...
NOW, NOW, DON'T FUSS!
MRMR
AAAAH!
HEY, DON'T PUSH ME!
...
DOMP
UH-OH!
DID YOU SPRAIN YOUR ANKLE?
N-NO.
VICE PRESIDENT! A MINUTE, PLEASE.
TUG
PSST
YOU ATTRACTED ALL THESE GIRLS! I HOPE YOU'RE NOT GOING TO EAT THEM LATER!
HOW RUDE. I'M ONLY BEING NICE.
IT'S A PEACE-KEEPING MISSION.
PSST

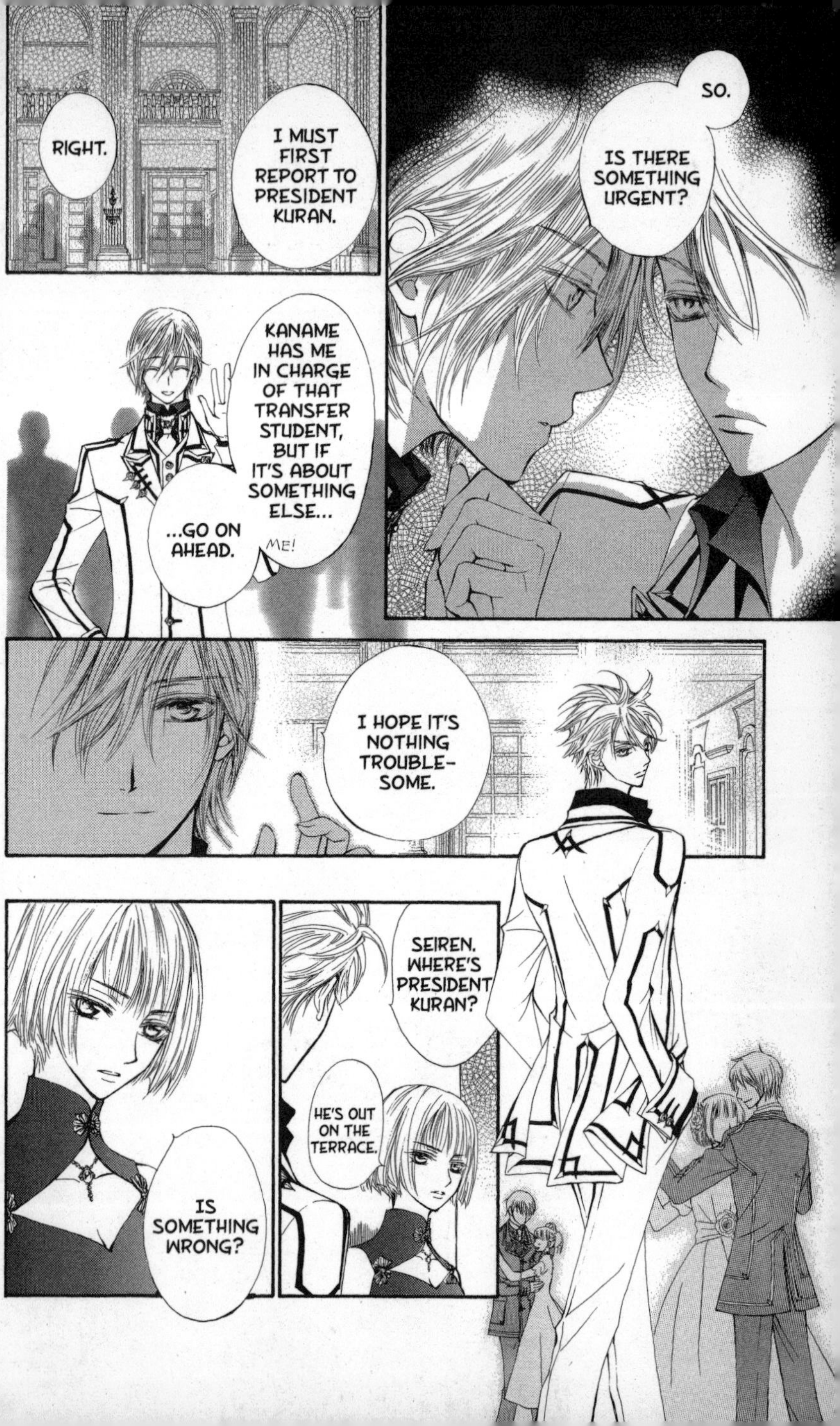
SO.
IS THERE SOMETHING URGENT?
I MUST FIRST REPORT TO PRESIDENT KURAN.
RIGHT.
KANAME HAS ME IN CHARGE OF THAT TRANSFER STUDENT, BUT IF IT'S ABOUT SOMETHING ELSE...
ME!
...GO ON AHEAD.
I HOPE IT'S NOTHING TROUBLE-SOME.
SEIREN. WHERE'S PRESIDENT KURAN?
HE'S OUT ON THE TERRACE.
IS SOMETHING WRONG?

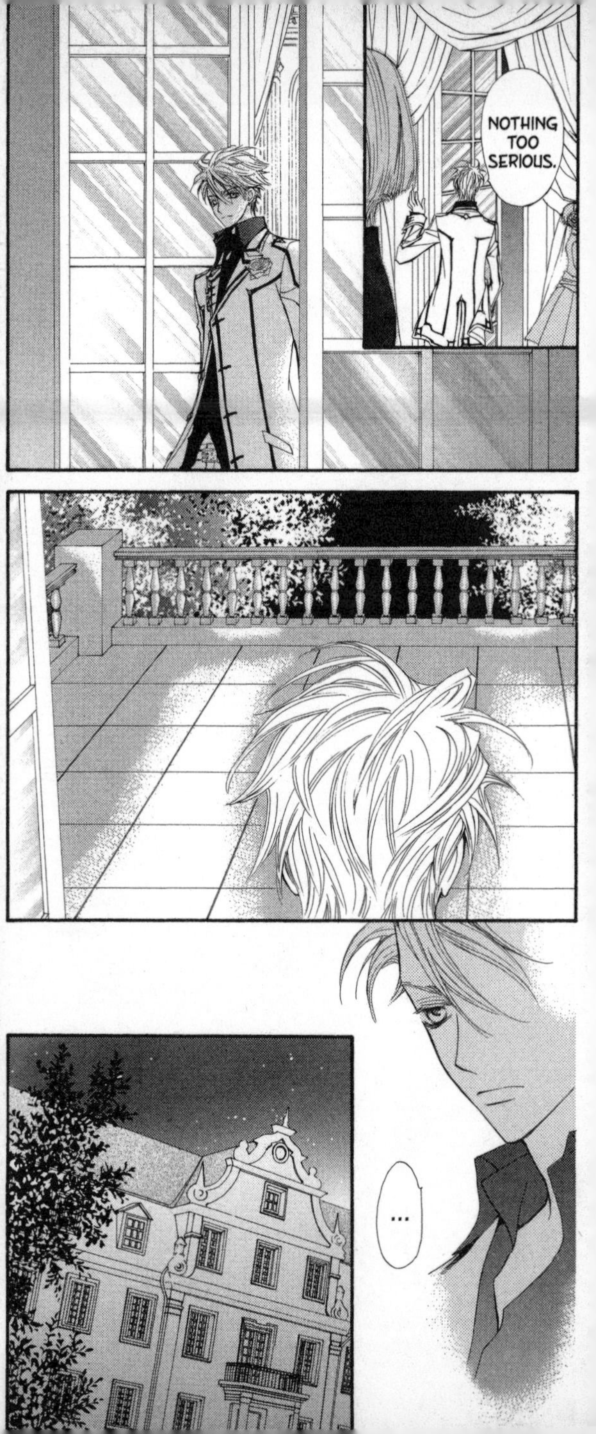
NOTHING TOO SERIOUS.
...

(continued)

↳So after consulting with my editor, I decided to extend the Shizuka arc a bit. Once it's over, various things will change, so please bear with it a little longer!!

In the October issue of *LaLa*, the results of the character popularity poll were announced. The change in this last poll was the reversing of the top two positions. Thus, first is Kaname, second is Zero, and third is Yuki. Yuki did pretty well, holding on against the guys. There wasn't that big a difference between each character. I'm looking forward to how the rankings will change in the future.♥ The characters will grow and change. I will do my best to make that possible.

More results from the poll will be published in volume 5, probably on the page following the Twentieth Night chapter title page. ₰ >

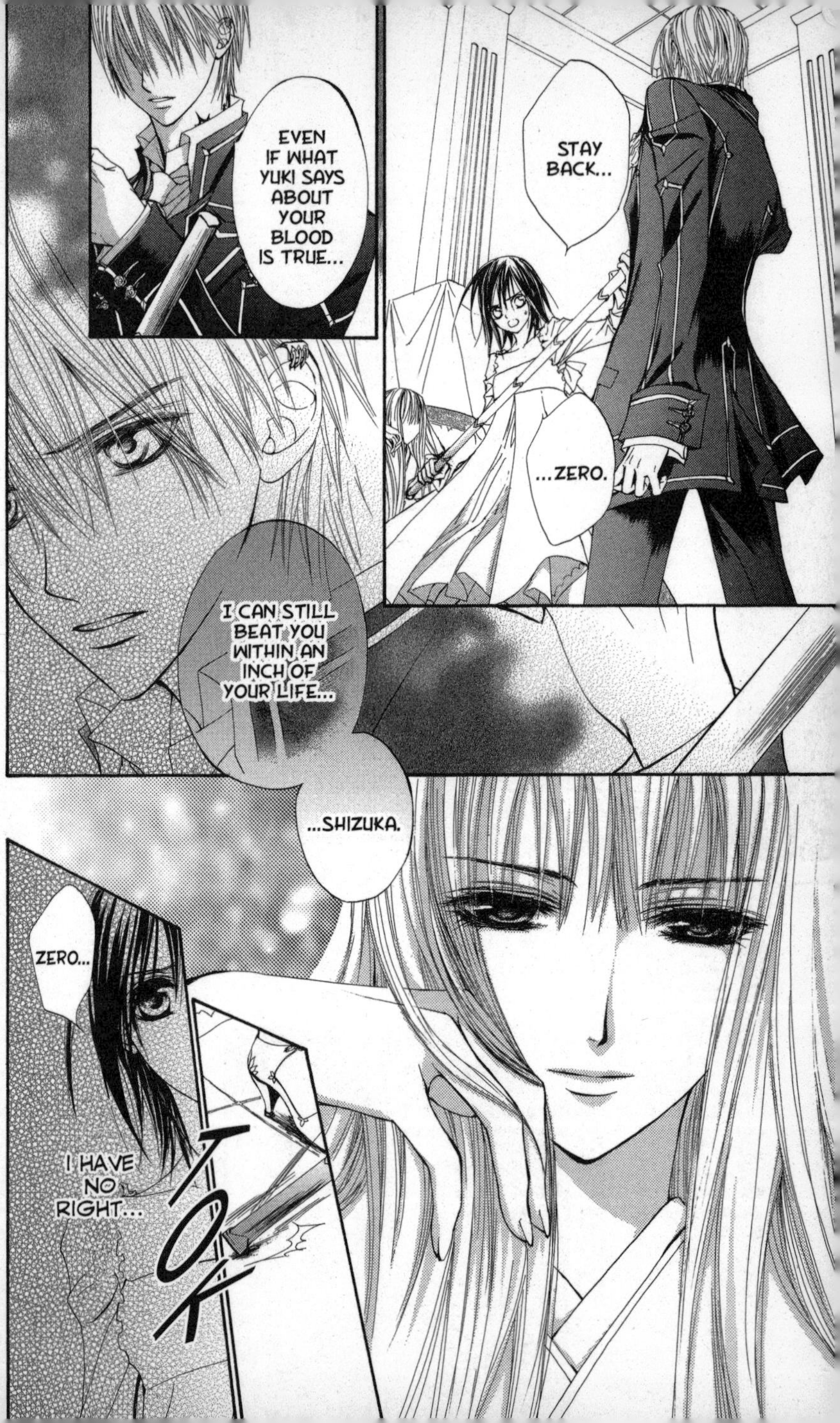
STAY BACK...
...ZERO.
EVEN IF WHAT YUKI SAYS ABOUT YOUR BLOOD IS TRUE...
I CAN STILL BEAT YOU WITHIN AN INCH OF YOUR LIFE...
...SHIZUKA.
ZERO...
I HAVE NO RIGHT...
TOK

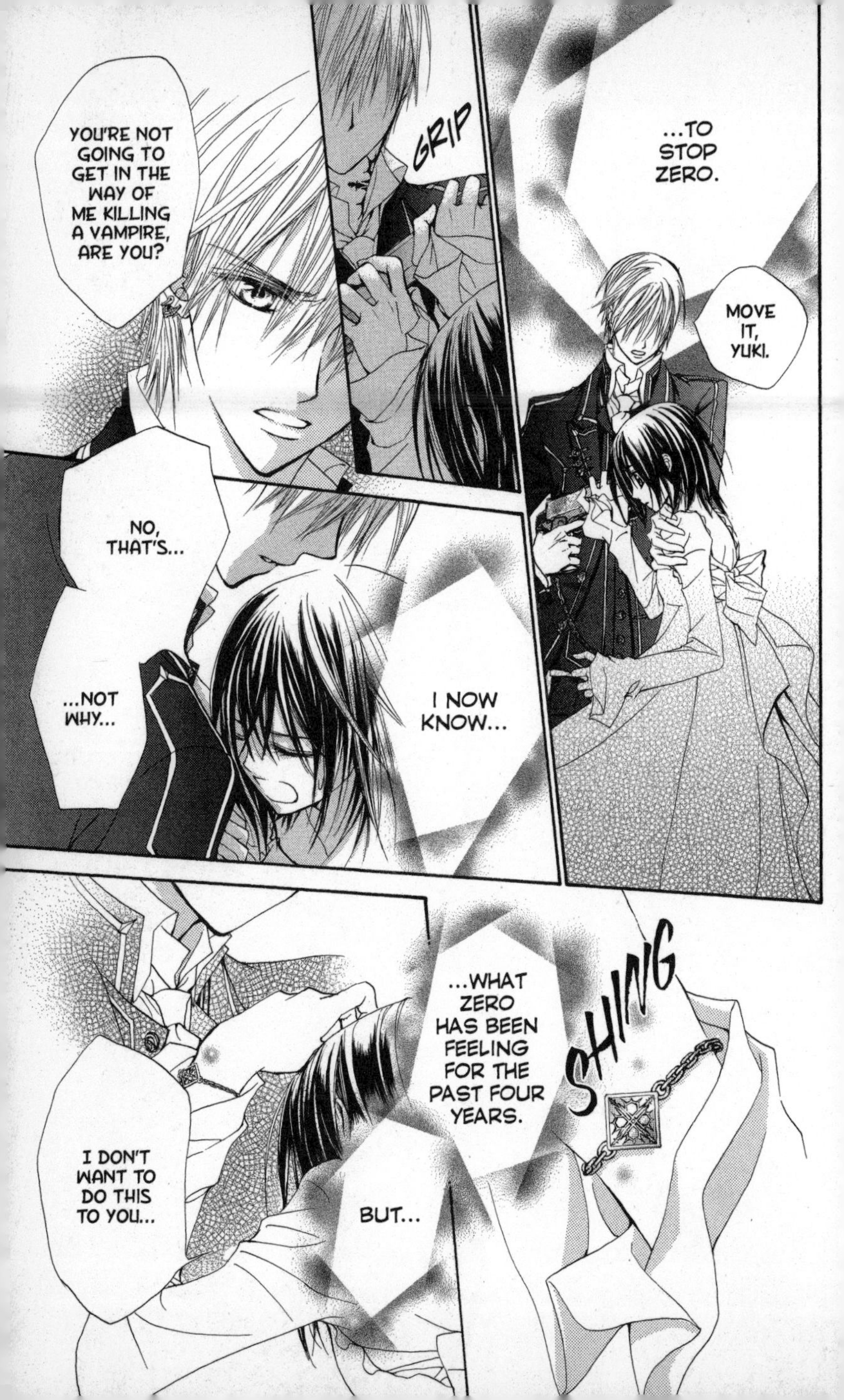
...TO STOP ZERO.
MOVE IT, YUKI.
GRIP
YOU'RE NOT GOING TO GET IN THE WAY OF ME KILLING A VAMPIRE, ARE YOU?
NO, THAT'S...
...NOT WHY...
I NOW KNOW...
SHING
...WHAT ZERO HAS BEEN FEELING FOR THE PAST FOUR YEARS.
BUT...
I DON'T WANT TO DO THIS TO YOU...

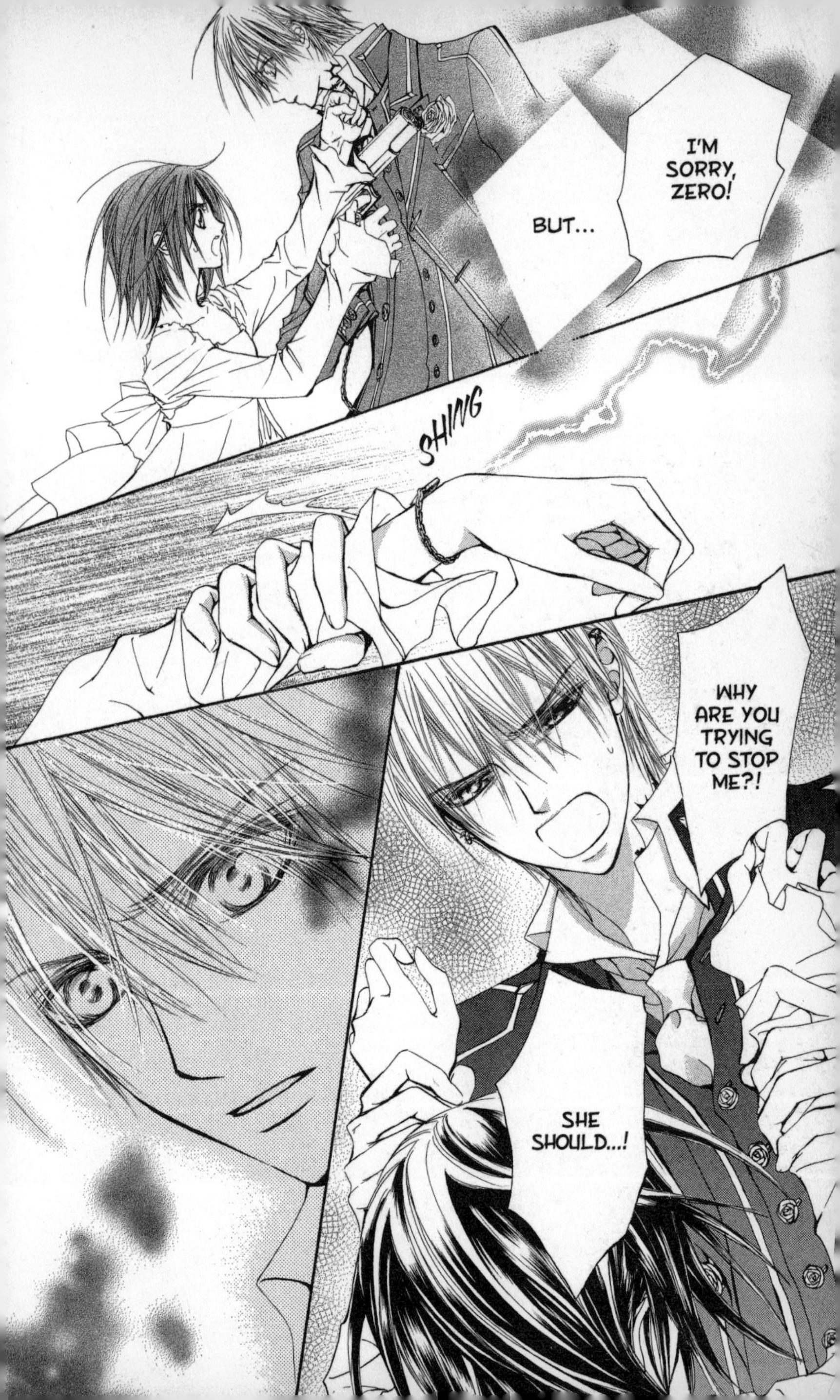
I'M SORRY, ZERO!
BUT...
SHING
WHY ARE YOU TRYING TO STOP ME?!
SHE SHOULD...!

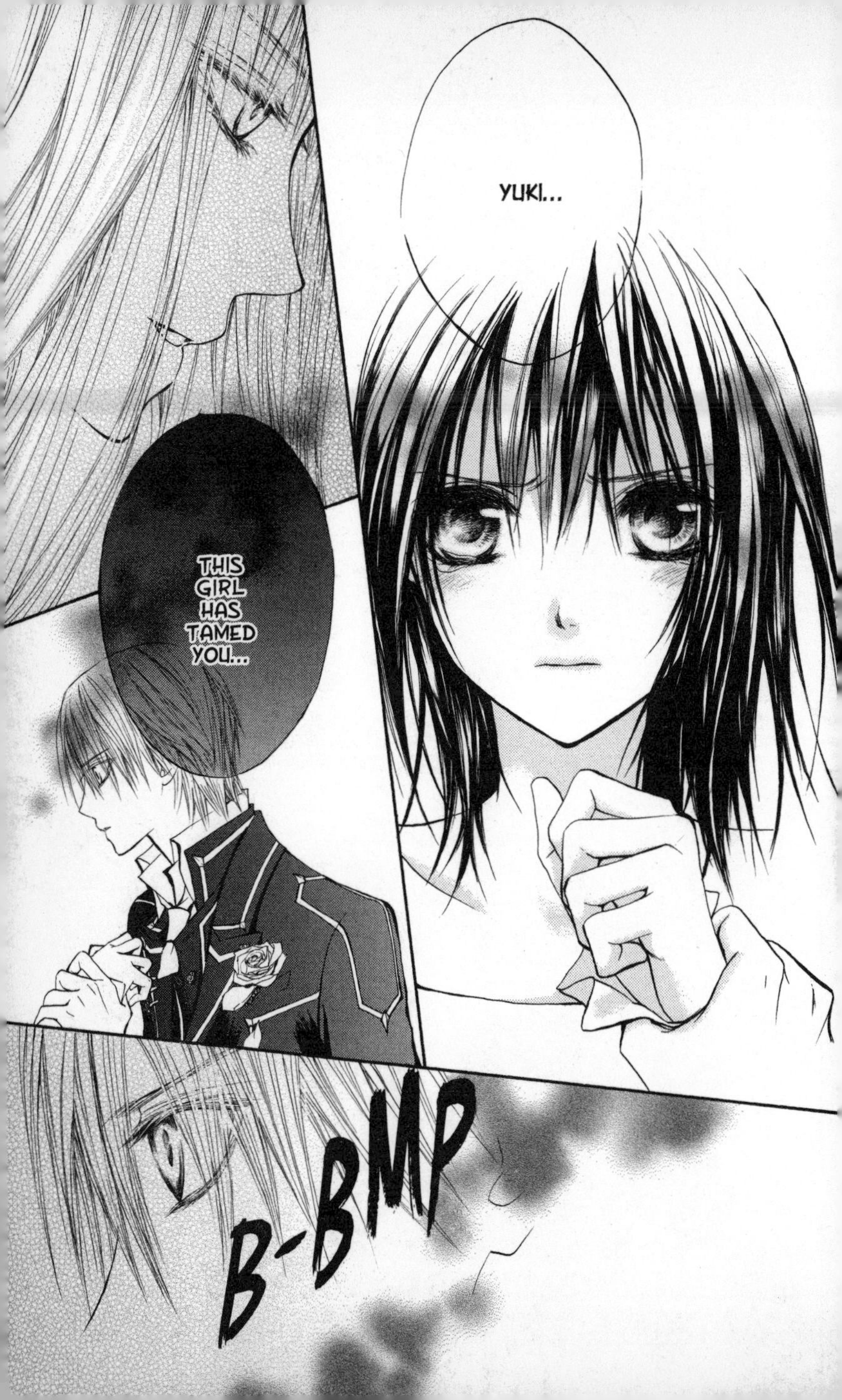
YUKI...
THIS GIRL HAS TAMED YOU...
B-BMP

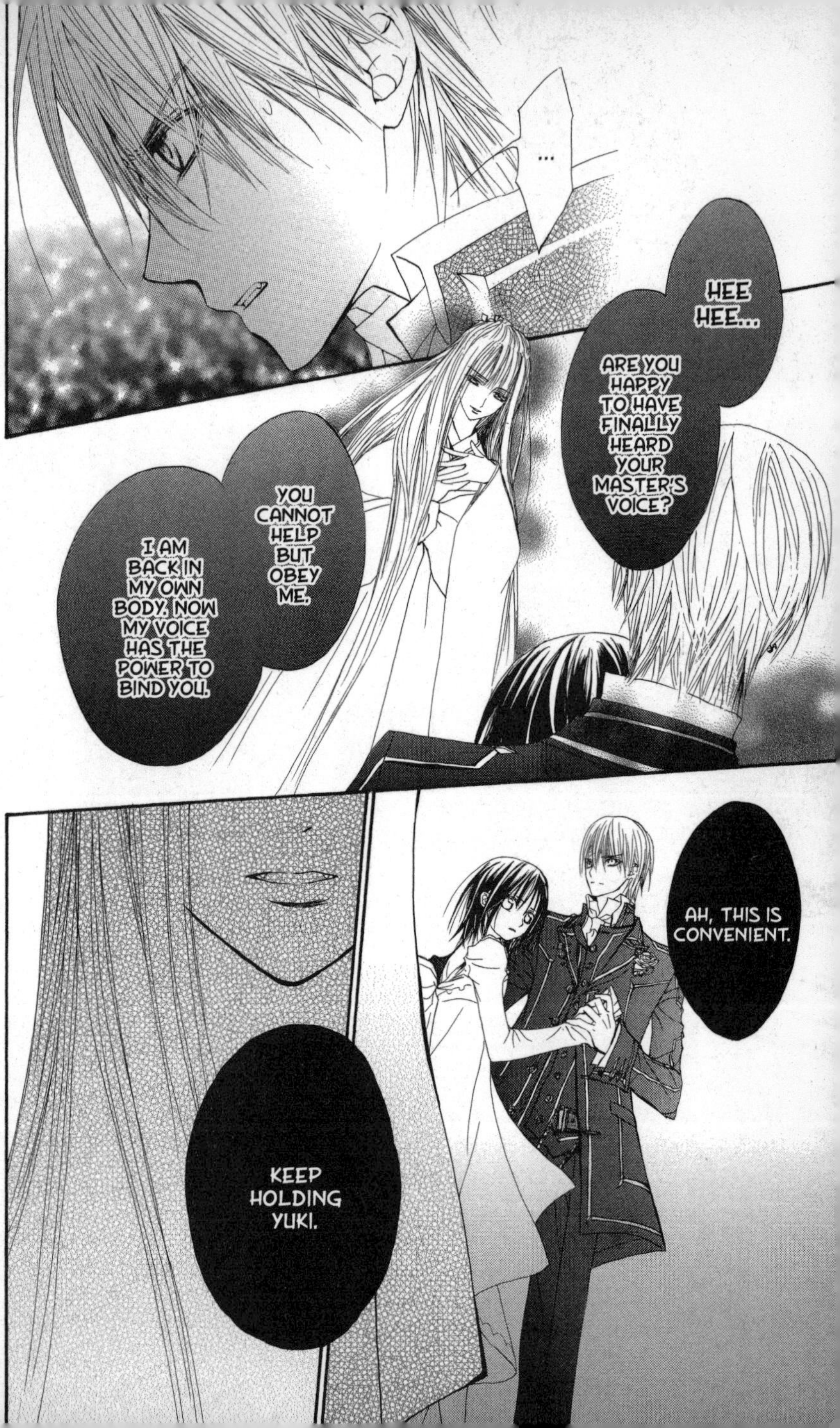
...
HEE HEE...
ARE YOU HAPPY TO HAVE FINALLY HEARD YOUR MASTER'S VOICE?
YOU CANNOT HELP BUT OBEY ME.
I AM BACK IN MY OWN BODY. NOW MY VOICE HAS THE POWER TO BIND YOU.
AH, THIS IS CONVENIENT.
KEEP HOLDING YUKI.

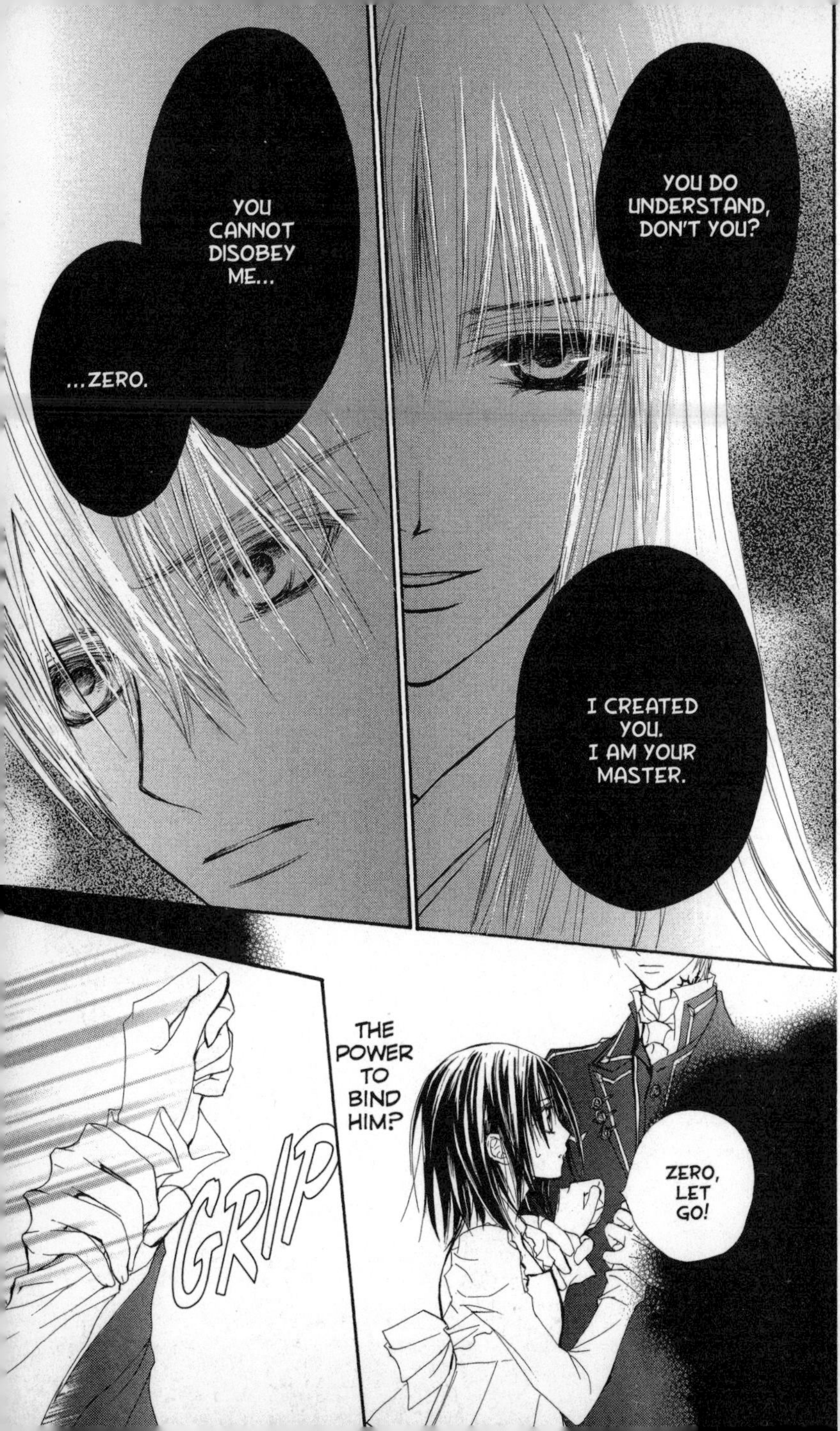
YOU DO UNDERSTAND, DON'T YOU?
I CREATED YOU. I AM YOUR MASTER.
YOU CANNOT DISOBEY ME...
...ZERO.
THE POWER TO BIND HIM?
ZERO, LET GO!
GRIP

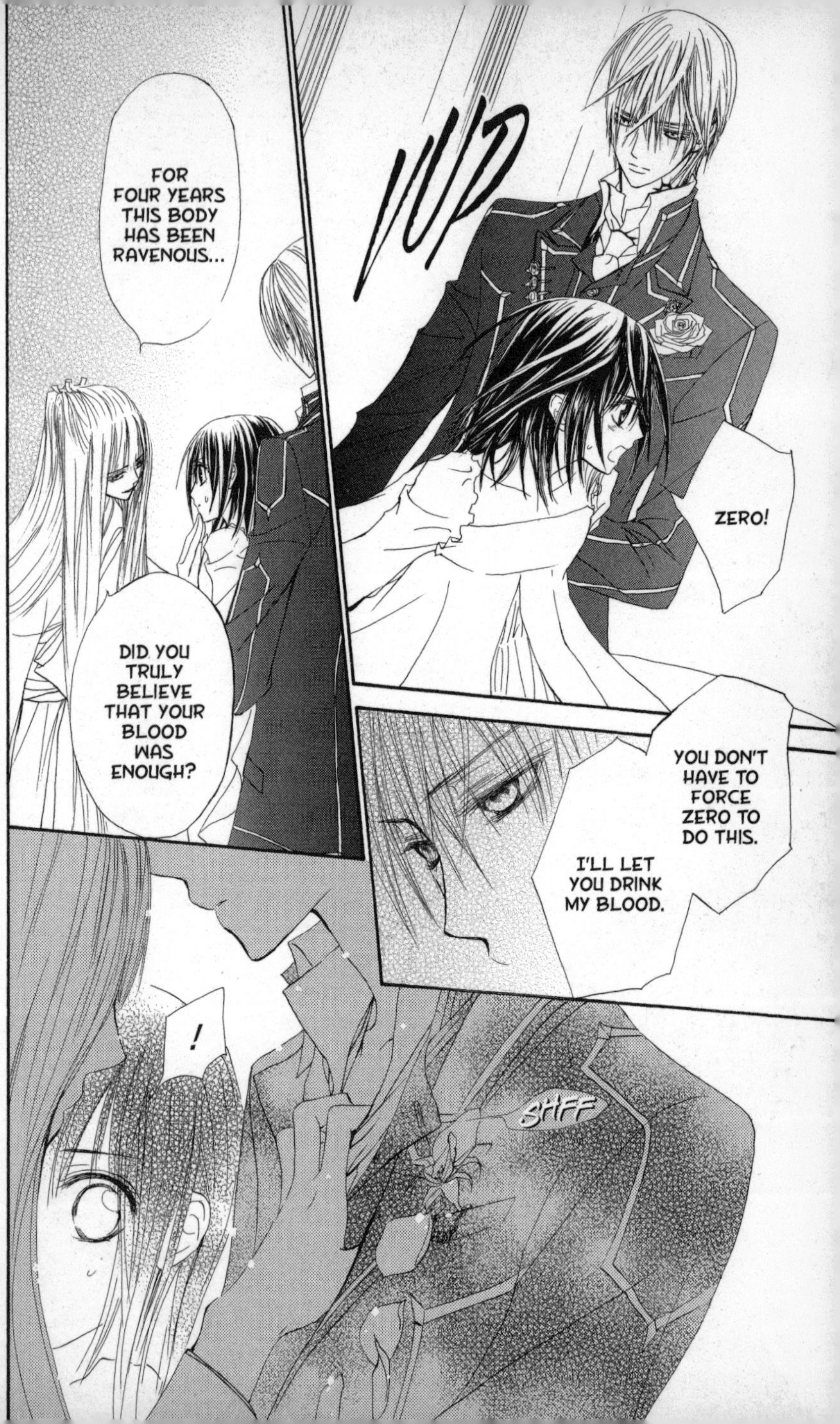
ZERO!
YOU DON'T HAVE TO FORCE ZERO TO DO THIS.
I'LL LET YOU DRINK MY BLOOD.
FOR FOUR YEARS THIS BODY HAS BEEN RAVENOUS...
DID YOU TRULY BELIEVE THAT YOUR BLOOD WAS ENOUGH?
!
SHFF

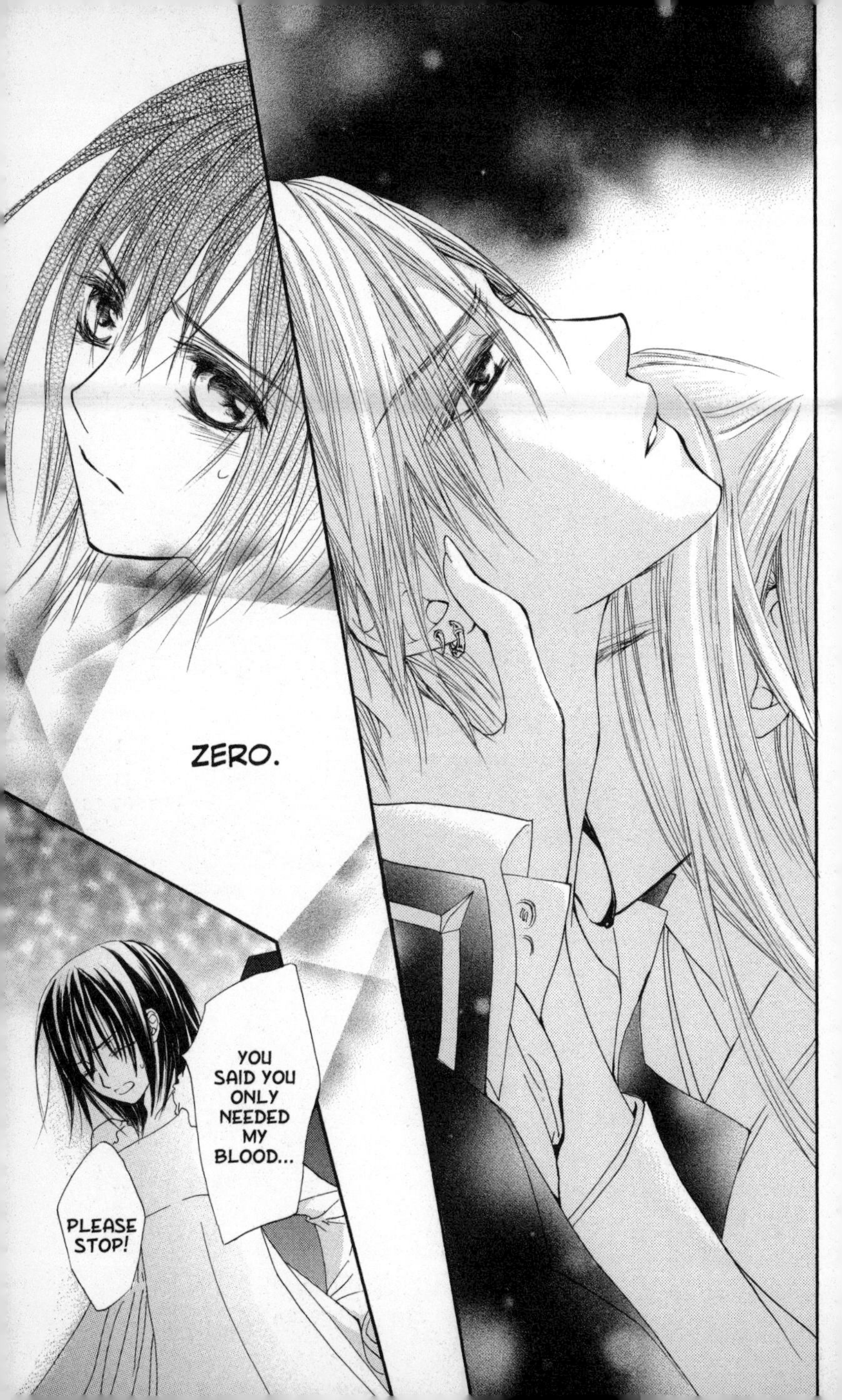
ZERO.
YOU SAID YOU ONLY NEEDED MY BLOOD...
PLEASE STOP!

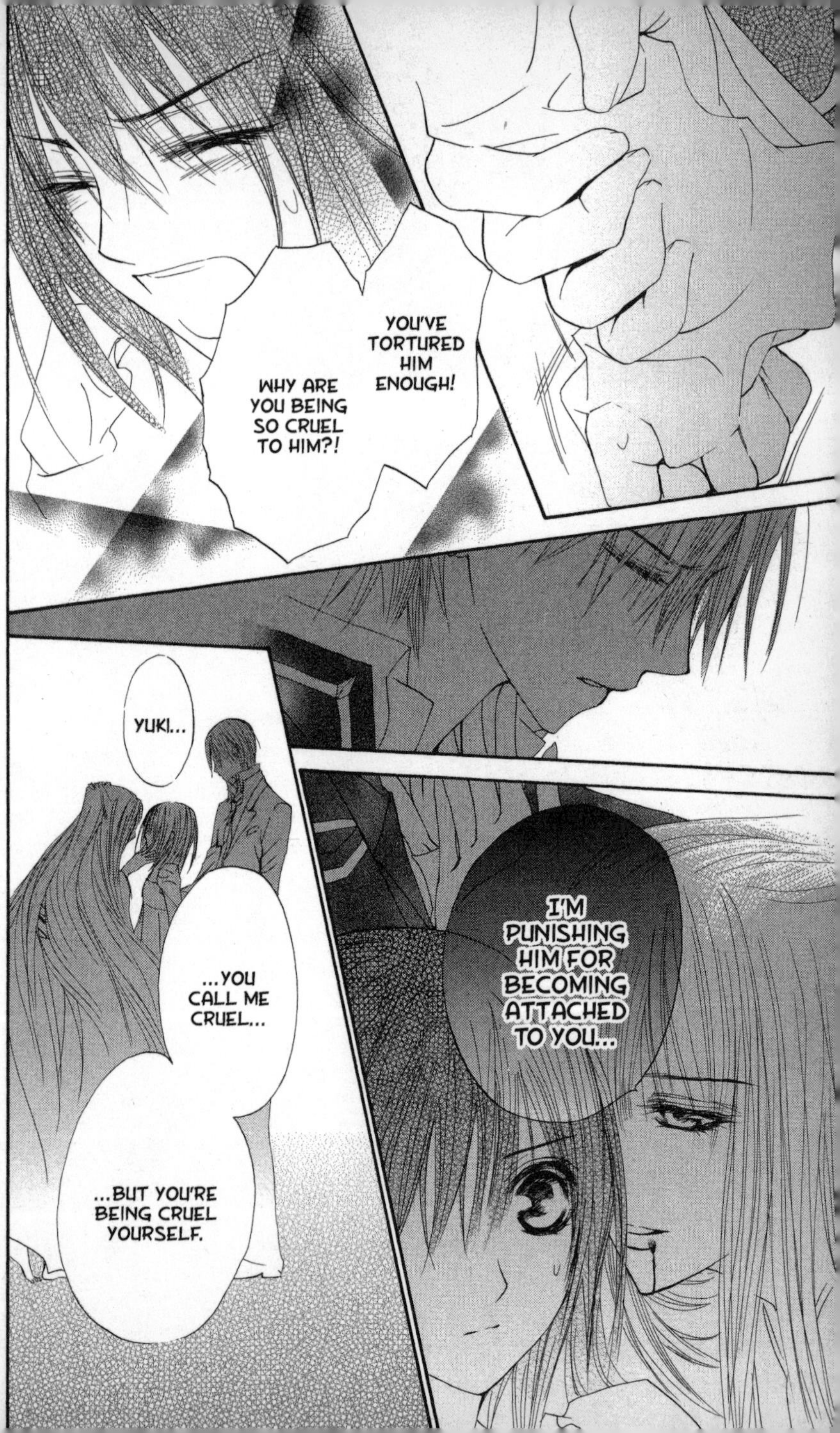
YOU'VE TORTURED HIM ENOUGH!
WHY ARE YOU BEING SO CRUEL TO HIM?!
YUKI...
...YOU CALL ME CRUEL...
...BUT YOU'RE BEING CRUEL YOURSELF.
I'M PUNISHING HIM FOR BECOMING ATTACHED TO YOU...

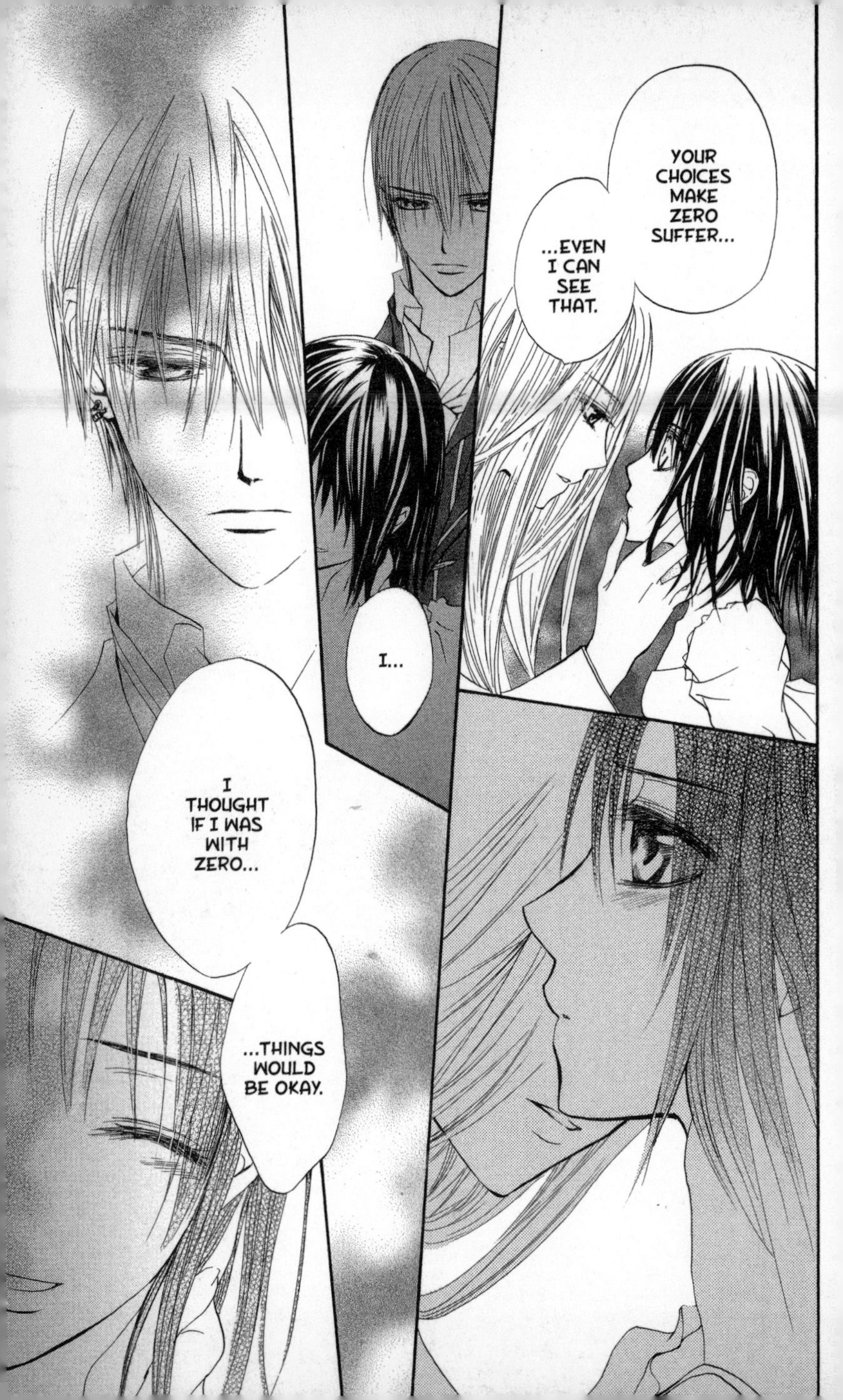
YOUR CHOICES MAKE ZERO SUFFER...
...EVEN I CAN SEE THAT.
I...
I THOUGHT IF I WAS WITH ZERO...
...THINGS WOULD BE OKAY.

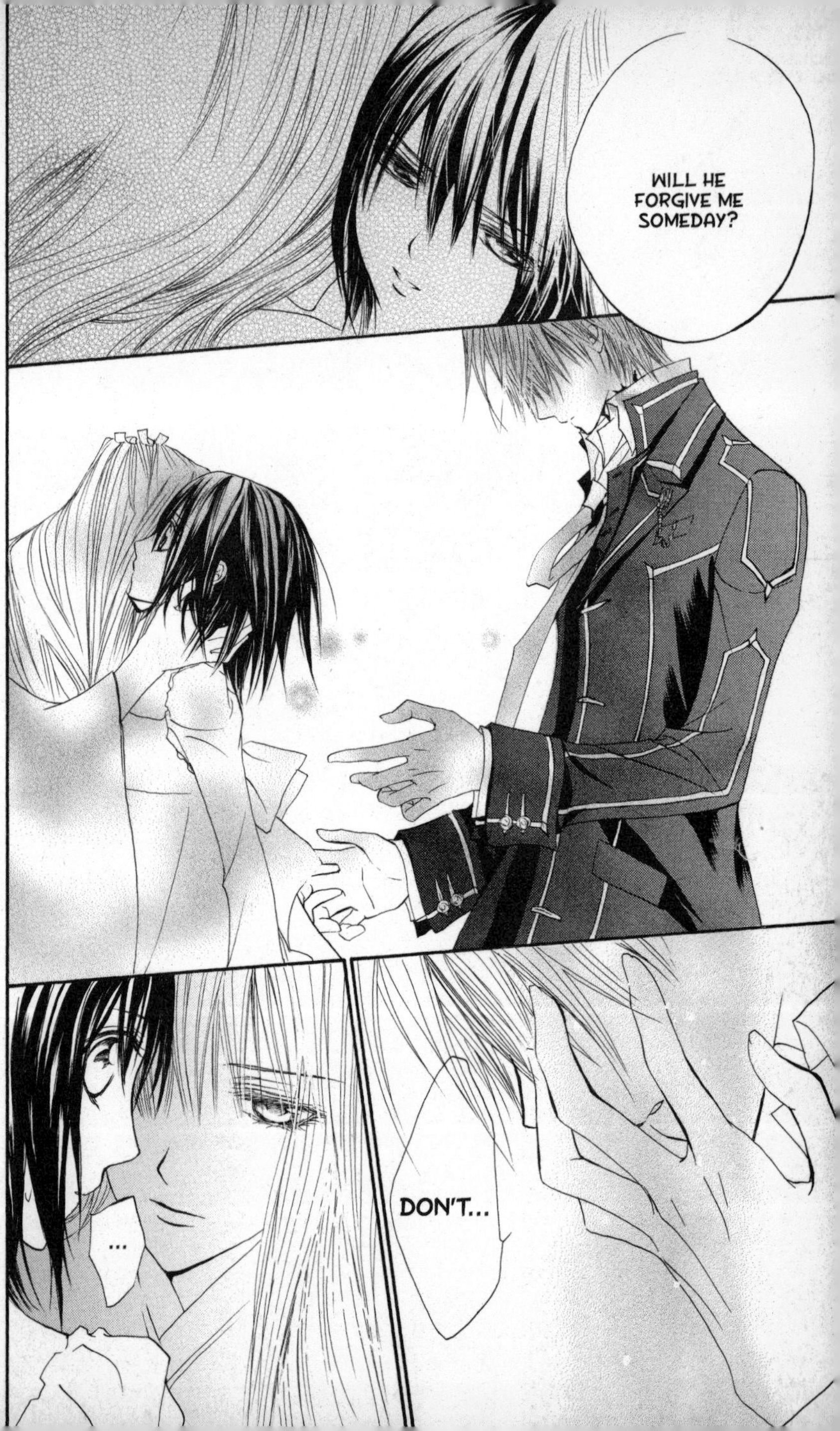
WILL HE
FORGIVE ME
SOMEDAY?
DON'T...
...

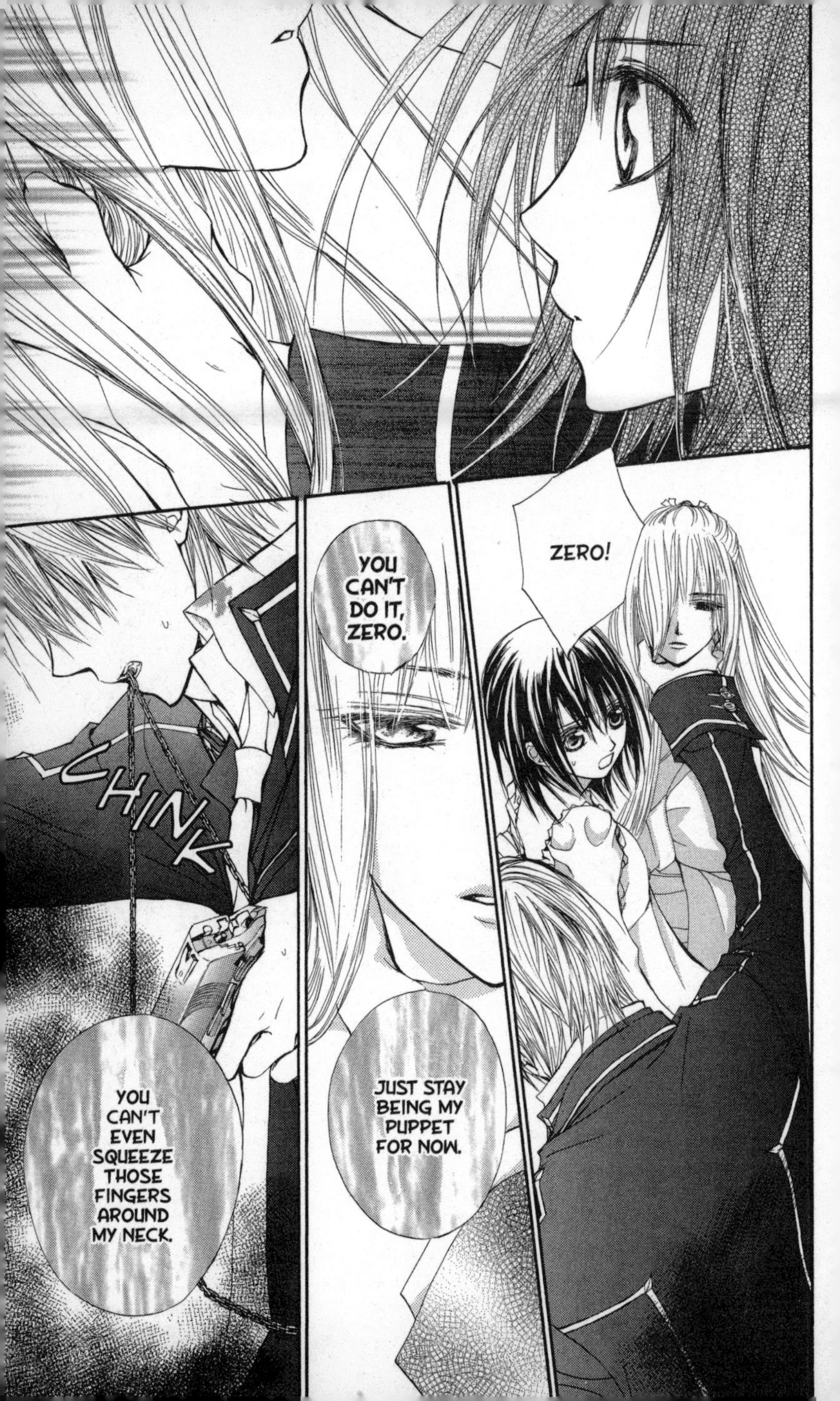
ZERO!
YOU CAN'T DO IT, ZERO.
JUST STAY BEING MY PUPPET FOR NOW.
CHINK
YOU CAN'T EVEN SQUEEZE THOSE FINGERS AROUND MY NECK.

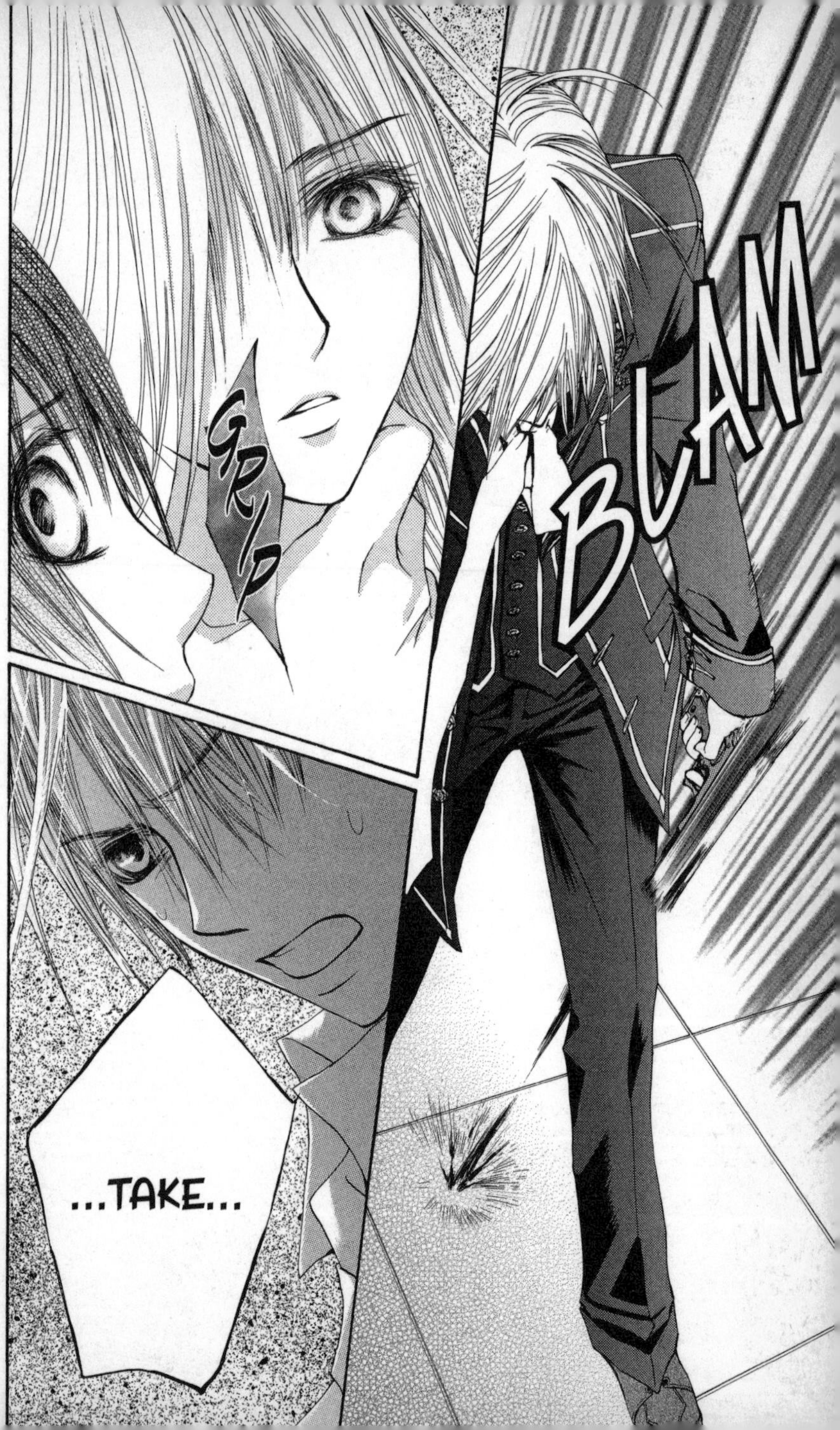
BLAM
GRIP
...TAKE...

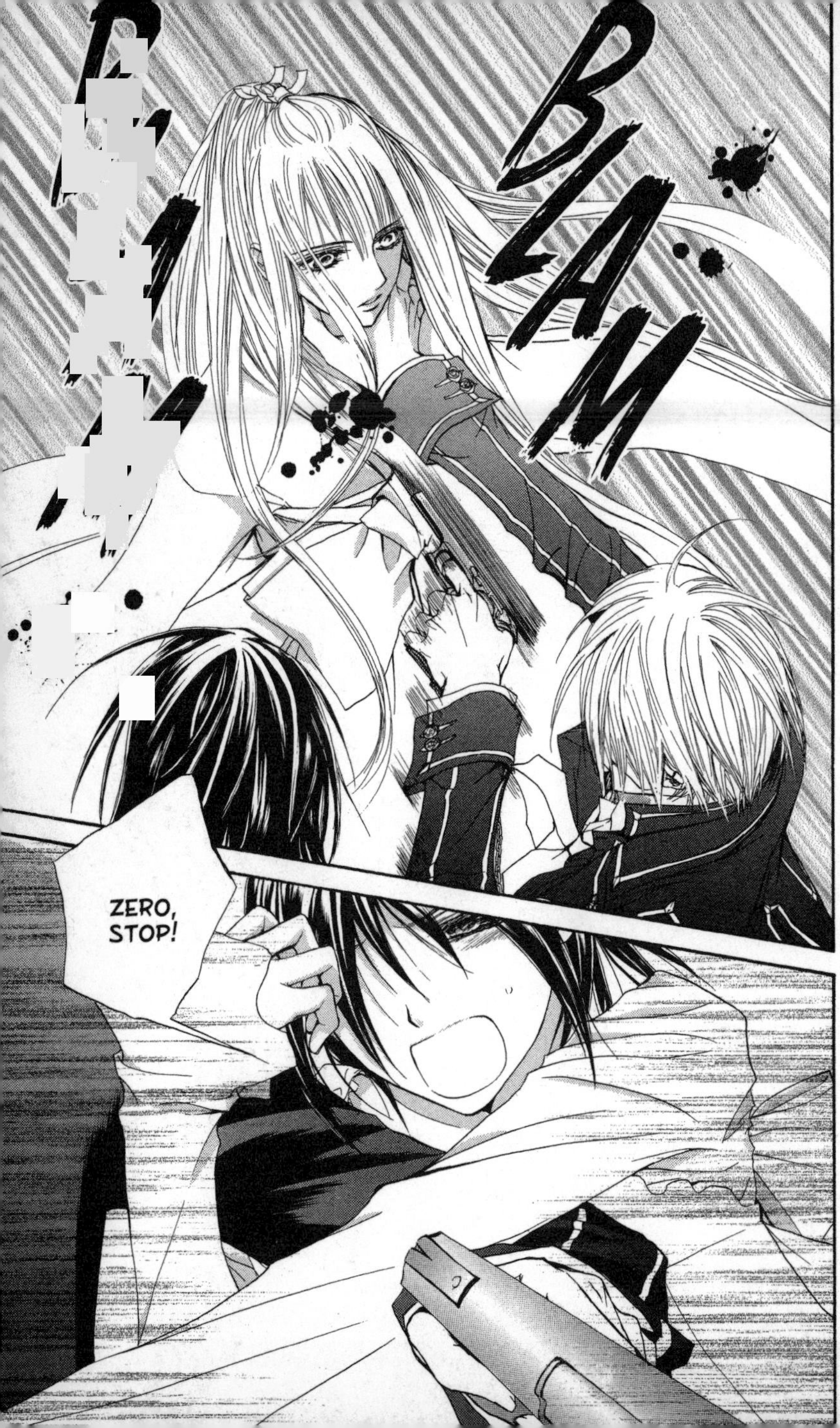
BLAM
ZERO, STOP!

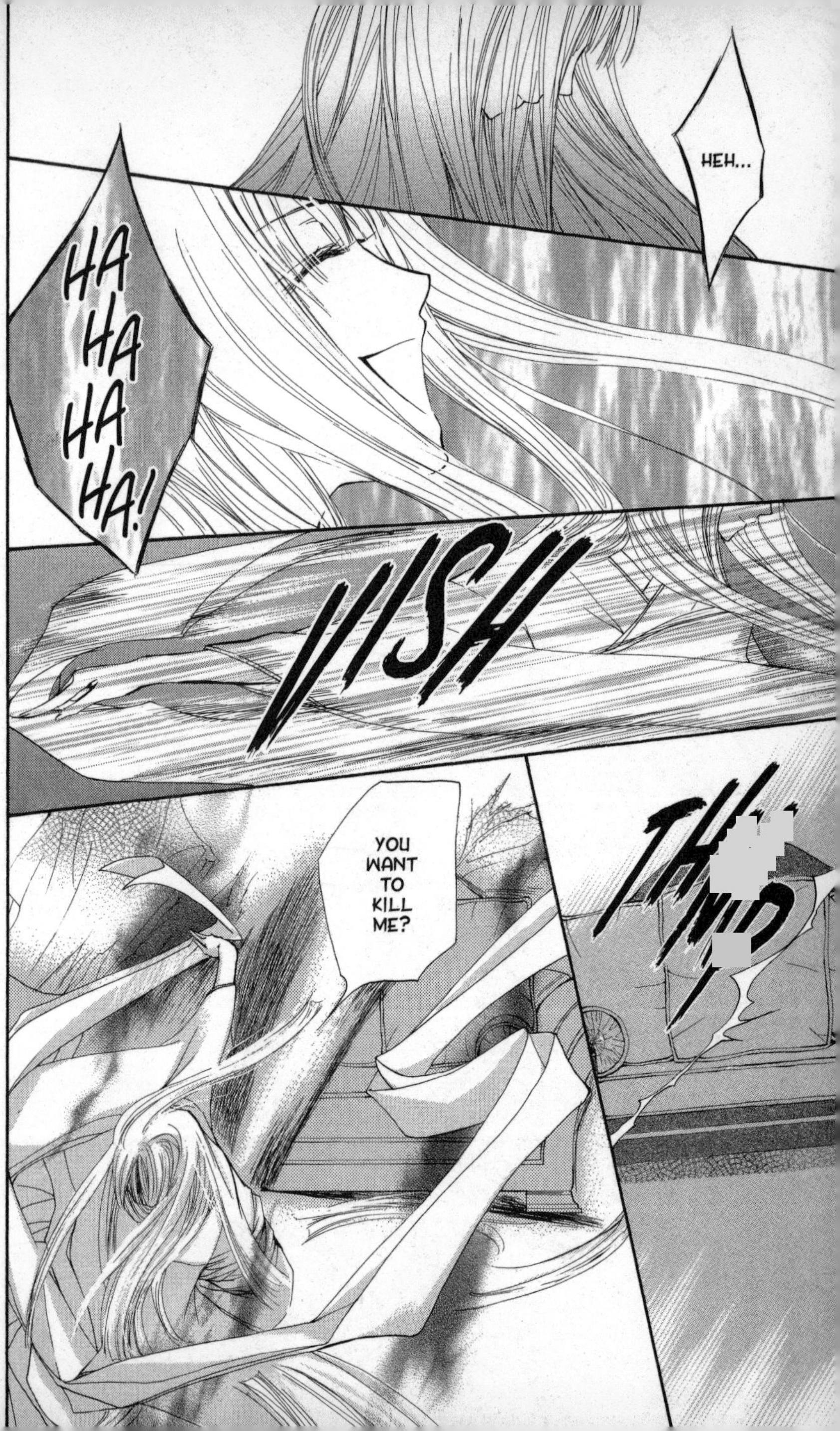
HEH...
HA HA HA HA HA!
VISH
YOU WANT TO KILL ME?

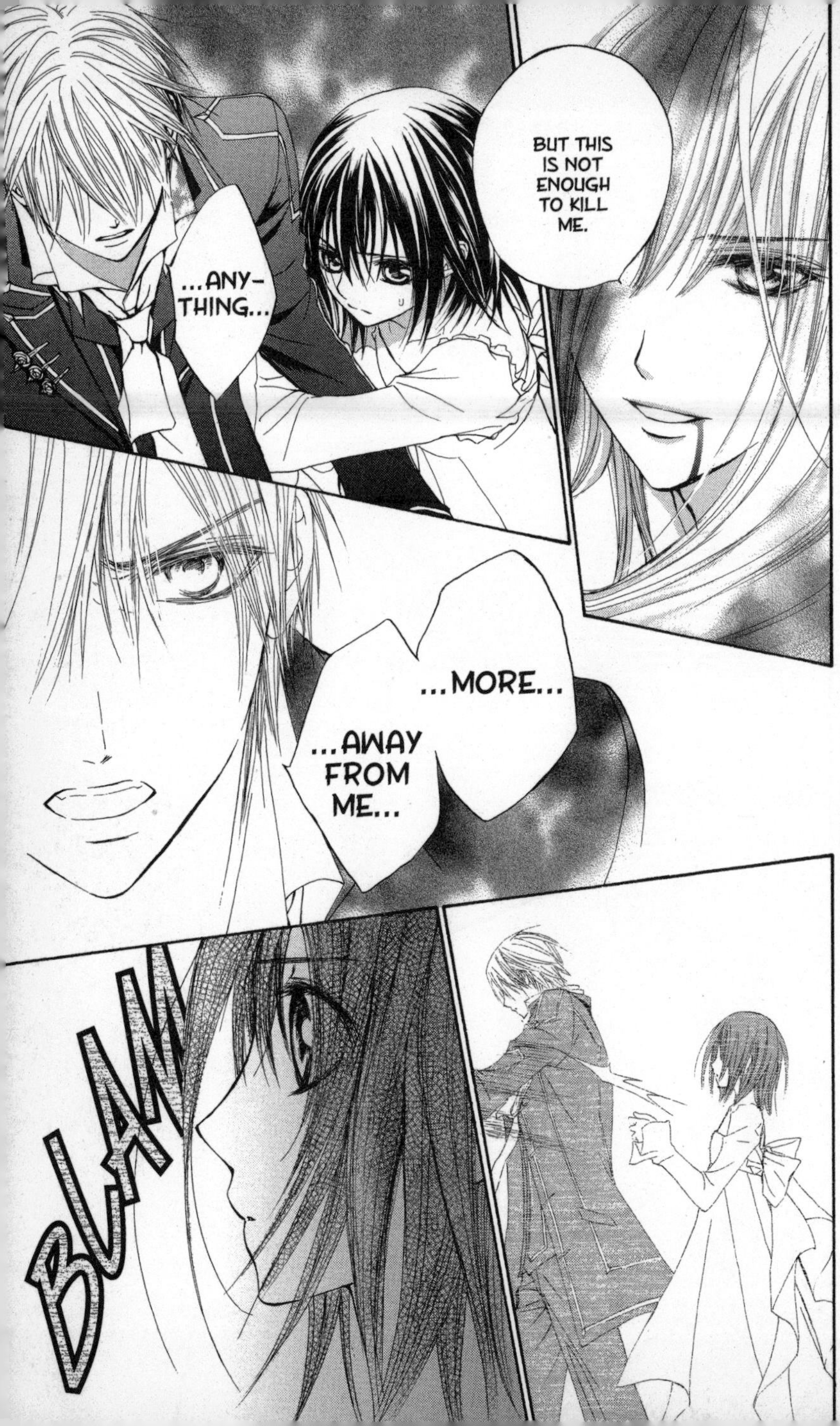
BUT THIS IS NOT ENOUGH TO KILL ME.
...ANY-THING...
...MORE...
...AWAY FROM ME...
BLAM

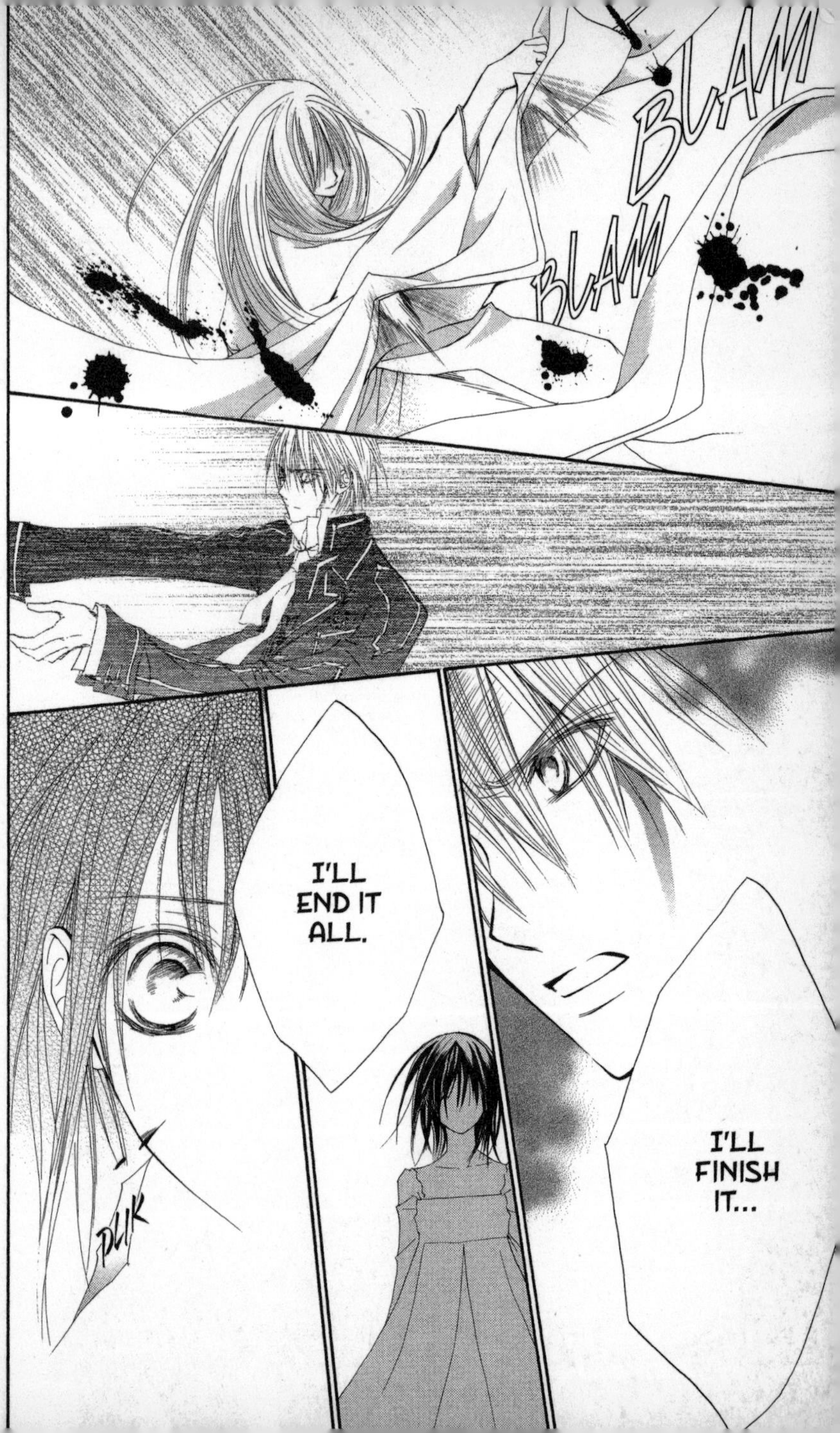
BLAM
BLAM
I'LL FINISH IT...
I'LL END IT ALL.
PLIK

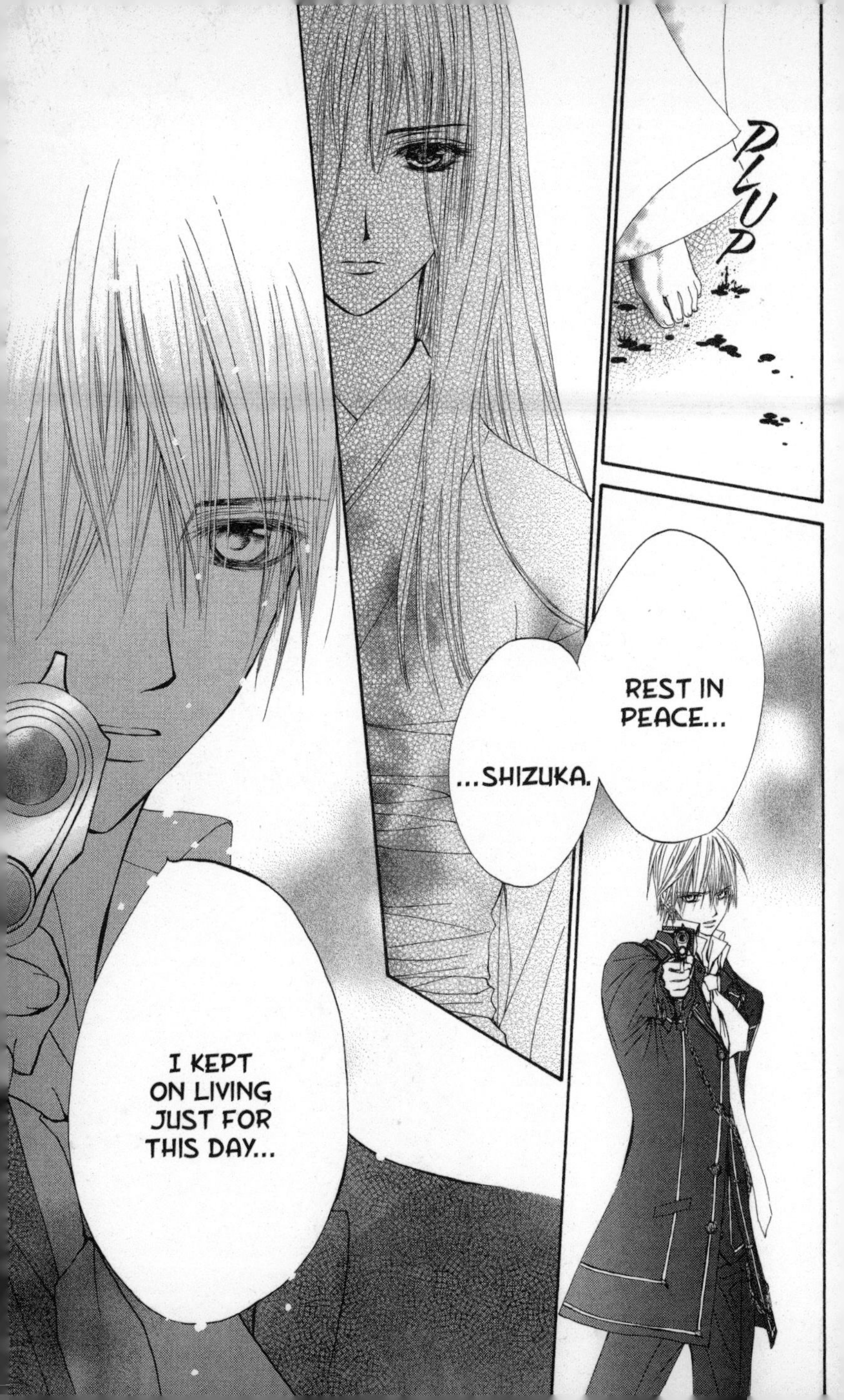
PLUP
REST IN PEACE...
...SHIZUKA.
I KEPT ON LIVING JUST FOR THIS DAY...

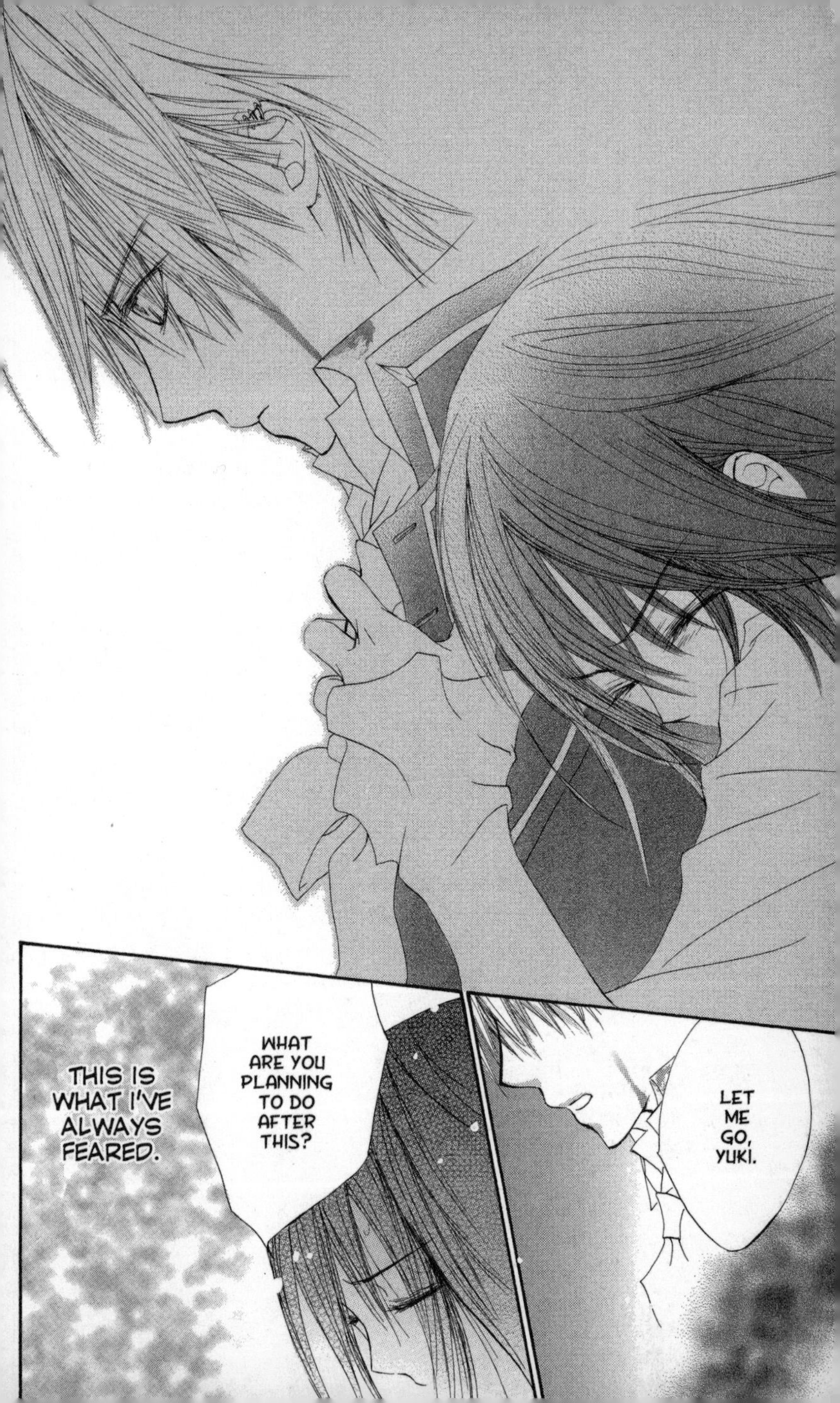
LET ME GO, YUKI.
WHAT ARE YOU PLANNING TO DO AFTER THIS?
THIS IS WHAT I'VE ALWAYS FEARED.

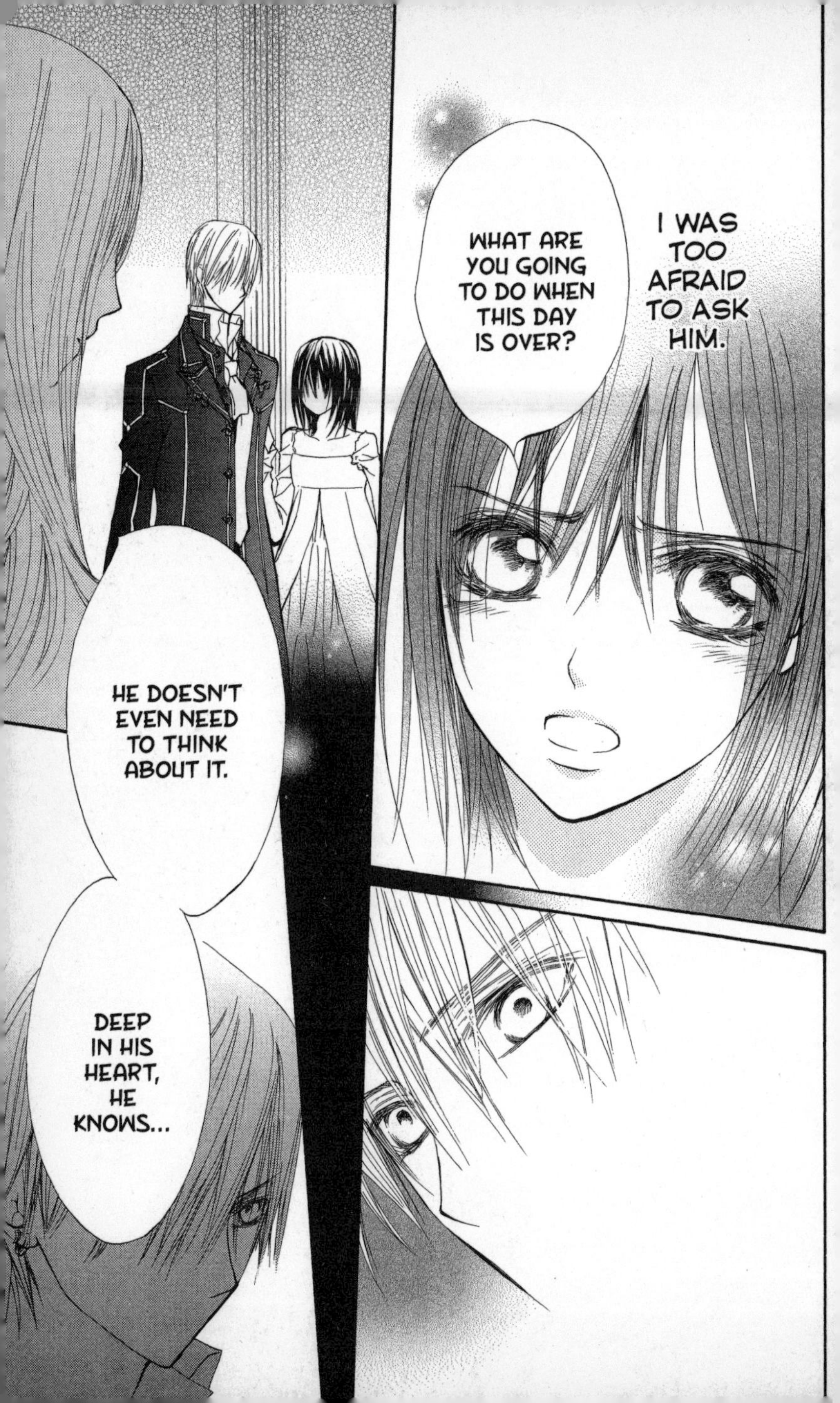
WHAT ARE YOU GOING TO DO WHEN THIS DAY IS OVER?
I WAS TOO AFRAID TO ASK HIM.
HE DOESN'T EVEN NEED TO THINK ABOUT IT.
DEEP IN HIS HEART, HE KNOWS...

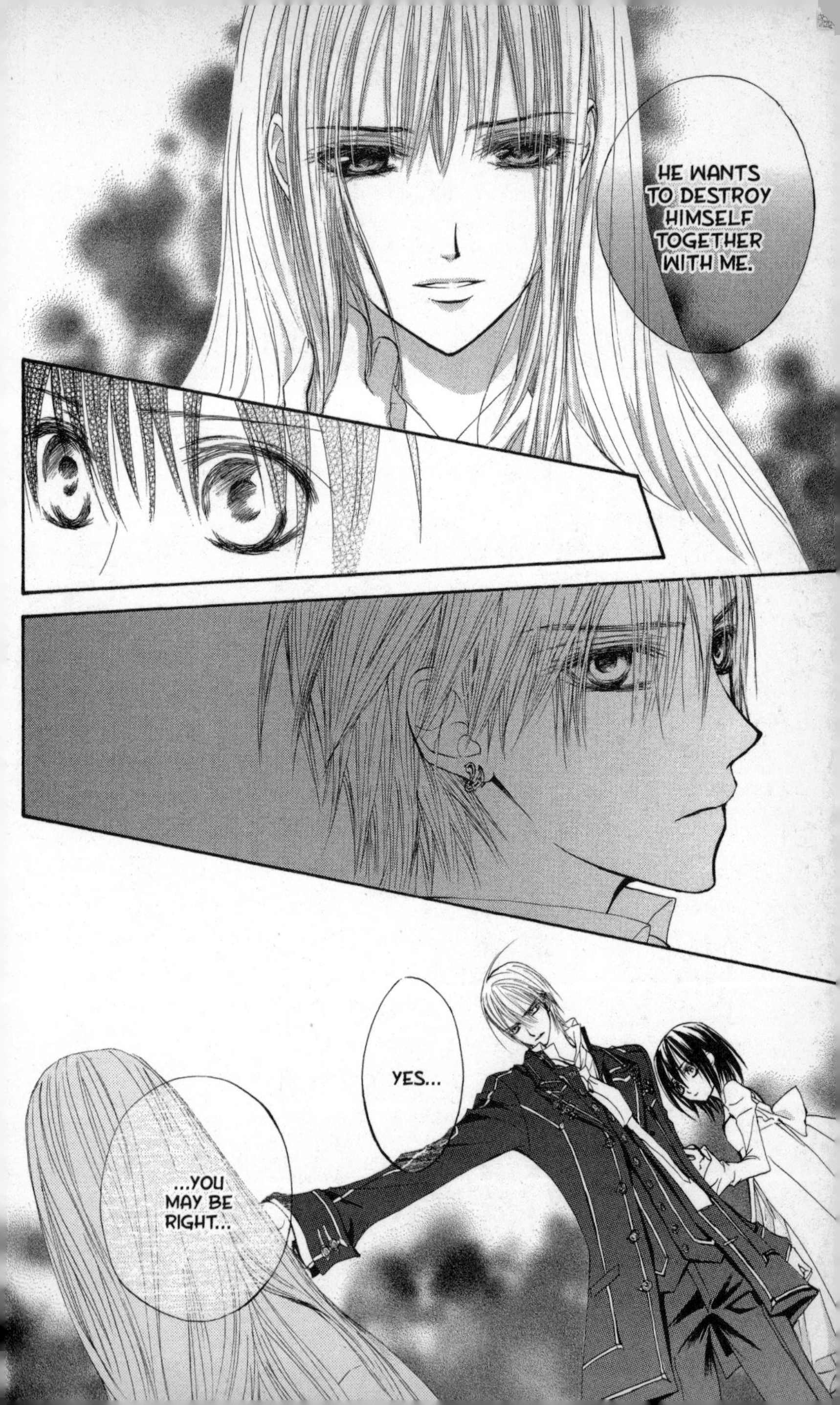
HE WANTS TO DESTROY HIMSELF TOGETHER WITH ME.
YES...
...YOU MAY BE RIGHT...

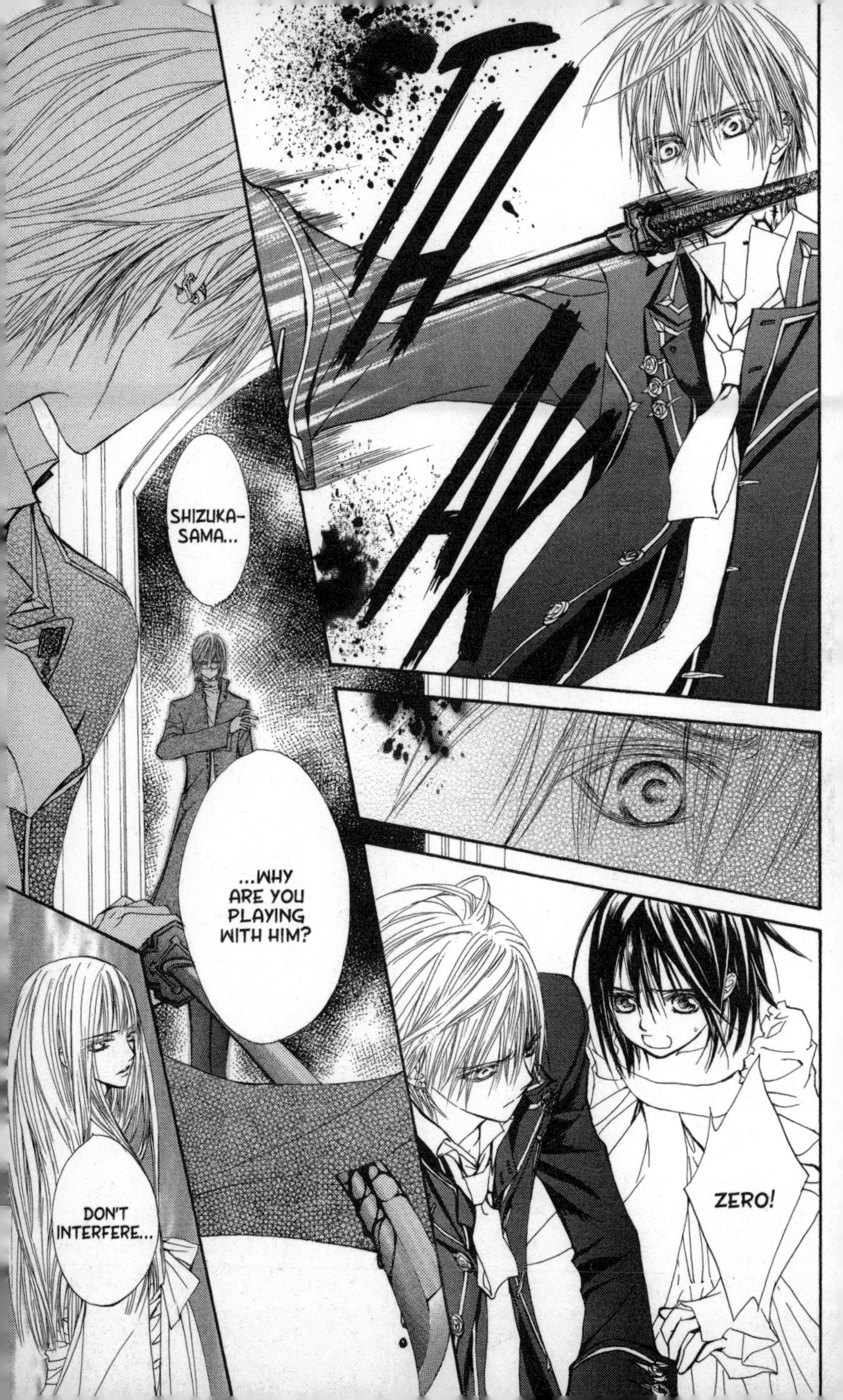
ZERO!
SHIZUKA-SAMA...
...WHY ARE YOU PLAYING WITH HIM?
DON'T INTERFERE...

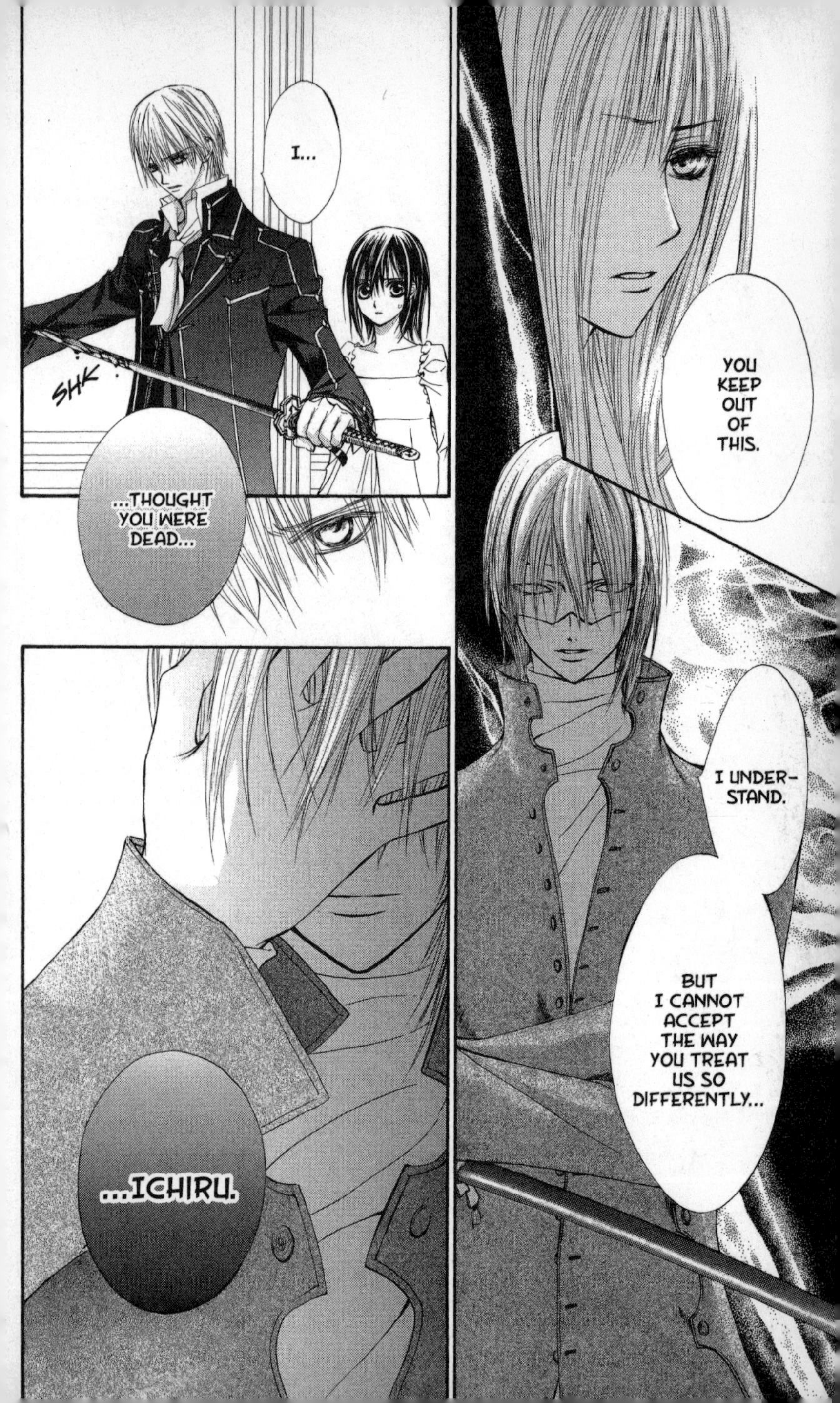
YOU KEEP OUT OF THIS.
I UNDERSTAND.
BUT I CANNOT ACCEPT THE WAY YOU TREAT US SO DIFFERENTLY...
I...
SHK
...THOUGHT YOU WERE DEAD...
...ICHIRU.

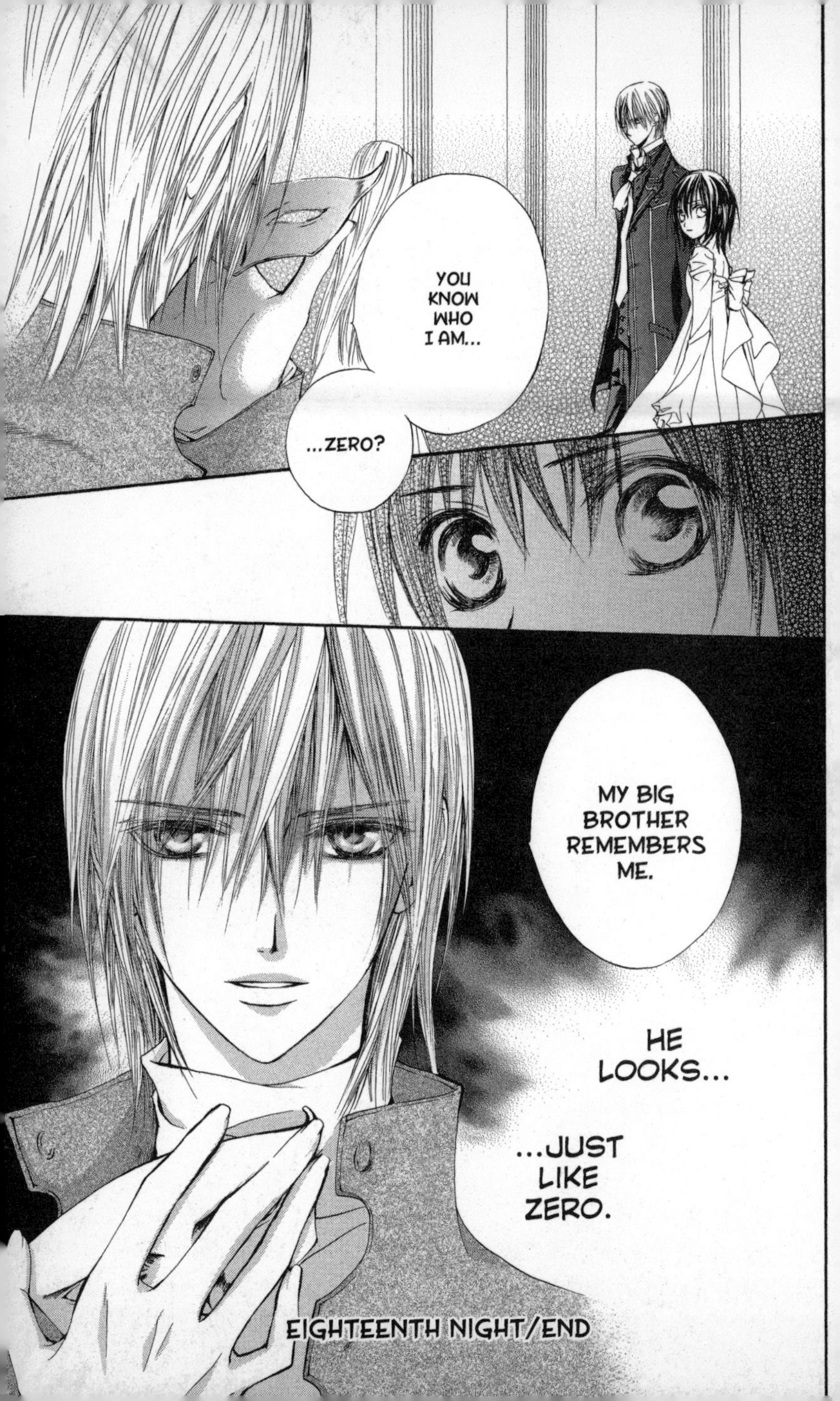
YOU KNOW WHO I AM...
...ZERO?
MY BIG BROTHER REMEMBERS ME.
HE LOOKS...
...JUST LIKE ZERO.
EIGHTEENTH NIGHT/END

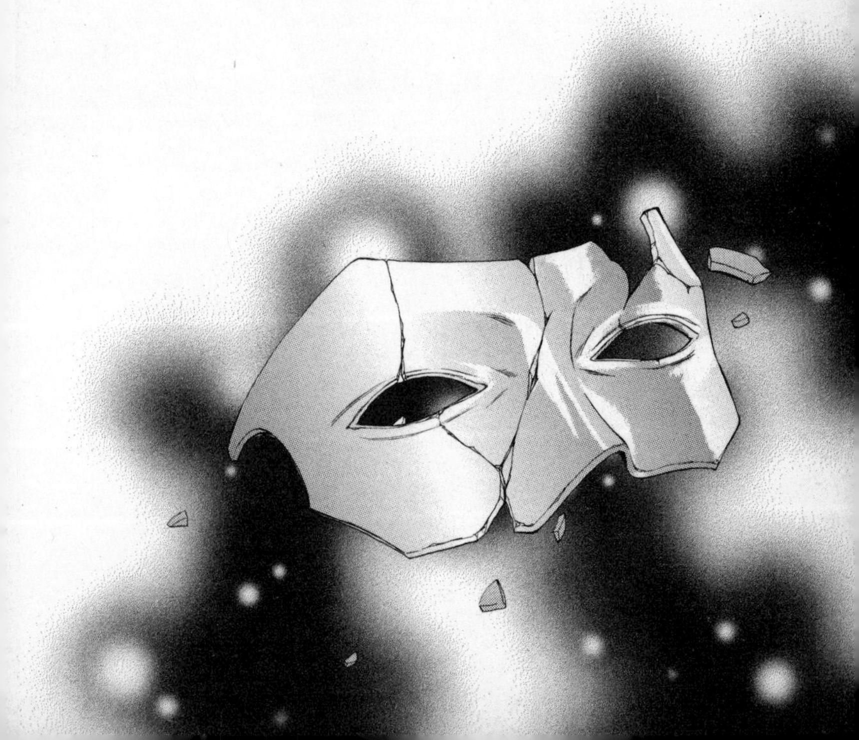

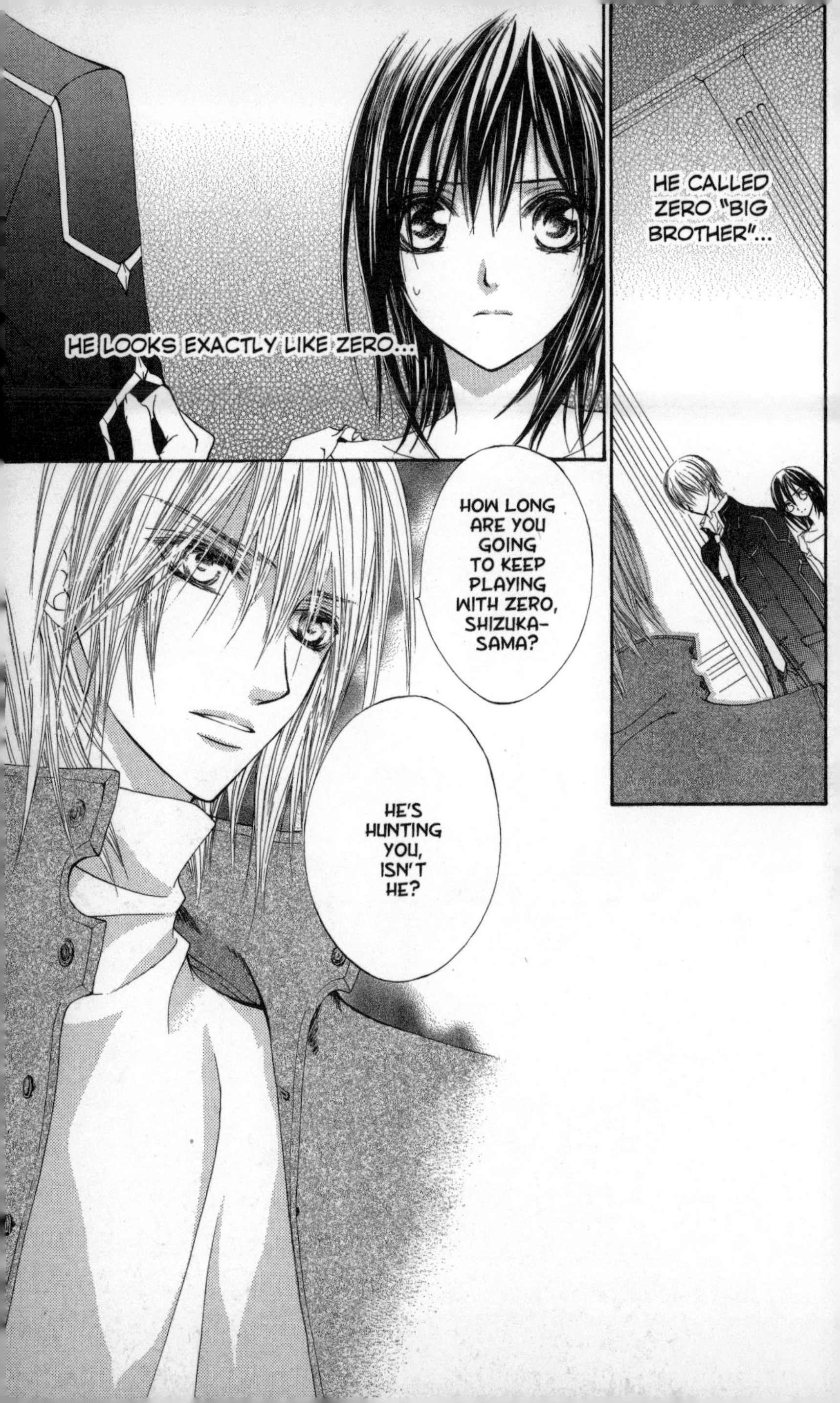
HE CALLED ZERO "BIG BROTHER"...
HE LOOKS EXACTLY LIKE ZERO...
HOW LONG ARE YOU GOING TO KEEP PLAYING WITH ZERO, SHIZUKA-SAMA?
HE'S HUNTING YOU, ISN'T HE?

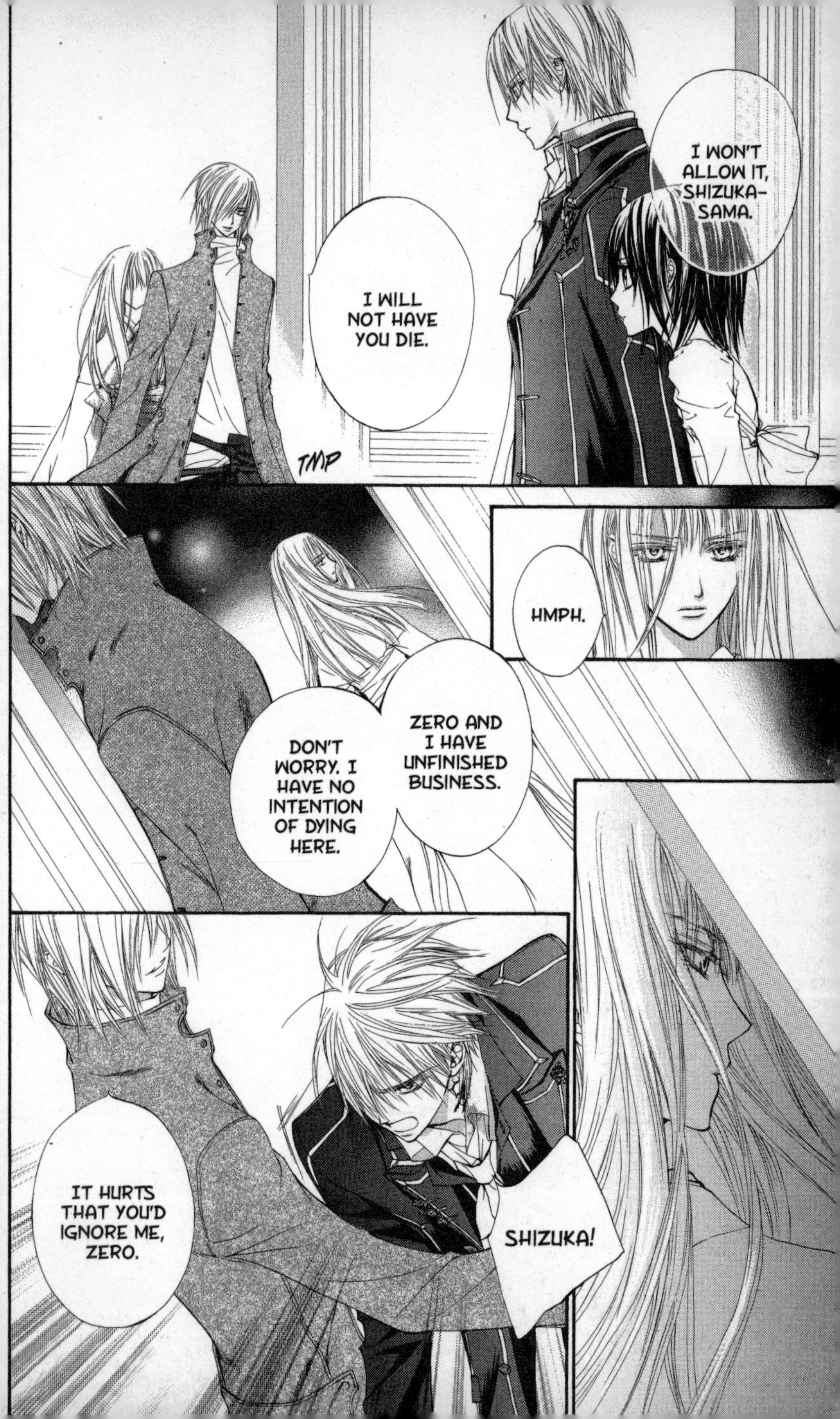
I WON'T ALLOW IT, SHIZUKA-SAMA.
I WILL NOT HAVE YOU DIE.
TMP
HMPH.
ZERO AND I HAVE UNFINISHED BUSINESS.
DON'T WORRY. I HAVE NO INTENTION OF DYING HERE.
SHIZUKA!
IT HURTS THAT YOU'D IGNORE ME, ZERO.

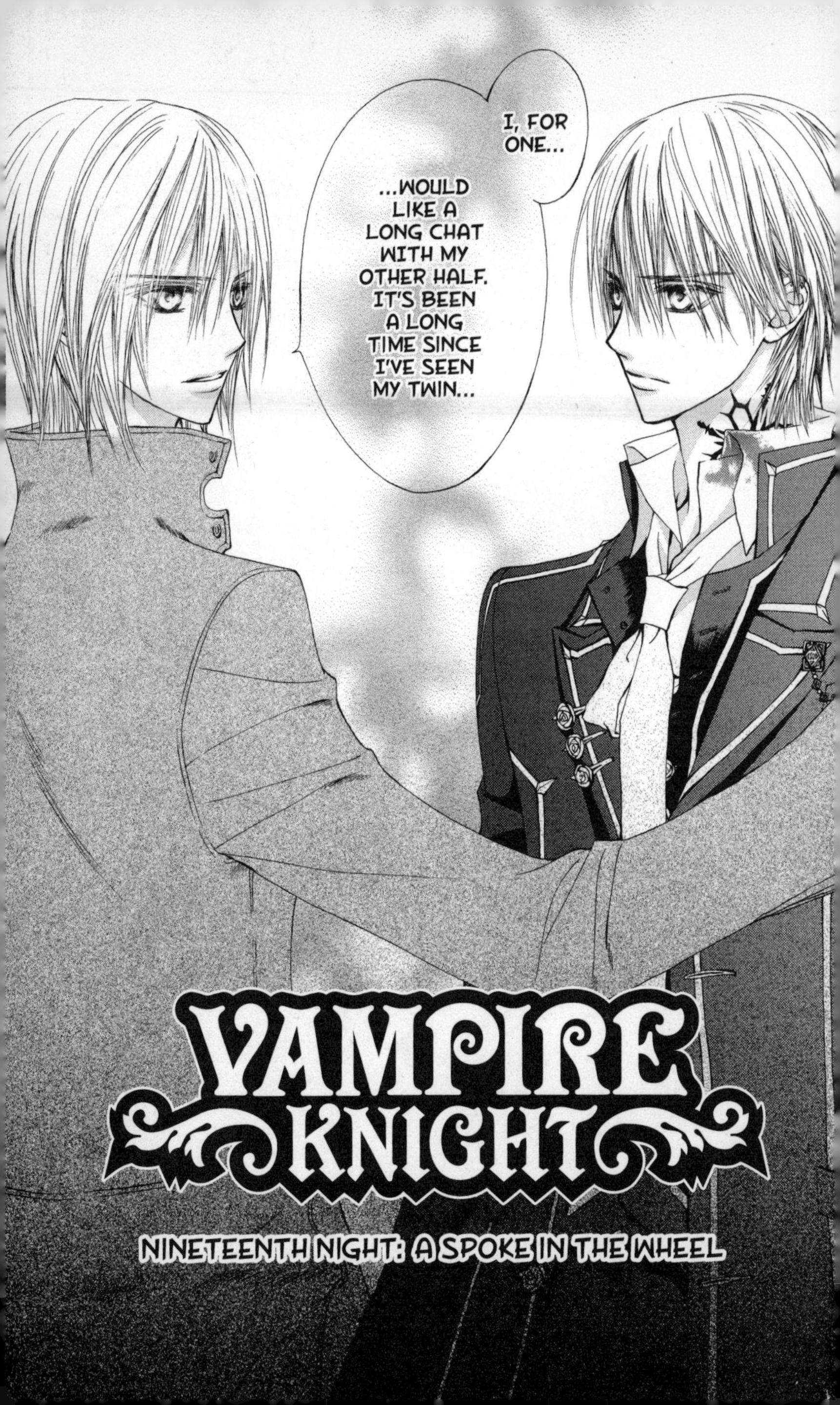
I, FOR ONE...
...WOULD LIKE A LONG CHAT WITH MY OTHER HALF. IT'S BEEN A LONG TIME SINCE I'VE SEEN MY TWIN...
VAMPIRE KNIGHT
NINETEENTH NIGHT: A SPOKE IN THE WHEEL

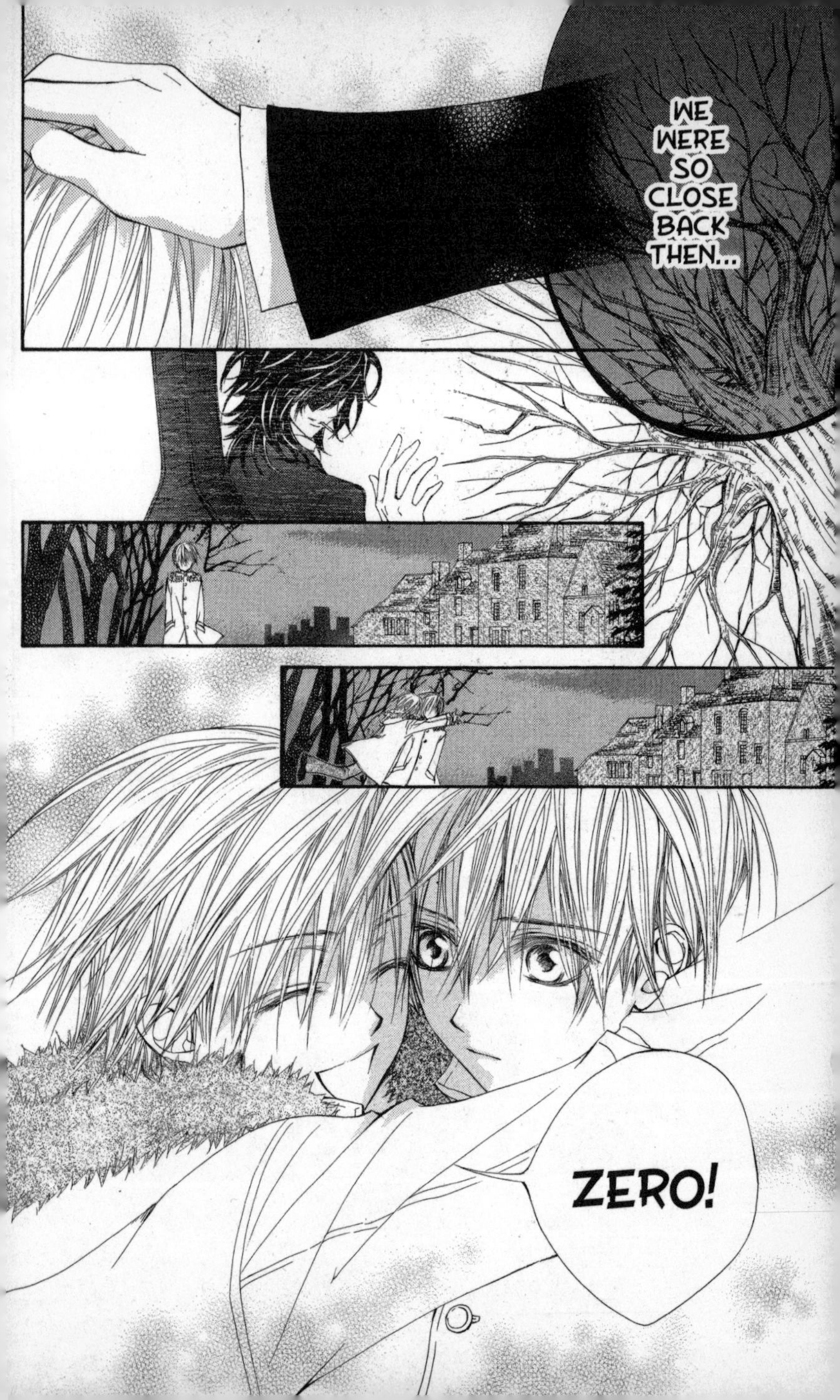
WE WERE SO CLOSE BACK THEN...
ZERO!

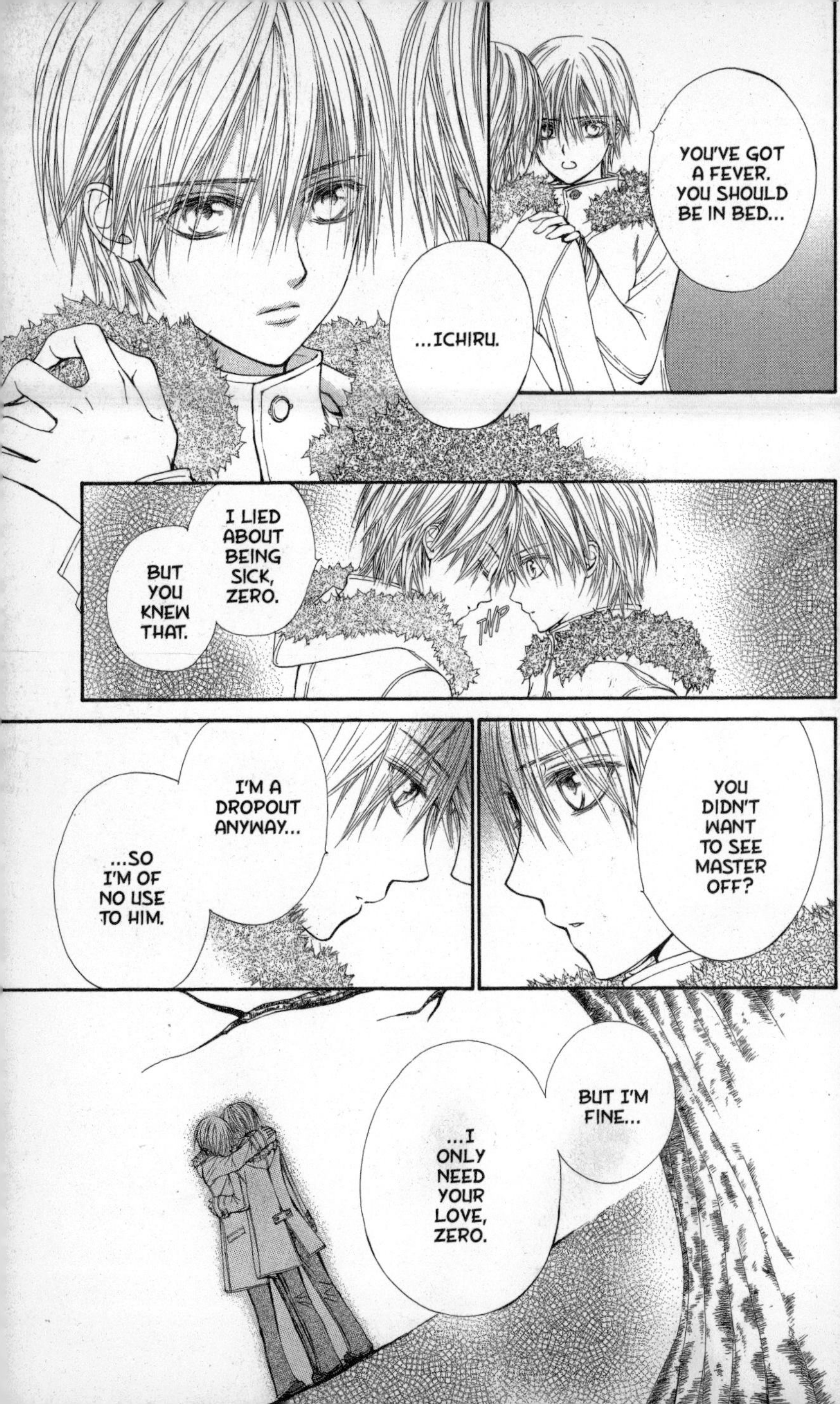
YOU'VE GOT A FEVER. YOU SHOULD BE IN BED...
...ICHIRU.
I LIED ABOUT BEING SICK, ZERO.
BUT YOU KNEW THAT.
TMP
YOU DIDN'T WANT TO SEE MASTER OFF?
I'M A DROPOUT ANYWAY...
...SO I'M OF NO USE TO HIM.
BUT I'M FINE...
...I ONLY NEED YOUR LOVE, ZERO.

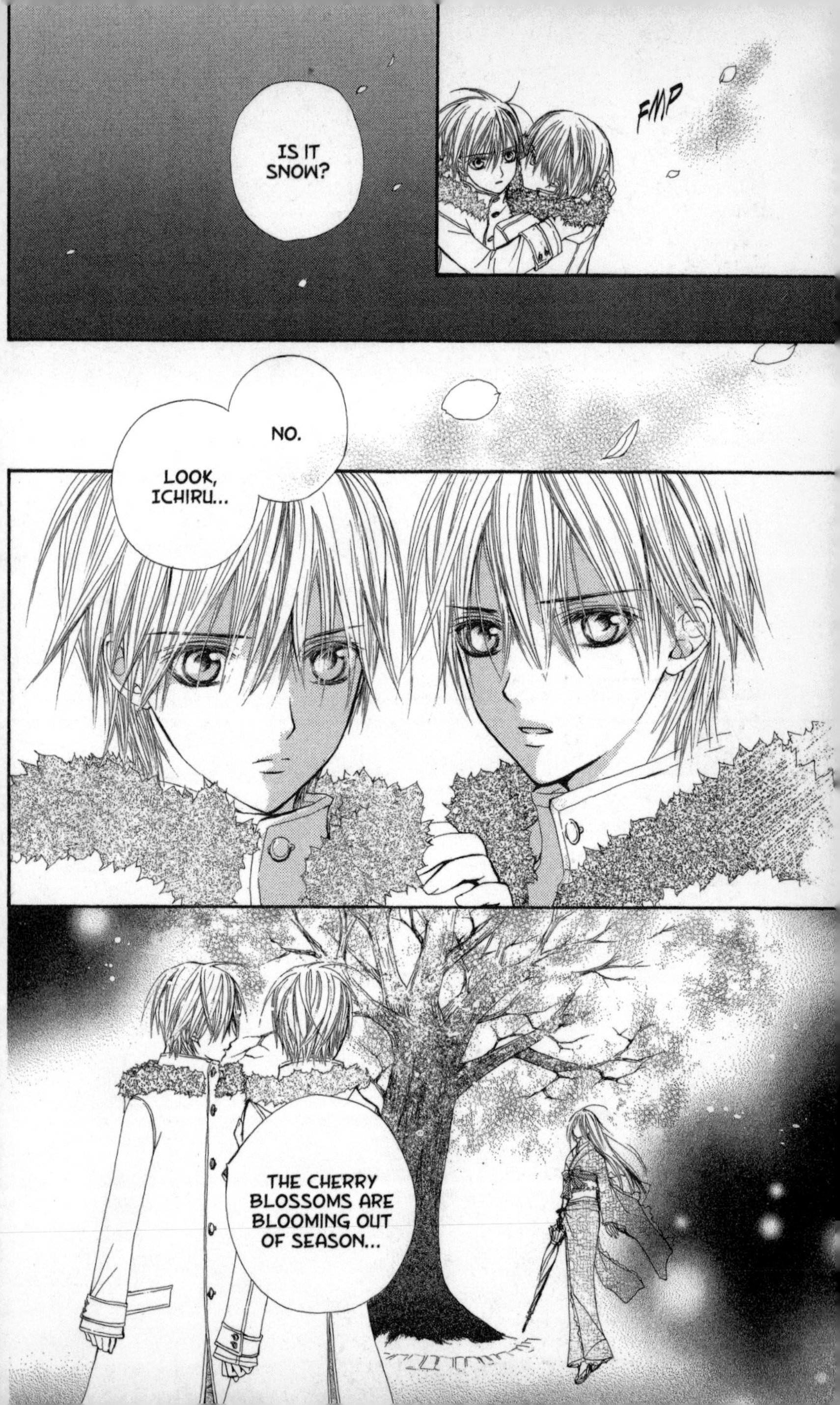
FMP
IS IT SNOW?
NO.
LOOK, ICHIRU...
THE CHERRY BLOSSOMS ARE BLOOMING OUT OF SEASON...

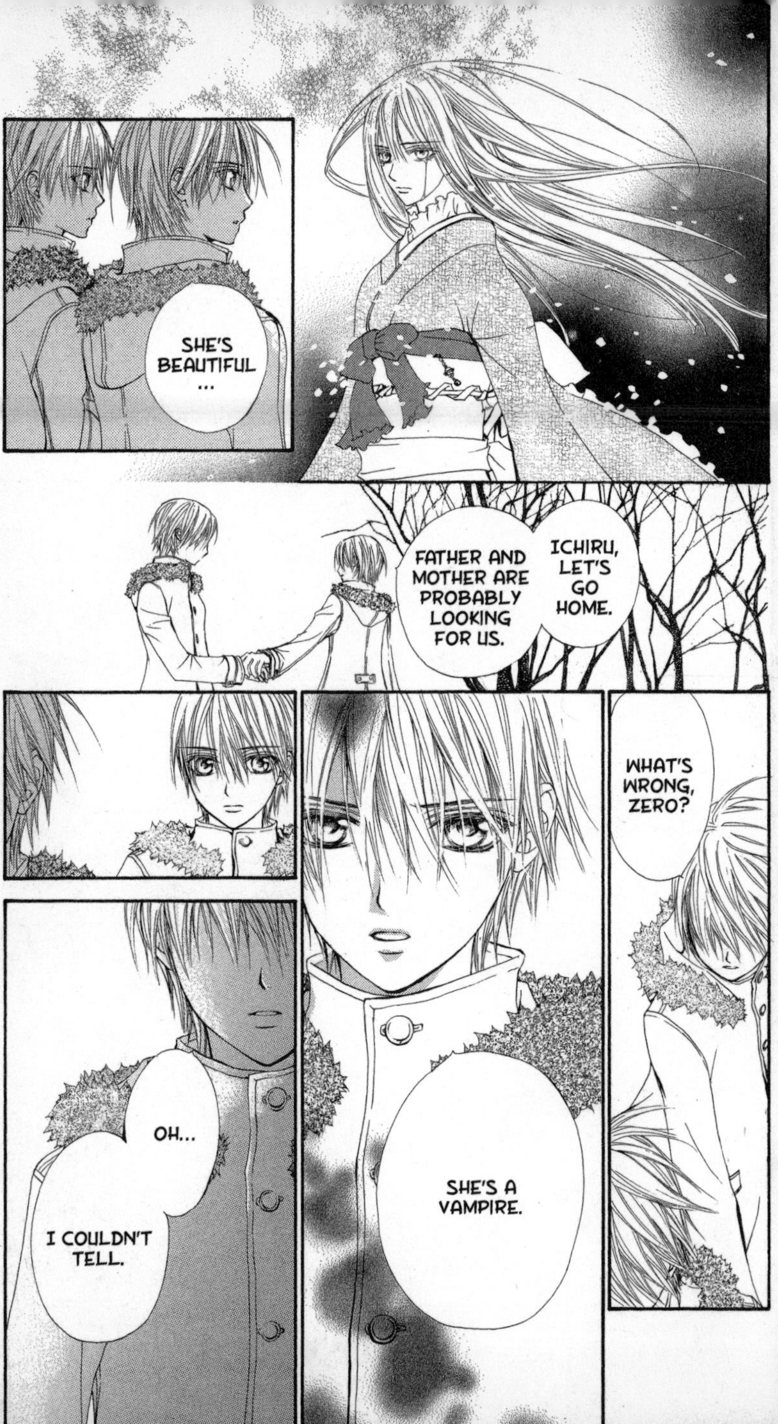
SHE'S BEAUTIFUL ...
ICHIRU, LET'S GO HOME.
FATHER AND MOTHER ARE PROBABLY LOOKING FOR US.
WHAT'S WRONG, ZERO?
SHE'S A VAMPIRE.
OH...
I COULDN'T TELL.

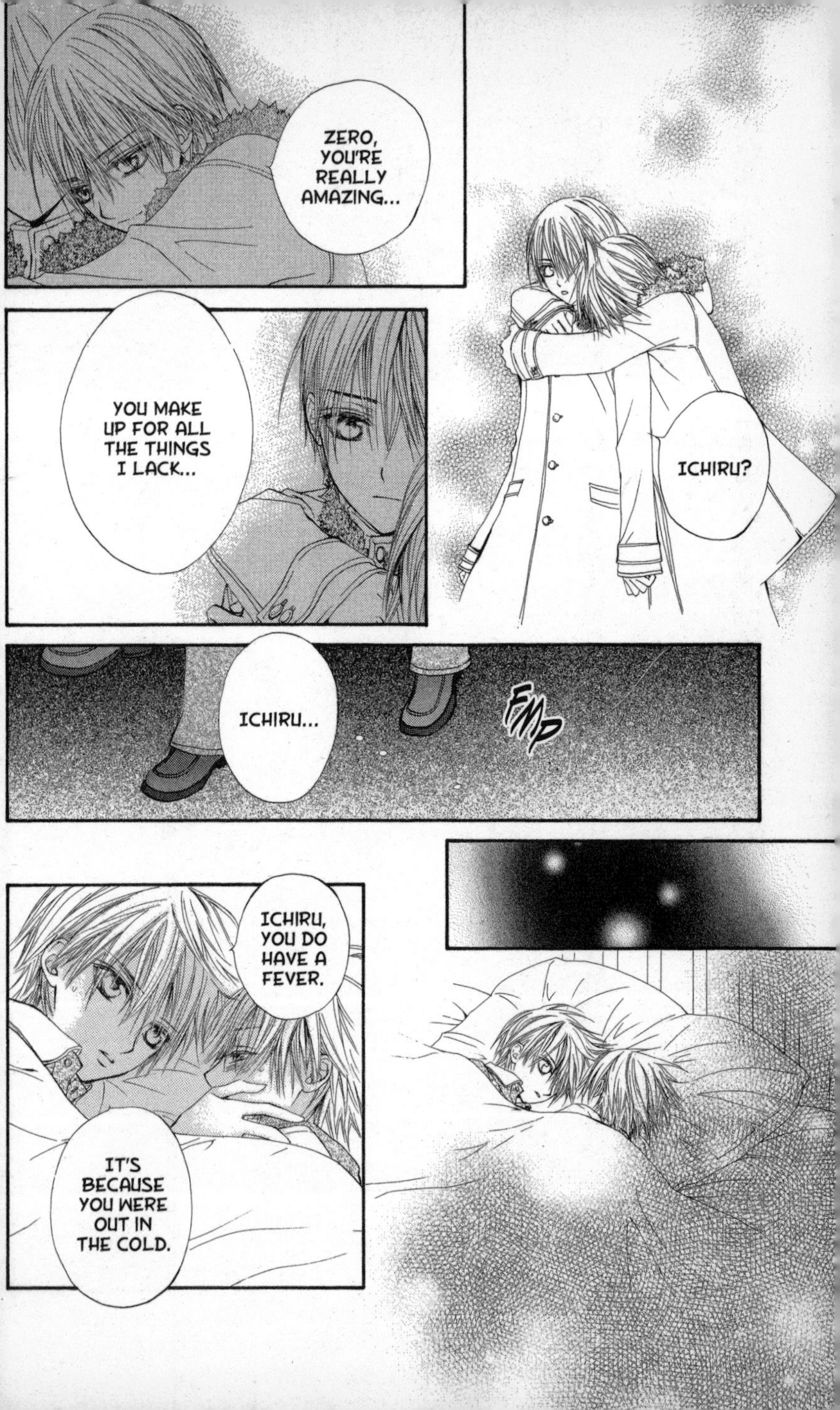
ICHIRU?
ZERO, YOU'RE REALLY AMAZING...
YOU MAKE UP FOR ALL THE THINGS I LACK...
FMP
ICHIRU...
ICHIRU, YOU DO HAVE A FEVER.
IT'S BECAUSE YOU WERE OUT IN THE COLD.

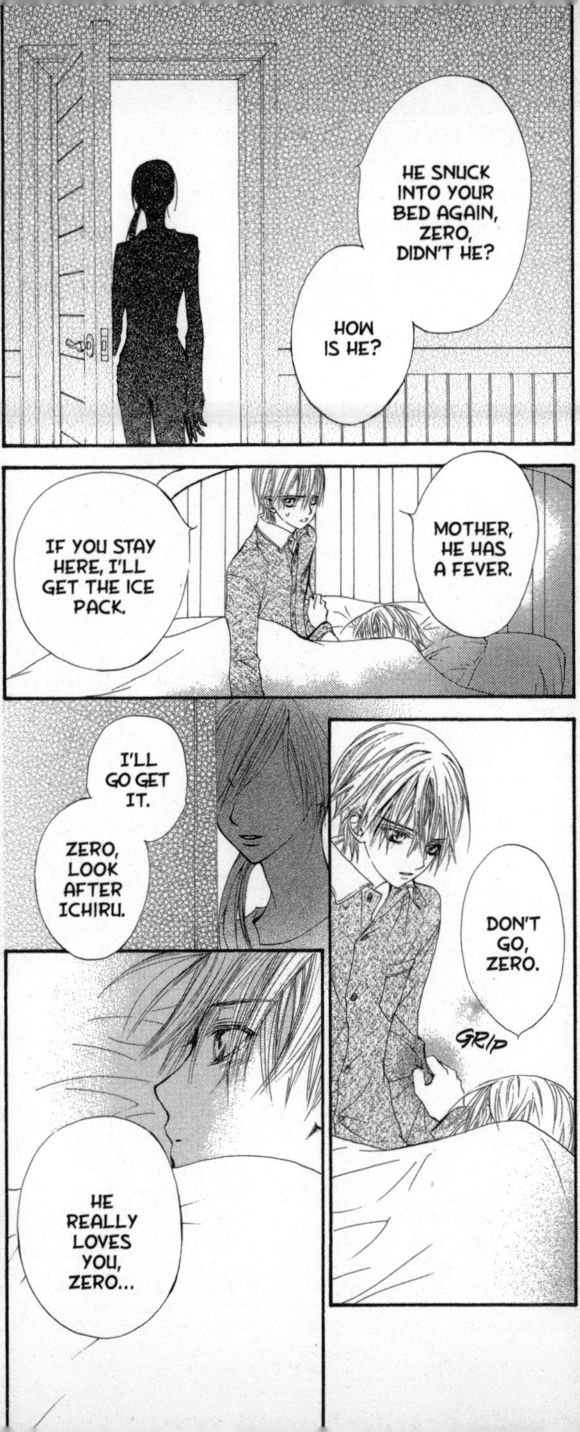
HE SNUCK INTO YOUR BED AGAIN, ZERO, DIDN'T HE?
HOW IS HE?
MOTHER, HE HAS A FEVER.
IF YOU STAY HERE, I'LL GET THE ICE PACK.
I'LL GO GET IT.
ZERO, LOOK AFTER ICHIRU.
DON'T GO, ZERO.
GRIP
HE REALLY LOVES YOU, ZERO...

## VI

This volume ends with a really surprising scene♪ that continues in volume 5. I'd be happy if you'd wait for the next volume.

And... Thank you to all the readers of Vampire Knight.

Thanks to my editor and everyone at LaLa. I made them worry and inconvenienced them...

Thanks to O. Mio-sama, K. Midori-sama, M. Kaoru-sama, who help me with my manuscripts.

And thanks to my family and friends.

I'm full of gratitude for everybody.

Because of your help, another volume made it to the world. Thank you!!

樋野まつり
Matsuri Hino

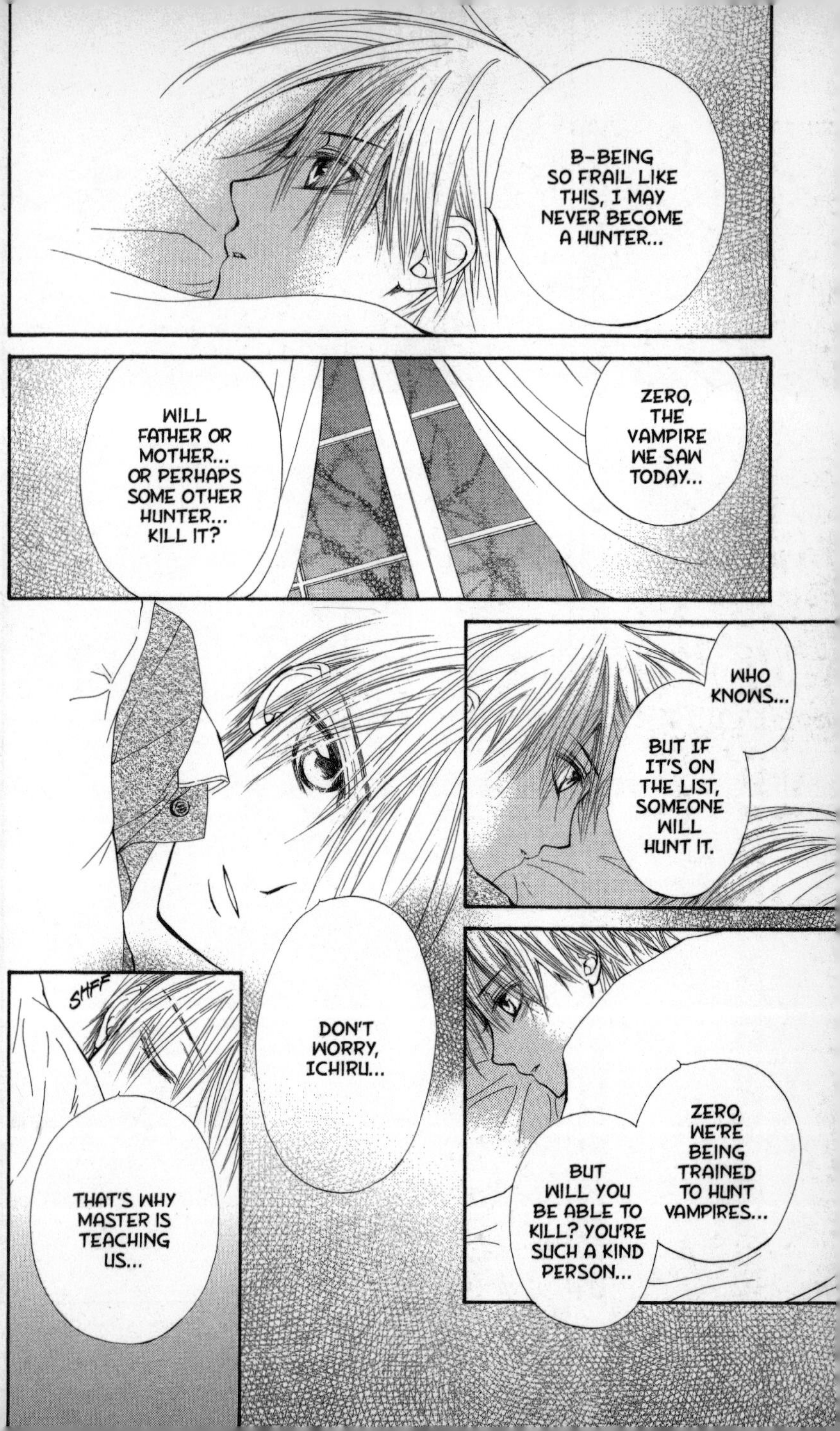
B-BEING SO FRAIL LIKE THIS, I MAY NEVER BECOME A HUNTER...
ZERO, THE VAMPIRE WE SAW TODAY...
WILL FATHER OR MOTHER... OR PERHAPS SOME OTHER HUNTER... KILL IT?
WHO KNOWS...
BUT IF IT'S ON THE LIST, SOMEONE WILL HUNT IT.
ZERO, WE'RE BEING TRAINED TO HUNT VAMPIRES...
BUT WILL YOU BE ABLE TO KILL? YOU'RE SUCH A KIND PERSON...
DON'T WORRY, ICHIRU...
SHFF
THAT'S WHY MASTER IS TEACHING US...

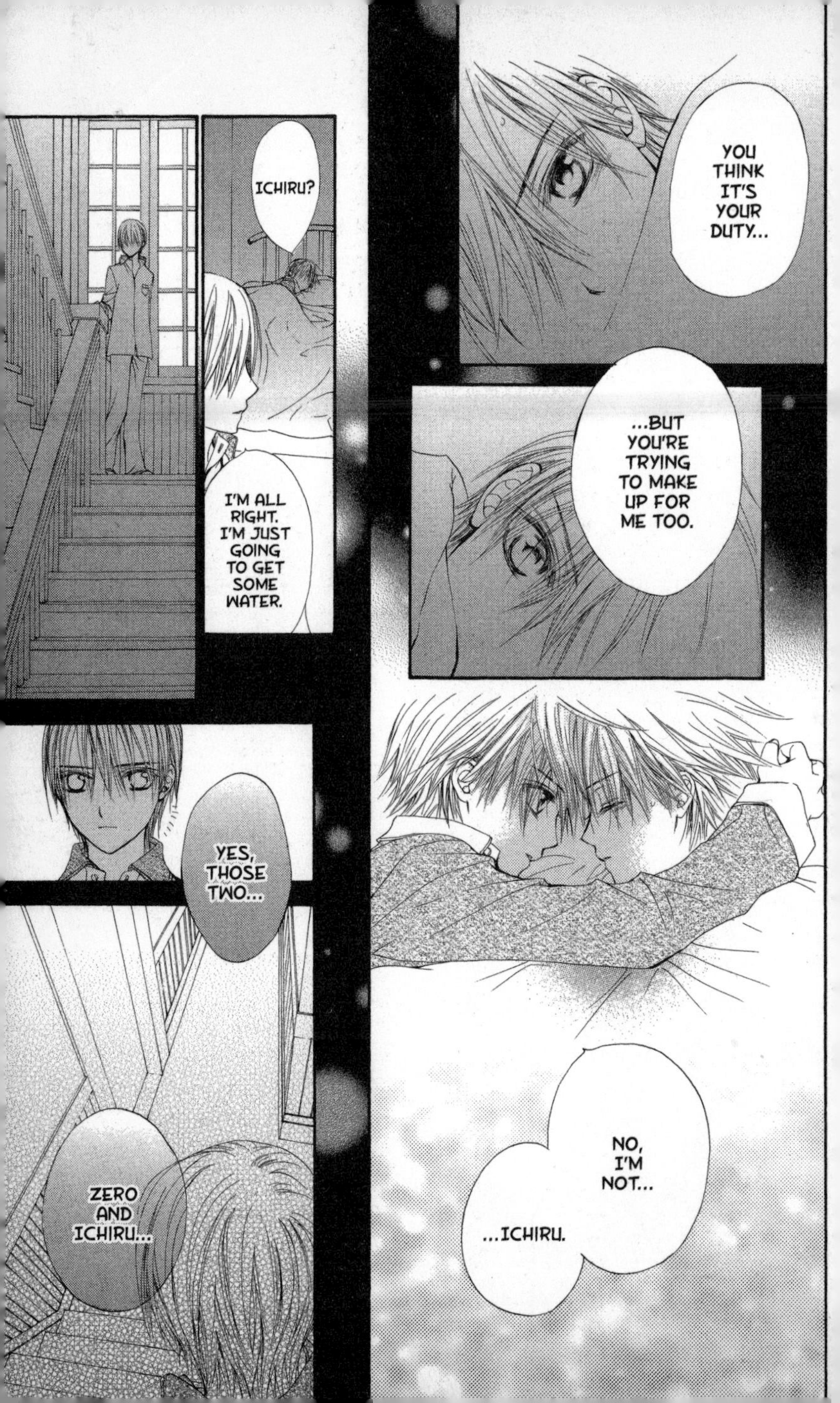
YOU THINK IT'S YOUR DUTY...
...BUT YOU'RE TRYING TO MAKE UP FOR ME TOO.
NO, I'M NOT...
...ICHIRU.
ICHIRU?
I'M ALL RIGHT. I'M JUST GOING TO GET SOME WATER.
YES, THOSE TWO...
ZERO AND ICHIRU...

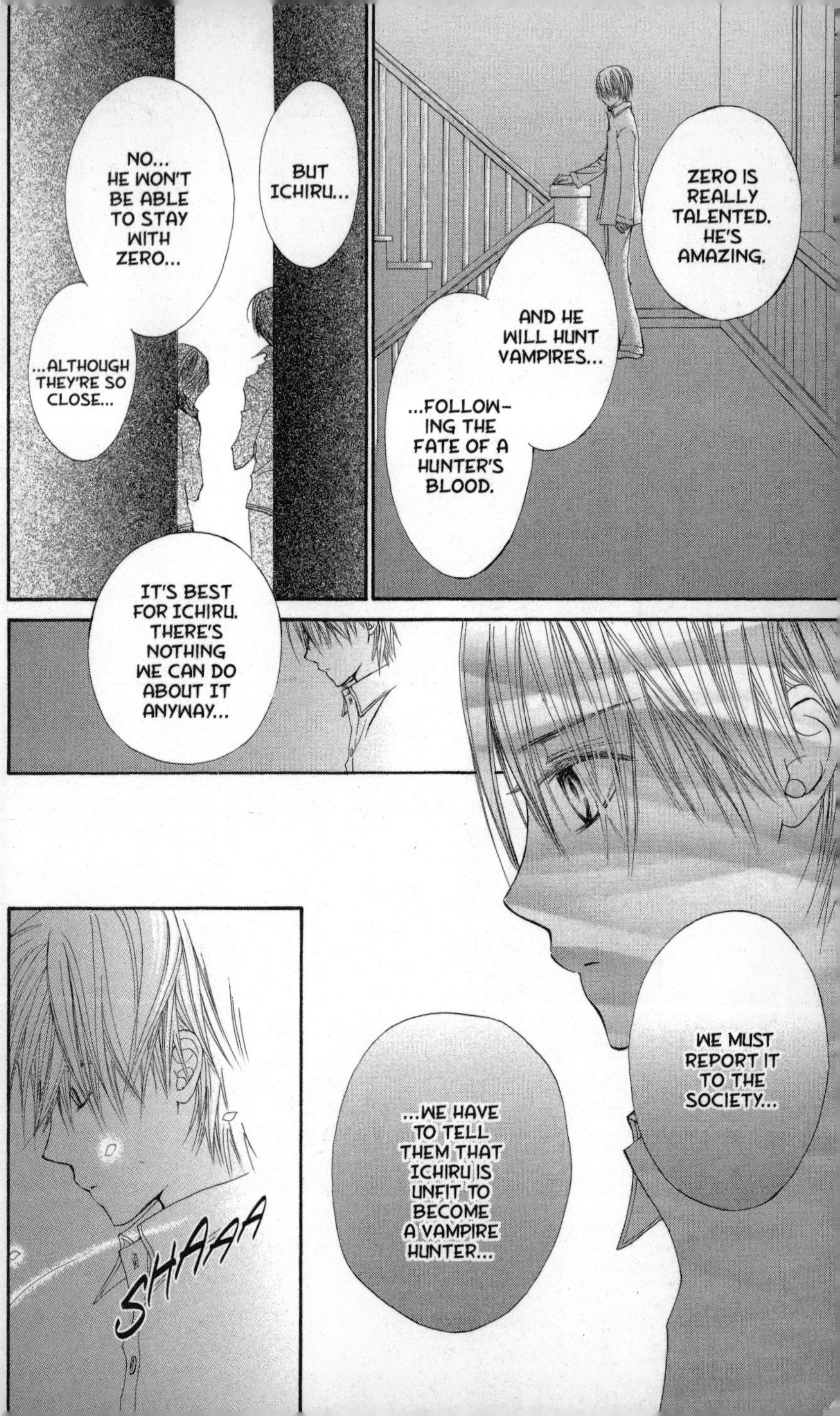
ZERO IS REALLY TALENTED. HE'S AMAZING.
AND HE WILL HUNT VAMPIRES...
...FOLLOW-ING THE FATE OF A HUNTER'S BLOOD.
BUT ICHIRU...
NO... HE WON'T BE ABLE TO STAY WITH ZERO...
...ALTHOUGH THEY'RE SO CLOSE...
IT'S BEST FOR ICHIRU. THERE'S NOTHING WE CAN DO ABOUT IT ANYWAY...
WE MUST REPORT IT TO THE SOCIETY...
...WE HAVE TO TELL THEM THAT ICHIRU IS UNFIT TO BECOME A VAMPIRE HUNTER...
SHAAA

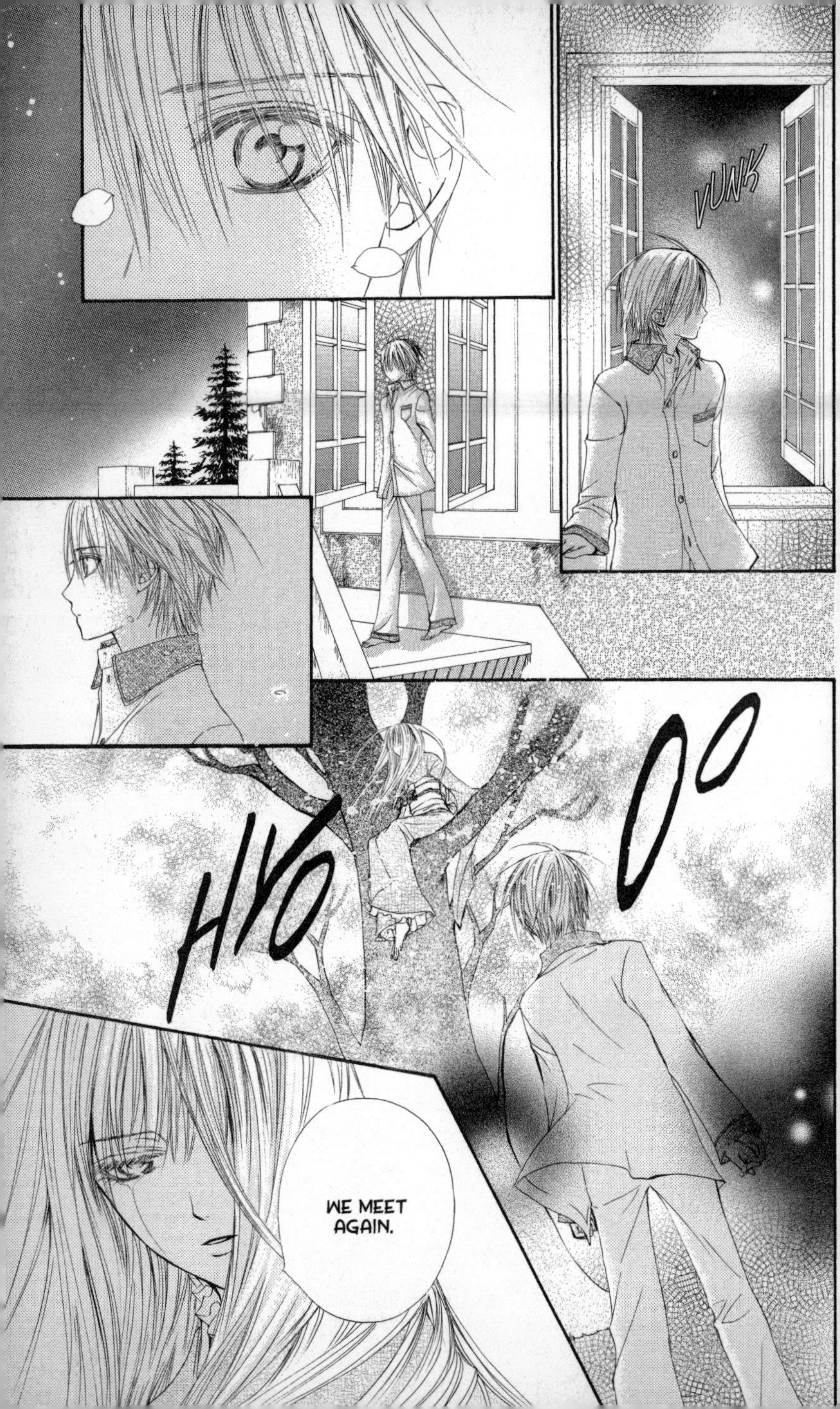
VUNK
HYO
OO
WE MEET AGAIN.

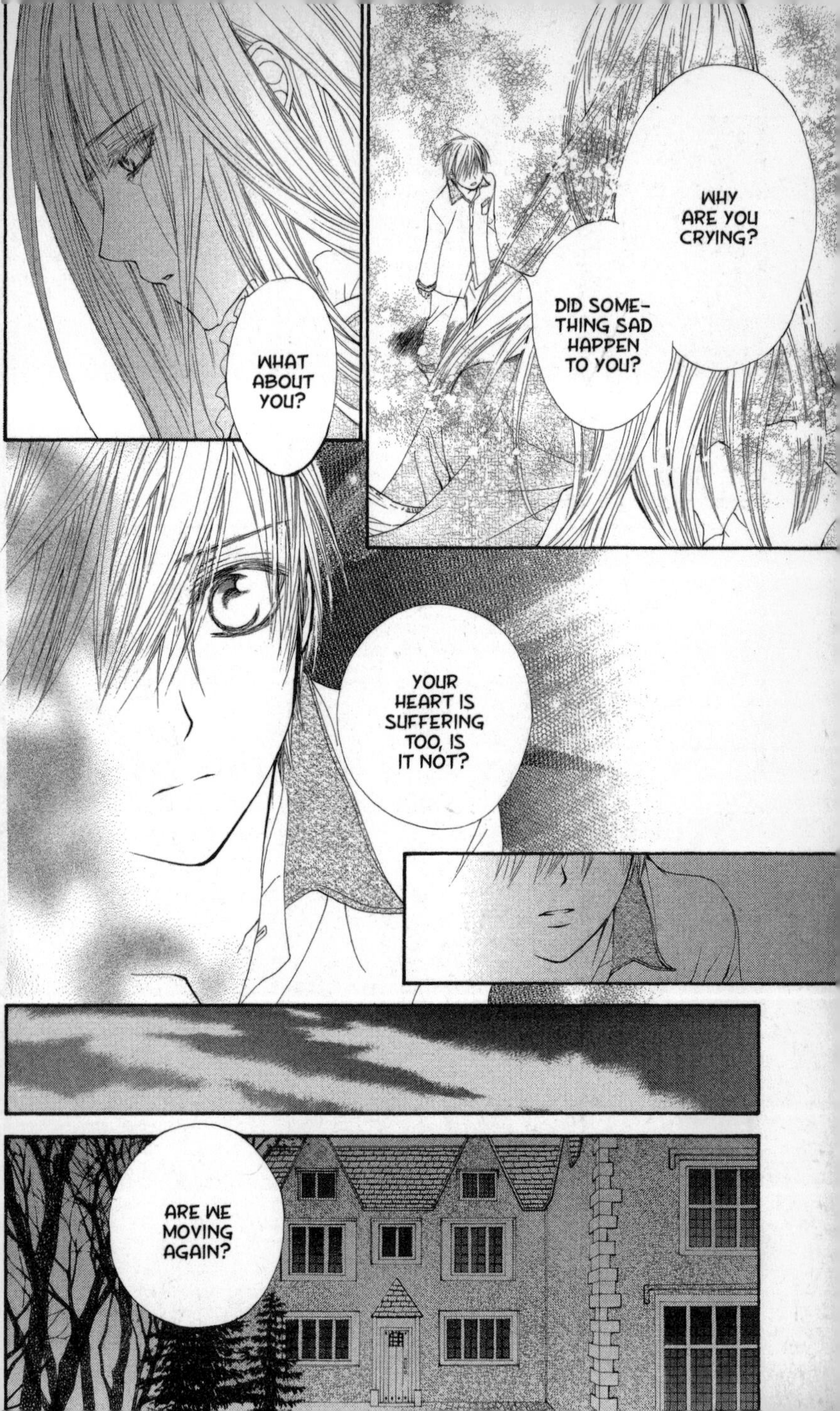
WHY ARE YOU CRYING?
DID SOME-THING SAD HAPPEN TO YOU?
WHAT ABOUT YOU?
YOUR HEART IS SUFFERING TOO, IS IT NOT?
ARE WE MOVING AGAIN?

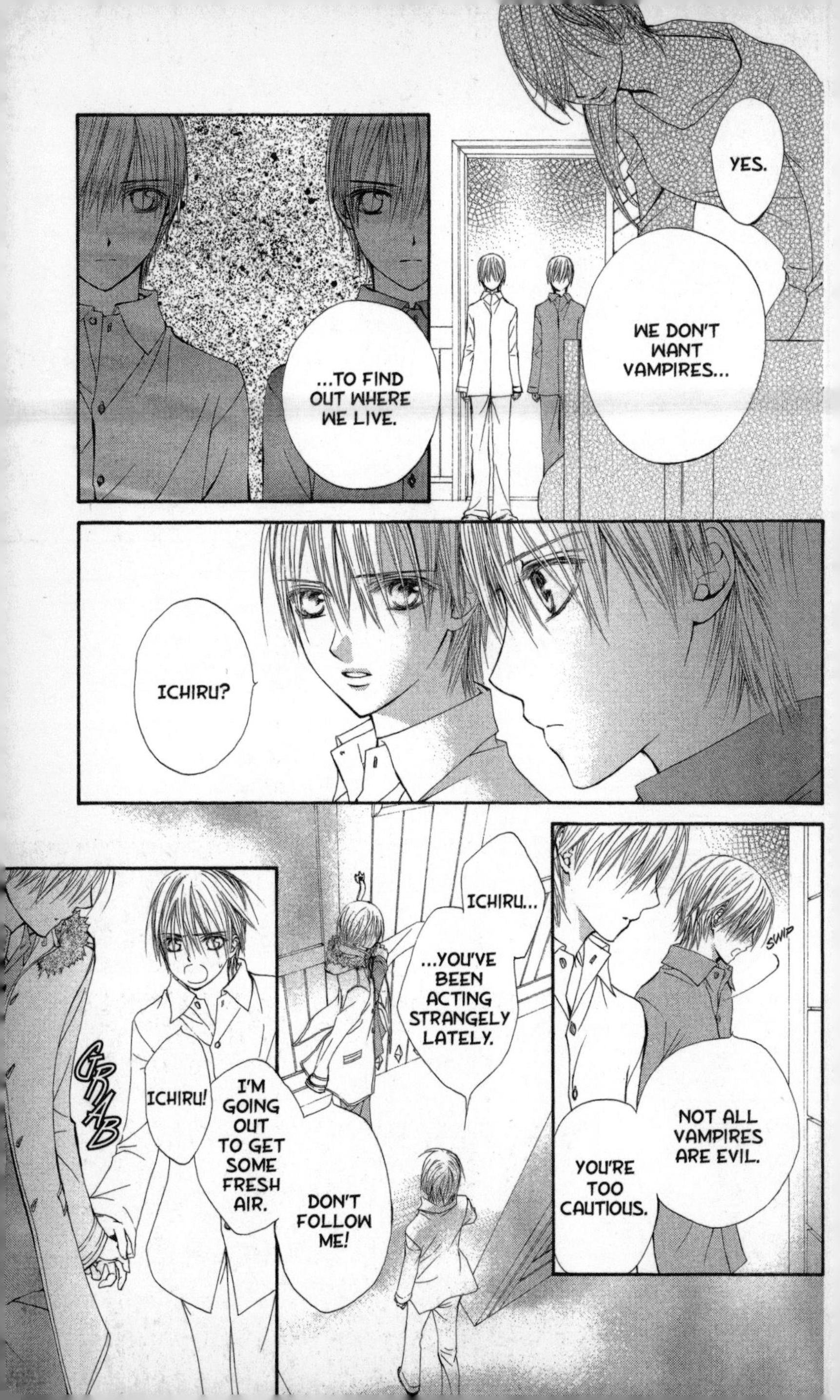
YES.
WE DON'T WANT VAMPIRES...
...TO FIND OUT WHERE WE LIVE.
ICHIRU?
SWIP
NOT ALL VAMPIRES ARE EVIL.
YOU'RE TOO CAUTIOUS.
ICHIRU...
...YOU'VE BEEN ACTING STRANGELY LATELY.
I'M GOING OUT TO GET SOME FRESH AIR.
DON'T FOLLOW ME!
ICHIRU!
GRAB

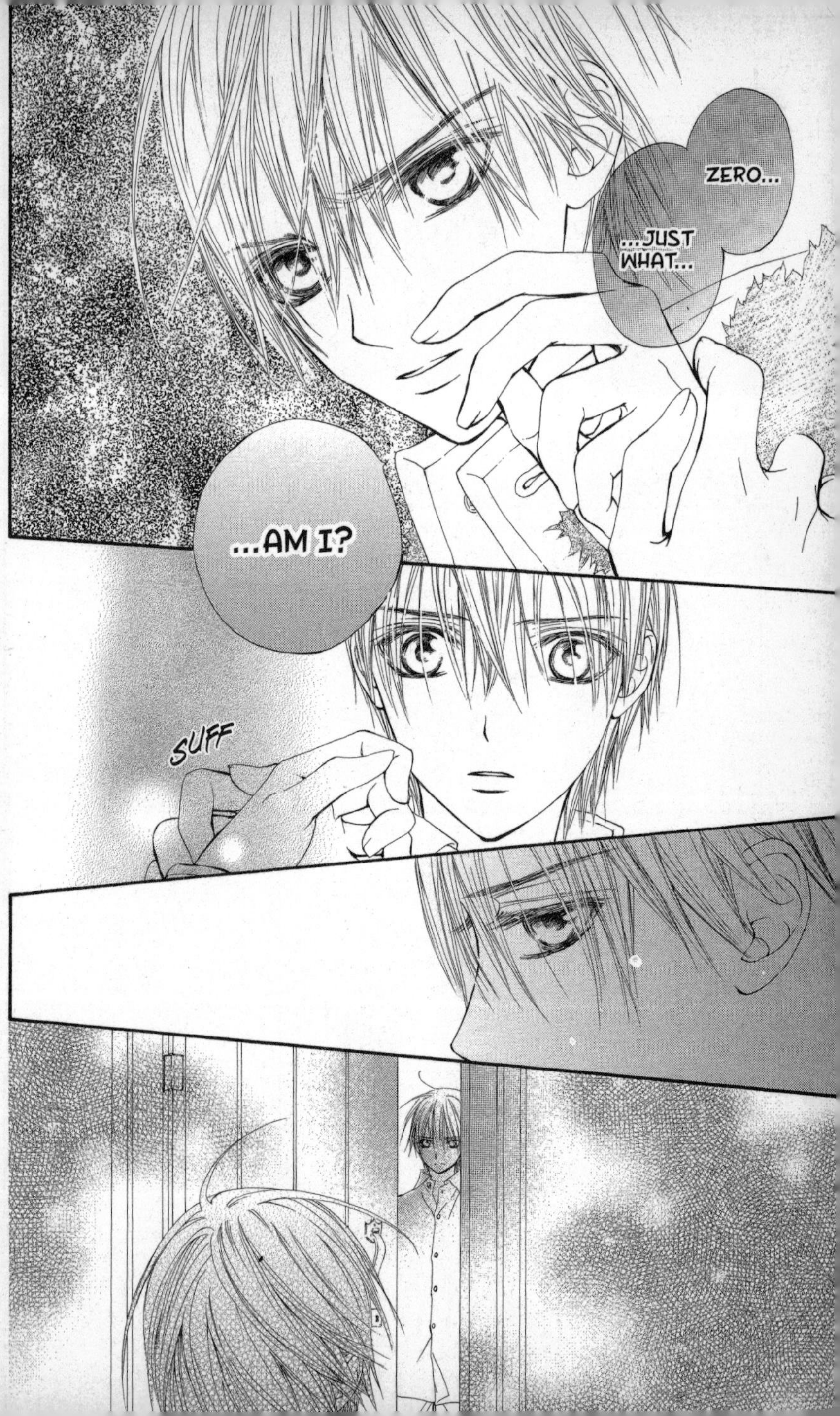
ZERO...
...JUST WHAT...
...AM I?
SUFF

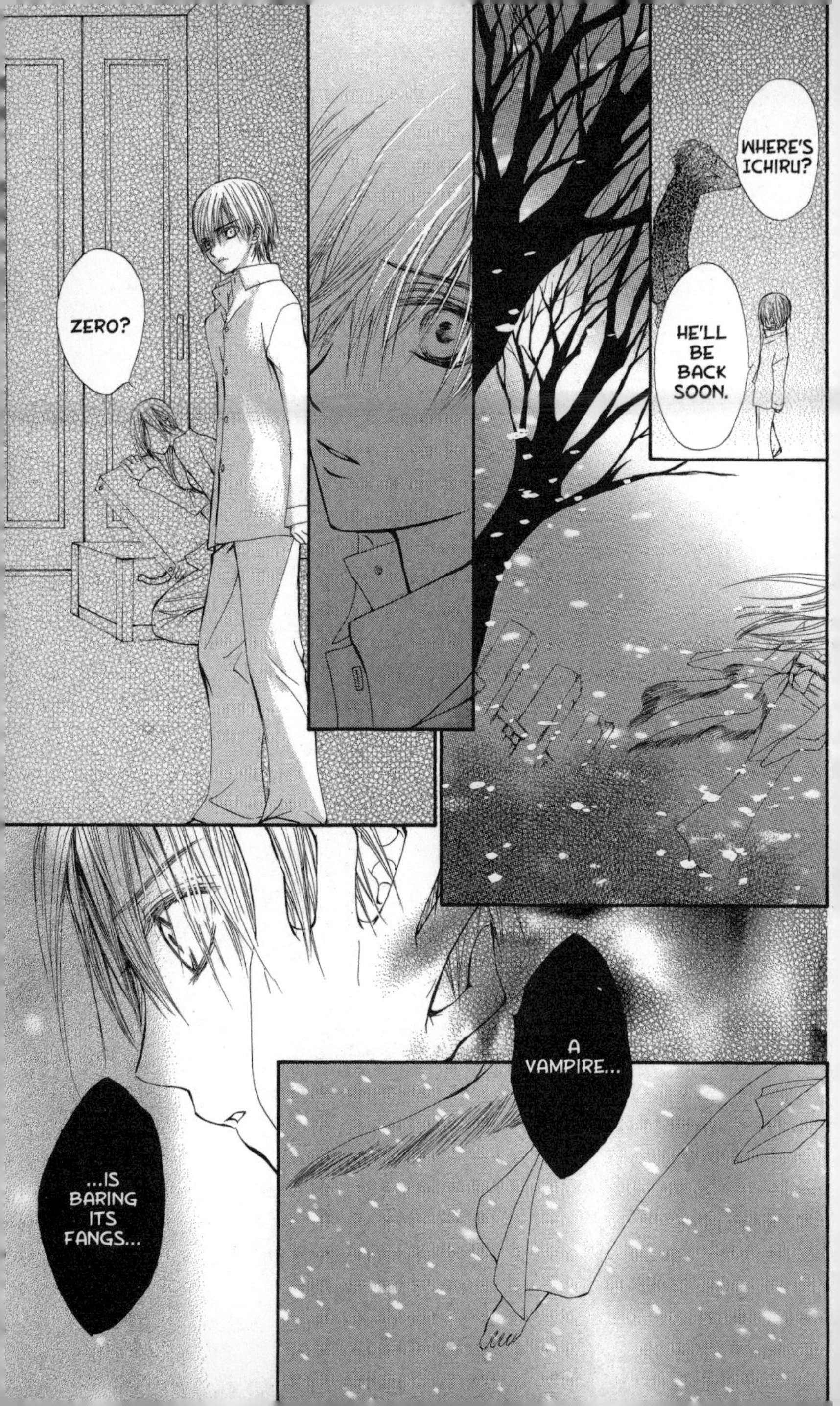
WHERE'S ICHIRU?
HE'LL BE BACK SOON.
ZERO?
A VAMPIRE...
...IS BARING ITS FANGS...

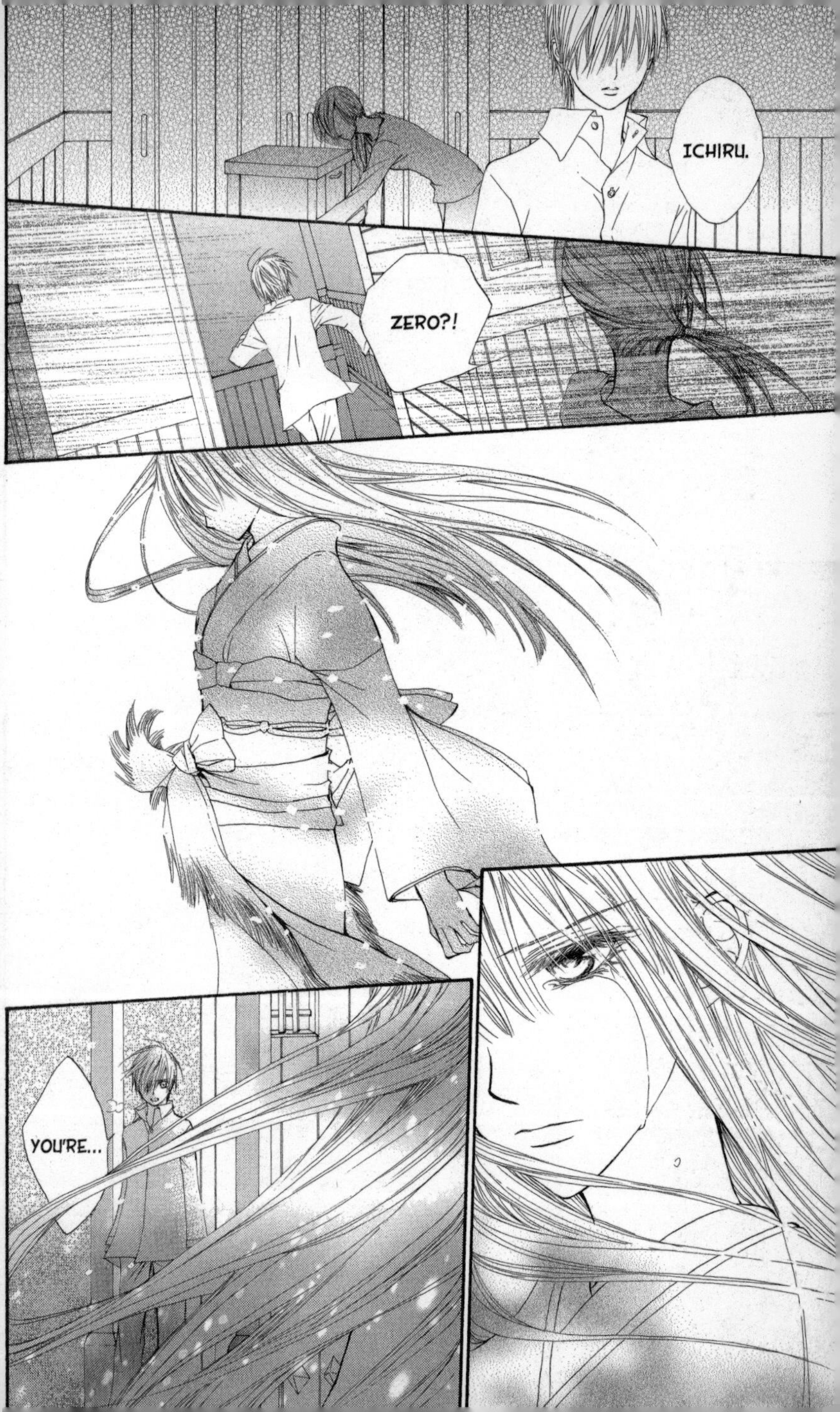
ICHIRU.
ZERO?!
YOU'RE...

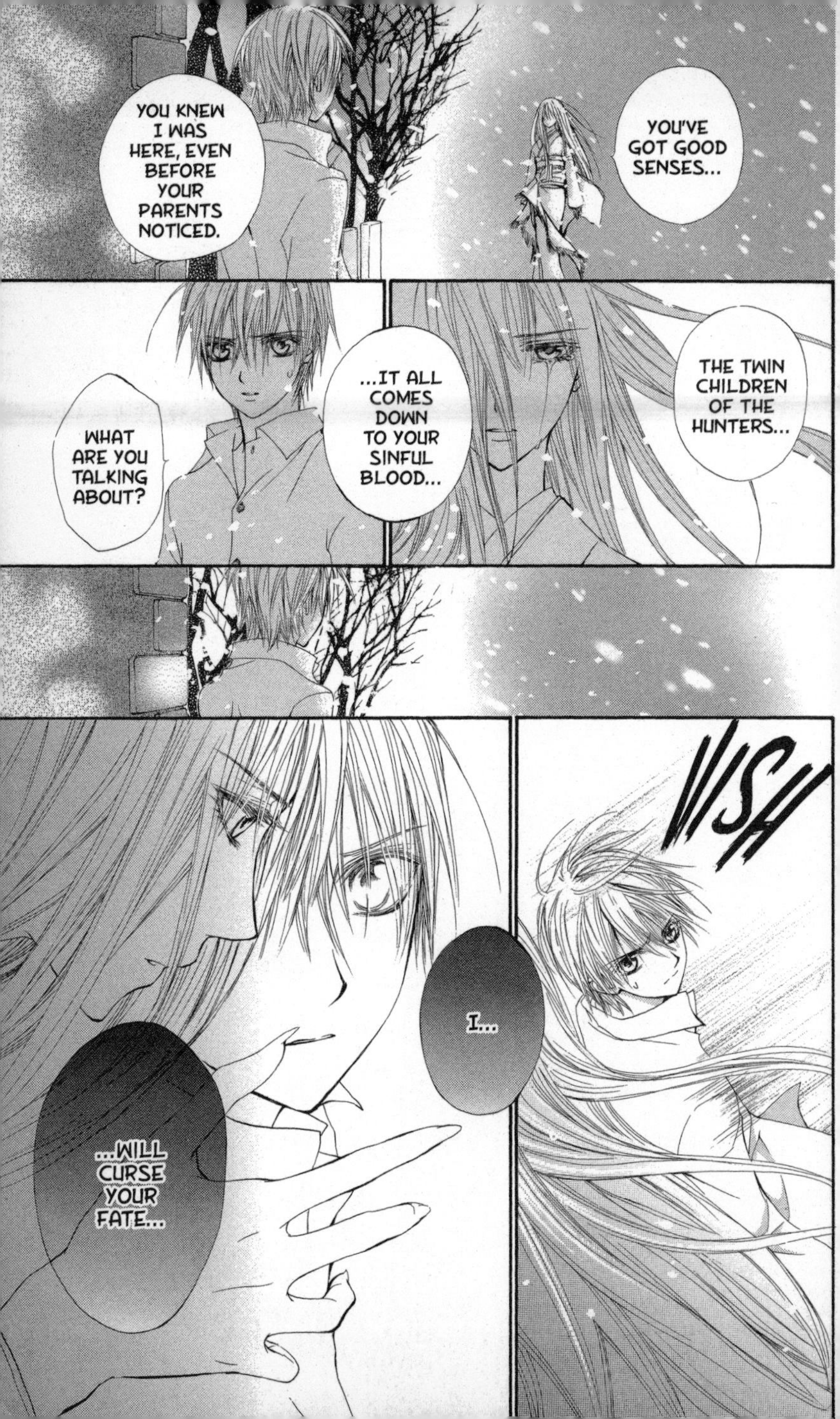
YOU'VE GOT GOOD SENSES...
YOU KNEW I WAS HERE, EVEN BEFORE YOUR PARENTS NOTICED.
THE TWIN CHILDREN OF THE HUNTERS...
...IT ALL COMES DOWN TO YOUR SINFUL BLOOD...
WHAT ARE YOU TALKING ABOUT?
VISH
I...
...WILL CURSE YOUR FATE...

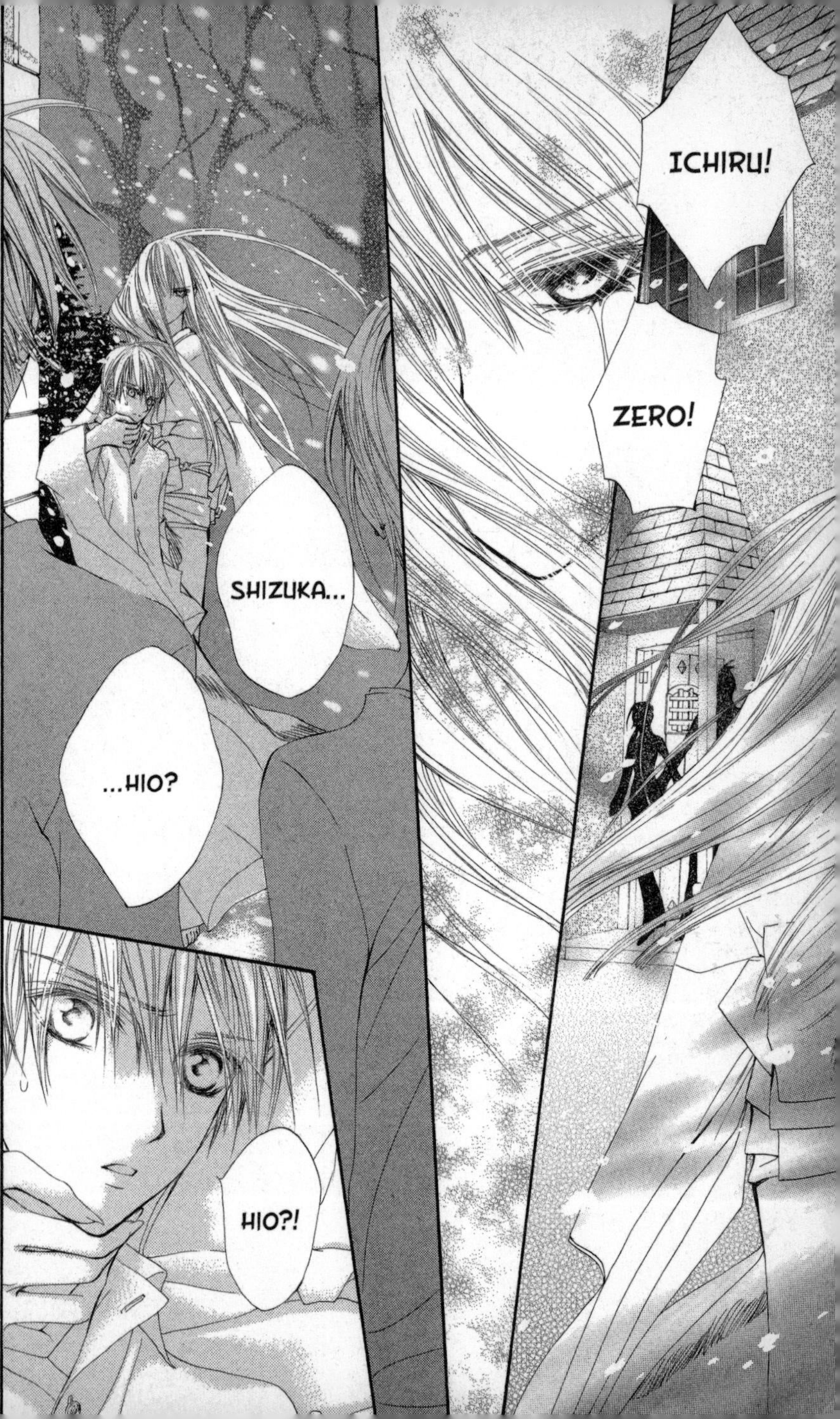
ICHIRU!
ZERO!
SHIZUKA...
...HIO?
HIO?!

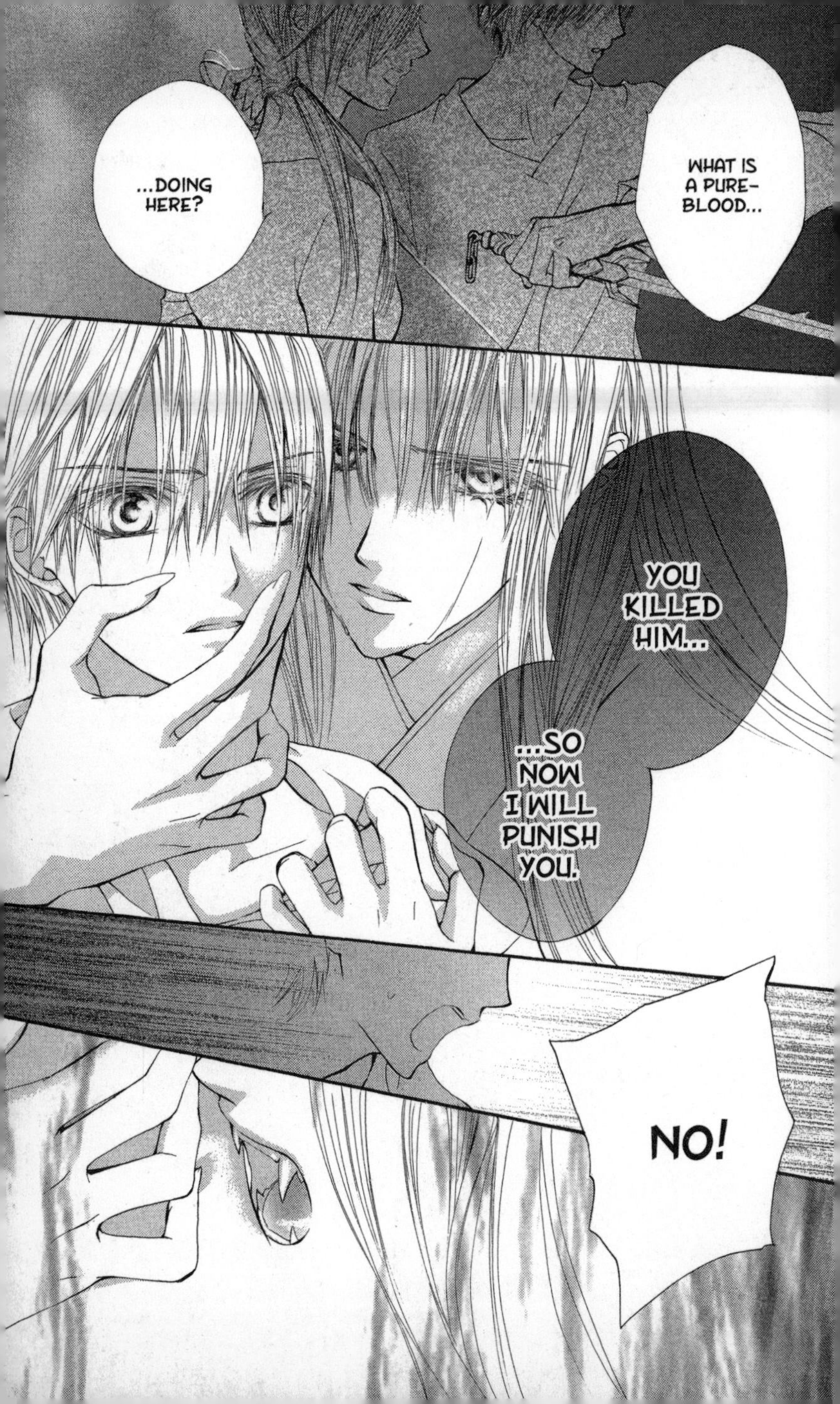
WHAT IS A PURE-BLOOD...
...DOING HERE?
YOU KILLED HIM...
...SO NOW I WILL PUNISH YOU.
NO!

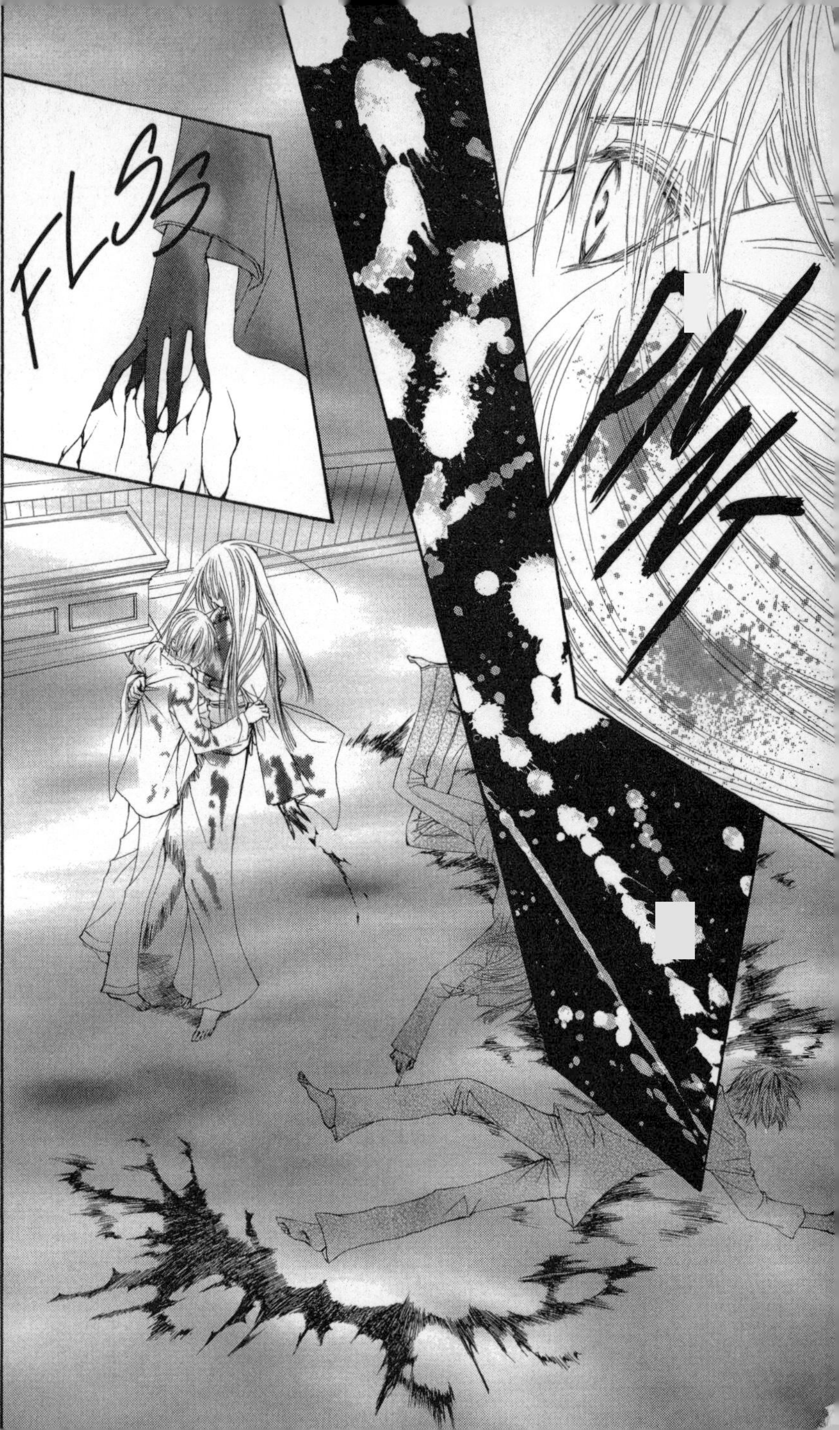
FLSS

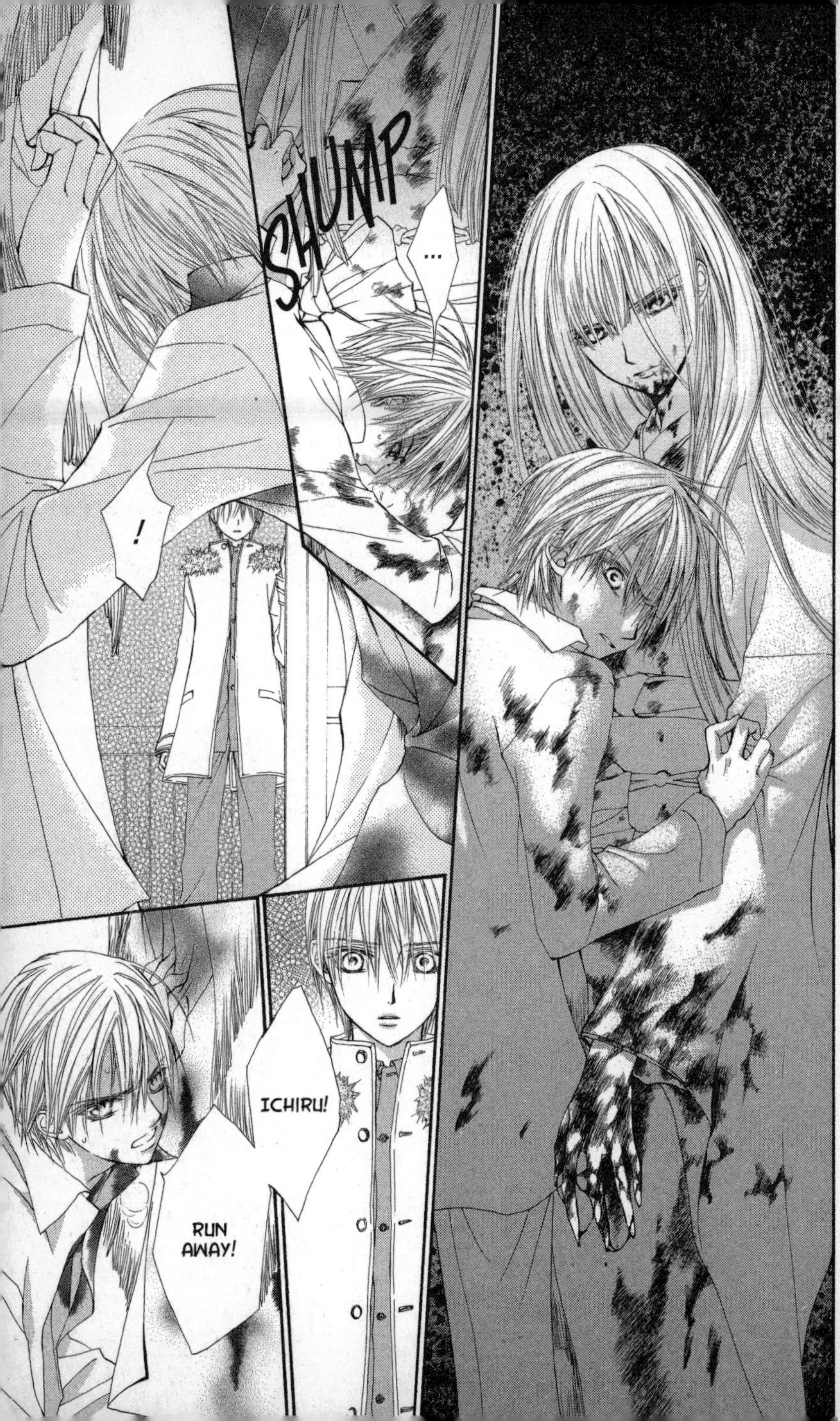
SHUMP
...
!
ICHIRU!
RUN AWAY!

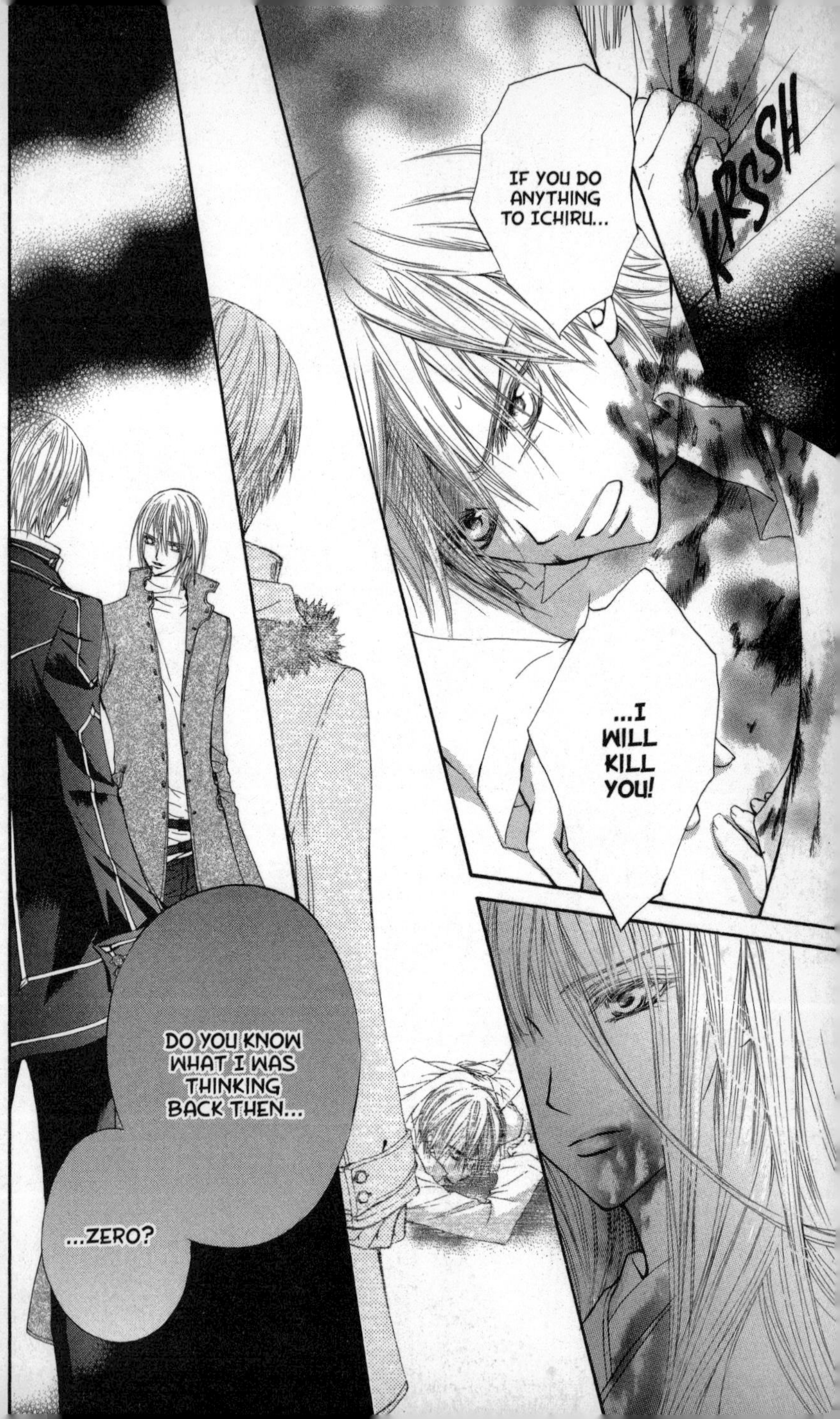

KRSSH
IF YOU DO ANYTHING TO ICHIRU...
...I WILL KILL YOU!
DO YOU KNOW WHAT I WAS THINKING BACK THEN...
...ZERO?

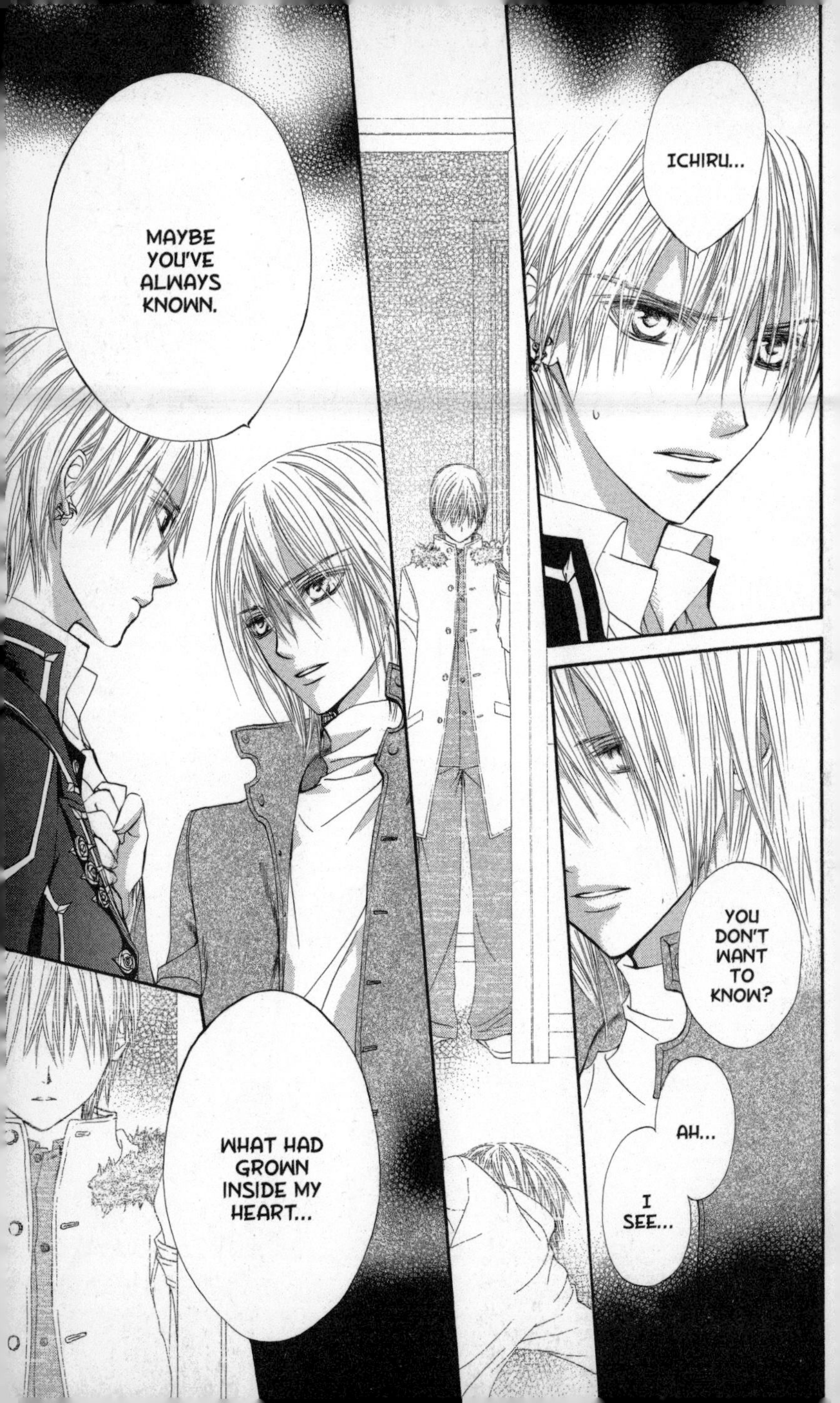
ICHIRU...
YOU DON'T WANT TO KNOW?
AH...
I SEE...
MAYBE YOU'VE ALWAYS KNOWN.
WHAT HAD GROWN INSIDE MY HEART...

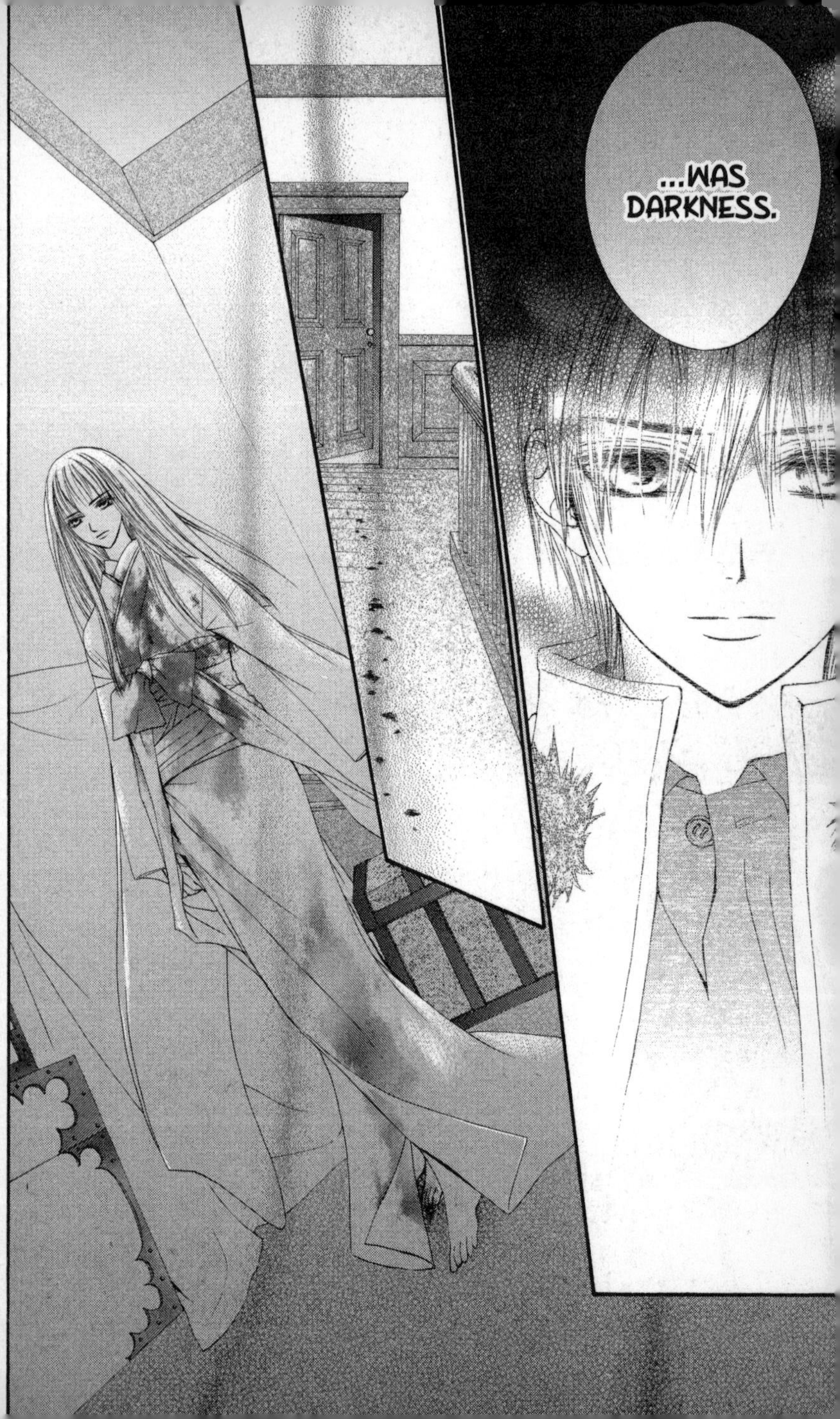
...WAS DARKNESS.

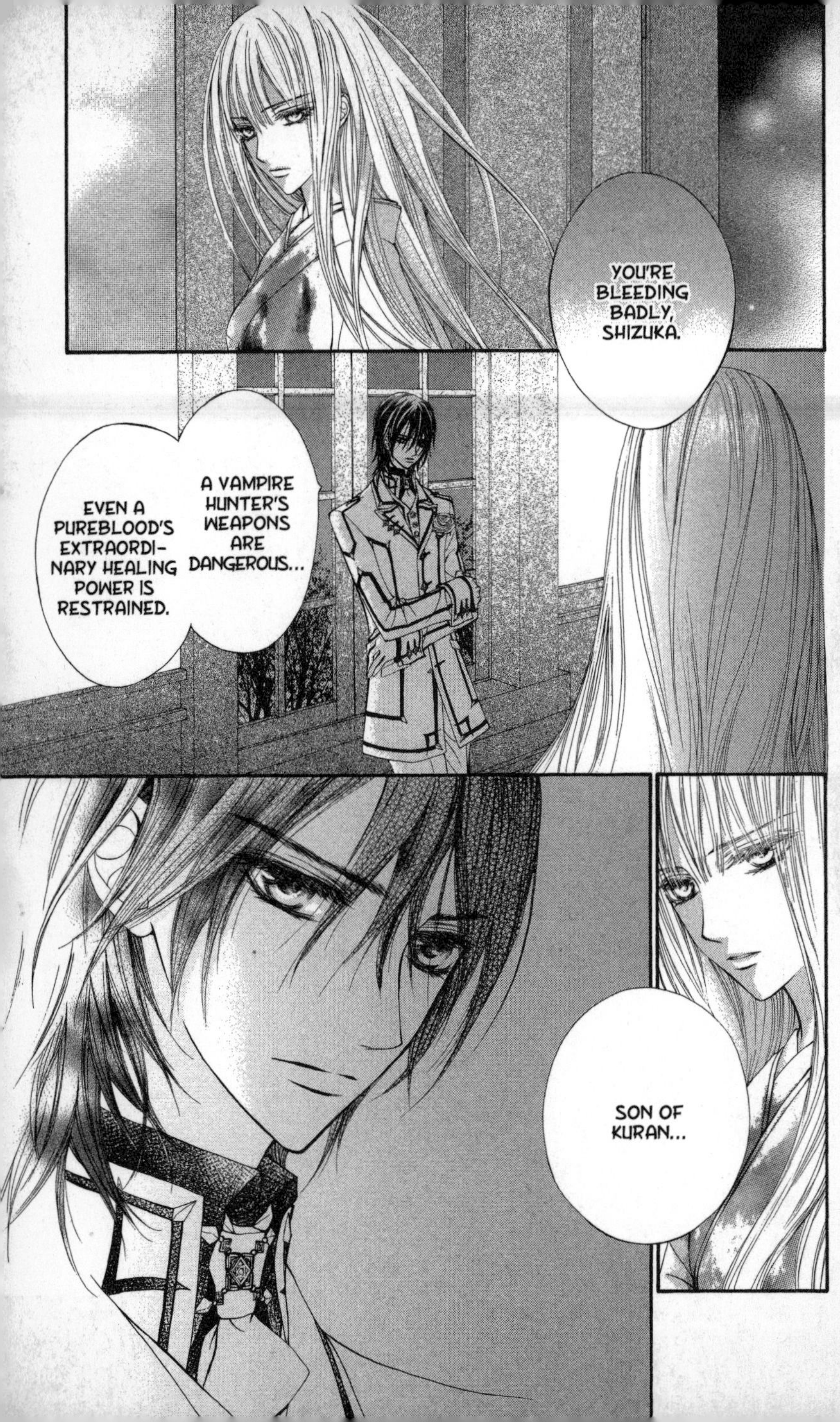
YOU'RE BLEEDING BADLY, SHIZUKA.
A VAMPIRE HUNTER'S WEAPONS ARE DANGEROUS...
EVEN A PUREBLOOD'S EXTRAORDI-NARY HEALING POWER IS RESTRAINED.
SON OF KURAN...

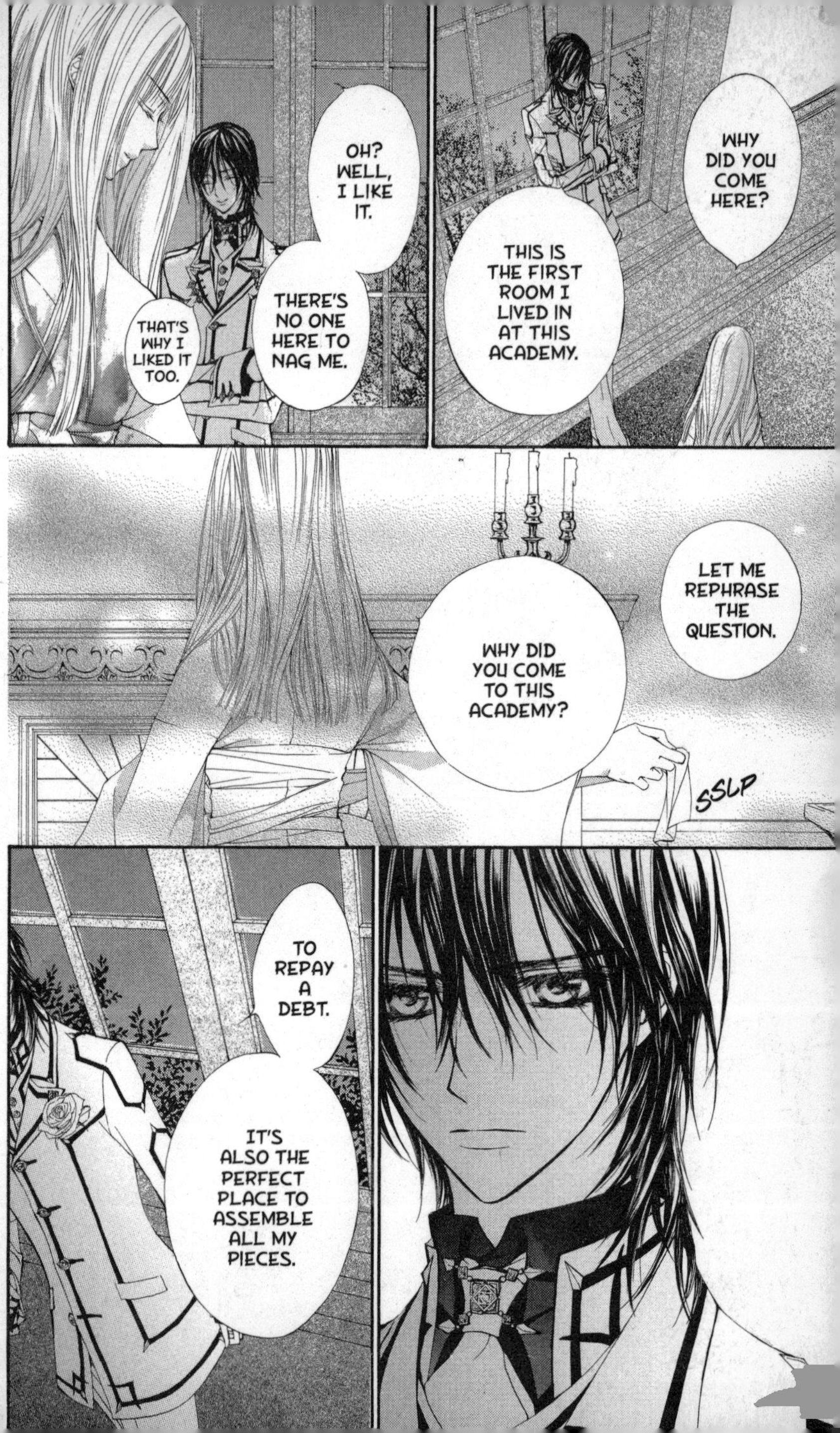
WHY DID YOU COME HERE?
THIS IS THE FIRST ROOM I LIVED IN AT THIS ACADEMY.
OH? WELL, I LIKE IT.
THERE'S NO ONE HERE TO NAG ME.
THAT'S WHY I LIKED IT TOO.
LET ME REPHRASE THE QUESTION.
WHY DID YOU COME TO THIS ACADEMY?
SSLP
TO REPAY A DEBT.
IT'S ALSO THE PERFECT PLACE TO ASSEMBLE ALL MY PIECES.

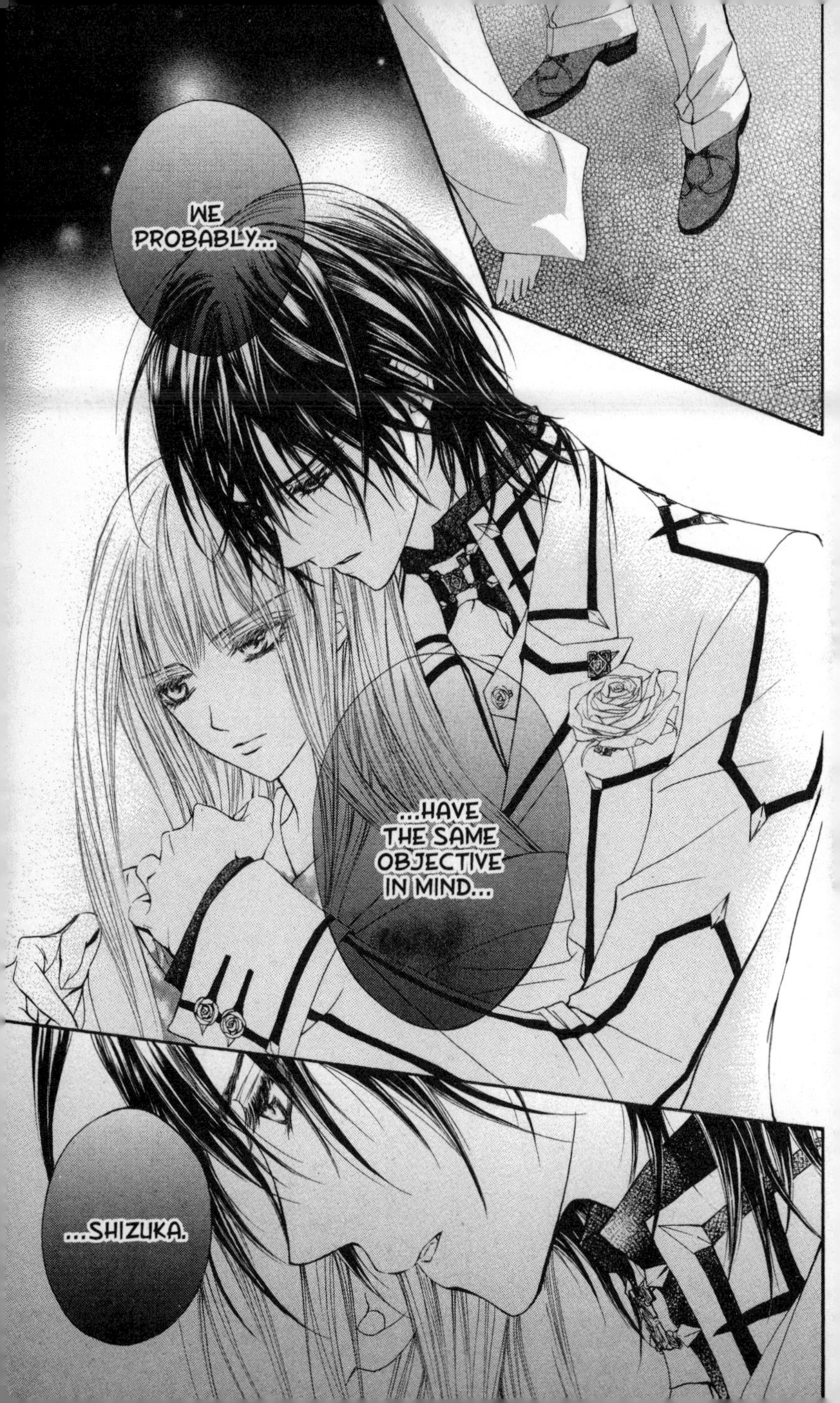
WE PROBABLY...
...HAVE THE SAME OBJECTIVE IN MIND...
...SHIZUKA.

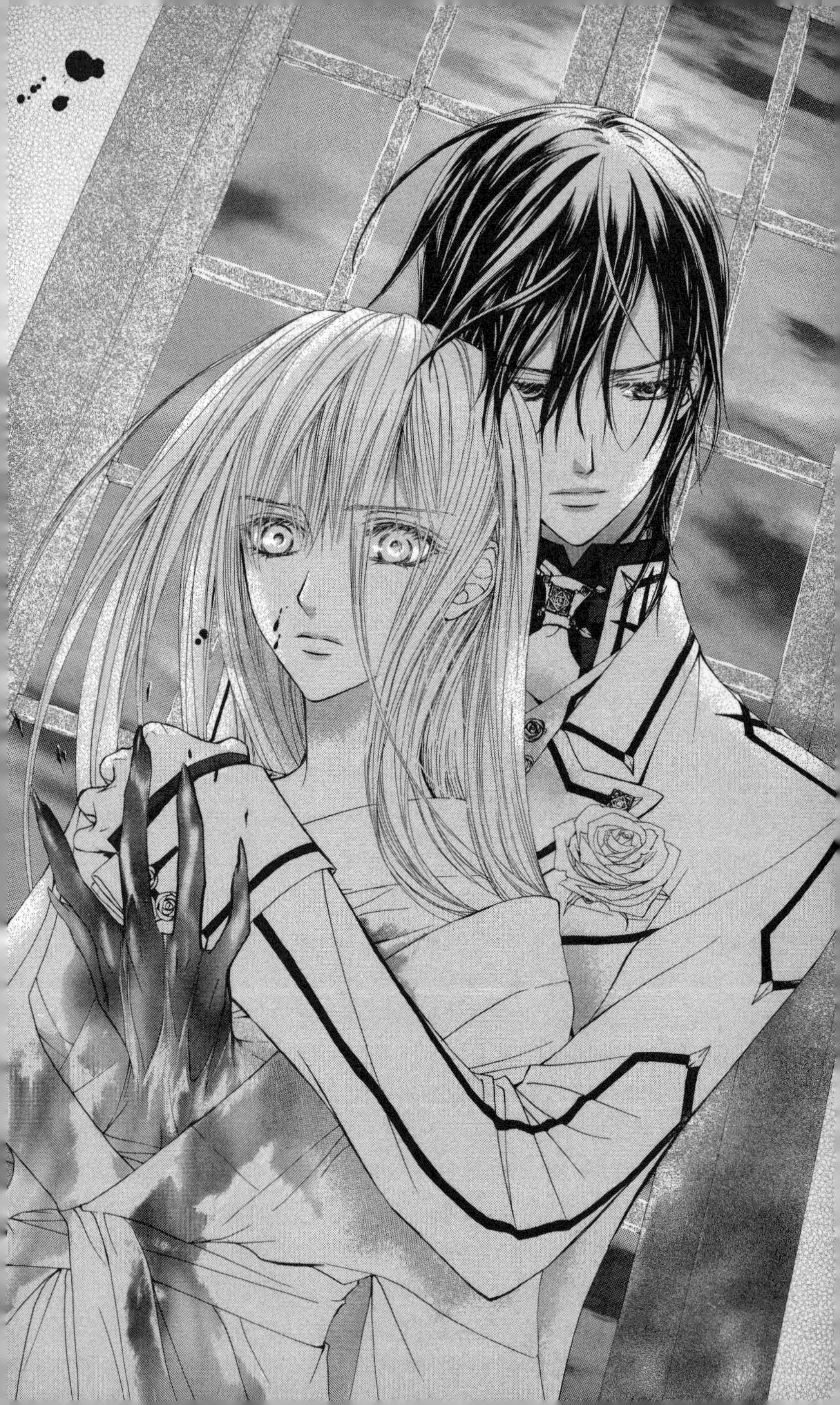

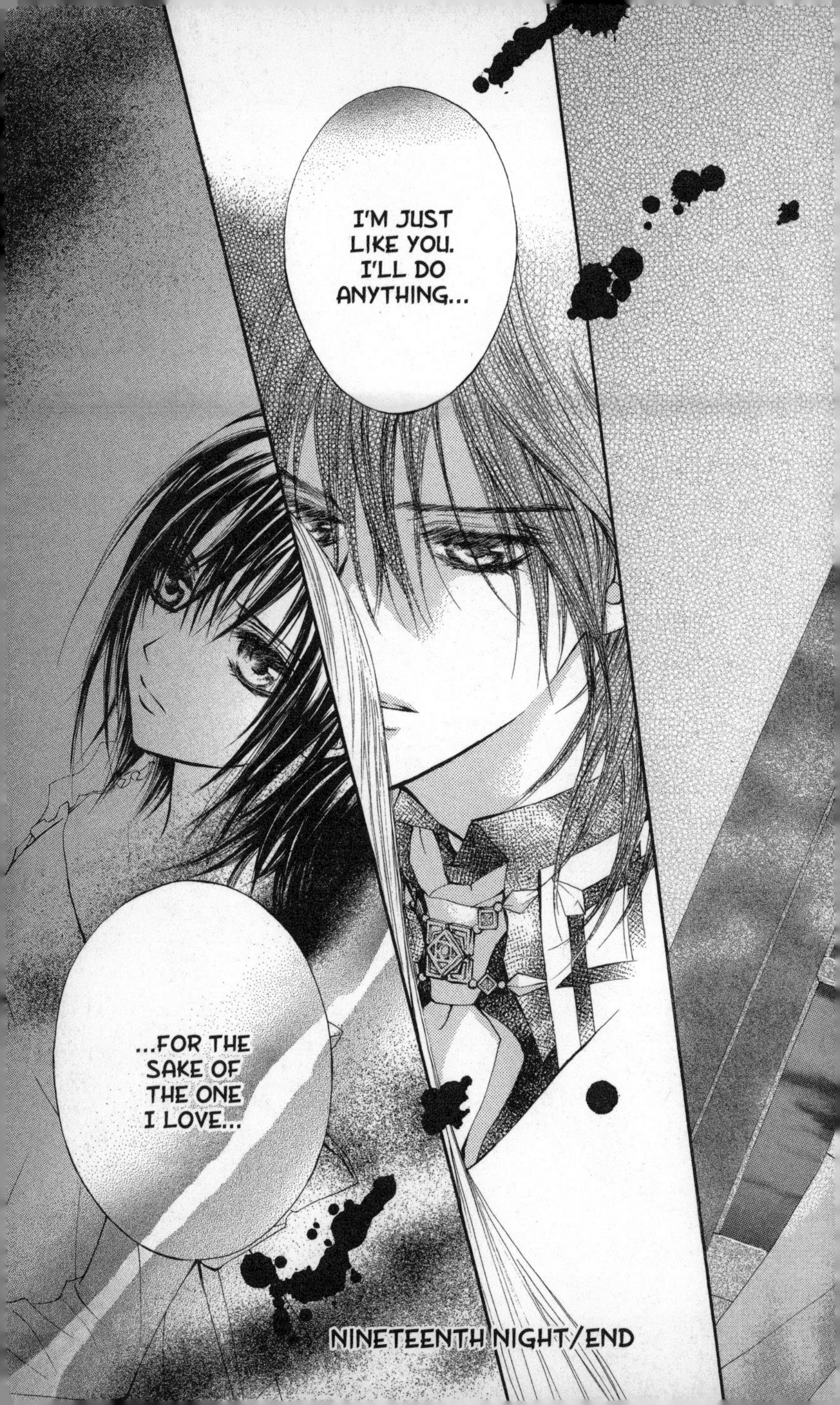
I'M JUST LIKE YOU. I'LL DO ANYTHING...
...FOR THE SAKE OF THE ONE I LOVE...
NINETEENTH NIGHT/END

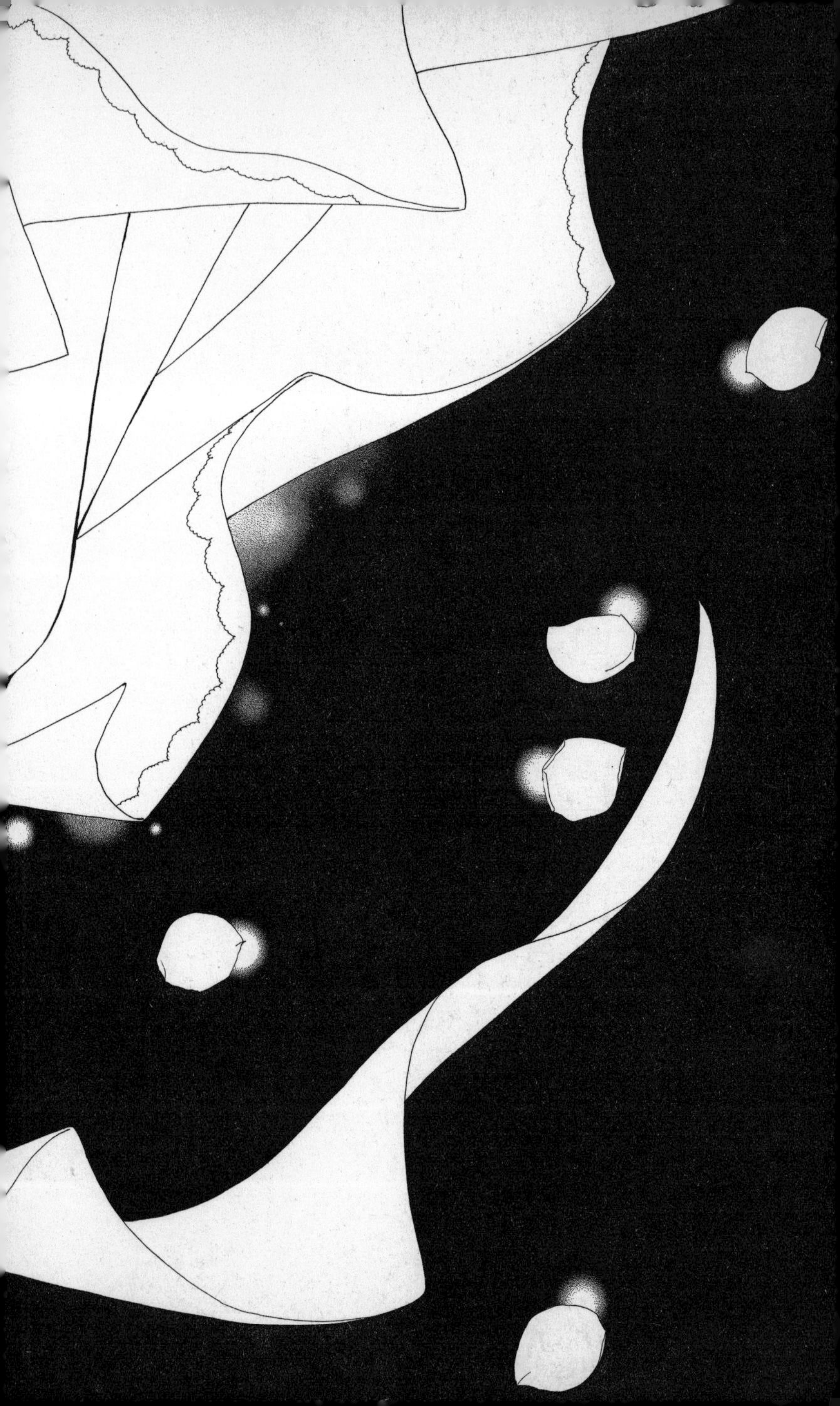

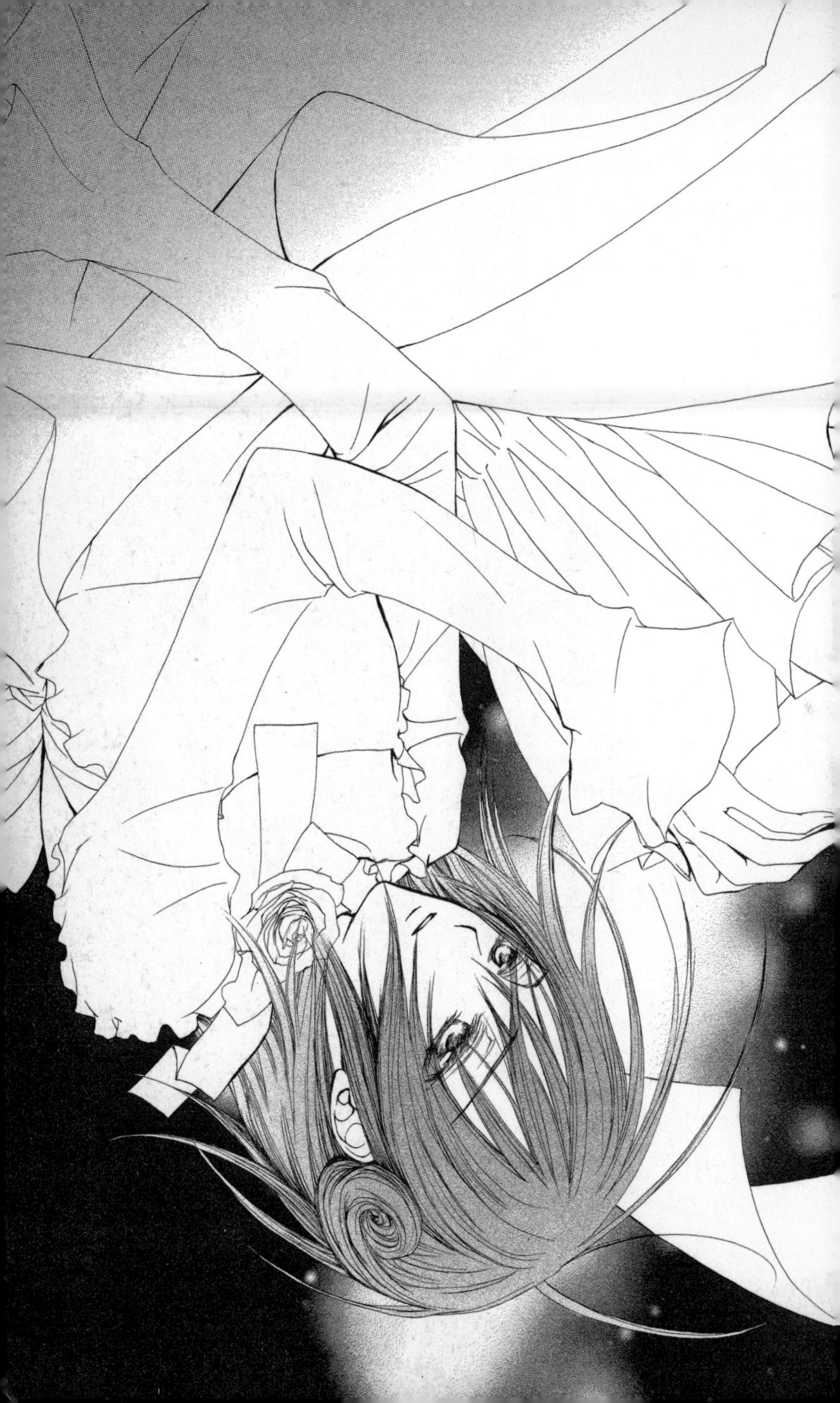

# VAMPIRES COVERED IN BLOOD ARE PROHIBITED FROM ENTERING THIS PAGE!!

✿SOME DAYS ARE NOT INTENSE AT ALL...✿

ZERO!
YOU JERK!
VEEN
DOES SHE...
...THINK SHE'S THREATENING ME?
LIKE THIS?
NOT SCARED
JERK! JERK! JERK! JERK! JERK!
FUMP FUMP
FUMP FUMP
FUMP FUMP
FUMP FUMP
...
JERK! JERK! JERK! JERK! JERK! JERK! JERK! JERK! JERK! JERK! JERK! JERK! JERK!
YUKI...
IT'S BECAUSE SHE'S SO SHORT...
SORRY.
YUKI'S!
I WAS THE ONE WHO ATE YOUR PUDDING, YUKI. IT WASN'T KIRYU.

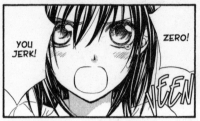

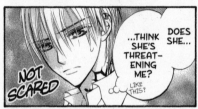

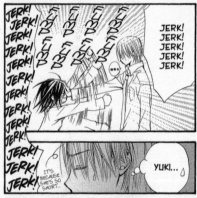

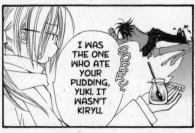

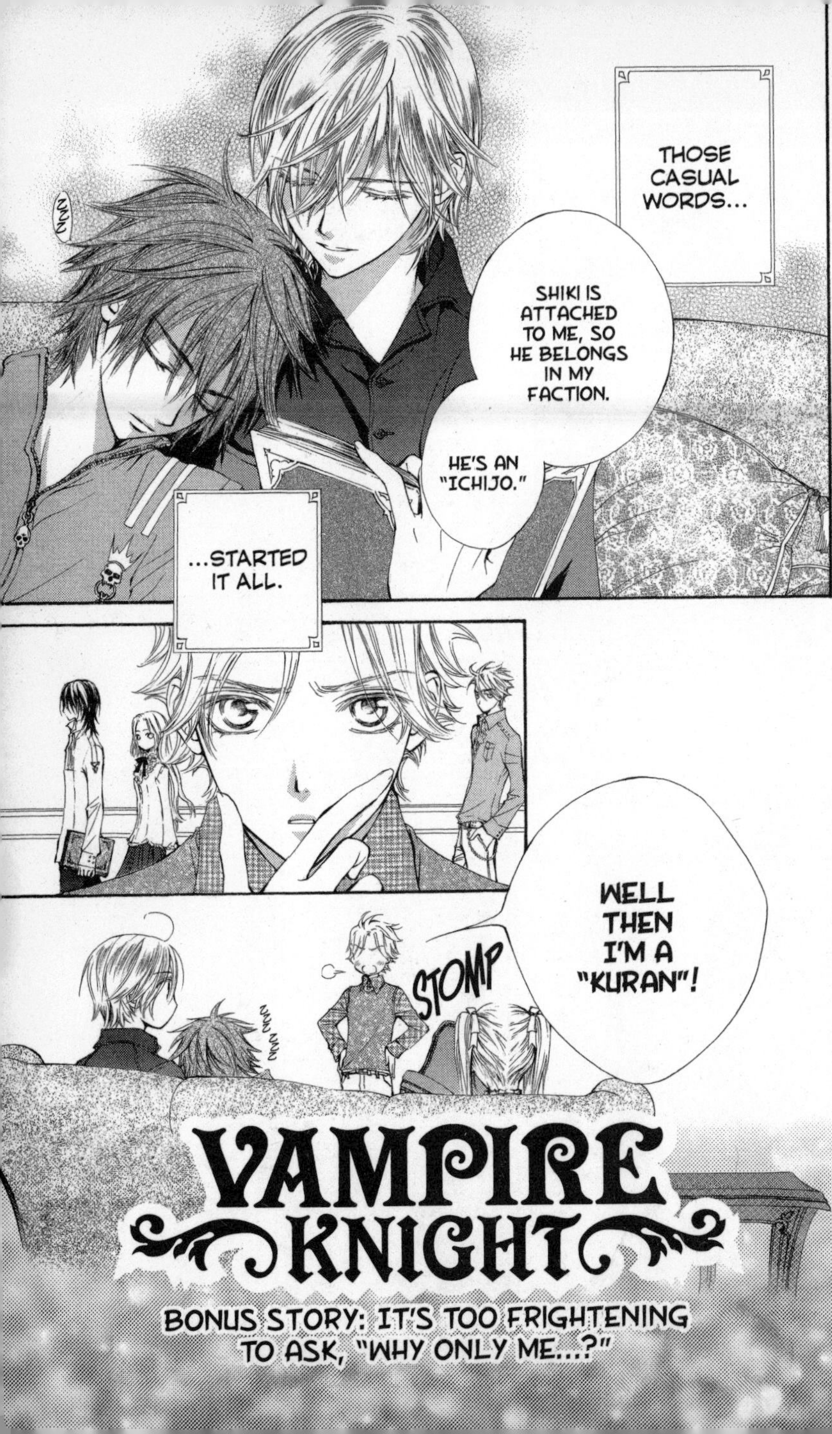
THOSE CASUAL WORDS...
SHIKI IS ATTACHED TO ME, SO HE BELONGS IN MY FACTION.
HE'S AN "ICHIJO."
...STARTED IT ALL.
ZZZ
WELL THEN I'M A "KURAN"!
STOMP
ZZZ ZZZ
VAMPIRE KNIGHT
BONUS STORY: IT'S TOO FRIGHTENING TO ASK, "WHY ONLY ME...?"

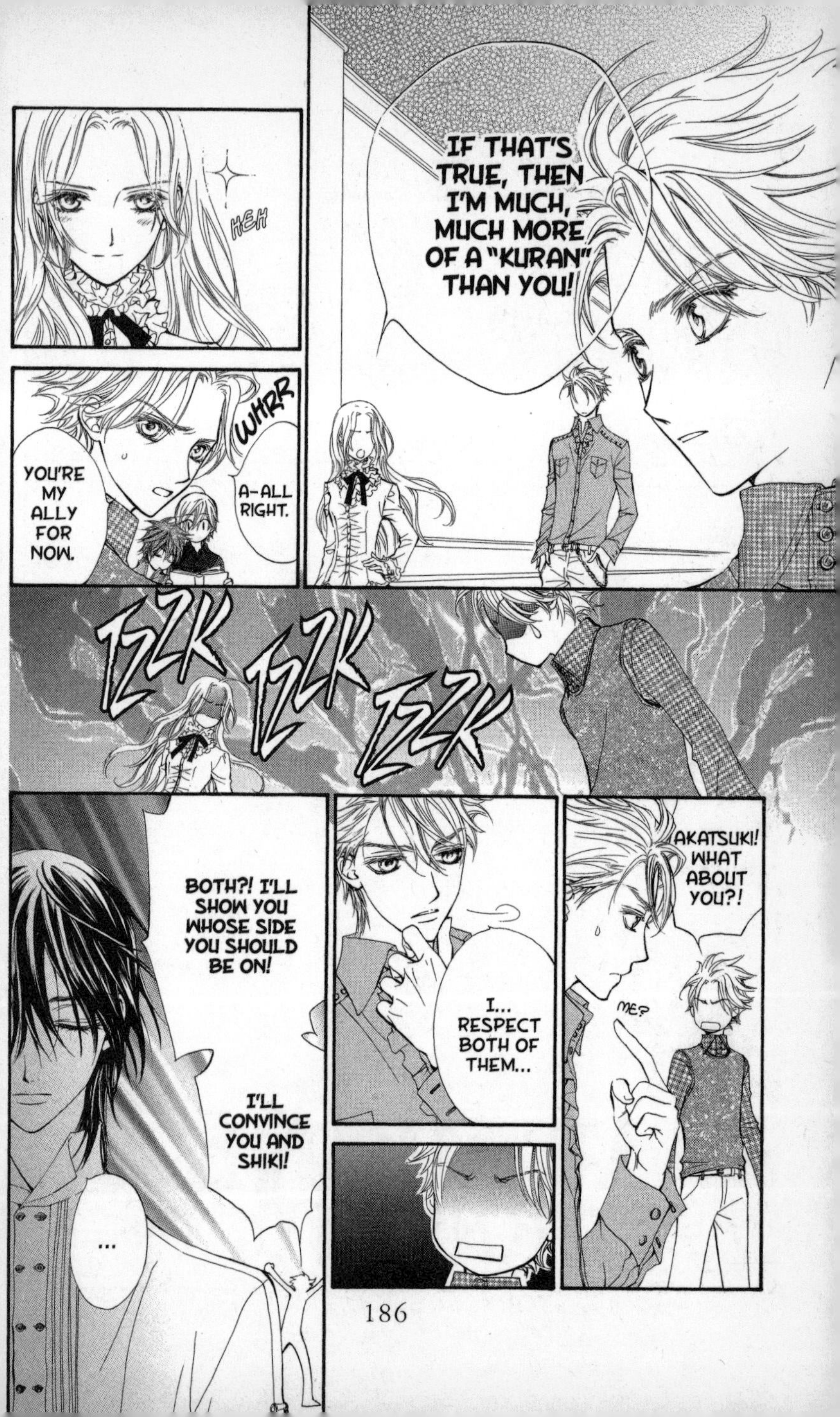
IF THAT'S TRUE, THEN I'M MUCH, MUCH MORE OF A "KURAN" THAN YOU!
HEH
WHRR
A-ALL RIGHT.
YOU'RE MY ALLY FOR NOW.
TZZK TZZK TZZK
AKATSUKI! WHAT ABOUT YOU?!
ME?
I... RESPECT BOTH OF THEM...
BOTH?! I'LL SHOW YOU WHOSE SIDE YOU SHOULD BE ON!
I'LL CONVINCE YOU AND SHIKI!
...

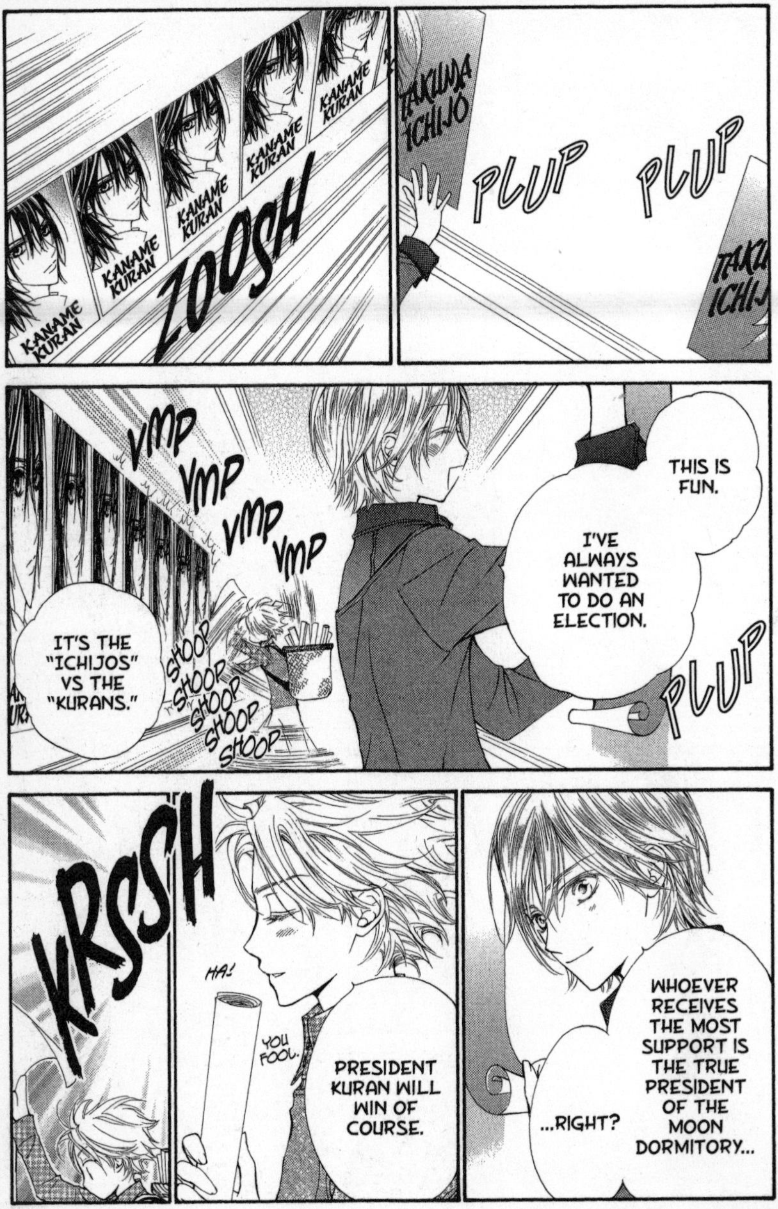
TAKUMA ICHIJO
PLUP
PLUP
KANAME KURAN
KANAME KURAN
KANAME KURAN
KANAME KURAN
KANAME KURAN
KANAME KURAN
ZOOSH
VMP VMP VMP VMP
THIS IS FUN.
I'VE ALWAYS WANTED TO DO AN ELECTION.
PLUP
IT'S THE "ICHIJOS" VS THE "KURANS."
SHOOP SHOOP SHOOP SHOOP SHOOP
WHOEVER RECEIVES THE MOST SUPPORT IS THE TRUE PRESIDENT OF THE MOON DORMITORY...
...RIGHT?
HA!
YOU FOOL.
PRESIDENT KURAN WILL WIN OF COURSE.
KRSSH

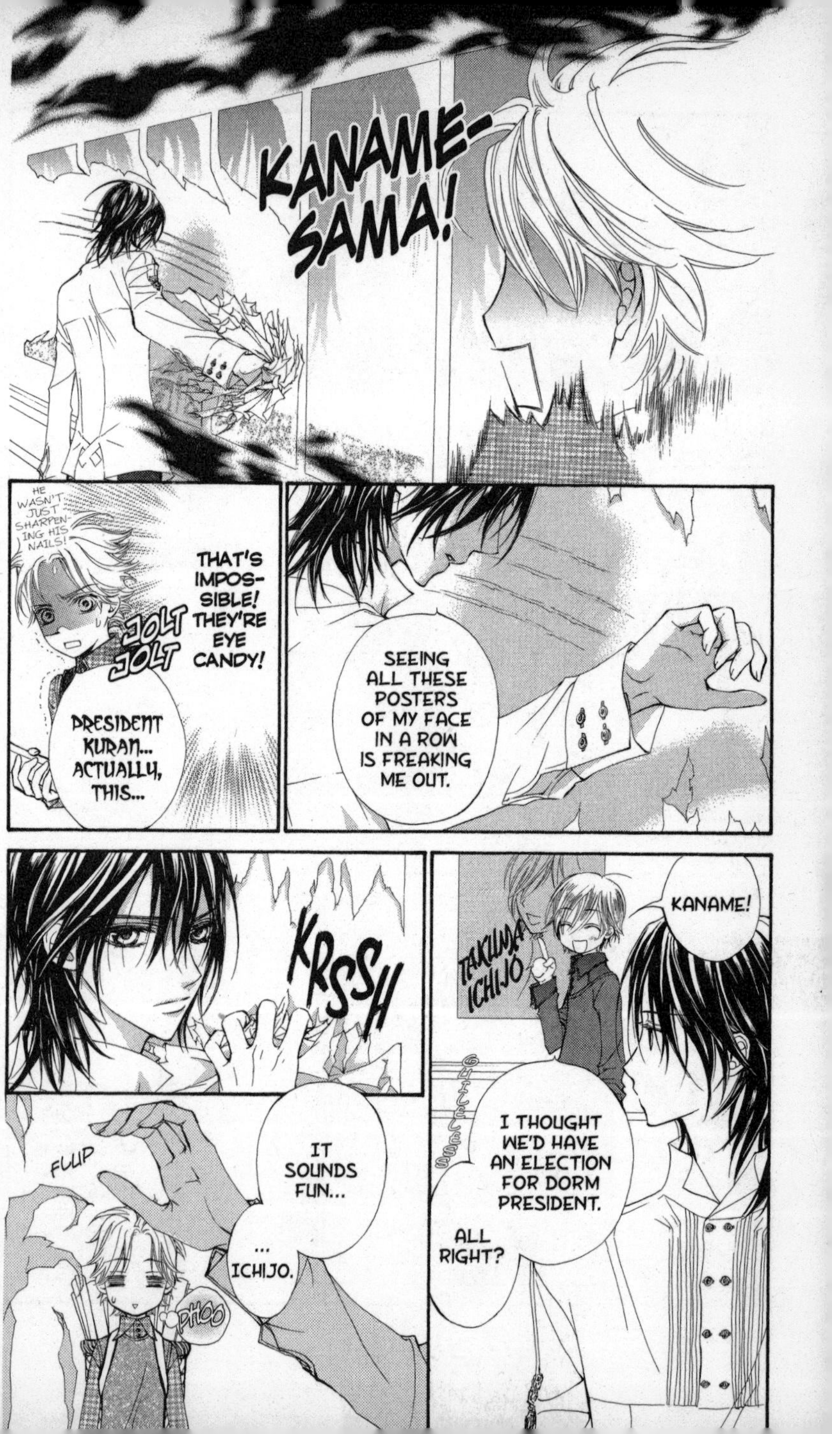
KANAME-SAMA!
SEEING ALL THESE POSTERS OF MY FACE IN A ROW IS FREAKING ME OUT.
THAT'S IMPOS-SIBLE! THEY'RE EYE CANDY!
HE WASN'T JUST SHARPEN-ING HIS NAILS!
JOLT JOLT
PRESIDENT KURAN... ACTUALLY, THIS...
KANAME!
TAKUMA ICHIJO
GUILELESS
I THOUGHT WE'D HAVE AN ELECTION FOR DORM PRESIDENT.
ALL RIGHT?
KRSSH
FLLIP
IT SOUNDS FUN...
... ICHIJO.
PHOO

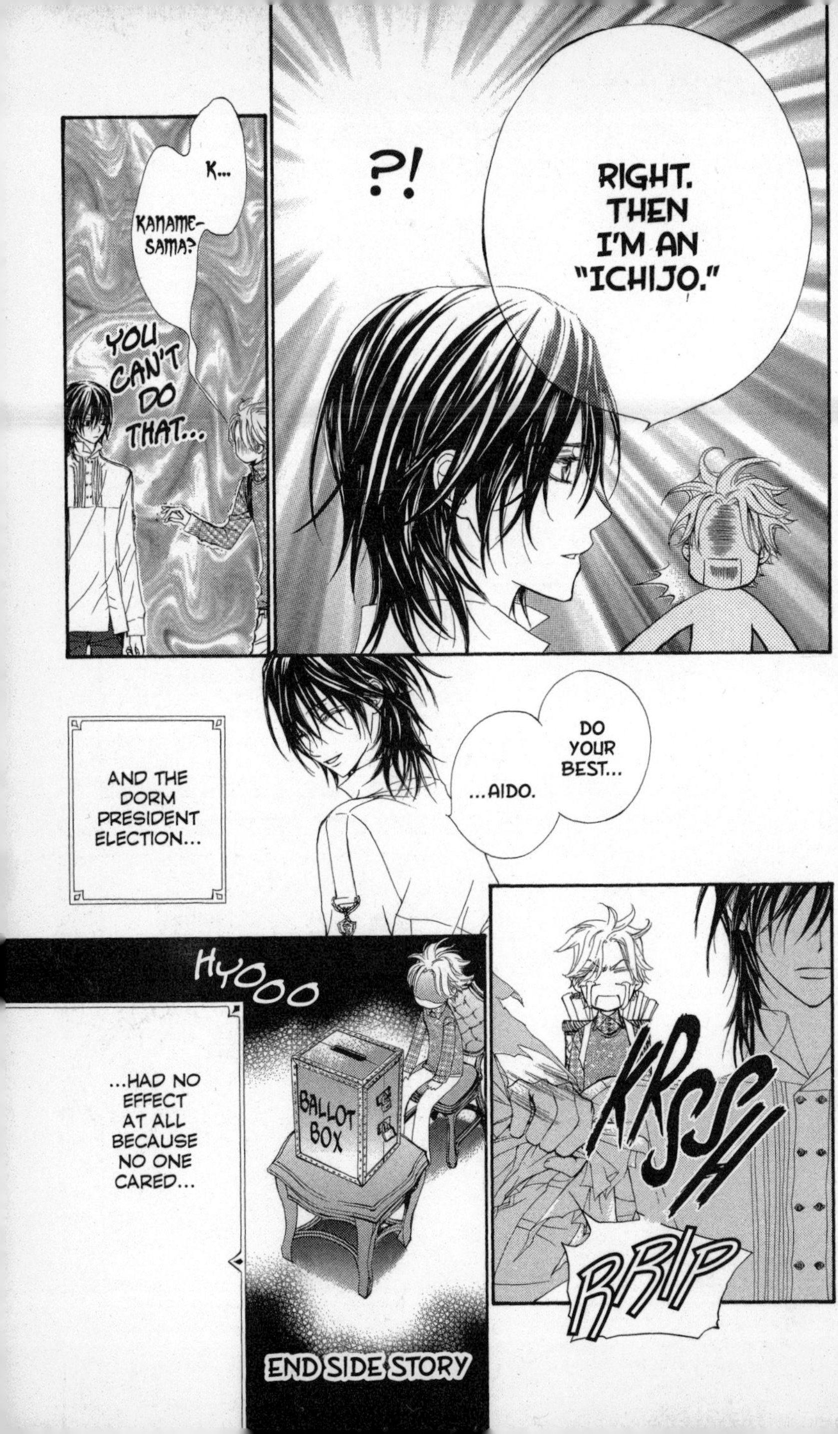
RIGHT. THEN I'M AN "ICHIJO."
?!
K...
KANAME-SAMA?
YOU CAN'T DO THAT...
DO YOUR BEST...
...AIDO.
AND THE DORM PRESIDENT ELECTION...
KRSH
RRIP
HYOOO
...HAD NO EFFECT AT ALL BECAUSE NO ONE CARED...
BALLOT BOX
END SIDE STORY

## CLEANING UP AFTER THE DORM ELECTION

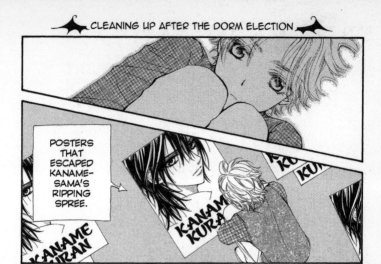

POSTERS THAT ESCAPED KANAME-SAMA'S RIPPING SPREE.
KANAME KURAN
UM.
SELL ME SOME POSTERS.
HURRY, BEFORE KANAME-SAMA FINDS OUT!
BLUSH
RUKA, YOU...
...REALLY LIKE KANAME-SAMA.
SOMEHOW I KNOW THAT.
HURRY UP!
SHE WANTS THESE?
FINE, HERE YOU GO.

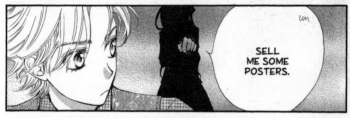

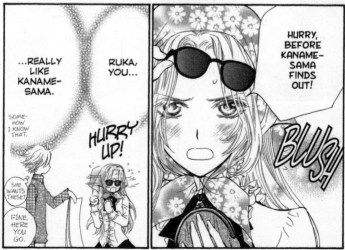

# *EDITOR'S NOTES*

## *Characters*

Matsuri Hino puts careful thought into the names of her characters in *Vampire Knight*. Below is the collection of characters through volume 4. Each character's name is presented family name first, per the kanji reading.

黒主優姫

**Cross Yuki**

Yuki's last name, *Kurosu*, is the Japanese pronunciation of the English word "cross." However, the kanji has a different meaning—*kuro* means "black" and *su* means "master." Her first name is a combination of *yuu*, meaning "tender" or "kind," and *ki*, meaning "princess."

錐生零

**Kiryu Zero**

Zero's first name is the kanji for *rei*, meaning "zero." In his last name, *Kiryu*, the *ki* means "auger" or "drill," and the *ryu* means "life."

# 玖蘭枢

**Kuran Kaname**

*Kaname* means "hinge" or "door." The kanji for his last name is a combination of the old-fashioned way of writing *ku*, meaning "nine," and *ran*, meaning "orchid": "nine orchids."

# 藍堂英

**Aido Hanabusa**

*Hanabusa* means "petals of a flower." *Aido* means "indigo temple." In Japanese, the pronunciation of *Aido* is very close to the pronunciation of the English word *idol*.

# 架院暁

**Kain Akatsuki**

*Akatsuki* means "dawn," or "daybreak." In *Kain*, *ka* is a base or support, while *in* denotes a building that has high fences around it, such as a temple or school.

# 早園瑠佳

**Souen Ruka**

In *Ruka*, the *ru* means "lapis lazuli" while the *ka* means "good-looking," or "beautiful." The *sou* in Ruka's surname, *Souen*, means "early," but this kanji also has an obscure meaning of "strong fragrance." The *en* means "garden."

# 一条拓麻

**Ichijo Takuma**

*Ichijo* can mean a "ray" or "streak." The kanji for *Takuma* is a combination of *taku*, meaning "to cultivate" and *ma*, which is the kanji for *asa*, meaning "hemp" or "flax," a plant with blue flowers.

# 支葵千里

**Shiki Senri**

Shiki's last name is a combination of *shi*, meaning "to support" and *ki*, meaning "mallow"—a flowering plant with pink or white blossoms. The *ri* in *Senri* is a traditional Japanese unit of measure for distance, and one *ri* is about 2.44 miles. *Senri* means "1,000 *ri*."

# 夜刈十牙

**Yagari Toga**

*Yagari* is a combination of *ya*, meaning "night," and *gari*, meaning "to harvest." *Toga* means "ten fangs."

# 一条麻遠, 一翁

**Ichijo Asato, aka "Ichio"**

*Ichijo* can mean a "ray" or "streak." Asato's first name is comprised of *asa*, meaning "hemp" or "flax," and *tou*, meaning "far off." His nickname is *ichi*, or "one," combined with *ou*, which can be used as an honorific when referring to an older man.

# 若葉沙頼

**Wakaba Sayori**

Yori's full name is Sayori Wakaba. *Wakaba* means "young leaves." Her given name, *Sayori*, is a combination of sa, meaning "sand," and *yori*, meaning "trust."

# 星煉
**Seiren**

*Sei* means "star" and *ren* means
"to smelt" or "refine." *Ren* is also
the same kanji used in *rengoku*, or
"purgatory."

# 遠矢莉磨
**Toya Rima**

*Toya* means a "far-reaching arrow."
Rima's given name is a combination
of *ri*, or "jasmine," and *ma*, which
signifies enhancement by wearing
away, such as by polishing or
scouring.

# 紅まり亜
**Kurenai Maria**

*Kurenai* means "crimson." The kanji
for the last *a* in Maria's given name
is the same that is used in "Asia."

# 錐生壱縷

**Kiryu Ichiru**

*Ichi* is the old-fashioned way of writing "one," and *ru* means "thread." He shares the same surname as his twin, Zero.

# 緋桜閑, 狂咲姫

**Hio Shizuka, Kuruizaki-hime**

*Shizuka* means "calm and quiet." In Shizuka's family name, *hi* is "scarlet," and *ou* is "cherry blossoms." Shizuka Hio is also referred to as the "Kuruizaki-hime." *Kuruizaki* means "flowers blooming out of season," and *hime* means "princess."

## Terms

**Junketsu no kimi**: In the Japanese version, Aido tells Zero to address Shizuka Hio as *junketsu no kimi*, or "Lady Pureblood."

**-sama**: The suffix *sama* is used in formal address for someone who ranks higher in the social hierarchy. The vampires call their leader "Kaname-sama" only when they are among their own kind.

Matsuri Hino burst onto the manga scene with her series *Kono Yume ga Sametara* (When This Dream Is Over), which was published in *LaLa DX* magazine. Hino was a manga artist a mere nine months after she decided to become one.

With the success of her popular series *Captive Heart* and *MeruPuri*, Hino has established herself as a major player in the world of shojo manga. *Vampire Knight* is currently serialized in *LaLa* and *Shojo Beat* magazines.

Hino enjoys creative activities and has commented that she would have been either an architect or an apprentice to traditional Japanese craft masters if she had not become a manga artist.

# *VAMPIRE KNIGHT*

**Vol. 4**

The Shojo Beat Manga Edition

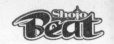

This manga contains material that was originally published in English in *Shojo Beat* magazine, September 2007–January 2008 issues. Artwork in the magazine may have been slightly altered from that presented here.

**STORY AND ART BY**
MATSURI HINO

**Translation & English Adaptation**/Tomo Kimura
**Touch-up Art & Lettering**/George Caltsoudas
**Graphic Design**/Nozomi Akashi
**Editor**/Nancy Thistlethwaite

**Editor in Chief, Books**/Alvin Lu
**Editor in Chief, Magazines**/Marc Weidenbaum
**VP of Publishing Licensing**/Rika Inouye
**VP of Sales**/Gonzalo Ferreyra
**Sr. VP of Marketing**/Liza Coppola
**Publisher**/Hyoe Narita



Printed in Canada

Published by VIZ Media, LLC
P.O. Box 77010
San Francisco, CA 94107

Shojo Beat Manga Edition
10 9 8 7 6 5 4 3 2 1
First printing, April 2008

RATED T+ FOR OLDER TEEN

**PARENTAL ADVISORY**
VAMPIRE KNIGHT is rated T+ for Older Teen and is recommended for ages 16 and up. This volume contains sexual themes and violence.

ratings.viz.com

store.viz.com

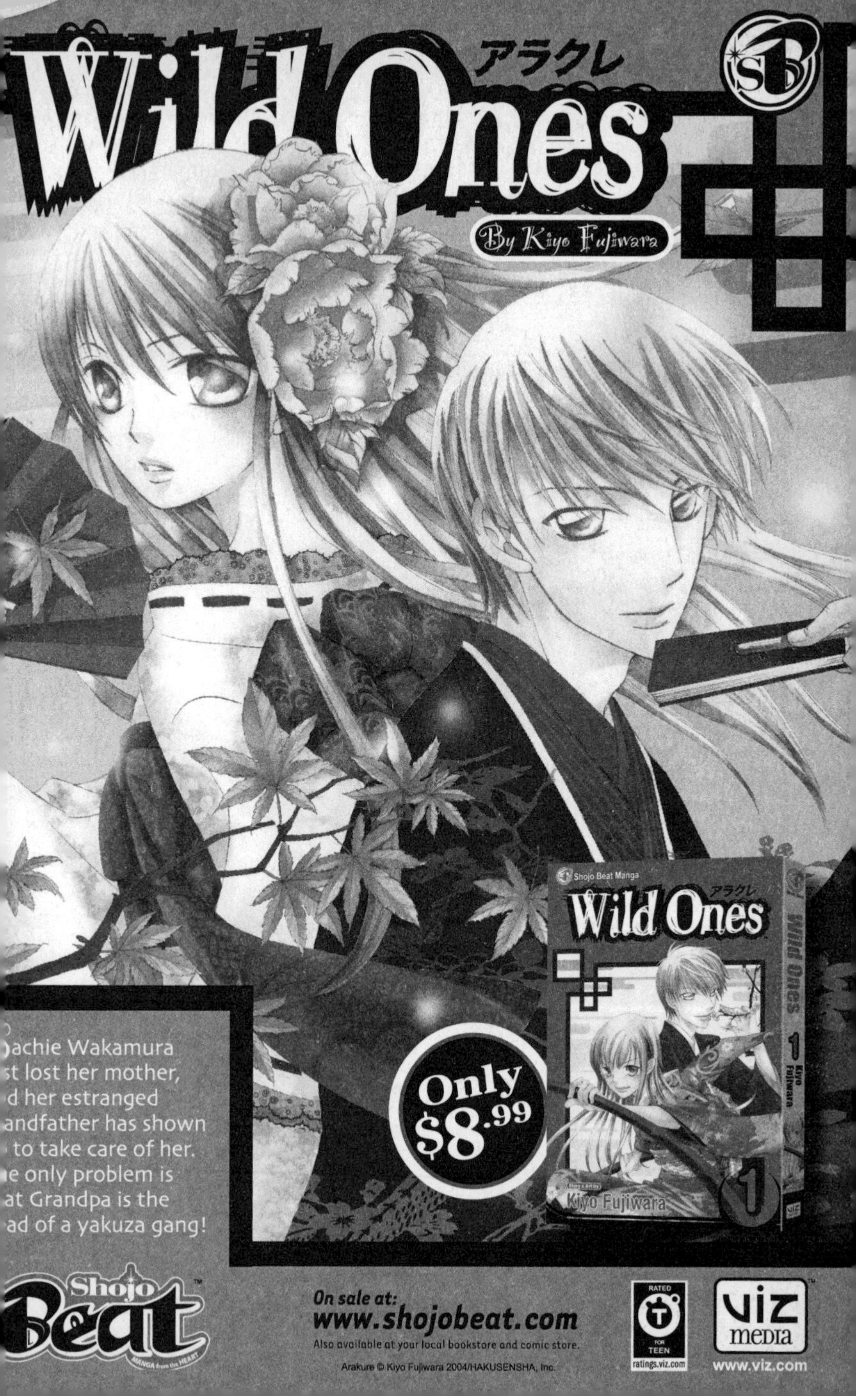
Wild Ones
アラクレ
By Kiyo Fujiwara
Sachie Wakamura
st lost her mother,
d her estranged
andfather has shown
to take care of her.
e only problem is
at Grandpa is the
ad of a yakuza gang!
Only $8.99
Shojo Beat Manga
Wild Ones
アラクレ
Kiyo Fujiwara
1
Shojo Beat
MANGA from the HEART
On sale at:
www.shojobeat.com
Also available at your local bookstore and comic store.
Arakure © Kiyo Fujiwara 2004/HAKUSENSHA, Inc.
RATED T FOR TEEN
ratings.viz.com
viz media
www.viz.com

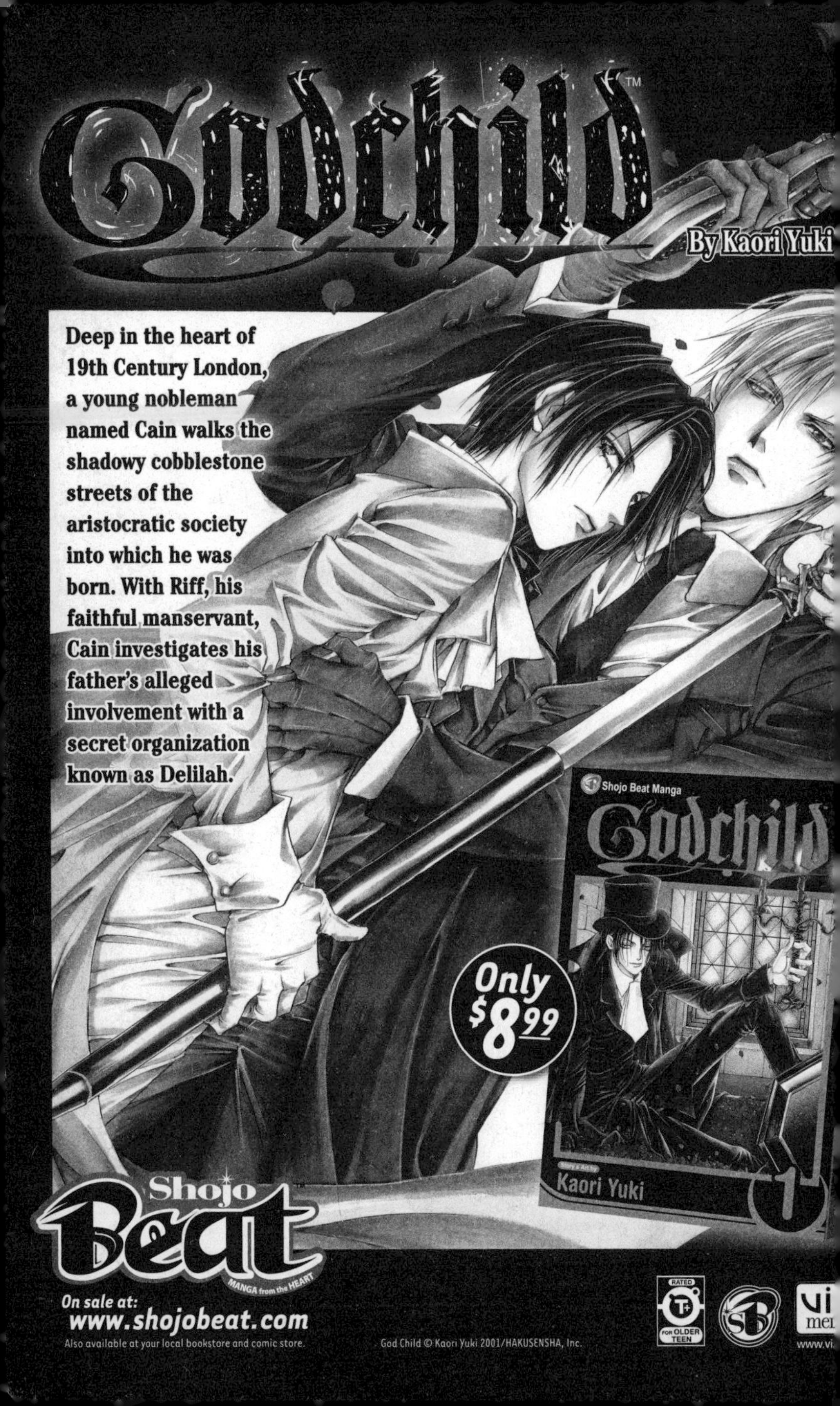
Godchild™
By Kaori Yuki
Deep in the heart of 19th Century London, a young nobleman named Cain walks the shadowy cobblestone streets of the aristocratic society into which he was born. With Riff, his faithful manservant, Cain investigates his father's alleged involvement with a secret organization known as Delilah.
Shojo Beat Manga
Godchild
Kaori Yuki
1
Only $8.99
Shojo Beat
MANGA from the HEART
On sale at:
www.shojobeat.com
Also available at your local bookstore and comic store.
God Child © Kaori Yuki 2001/HAKUSENSHA, Inc.
RATED T+ FOR OLDER TEEN

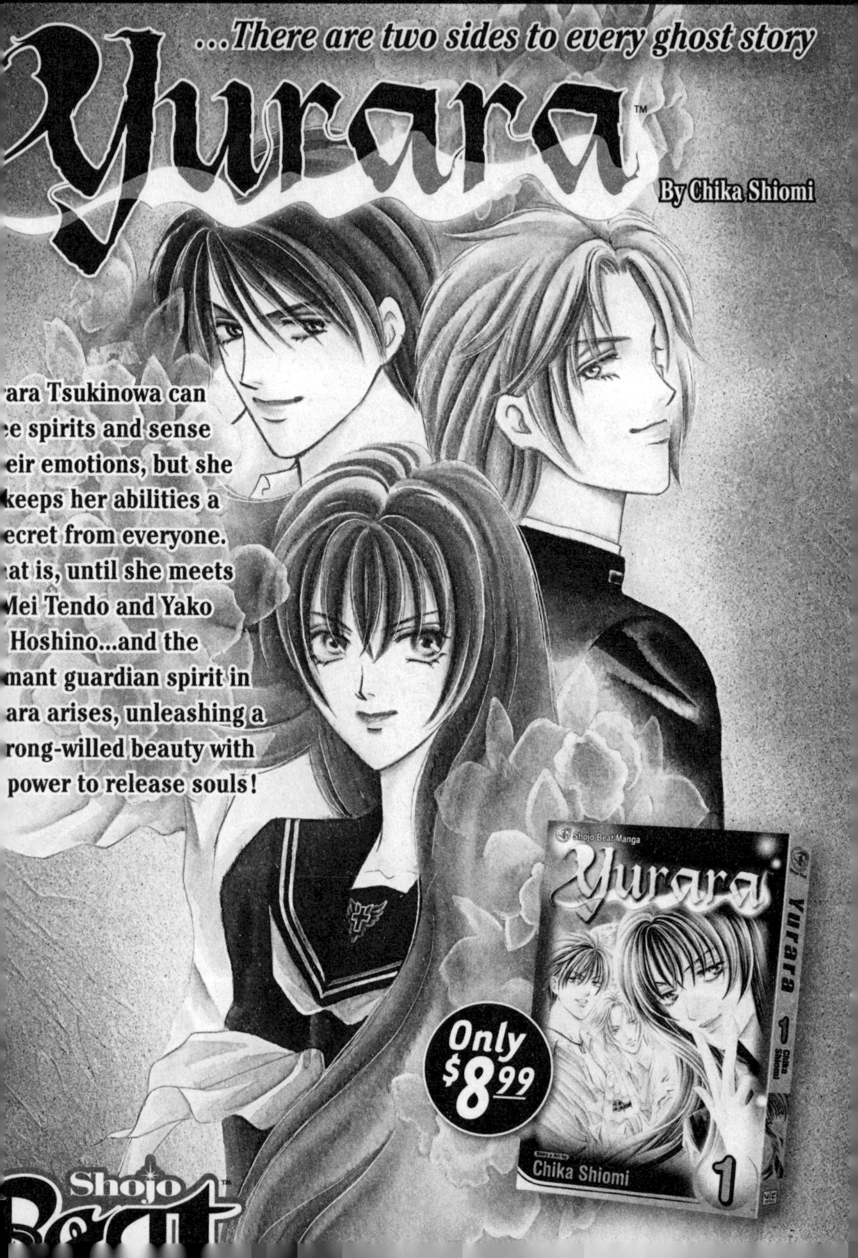

...There are two sides to every ghost story
Yurara™
By Chika Shiomi
ara Tsukinowa can
e spirits and sense
eir emotions, but she
keeps her abilities a
ecret from everyone.
at is, until she meets
Mei Tendo and Yako
Hoshino...and the
mant guardian spirit in
ara arises, unleashing a
rong-willed beauty with
power to release souls!
Shojo Beat Manga
Yurara
Yurara 1 Chika Shiomi
Chika Shiomi
1
Only $8.99
Shojo Beat™

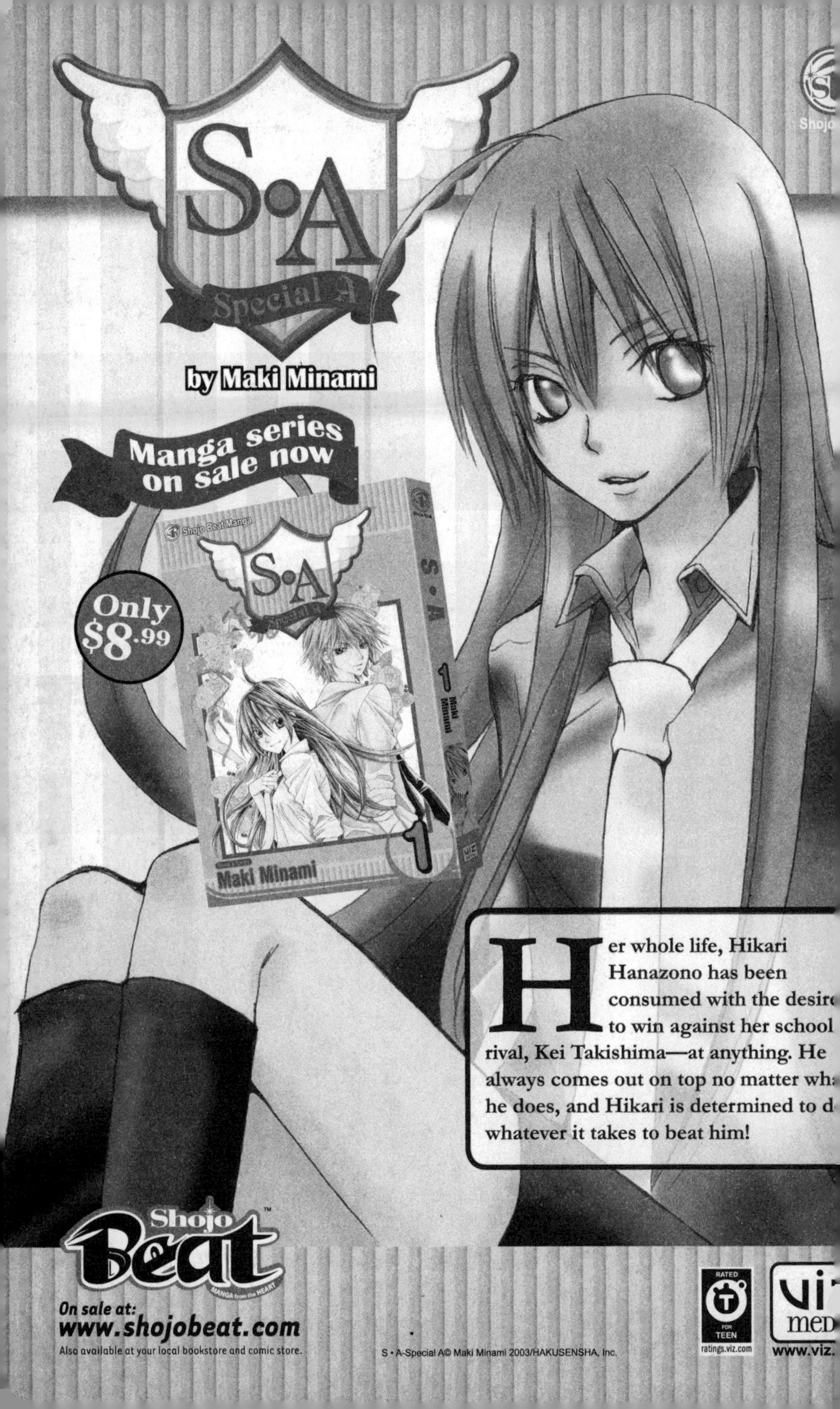
S·A
Special A
by Maki Minami
Manga series on sale now
Shojo Beat Manga
S·A
Only $8.99
S·A
1
Maki Minami
Maki Minami
Her whole life, Hikari Hanazono has been consumed with the desir to win against her school rival, Kei Takishima—at anything. He always comes out on top no matter wh he does, and Hikari is determined to d whatever it takes to beat him!
Shojo Beat™
MANGA from the HEART
On sale at:
www.shojobeat.com
Also available at your local bookstore and comic store.
S · A-Special A© Maki Minami 2003/HAKUSENSHA, Inc.
RATED
T
FOR TEEN
ratings.viz.com
www.viz.

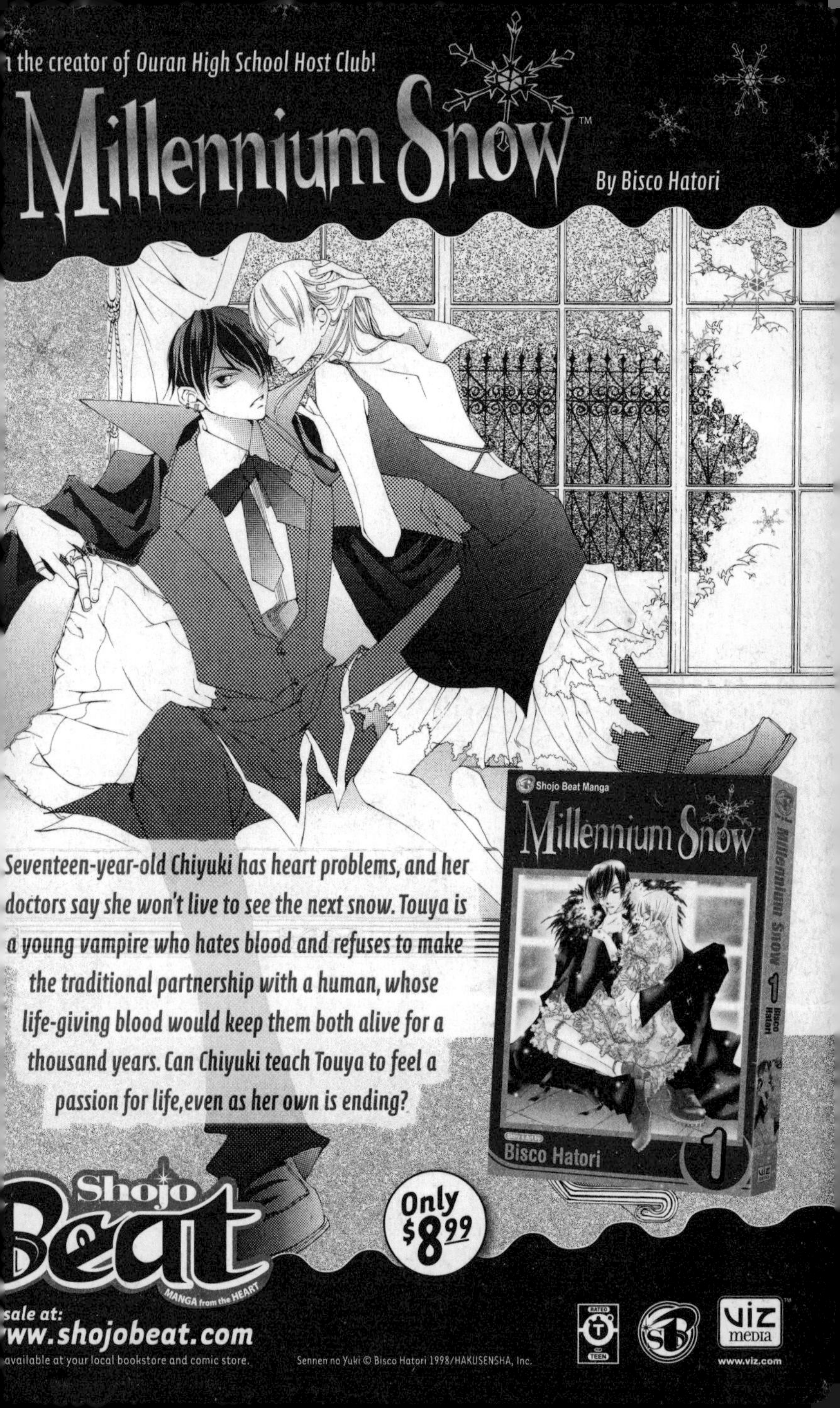

n the creator of Ouran High School Host Club!
Millennium Snow™
By Bisco Hatori
Shojo Beat Manga
Millennium Snow
Millennium Snow 1 Bisco Hatori
Bisco Hatori
1
Seventeen-year-old Chiyuki has heart problems, and her doctors say she won't live to see the next snow. Touya is a young vampire who hates blood and refuses to make the traditional partnership with a human, whose life-giving blood would keep them both alive for a thousand years. Can Chiyuki teach Touya to feel a passion for life, even as her own is ending?
Shojo Beat
MANGA from the HEART
Only $8.99
sale at:
ww.shojobeat.com
available at your local bookstore and comic store.
Sennen no Yuki © Bisco Hatori 1998/HAKUSENSHA, Inc.
RATED T TEEN
viz media
www.viz.com

Save OVER **50%** off the cover price!

Shojo Beat

MANGA from the HEART

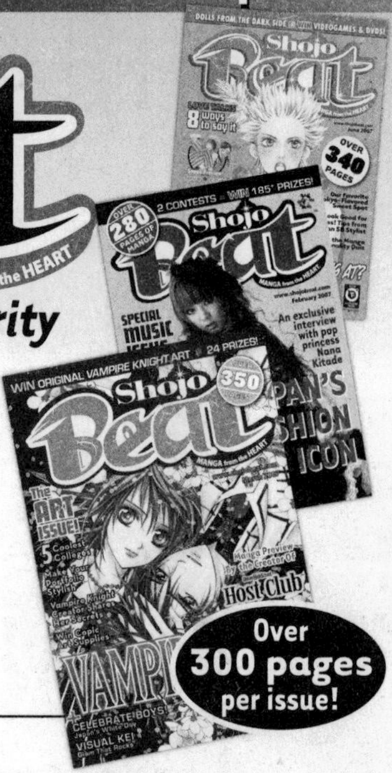
DOLLS FROM THE DARK SIDE
Shojo Beat
OVER 340 PAGES
2 CONTESTS = WIN 185+ PRIZES!
OVER 280 PAGES OF MANGA
Shojo Beat
SPECIAL MUSIC
An exclusive interview with pop princess Nana Kitade
WIN ORIGINAL VAMPIRE KNIGHT ART
24 PRIZES!
Shojo Beat
350
The ART ISSUE!
Host Club
CELEBRATE BOYS!
VISUAL KEI
Over
300 pages
per issue!

## *The Shojo Manga Authority*

This monthly magazine is injected with the most **ADDICTIVE** shojo manga stories from Japan. PLUS, unique editorial coverage on the arts, music, culture, fashion, and much more!

☑ **YES!** Please enter my one-year subscription (12 GIANT issues) to ***Shojo Beat*** at the LOW SUBSCRIPTION RATE of **$34.99!**

**NAME**

**ADDRESS**

**CITY** **STATE** **ZIP**

**E-MAIL ADDRESS** P7GNC1

☐ **MY CHECK IS ENCLOSED (PAYABLE TO *Shojo Beat*)** ☐ **BILL ME LATER**

**CREDIT CARD:** ☐ **VISA** ☐ **MASTERCARD**

**ACCOUNT #** **EXP. DATE**

**SIGNATURE**

CLIP AND MAIL TO

SHOJO BEAT
Subscriptions Service Dept.
P.O. Box 438
Mount Morris, IL 61054-0438

Canada price for 12 issues: $46.99 USD, including GST, HST and QST. US/CAN orders only. Allow 6-8 weeks for delivery. Must be 16 or older to redeem offer. By redeeming this offer I represent that I am 16 or older.



RATED T+ FOR OLDER TEEN
ratings.viz.com

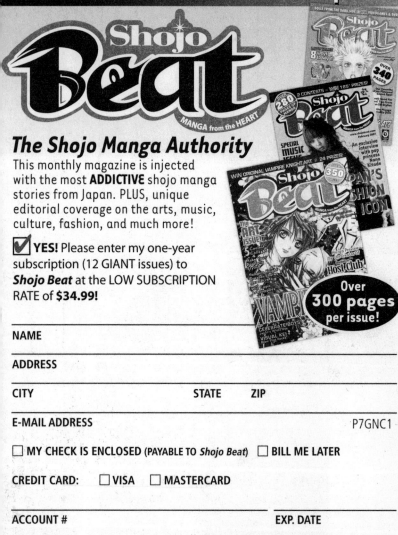